Yoga inFocus

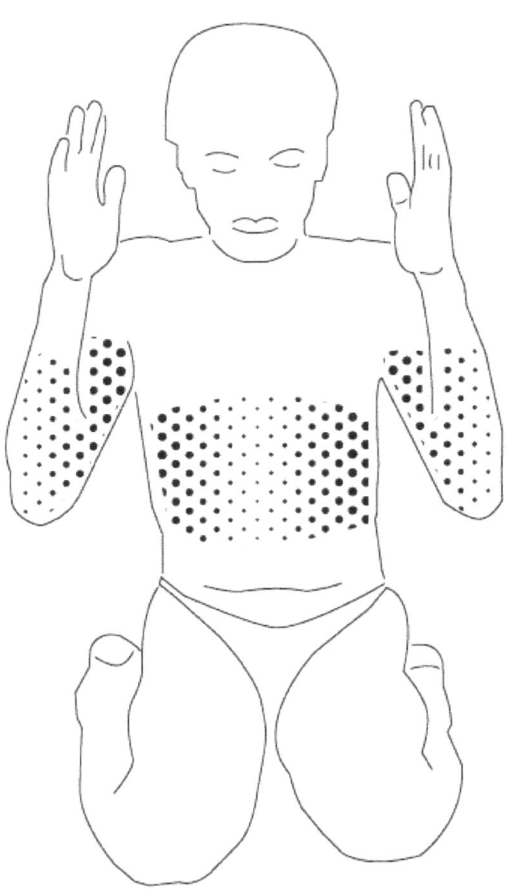

Michael Beloved

Illustrations: Author

Correspondence:
Michael Beloved
7211 41ST CT E
Sarasota FL 34243
USA
Email: axisnexus@gmail.com
michaelbelovedbooks@gmail.com

Paperback ISBN: **9781942887614**

eBook ISBN: **9781942887621**

LCCN: **2026904519**

Mi-Beloved

Contents

Introduction

On March 23, 2025, Yogeshwarananda requested that I publish a book with illustrations of the movements of energy in the subtle body. This concerned showing how energy flows in various postures while doing breath infusion and/or meditation.

Some years prior, when this body was in its young adult stage, Sir Paul Castagna took some photos of my postures while I was in Brooklyn, NY. Later, some other photos were acquired. I will use some of those images and some recent ones to construct the diagrams.

There is a misconception about yoga, where the *asana* postures are regarded as a curbing action for the physical body. However, the reason is the toning of the physical system to reform the subtle body. This is to make the subtle body lose interest in its physical copy. Yoga is for targeting the subtle system, the psychic version of self. The *asana* portion of yoga, is for making the physical body efficient in its use of psychic energy.

It is *pranayama* breath infusion which helps to make the shift of interest from the physical to subtle body. *Asana* helps, because it gives insight about the energy flow through the physical form. The more efficient the energy flows in the physical form, the less energy expenditure will be exerted for the physical system's maintenance by the subtle body.

There is no set arrangement of postures in this book. Any posture from any page can be done as instructed. This is not an orderly layout for mastery of doing stretches. This shows that no matter which posture is done, regardless of when it is assumed, there should be focus within the psyche, to isolate and target the energy movements, which that particular posture produces.

The energy movement in a posture is itself the target. That movement is real. The yogi applies his focus to that. He/She becomes focused on that, absorbed into that. Such focus is the *samyama,* three highest stages of yoga.

Samyama is *dharana* deliberate focus, shifting into *dhyana* spontaneous focus, and peaking in *samadhi* continuous spontaneous focus. This could be an upward progress or a degression, where the yogi is elevated or lowered. The only part of that three stepped process which requires the application of willpower is *dharana* deliberate focus.

If, however a yogi is in *samadhi,* that is a spontaneous focus from which he may be lowered instantly or gradually, to *dhyana* momentary focus. Then he will arrive in *dharana* where he will discover that to keep the focus, he must apply willpower.

Yogeshwarananda wanted to bring it to someone's attention, that in a posture, there is already some absorption or *samadhi* happening. To locate that, one has to inFocus. One must check to see where the energy converges. The mind conglomerate will automatically go to that place. If it does not, the yogi may assume *dharana* deliberate focus to link to it.

The technique is to train the mind to locate the energy shifts in any posture. This is how the mind is trained to do *dharana* and *dhyana.* Use the inner energy formats which occur naturally during a posture, to train the mind in *samadhi* practice.

Abdomen Uplift in Lotus Posture

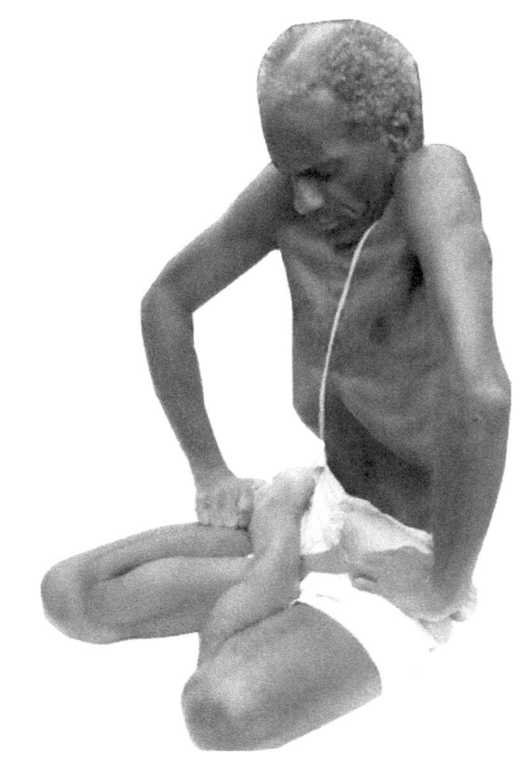

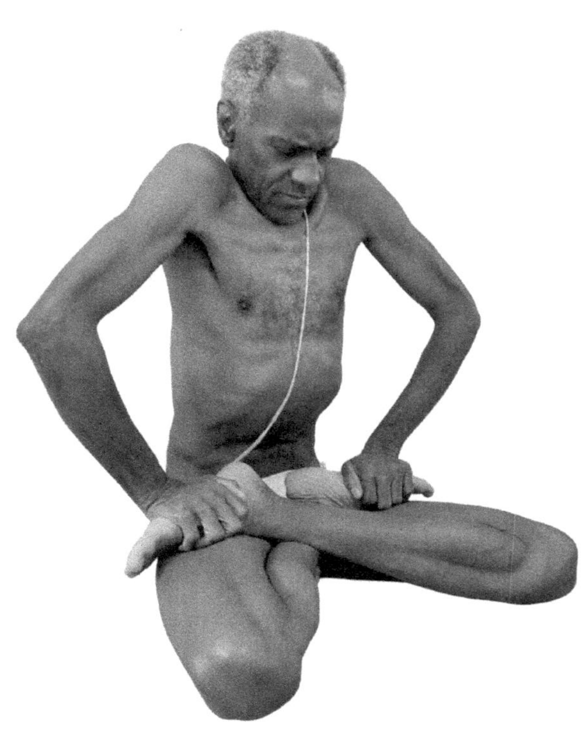

For this *Abdomen Uplift in Lotus Posture,* one should be proficient in the lotus posture. Assume the position. Lift the body to be sure that it is centered on the hips and pelvic cage. Press hands on upturned feet. Let elbows tense by attempting to straighten elbows. This is an attempt only. The elbows will not straighten. They will remain under tension.

Close eyes. Focus within the body-psyche. Pull the organs up from the lower abdomen. Pull up and back. If there is food in the intestinal tubing, that will fully or partially obstruct the contraction. Check the chin/neck lock. Be sure that it is applied efficiently with the chin pulled to the throat but with the head not being tilted forward.

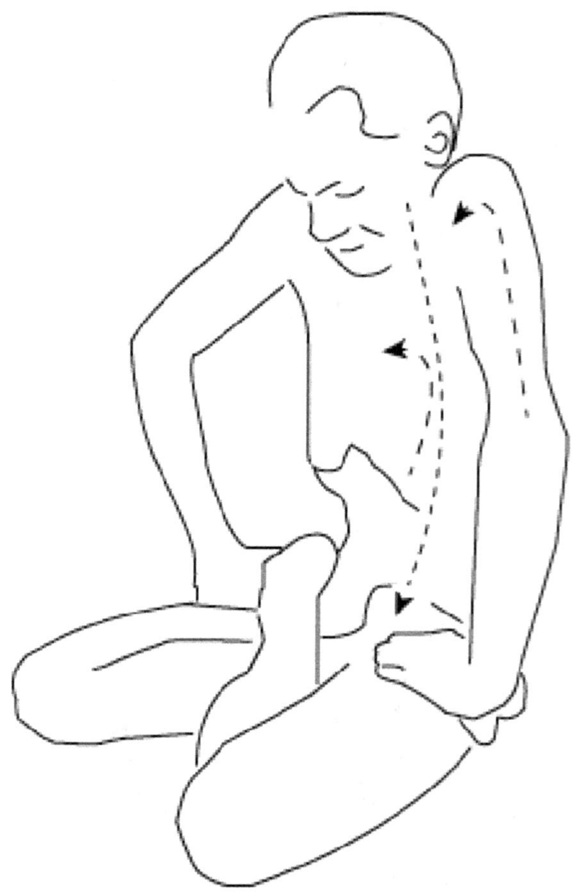

Focus down through the body. Check here and there to note the movement or arrest of subtle energy. Finally, check the base chakra. If it is relaxed, pull it up. Let energy fall like rain from the top portion of the psyche to the base. Keep the focus.

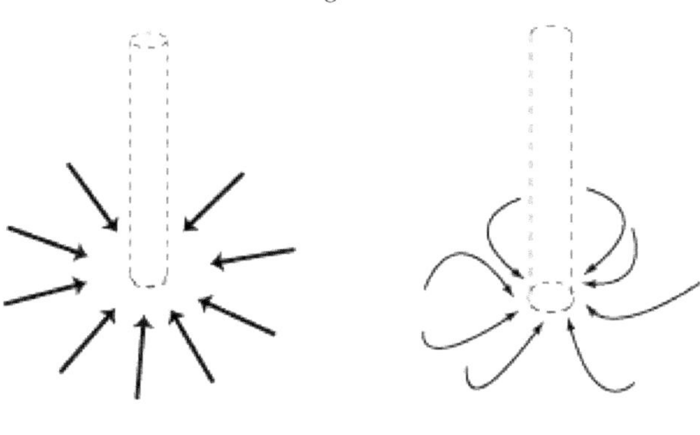

relaxed base chakra active base chakra

Focus Connection

In each posture the discovered energy configuration, accumulation, and movement, should be noted. I will report on discoveries made and psychic events which may occur in a posture.

- Is there a struggle to link focus to the energy which was noted?
- Is there a spontaneous connection of the focusing power to the energy.

For this A*bdomen Uplift in Lotus Posture,* the chin lock should be held. This means that the chin is pulled to the throat. The abdomen is up-locked under the rib cage, being drawn back to the spine. The breath is not held. The breathing continues but with very little air entering and leaving the nostrils. This will happen because the diaphragm is restricted.

The attention which is a focusing beam of interest, will go to the throat. It will discover a circular entrance there. That will have some transparent light with a clear transparent feel to it. Hold the focus. Look through that energy downward. Some long lost memories may arise. Some of these may be from past existences. Some may be from the childhood years.

When the lost memories arise, there will be corresponding images but these may be transparent, like bubbles rising in water, where those formations cannot be seen, because of a lack of contrast. A yogi may decipher these but he may be unable to do so. This is a case of experiencing a *siddhi* perfectional power, but not being able to make coherent sense of it. It does happen that a yogi experiences a mystic skill, but he is unable to understand it.

During this practice, there was a memory from a past life. It opened as a scene. I was an invisible person in a city which had an earthquake. The place was besieged. I was in a royal family. We had an escape tunnel which was dug many years prior. Knowing that the battle was lost, and that the enemy would soon ram through the city walls, some members of the royal family and myself, headed for the escape tunnel.

There was a slipway. It was designed to cause collapse of the tunnel, so that the enemy could not trace the escape route. My responsibility was to trigger the collapse, which I did. There was some fear that the enemy would somehow or the other, figure the route. After that the awareness of that incidence ceased. I could no longer perceive it.

Lifting Lotus-Posture on Palms

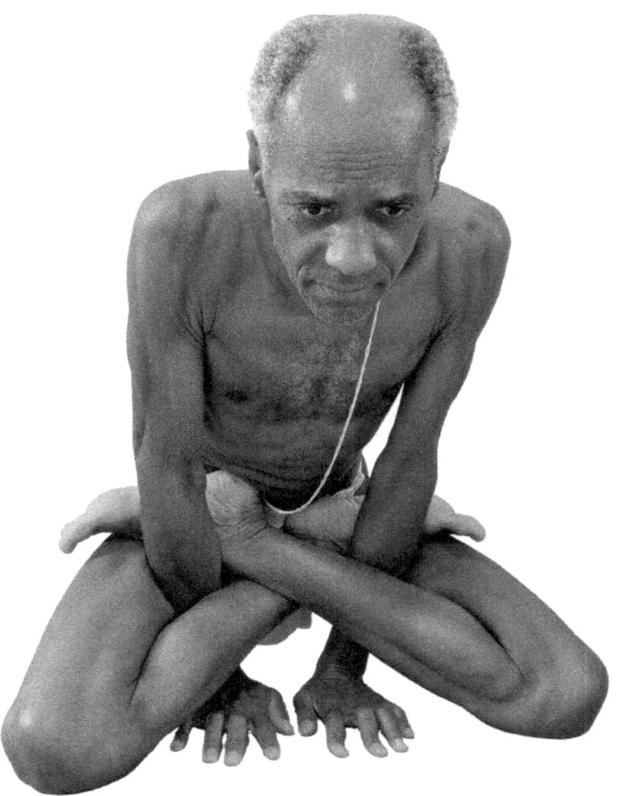

For this *Lifting Lotus-Posture on Palms,* the knees may or may not touch floor, but the weight of body should be borne through wrists, forearms, and arms. Even when the eyelids are open, focus of attention should be within the body/psyche. Odd feelings within the wrist, forearms, and arms, should travel to the area within the lower part of the shoulders.

Breath infusion is done in this posture, while the infused energy rushes to the dual electric tension, which is represented in the following illustration.

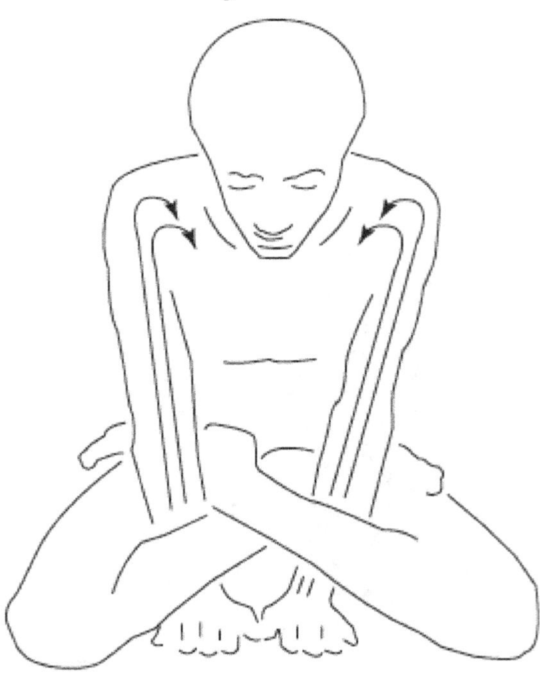

This, is impractical for those who are uncomfortable in the lotus pose. If when pushing the hands and forearms through the space between the thighs and calves, there is friction, one may wet those areas to lubricate it. This posture is a lotus lift event.

Focus Connection

This position is summarized internally as stress in the wrist and shoulders. It may produce shivering. That may be here or there or everywhere. When the stress can no longer be tolerated, the yogi should slowly lower the buttocks to the floor. This will provide instant relief, but there may be a tinkling energy which is like ice-crystals in the wrists. Do not shift the shoulders. Look down, through the arms and forearms. There may be a focusing beam running through each forearm, and flaring when it reaches the wrists. Lock the focus into that energy, which may be like clear crystal, twinkling in moonlight.

Check in the body for energy bricks. Some may vibrate and flicker in the buttocks. Tighten the chin to the throat. Draw energies to the back of the neck. Focus on pulling the energies there. It will not accumulate. The energies may reach the back of the neck and then disappear.

Energy will radiate from the back of neck, doing so with a sober intent, without a bliss aspect. At some point when the body requires release from tension, the buttocks should be relaxed on the floor. The wrists will still be interlocked between the thighs and legs.

A check should be made to be sure that the spine is upright, not curved. Again, the yogi should check for inner focus. There may be no visual perception but there may be no thought harassment either. Only the steady radiant energy will sparkle in every direction.

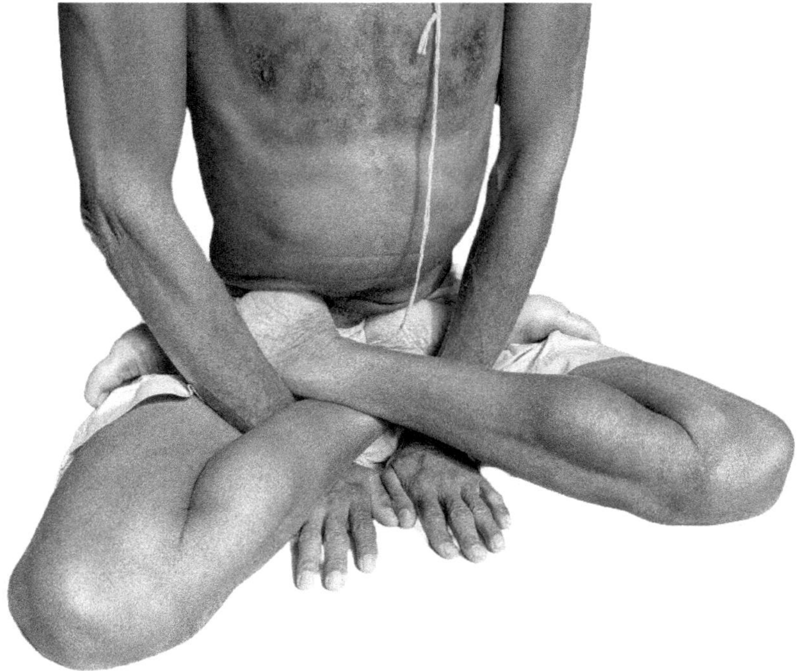

With knees touching the floor or with knees floating above the floor, lower the buttock to the floor. Keep the forearms as they were with the wrist pushed through the lotus lock. Focus through the shoulders, arms, forearms and wrists.

Sitting on Soles Together

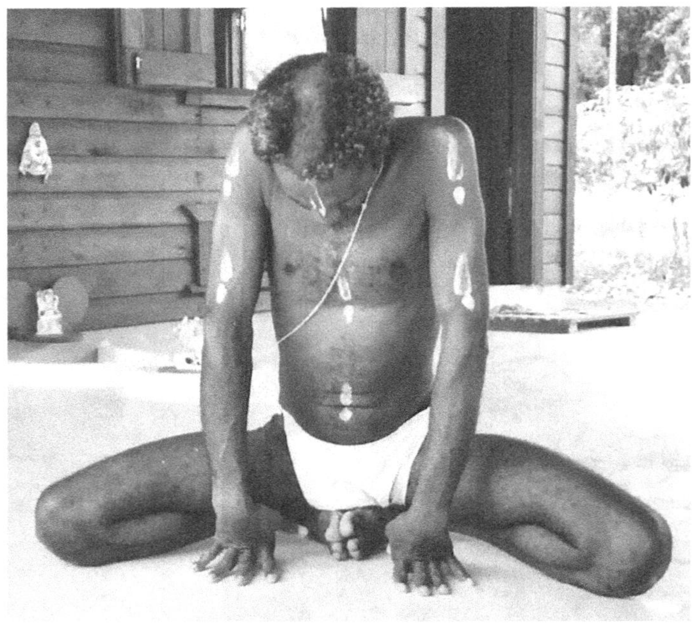

There are many postures for the *asana* process. The legend has it that there are as many postures as there are species of life, with each species naturally using a specific posture in its ideal format. Today there are many lifeforms. Many more which we do not see, are extinct.

Some yogis who became proficient in postures, recommended a particular sequence, for assumption of one posture after the other, with a special one being used, for the conclusion of a session.

In this book no series is given. The names of each posture were assigned by the author in terms of how it describes what the posture achieves.

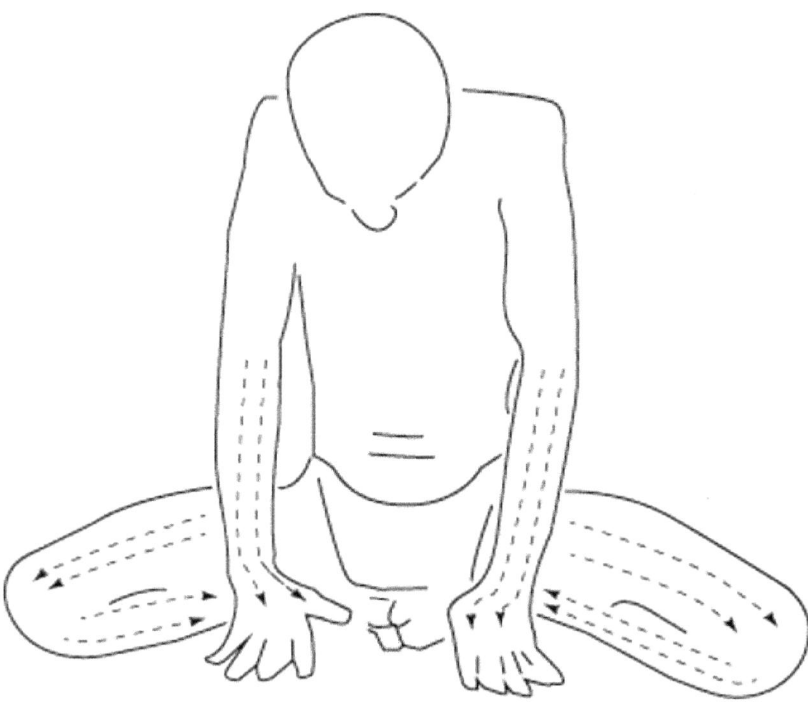

For this Sitting on Soles Together position, there is emphasis caused by the pressure on the fingers. The thumb floats. It is not tensioned, except that the pressure applied to the fingers, causes the thumbs to stick out. The places where the finger-bones connect to the palms do not touch the floor. There is tension which runs through the forearms into the palms.

The soles of the feet are pulled together. The yogi sits on that. He may have to push the knees to the floor. Then he may press the fingers down as illustrated. This posture may be difficult. When it is done, there will be tension and energy flow into the knees, and from the knees to the soles and toes.

This is a super-posture for finding the centralized *muladhara* base of the spine chakra complex of energies. Doing this posture with breath infusion is grand. Some *hatha* yogis do this with regular breath intake, while they focus intently on the space in the center of the base *muladhara,* spine-ending chakra. After a time, a flash of white-minus light may occur there. That is not a white light like star or moon light. It is negative to that, but it is a light nevertheless.

Focus Connection

When *Sitting on Soles Together* posture, the knees may be relaxed or tense. If they are tense, those knees may float above the floor. This may be painful. One should hold the posture for a time. If, however, one cannot bear the discomfort from the ankles, one may use a cushion. The chin lock should be applied. The head may be tilted forward slightly. After there is much tension, and the posture becomes unbearable, the yogi may remove the hands from the floor and place them on the floor in the back of the body, near the buttocks.

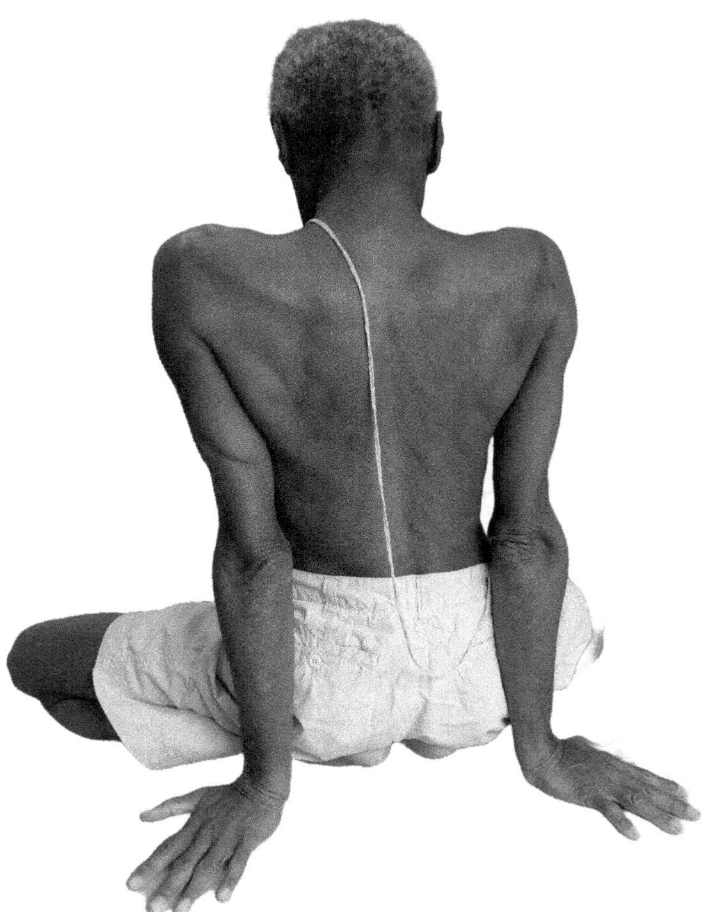

The yogi should check the chin to be sure, that it is pulled to the throat. The head however should be slightly tilted. The chest region should be raised a bit, so that the chin locks against the throat.

A yogi should internalize to note the condition of the bio-electric energy. It should be that the energy in the torso moves upward like water moving in a fountain. The energy will evaporate into the neck where it will disappear.

The ankles should be checked. These may seem to be filled with energy, but as if they are swollen. They will cry for relief. The yogi should note that but he should ignore it for the time being. Instead, he should check to find thoughts in the mind. The spontaneous process of generating thoughts may cease. A yogi should note that. He should make an effort to resume thinking. He will find however that the mind does not create nor expand ideas. Instead, it exhibits no interest in thought production or thought continuation.

Due to demands for attention in the ankles, the thought generation and maintenance system became latent. It does not operate. This is important in higher yoga, to know that the mind can abandon its thought generation system for some time. If there is a painful experience, the mind may abandon its natural process for a time. This happens as well during some unconscious states, but as experienced in this pose, it can happen even in conscious conditions.

Palm-Sole Half-Body Support

This *Palm-Sole Half-Body Support* pose, is a body support position which shifts the mind focus to tendons, muscles, and nerves, which are hard to locate otherwise. The focal areas are shown in the diagram.

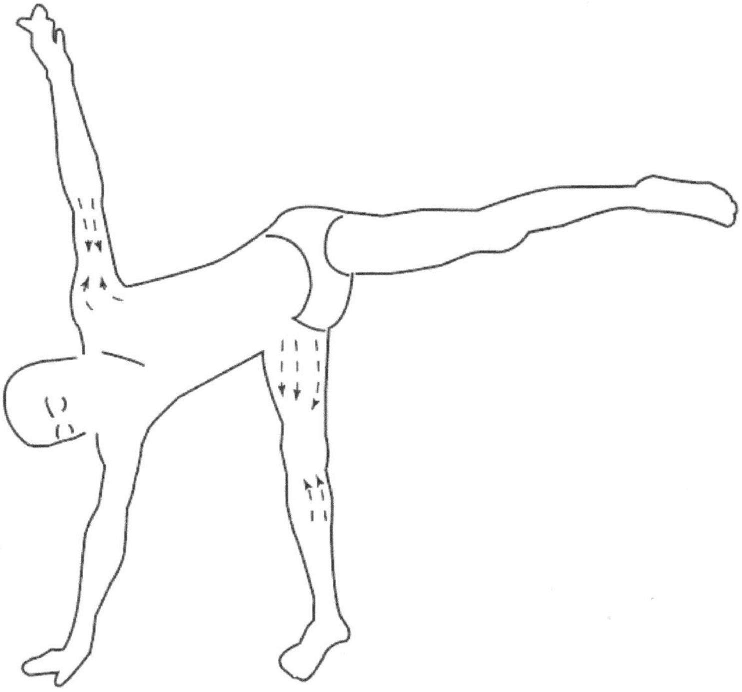

A yogi is required to disconnect from the physical world and its supportive psychic framework. But it is also necessary to cause the mind to focus on the design of the psyche. There are three focuses which become a challenge but which are relevant.

- deliberate forceful extraction of sensual and whimsical interest in what is outside the physical body.
- stabilization of internal interest which was withdrawn previously, and which lost the desire to target what is external.
- discovery of territories or zones which are internal, but which were of no concern previously.

Postures with regular breathing can yield results if the internal focus is firm, and if the yogi has outgrown the need for the external excitements. The same postures can yield different realization if rapid breathing is done, when the postures are assumed. The idea is to surcharge, target, or stress, areas which are within the psyche, and which become energized by the infused breath energy. One should be sure to access fresh air when doing breath infusion.

Focus Connection

The *Palm-Sole Half-Body Support* posture produces a no-thoughts attitude in the psyche. In this pose, even deliberate thinking is squelched. It is a difficult pose but it allows and renders focus in the thighs, knees, and calves. There may be shivering in the raised forearm, arm, and chest. When this pose becomes unbearable, the yogi may lower the raised foot to the floor. This should be done gradually, not jerking any part of the body. A yogi may hold the pose for seconds or minutes. It depends on the conditions of the muscles engaged. When it is no longer tolerable, he should lower the raise foot to the floor.

There he should wait for stability. He should move slowly into an easier pose. As for example, he may sit on the heels.

The absorption should continue in that posture. He should note what changes occur within the psyche. Sitting on the heels he should check the mind space. He should search for the thought-generating apparatus. That is the intellect. It may be hidden. The yogi should discover where it is. He should make the effort to understand why it ceased.

Stand / Hands on Back Thighs

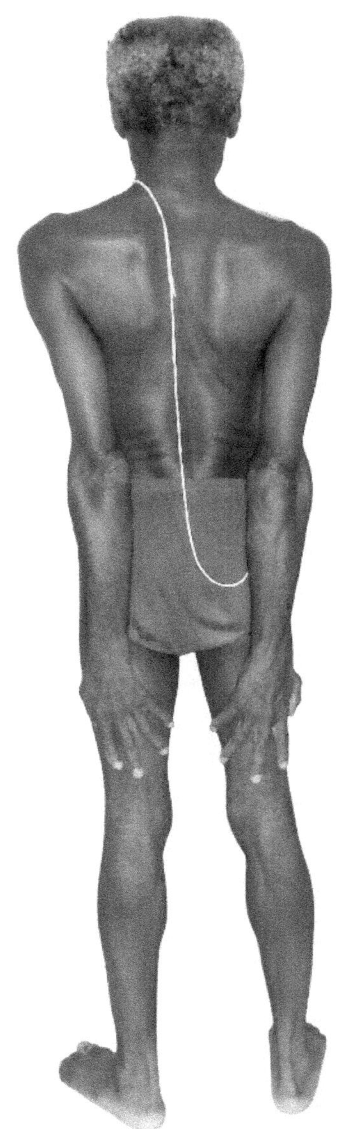

In this *Stand / Hands on Back Thighs* posture, the yogi stands with hands pressing on the back of each thigh. The chest is raised, while the chin is pressed against the throat. The internal focus is applied to the neck to discover the focal point where the energies centralize to resolve the tensions.

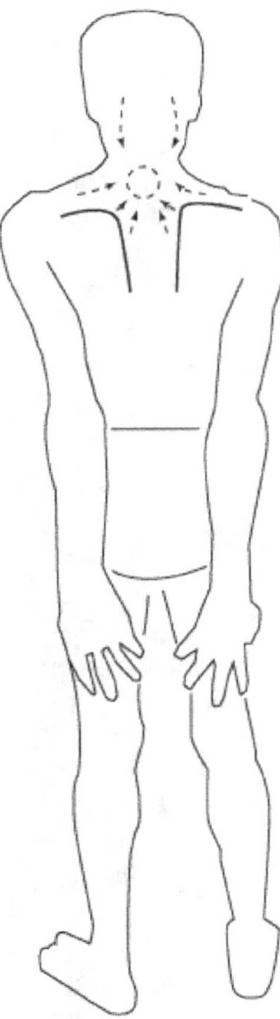

A yogi may feel a vortex in the throat. The energies in the neck and chest will converge at this vortex. The yogi should focus to map the operations.

Focus Connection

This *Stand / Hands on Back Thighs* pose, allows checking the stability, the balance. It measures physical gravity. In this pose, a yogi should check to be sure that the feet are positioned firmly. The hands should slightly grip the back of the thighs. The knees should be locked. An internal check should be made for the chin being pulled to the throat and the sternum. The front of the chest is lifted and contracted.

After that check, an internal tally should be made to check that the anus is up-drawn. The abdomen is firm. The centralizing energy in the head should be focused into the throat. There should be a blank circular space in the center of the throat. It should be hollow. The yogi should focus into it.

He should check periodically to be sure that balance is maintained. There may be a swaying this way and that way, like the swing of a pendulum. The yogi should notice how the system does that involuntarily, with no input from the coreSelf.

After a time, when the yogi can no longer stand in this way, he may move his hands. The hands can be placed on the hips. The muscles which were tensed should be relaxed. The internal focus should be maintained. Keeping the relaxation, the yogi should sit on a chair or floor. He should do so without disturbing the energy configuration in the psyche. He should meditate.

Lifting the central chest and applying the chin to the throat, he should peer through the throat. There may be a circular opening under which may be clear space. Half-way down some cloudy energy may be discovered. If not, there may be blankness. There, a dark grey cloud may traverse horizontally.

Inner sound may blare. If it does, it will arrest the attention of the yogin. It will demand or simply arrest his attention. He will lose track of the energy below the throat. Only inner sound will be predominant, but with blank energy thereabout.

Hands Pressing on Lower Back

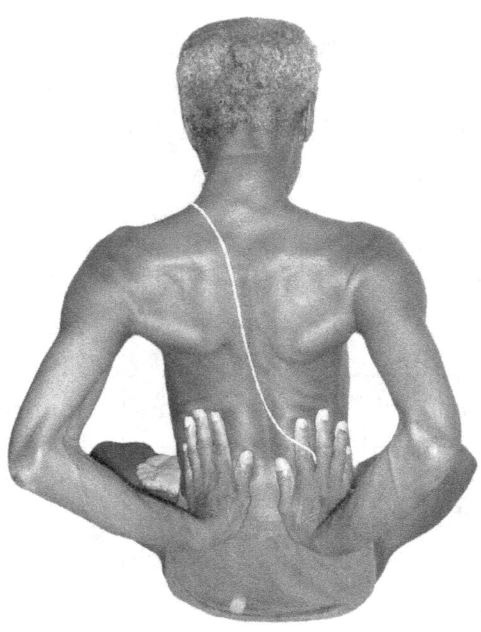

While *pressing palms on the lower back,* the yogi should keep the spine in an erect situation. The palms serve to brace the back. The shoulders provide a limit as they will yield only so much as the neck protrudes out of the body. Without tilting the head forward, the chin should be kept pressed back to the throat, but it should not touch the chest.

Once this posture is set, there will be a switch of focus to sense the movement of energy in the top of the torso, and in its median area. This energy will stir after a time. It will settle and begin flowing upwards through the neck, into the head.

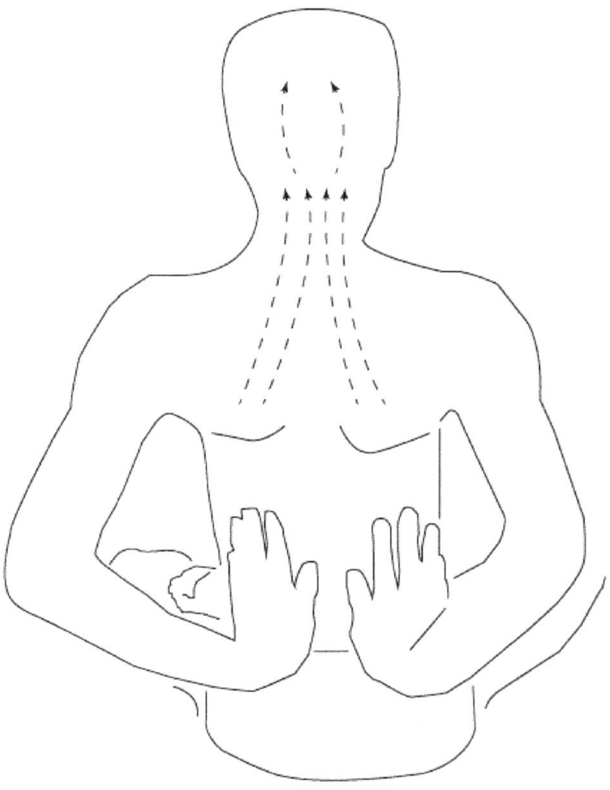

Focus Connection

This *Hands Pressing on Lower Back* posture may have a terrible pressure in the hands and wrists. It is pronounced. It could be used as a study of a nature-enforced painful or pleasurable feeling, where the attention of the yogi becomes absorbed in the affliction. If at the time just before the death of the physical body, there is serious injury which results in this kind of mandatory focus, the yogi may be forced to focus on the painful sensations. He can study that condition while assuming this posture. He should consider that as soon as the physical system is no longer a bio-electric mechanism, its trauma will end, if the subtle body does not have that anxiety embedded in it;

If it does, the trauma will continue on the subtle side. Until something is done which shifts the focus, or changes the condition, it will be sustained there.

It should be observed that when this mandatory attention is applied, no thoughts arise. Even the desire to think about this for the purpose of studying it, will be absent. Sometimes, the inner sound resonance will be heard. When this happens, the inner sound may arrest the attention, causing it to shift from the traumatic feeling. The feeling will continue but it will lack intensity.

Fingers Grabbed in Back with One Forearm over, and the other under, the Shoulder

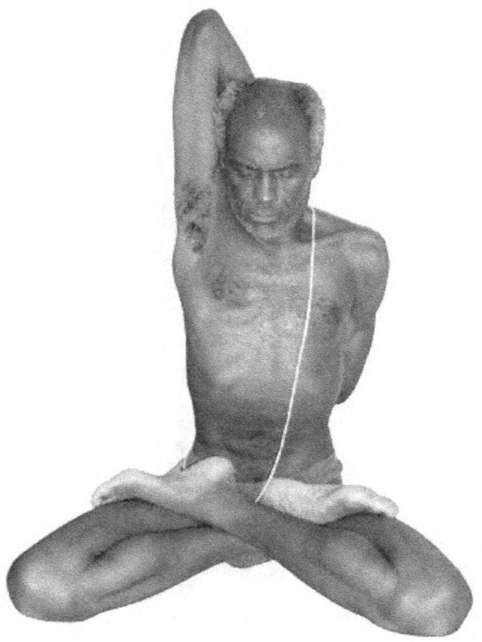

This *Fingers Grabbed in Back with One Forearm over and the other under the Shoulder* posture, is best done while the legs are intercrossed in lotus posture, with the spine squarely positioned. The lower torso is stretched to a limit which is set by each hand grabbing the other in the back. This is with one hand going over a shoulder, and the other passing under the other shoulder.

The abdomen is pulled up. The spine is centered. The eyelids are closed. The focus passes through the body into the thighs. Once there, the focus may reenter into the torso. Let it remain there but be attentive. Check the collar bones, shoulders, and arms. In the arms there will be tension energy. Focus on that.

Note that the fingers of each hand, tightly grips the fingers of the other hand. This hold is kept as the focusing energy of the yogi. It permeates through all tensions created by the posture.

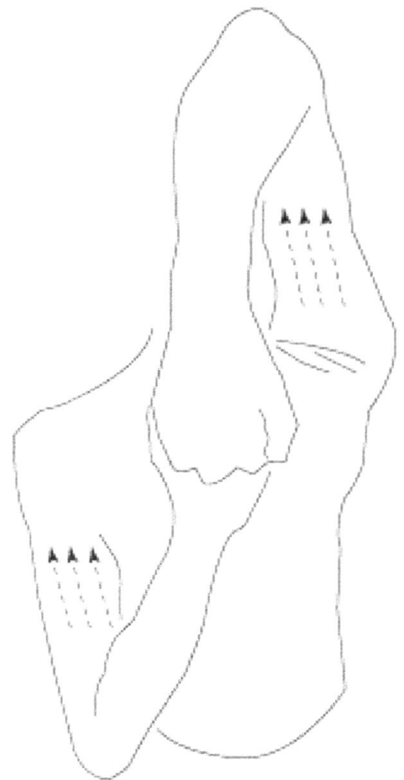

Focus Connection

When doing the *Fingers Grabbed in Back with One Forearm over and the other under the Shoulder*, a yogi may use a cushion under the buttocks. This eases the thighs, knees, and legs. If, however, the lotus posture is extreme, a yogi may sit on a chair or sit otherwise but with the torso upright. First one side is done, then the other, gripping the fingers firmly, and resituating the hands to get them into firm grasping. The spine alignment should be checked. The rib cage should be positioned firmly. The navel should be taut. The top chest area should be pulled up. One side is done. That side is held. The other side is done. That is held.

While doing this research, Yogi Bhajan visited on the astral side of existence. I explained that this was a project which I did as supervised by Yogeshwarananda. Yogi Bhajan said that in the old days, many yogis used specific postures while doing research. Each posture done was assumed with great care, being specific to note its advantages according to the objective of the yogi. He stated that how one degenerates from a higher state to a lower one, was studied.

Earlier that morning, Yogi Bhajan came with six persons who were his disciples when I lived at his Denver Colorado ashram in 1973. There was a teacher named Brian, one named Prem Kaur, the wives of these males, another man who was a mechanic, another one who was an Indian gourmet cook, and yet another who was a teacher of kundalini yoga in Kansas City, Missouri.

Yogi Bhajan said that failure in yoga is traceable to reducing the practice. He said that it was his fault as well, where he decreased personal practice. Then another disciple of his, arrived. This was a female who was a leading teacher in his 3HO organization for some time. He said something to me privately about this person, but he did not allow the others to hear the conversation. He explained.

> *"My energy leaked to her. This was detrimental because it caused my practice to be reduced. It was so bad that I gave up my practice completely. It is important to practice day by day. It does not matter if one is a renowned teacher. What has that to do with one's individual practice. One should practice."*
>
> *"Somehow, energy from my psyche, leaked into her psyche. I lost the impetus to practice. That should be studied as to how that happens. Anyway, it happened. I feel that now you are the one with the energy and authority to teach kundalini yogi. Once I taught somebody. That person showed you what it was. You practiced. You continued no matter what. Now I will learn from you."*
>
> *"These persons too, even the ones who ran yoga schools and were known teachers, they desisted. Now they can learn from you. It is more than learning the way to do it. It is learning how to continue it no matter what. I thought that I learned the whole thing, but I did not learn how to keep practicing. Imagine that! You can know many poses and how to absorb*

the breath energy, and still, you may not have the impetus to keep practicing. That is a specific power."

When a yogi does the *Fingers Grabbed in Back with One Forearm over and the other under the Shoulder* posture, he does one side. Then he does the other. Then he sits to meditate on its effects. He relaxes the body. He places the forearms on the thighs. He does *dhyana* inner focus on the shoulders and arms. At first there will be discomfort but it will gradually cease.

There will be a state of awareness, with ease everywhere in the psyche. The yogi will hear inner resonance. He will realize that there is thought interference, but he can banish the thoughts with the smallest energy. The thoughts will not have a power to fight the yogi or to resist him. And yet, thoughts will keep appearing like shadows of passing clouds on a windy day.

The thoughts will keep appearing. The yogi will hear inner sound, now and again. The thoughts will continue like flimsy formats coming into manifestation and disappearing. Yogi Bhajan said that it was important for each yogi to study how this happens, how the thoughts arise even the flimsy ones, and how the yogi may, or may not, have the power to shew them away.

- What controls that?

Plunge Forward – toes pressed forward-
hands aligned with body – fingers straight back

This is the *plunge with toes pressed forward*. The hands point backwards in alignment with the body. The head is help up with chin up and head cranked to the back of the neck.

This causes a focus within the thighs and legs. The thighs feel blank. There is tension in the legs.

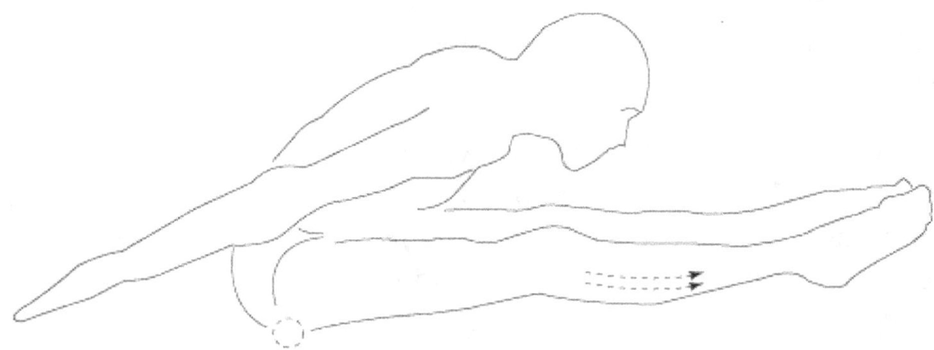

Two knob-like tubules of energy are experienced where each sit-bone makes contact with the floor. The energy of the sit-bones rotates. There should be focus on the tubules there. There is a tendency to avoid pressing the toes forward. Hence, special effort must be made to maintain the toes in a pressed downward position

Focus Connection

When doing the *Plunge Forward – toes pressed forward – hands aligned with body – fingers straight back* posture, a yogi may hear a lub-dub sound in the body. This is the pump action of the heart. Besides that, there may be other sounds which are steady or which are chaotic and hard to identify. Whatever it is, a yogi should accept that there are many motor-like, and lightning-like energies, which operate involuntarily. One should listen. If possible, one should identify each sound.

After holding this posture for a time, there may be a feeling as if it cannot be held any longer. There may be shivering, or shaking, which the yogi cannot reduce. This may occur in the forearms and arms. The yogi may be forced to abandon the posture. Gradually he should raise the torso and move the hands and forearms so that the hands are positioned on the floor. He may do so with the palms up or down. Either position of the hands may be assumed.

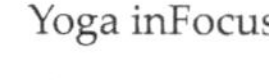

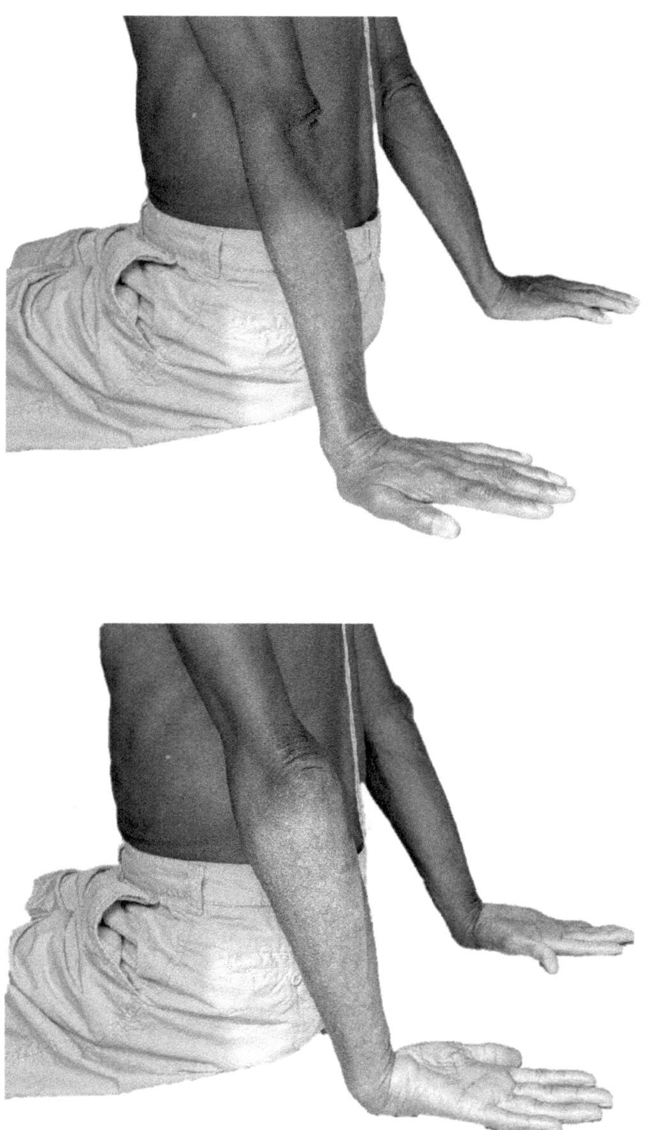

That will provide instant relief. Keeping the focus inside the body, the yogi will notice that energy from the abdomen, moves up through the neck, and permeates the face. It flushes the inner face. This will happen for a time. Inner sound will impress itself upon the yogi. He will hear it internally, and will be interested in what it communicates

Standing Rigid with Fist on Hip Bones

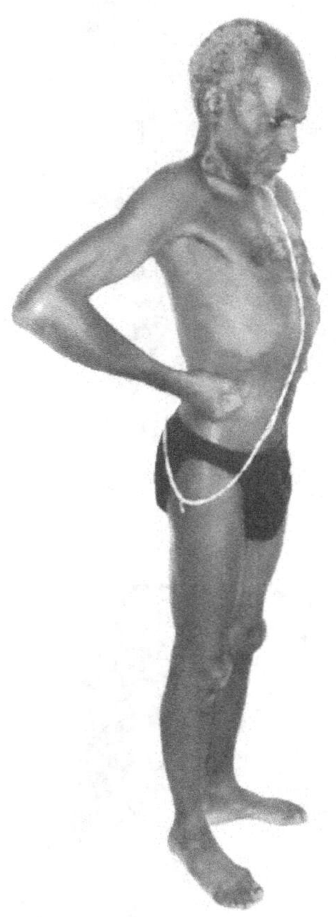

This *Standing Rigid with Fist on Hip Bones* posture, involves the lower trunk of the body, being drawn upwards in a taut configuration, but with the fists resting on the corresponding hip bones. In this, the eyelids are open. The yogi stares blankly into nowhere with his mental and sensual focus being restricted within the subtle body.

The abdomen is pulled under the rib cage. The chin lock is applied. This means that without the head tilting forward, the chin is drawn to the throat. From in the body, the anus is pulled up. With the fists, the yogi should push down the hip bones, while the trunk of the body is drawn upward. Once the yogi holds this position, he should focus internally to determine any shifts, or movements.

An energy may move from below the navel upward, as if a set of muscles give a slight shiver and attempt to run upward through the trunk. To observe this, the yogi should close the eyelids. He should check to be sure that the anus is retracted. Once that is secured, he should pull the perineum muscles backward and upward. With focus, he should maintain the inner observation.

Hatha yoga means both *asana* postures and *pranayama* breath infusion. These may be combined as a practice. Or they may be done as two separate procedures. However, in so far as one prefers to do *asana* postures, it is possible if it is done sincerely and with particular focus. This could yield higher realization about the energy flow in the physical and subtle bodies, as these forms are combined as one living system.

The posture which follows may yield an understanding of the relationship between the energy which rises into the shoulders, and which lunges through the neck into the head. When this energy is restricted so that it no longer flows freely, the person experiences forgetfulness, and lack of sharp focus.

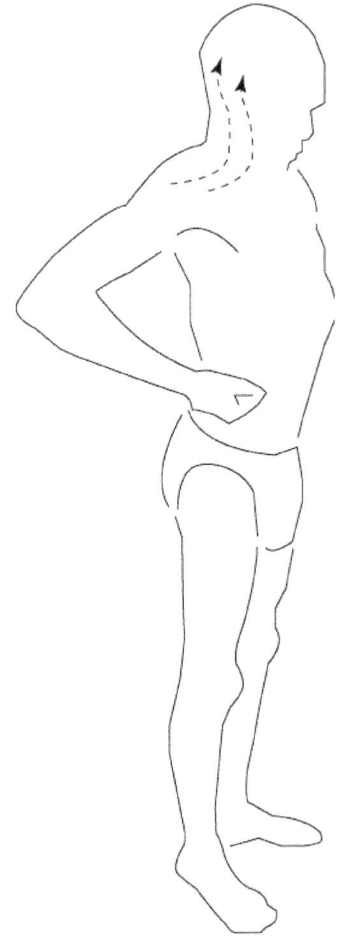

Focus Connection

When *Standing Rigid with Fist on Hip Bones,* the knees act as a demarcation. What is above the knees seem to float. What is below seems to be anchored. The abdomen should be pulled under the rib cage. The chin should be pulled to the throat. In the body, the yogi should do exploration. He should discover energy movements and stress expressions. These have corresponding flares in the subtle body.

The yogi should check for balance.

- Does the body float from the knees?
- Is it, like a kite swaying in the sky?
- Can the yogi hold the pose?

Though it is simple, this pose gives insight into the sense of balance which is expressed from the center of the earth. It is a force to recon with. It arrests everything on the planet.

While doing this meditation, I was aware of Yogi Bhajan in the astral vicinity.

He observed the posture. He said this.

> *"Previously, some rare yogi would do a pose. He would stay in that configuration for hours, days or months, continually, or now, and then. People misunderstood. They regarded the yogi as a gymnast. Some threw money at him. Some sat near him wishing for blessings. A yogi may stand for half day, from six in the morning to noon. Then he would leave the pose. Travel to a village. Get a restricted diet. Then do other things. Then again at six in the morning, he would assume the posture for six hours.*
>
> *"This was done for inner exploration. Most people misunderstood the practice. They assumed that it was a physical act. They had no idea about the psychic features.*
>
> - *Why would a yogi do this?*
>
> *"It was to discover how the mind focuses. If figured, that yogi would develop methods of curbing the mind from its natural way."*

After standing in this posture for a time, it will be necessary to sit. One can sit on a chair or floor. The fists can be left on the hips or be placed elsewhere. The yogi should check in the body for energy shifts.

Fold-Over-Grab-Shins

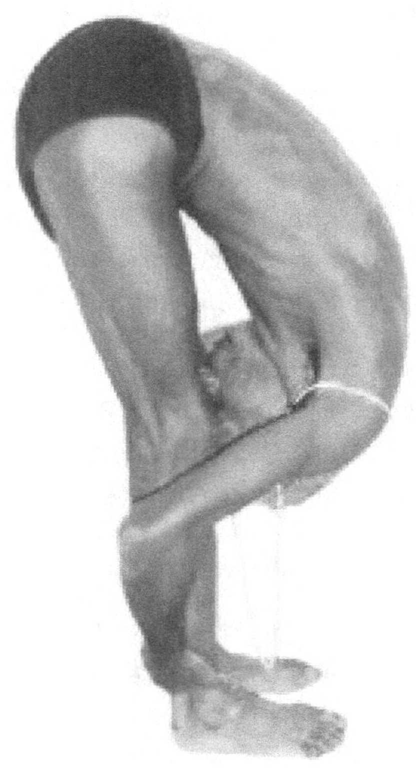

In this *Fold-Over-Grab-Shins* pose, the shins are grabbed. The face is braced against the knees, which are positioned firmly. The knees do not cave in. Care is taken to observe irregularities in the spine.

This position is held steady for a time, until the focus of attention settles in the calves. An energy will accumulate in the calves, but it will have a desire to move into the knees. When it does this, there will be resistance. The yogi should hold the focus in the calves, but allow some energy to be released upwards, into the knee complex of bones. This release will flash from the calves repeatedly. After a time, after five minutes, this flashing will cease. The energy in the calves will shimmer.

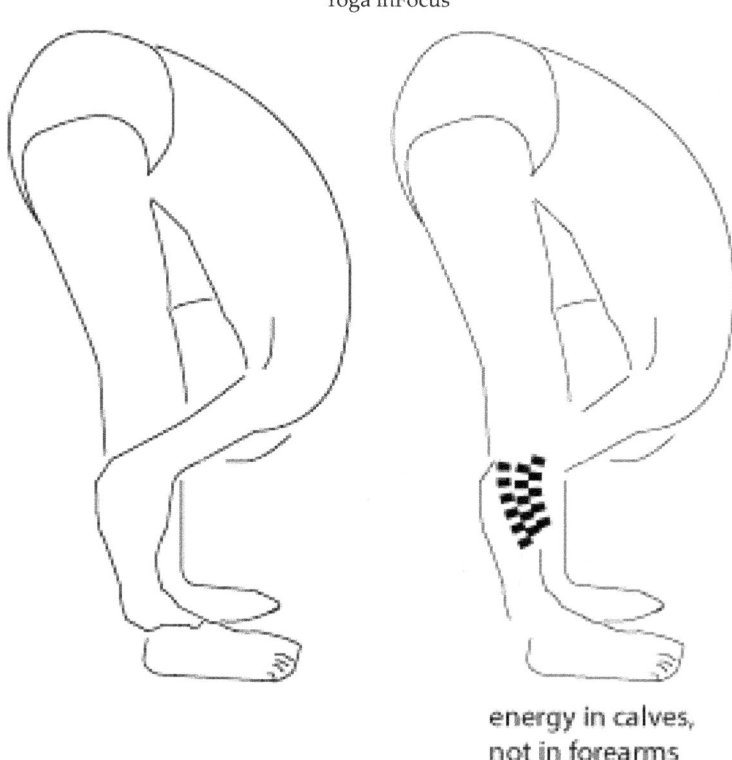

Focus Connection

The *Fold-Over-Grab-Shins* posture may be strenuous. There may also be the factor of reverse blood flow from the waist to the head. Some person may experience giddiness or fainting. Such individuals should not assume this pose.

After doing this for a time, for minutes or longer, there will be a shattering of energy. Then the yogi should make an adjustment to relieve the stress. Whatever movement one does at that time, should be done slowly, with the inner focus being maintained. If not, there is the likelihood of the body falling to the floor. One must keep the inner focus when shifting out of this pose. No sudden movements should be made.

This posture scrubs the area of the ankles. It is likely that a pain will spread from that zone. It may go to the buttocks and may be felt where the thighs fit the pelvic region. The energy there will be such that it is difficult to map, or determine its format.

During this pose there should be regular checking to be sure that the knees are pressed back. To come out of this pose, the hands may slide up the back of the legs and thighs to rest where the thighs meet the buttocks. That will provide a degree of relief.

From that position, the yogi may again resume the posture with the hands holding the insteps, with the head pulled to the body. Again, there will be tensions and electric feelings. When these can no longer be tolerated, the yogi should squat with the hands holding the lowest part of the shins. This gives relief.

In the squat, the yogi should meditate. He should map all energy to determine what it is and where it traverses.

A check should be made, to inquire if the areas where the thighs meets the pelvic zone, are totally relieved.

- What is the attitude of that area?
- Can inner sound be heard?
- Are there thoughts?

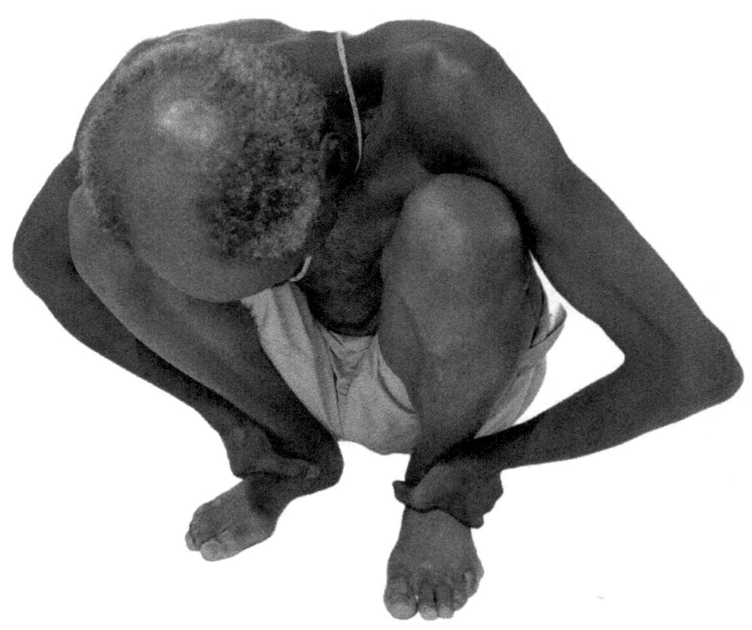

Brace Back Inclined Triangular

This *Brace Back Inclined Triangular* is a relaxation pose. To assume it, one should place the hands as in the photo above. Do this while sitting. Then stretch the feet forward. Press the toes down. Lift the body. As necessary, according to how it feels, extend the hands further out from the body. Lift the torso, lower trunk and buttocks.

Once you are positioned, close the eyelids. Lift the lower trunk higher. Focus internally with the eyelids closed. Check to be sure that the chin is pulled toward the throat. Keep the posture with focus. Slowly lower the trunk. Lower the body so that the buttocks rest on the floor.

Again, assume the posture. As soon as the lower trunk is raised, focus in the body. Notice any areas which are tensioned or which shiver. Keep the focus on those areas. Again, lower the body with buttocks on the floor.

Keep the eyelids closed so as to intensify the focus. Raise the body again. Focus in the trunk. There may be subtle energy vacillating upwards. This may have a white silver color. It may be in the area with the black pods in the illustration below.

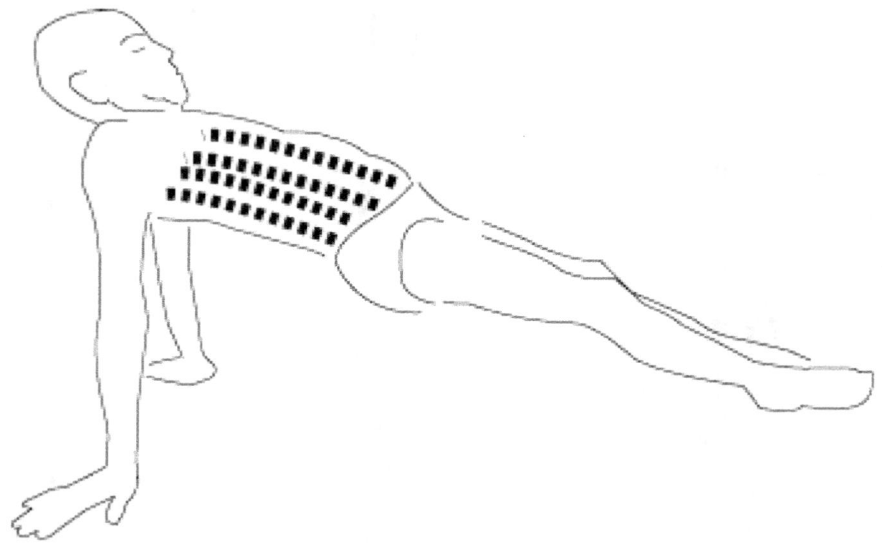

Focus Connection

The *Brace Back Inclined Triangular* is a relatively easy posture. It would be a challenge for anyone who has a heavy body which would strain the upper and lower limbs. I suggest that persons who regard their bodies as being over-weight, should not assume this pose. There are many other poses which can be done without the degree of strain of this one. Those other positions will suffice for the practice of inner research.

The balance must be set in this pose. There are two aspects to it, being the position of the hands, and that of the heels. As soon as this pose is assumed, the yogi should check to be sure that the heels are positioned, to assist in bearing the weight of the body. The heels should be moved forward, backward, to the right or left, to put them in the optimum location. The second aspect for balance is the hands. These should be relocated to the right or left, up or down, so that they are in the best position, to assist in transferring the weight to the floor. While doing this, the attention should be within the body. It should check from the inside.

At last, once the yogi is confident that he has the hands and heels at the best location, he should press the feet forward. The waist should be checked. It should be lifted. It should not sag. It may be that it requires a slight adjustment to lift and lock it. Without jerking the body, the yogi should adjust it.

There will be pressure in the arm muscles. That should be noted. The yogi should do the inner focus to check energy distribution, location and movement.

- Is there disturbance?
- Is there discomfort?
- For how long can it be tolerated?

After a time, when this posture cannot be held, the yogi should keep the hands where they are located. He should lower the rest of the body. When this is done the heels may slide. He should lower the buttocks, thighs, and legs, to the floor. That will provide relief.

The yogi should note the change in the energy configuration. He should map it. There may be movements in the arms and chest. These areas may have a sizzling energy. While doing this *Brace Back Inclined Triangular* posture, Yogeshwarananda, who inspired this book, arrived.

श्री 108 स्वामी योगेश्वरानन्दजी सरस्वती महाराज
Shri 108 Swami Yogeshwaranandji Saraswati Maharaj

He gave this information.

> *"This posture can be used for a samadhi discovery practice. That would require the yogi to remain in it, in focus within the psyche, for five hours. To achieve that, the yogi would begin by doing it for a time, for five minutes daily. Day by day, he would increase the time, until he can do it for one hour. Then he will increase it by fractions for a time. Then again, he would elevate the time to two hours. This will go on until he can do it for five hours.*

"Some yogis utilize a guard who watches the body for that time. Some do it on a cushion or padded area. Why? Because in the past some yogis lost control of the posture. The body fell to the floor. The guard who is employed is another yogi who is experienced in reviving yogis who enter trance states, or who may lose bodily awareness, and not be aware that the body will be injured.

"Here is an example. Once a yogi was in a similar posture. He began to have dream experience, but he had no idea that he was on the astral side. He was unaware of his physical body, which was kept in position by its kundalini lifeForce.

"However, even though the body remained upright for a time, suddenly kundalini released itself from the body. The body fell. He got a fractured forearm. It was painful. The checking factor is the head of the body. In that pose if the head does not stay in the upright position, the assistant yogi, should slowly lower parts of the body so that no part flips or moves suddenly and causes injury."

When I researched this posture, I found that in this posture, there is a silent movement in the intellect. It continues to process thinking energy, either thinking, replying to thinking, or sensing thinking messages, which are transmitted from the mind of another person.

Once in a while, there is a sharp ringing treble inner sound. Even if the yogi is captivated by a thought, the treble sound makes itself to be heard by the yogi. The thoughts are not emphatic. They are slight and quiet, but they run on and on, regardless.

Palms Up, Facing Out, Centralized on back of Chest

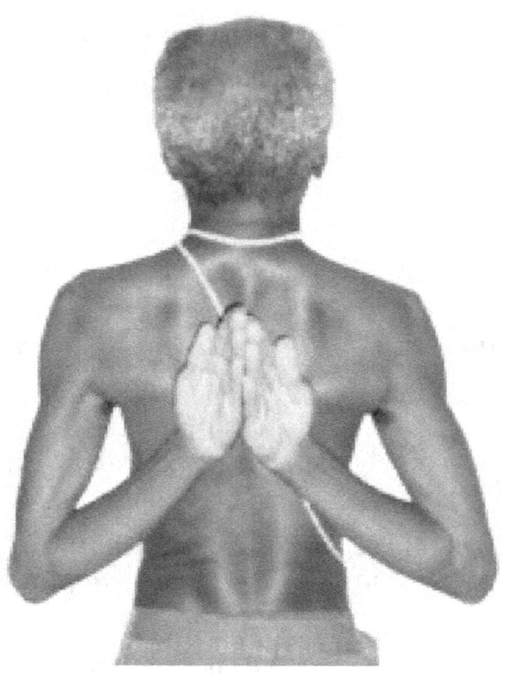

Assume this *Palms Up, Facing Out, Centralized on back of Chest* posture, while sitting or standing. With the palms facing outward, push the hands up the central back. The back of the hand is in contact with the back of the body. To discourage physical interruptions, the eyelids are closed. The interest in external objects is curtailed.

This posture will cause the spine to be erect. The chest will be lifted slightly by the pressure which is put on the spinal column. The head can be erect. Or it may be pushed backward, with the chin lifted as far as the neck allows.

In this posture, a rocking motion may be experienced. The body may go from left to right and from right to left. A yogi may experience drowsiness. If a yogi finds that he feels as if he drops through the sky, he should immediately arrest the mental state. He should sit and stabilize the mind. If one is not rested, one should not do this posture. It is a dangerous. It may induce the kundalini lifeForce to shift to the dulling influence.

The diagram which follows, shows where the energy may accumulate and flow when this pose is done in sober awareness.

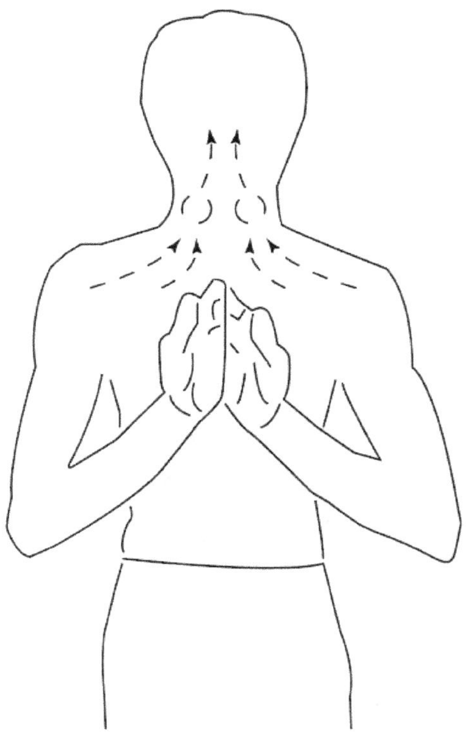

Focus Connection

The *Palms Up, Facing Out, centralized on back of Chest* posture should be done from a standing position. However, someone who is unable to assume it in that way, may use a sitting posture. In either case, it has a relaxed version which occurs from sitting. In this, the palms face out, but it can be done with the palms pressing against the body or with the palms against each other in a *hands-in-prayer-fashion*.

Once the hands are positioned facing out or facing the back of the body, the yogi should notice an electric jolting in the arms. This current of bio-electric energy will run into the shoulders. It should be a stout energy. When that standing position tires, the feet, legs and thighs will become uneasy. The yogi should check through the psyche to determine if he can stand any longer.

If he cannot, he should sit on a chair, or floor. This will relax the lower limbs. The hands would be released from the back and should be placed on the knees. The focus should be placed within the body. Then the yogi will realize that thoughts are absent. There will be sensations in the arms and shoulders. This energy will demand attention. The yogi should feel satisfied that there are no thoughts. No responses from invasive ideas are created.

Abdomen Up-Draw

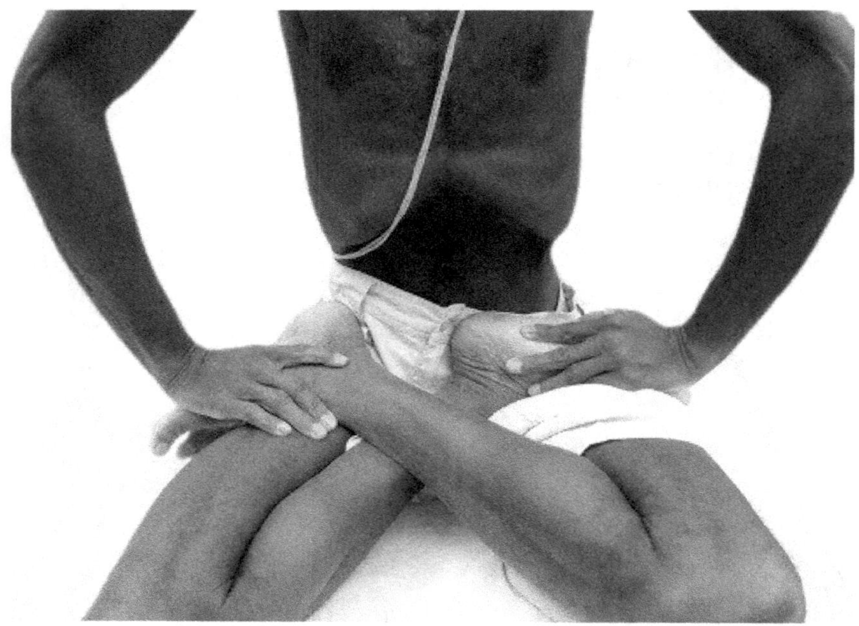

The *Abdomen Up-Draw* is done from several positions. It is done while sitting in lotus posture, cross-legged. It is done from a standing position with knees unbent. It is done with knees bent. It is required that a yogi should exhale abruptly and forcibly before doing this. However, the mandatory requirement is that the stomach should be empty. A yogi cannot do this posture properly if the stomach and intestines are loaded with food matter.

The area behind the navel, and the area just below the lowest ribs, should be clear of food waste, so that the skin of the abdomen is drawn back. Food intake must be carefully regulated by a yogi. Day by day, he/she should curb the food used, and the time of its ingestion. By all means it is best that a yogi should cook for himself/herself. This is due to the fact that each yogi is at a certain stage of advancement, that requires specific meals and time of eating, which suit and facilitate the practice of *asana* postures, and breath infusion *pranayama*.

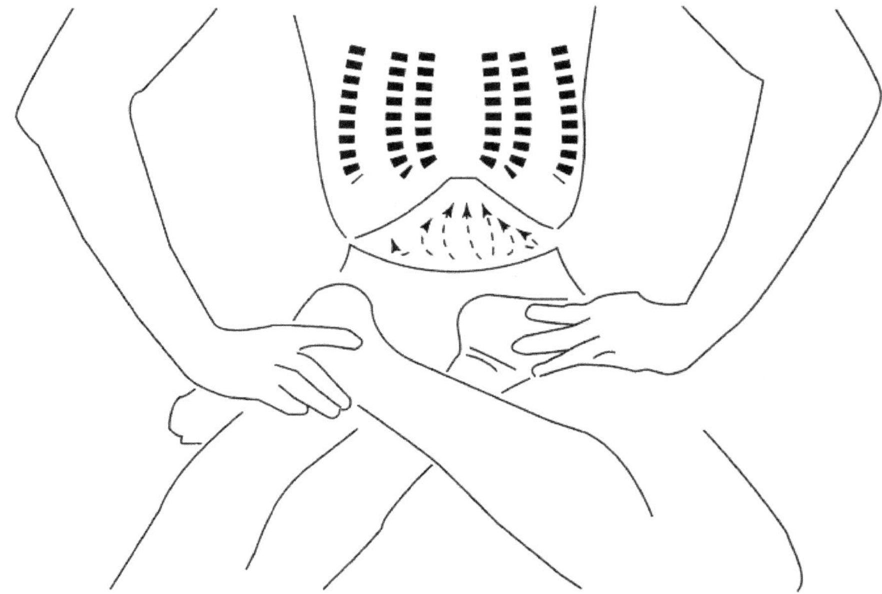

In that diagram, the arrow paths show where the updraw action is applied under the rib cage and to the spine. The energy from the abdomen, and vital organs in the chest, is felt as a pressure which is represented by the black pieces. This energy collective is prohibited from reaching the navel sector. It becomes a pressure force which is compressed by the infused breath energy during *kapalabhati* or *bhastrika* rapid breathing compression. In the subtle body, the black pieces are dark brown in color. As the fresh air is compressed in the body, its chunks become surcharged. They generate heat. They glow. Overtime, they ignite and assume a red brown color, then a yellow red color, then a white pink color. After this, if the yogi/yogini persists, this will change into crystal transparent color. This will result in changes in the subtle body, so that it will be transformed into a *siddhayoga* form.

Focus Connection

The *Abdomen Up-Draw* is a unique posture which uses the lower trunk contraction during meditation research. This is specific because the normal breathing ceases. Shallow breathing is used instead. This type of breathing provides less air than the body requires. Thus, it is not a breathing process which is usually recommended, except for yogis who want to enter trance states, or to alter consciousness for specific psychic transits.

To do this posture, one assumes a tight lotus. The hands are placed on the upturned feet, on the soles. The elbows are flared. There is an inbreath through the nostrils. There is an outbreath through the mouth. With that outbreath, the abdomen is pulled back and is not allowed to resume its relaxed position.

Breathing continues but with the abdomen up-drawn, or retracted upward under the rib cage. In that condition with the diaphragm restricted, the breathing continues. It is shallow and slight. Much air does not come into the lungs. Only a small percentage of the air which is usually absorbed is ingested. Breathing in and out continues in this shallow way.

The yogi switches to inner focus. He checks to find energy formations and movements. He may feel electric sensations in the elbows, arms and shoulders. With that the yogi should look through the neck. He should note energy which is unusual or sensational.

After being in this posture for a bit, noticing the bio-electric energy which darts here or there, the yogi should realize that he is engaged in thought production and response. Naad inner sound may touch the coreSelf, so that it realizes that it did not know that it was under an influence, that it responded to an influence. It had a conversation in which it participated.

Becoming aware of the thought would be like someone awakening from a deep sleep where over a period of moments, the sleeping person gradually becomes cognizant of the room and surroundings.

Naad would be like someone else who gently awakens that sleeping person, where he becomes aware of the room and also of the person who aroused him.

The yogi will find that he is aware of the thoughts which developed, but some of which already occurred, and which cannot be known in full. Then, the location of the present thought will be known, and the thoughts which are to follow will be suspected. The yogi will decide if he should engage with naad, or if he should shift his attention fully to the thought pattern, which like a video is displayed, but with a theme which is known partially only. A yogi should research this to determine the type of relationship he has with naad. He should query why in some instance, he is indifferent to naad, and treats it as if it has little or no importance.

Squat near one Foot with other Foot/Leg/Thigh out

This *Squat near one Foot with other Foot/Leg/Thigh out* posture, is done with buttocks touching floor, or with buttock not making contact. The focus during this pose is on the thigh of the outstretched limb. There will be a shivering of the outstretch limb (the arms, forearms and hands).

The focus is on the shivering energy. A yogi should check to see if the shivering runs to the hip joints, where the thighs connect below the hips. The eyes should be open with a blank stare, with no focus through the eyes, only focus through the shivering energy into the hip bone.

When this posture is done with the buttocks making no contact with the floor, the weight of the body is conveyed through the leg above the squatted foot. Conversely when it is done with the buttocks resting on the floor, the weight of the body is transferred to the opposing foot/leg/thigh combination. In the diagram which follows, the shivering energy is shown.

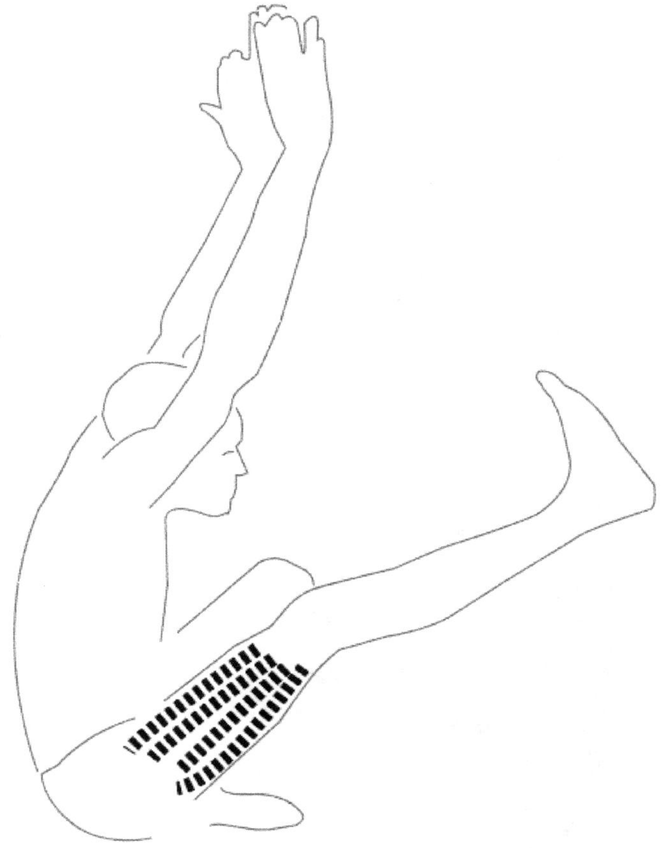

This posture is done with the toes pressed forward. It may be done with the arms/forearms/hands slanted instead of going straight up from shoulders. A yogi should remain in this posture, while studying the energy movements which are triggered.

Focus Connection

This *Squat near one Foot with other Foot/Leg/Thigh out* posture is difficult to assume if the buttocks with the lifted foot floats above the floor. When this posture is assumed, it should be completed with one foot outstretched. Then it should be done with the other foot. Then an easy pose should be assumed. If when that easy posture is done, there is a need for more relief, then even an easier posture should be done. Care should be taken so that there are no jerks nor rapid movement, which may cause energy shifts from the original pose.

A yogi should have time to do each posture, otherwise the inner focus will be haphazard. That will cause distraction, resulting in shattered insight into the benefit of the pose.

When the posture is assumed, there may be shivering in the lifted thigh. At first this may not happen. Eventually, either in a short space of time or after a while, there will be shivering. The yogi should monitor it. When it is intolerable, he should lower the lifted thigh. It may seem that light flashes, as the center of the thigh shivers. Then the yogi should lower the lifted thigh to the floor. This will provide partial relief.

As soon as the lowered thigh is normalized, the yogi should slowly switch, so that the other thigh is lifted and the first lifted one is positioned for squatting. After switching, the yogi should be attentive to the second thigh. He should keep it lifted. He should observe its energy actions. For this there should be a blindfold or the eyelids should be closed.

Again, when that lifted thigh shivers, the yogi should lower it. When it stabilizes, he should switch so that the other thigh which was lifted prior, is elevated. Switching like this, when it seems that both thighs are stressed, the yogi should sit on the floor with lower limbs outstretched. The hands should be on the legs near to the knee.

The yogi should execute inner focus, mentally looking through the neck. He should check to be sure that the spine is not arched. He should lift the waist, and keep the head and neck in alignment with the spine.

Meditation should be done by focusing mentally in the head of the subtle body, but with interest to know what happens elsewhere in the psyche.

- Are there inner sounds?
- Are there compelling thoughts and ideas?
- Is there a blank space, where the yogi can shelter from the attack of ideas?

One Foot Forward with one Knee in Back

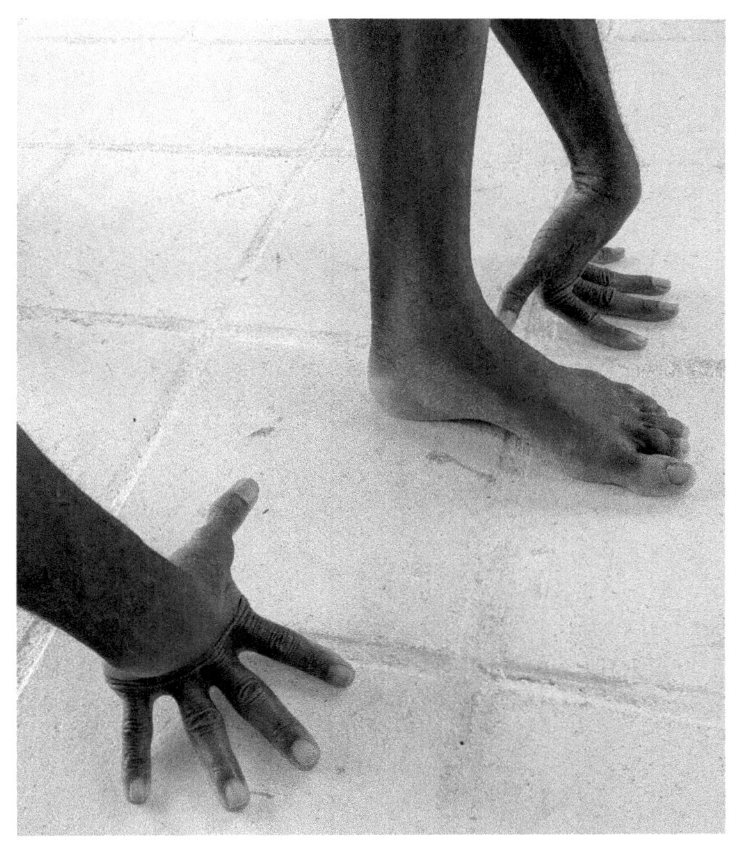

This *One Foot Forward with one Knee in Back* posture, is stepping forward with one foot. The other is positioned with the knee as the rear resting point. The leg and foot of that second food are positioned so that the knee serves as the support. Both hands are used as body supports. The fingers spread. The wrists, forearms and arms are vertical. These are taut. The head is held back with the chin raised as much as possible.

Within the body, there is focus of attention. A yogi may notice a random sweep of energy in the psyche, with a rushing to find a solution to the rapid shifting of energy. The head may be clear, but in the trunk of the body, the system will seek a resting place. It will decide that the energy of the forward thigh is where every other energy seeks to relocate.

In the rear thigh, some energy will shift but there will be no steadiness. The yogi should remain in the pose observing the flows.

After coming out of this pose, one should sit on the heels. Then, tilt the head back as far as can be tolerated. Remain in that position until the energies are relaxed and settled.

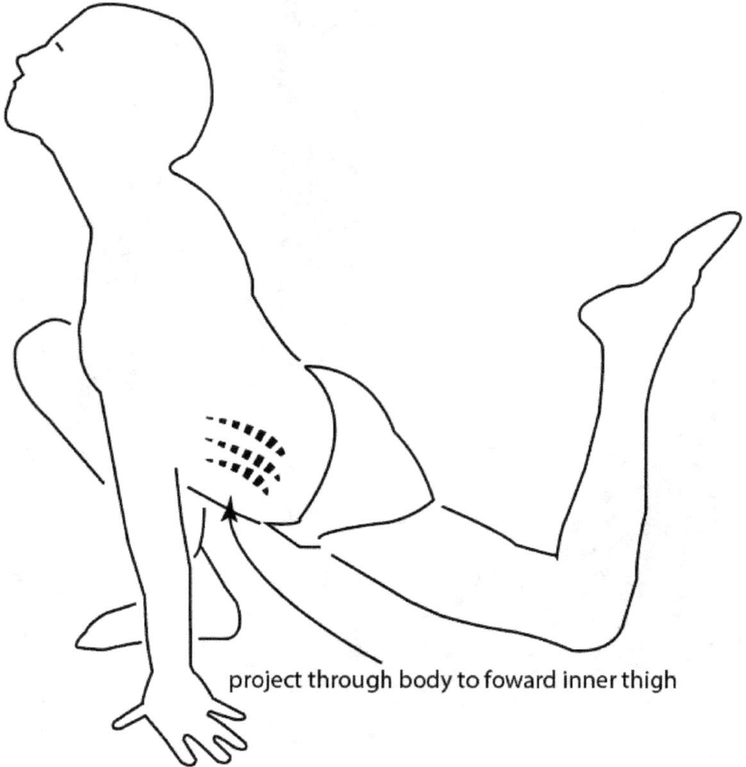

Focus Connection

For the *One Foot Forward with one Knee in Back* posture, the four fingers of each hand are held under tension. The thumbs are free of weight. The spine is pressed forward at the navel but the shoulders are held back. The head too is held back. The head may be situated to have the chin pressed to the throat or the head may be pushed backward as far as it can go. That is the backward neck lock.

In kundalini yoga, when doing breath infusion in various postures, the rear neck lock is discouraged for beginners. This is due to the fact, that as the kundalini passes through the neck and enters the brain, it is hard to control. For that the front neck lock, which is known as the chin lock, is efficient for checking and guiding kundalini safely, from the trunk of the body into the brain.

Yogis who become giddy when making movements or when doing breath infusion, are required to study the muscular locks for the physical body. These have a psychic counterpart which is in the subtle form. The physical application of muscular controls, translates into psychic control of various energy operations in the subtle body.

When doing the *One Foot Forward with one Knee in Back* posture, one side is done then the other side is used, when the first side becomes stressed. When the second side is stressed, the yogi can repeat the first side again. Following that, he may do the second one again. This can be repeated until he feels that the body should be rested.

For relaxing in this pose, he should go into any sitting position but he should do so without jerking the body or causing it to lose its energy configuration. In that pose he may sit on the heels or between the heels or sit in another easy pose. Then immediately, he should do inner focus to observe the energy movements. He must check to see if anything is facilitated, if thoughts are absent, if mental communication with others ceased.

Applying inner focus, he should continue sitting for a time. In whatever easy pose he assumed, he should be determined to meditate with observation. It may happen that he will drift into a refreshing sleep state or a state wherein there is partial sleep and partial alertness.

One Knee, one Heel and two Fingers Support

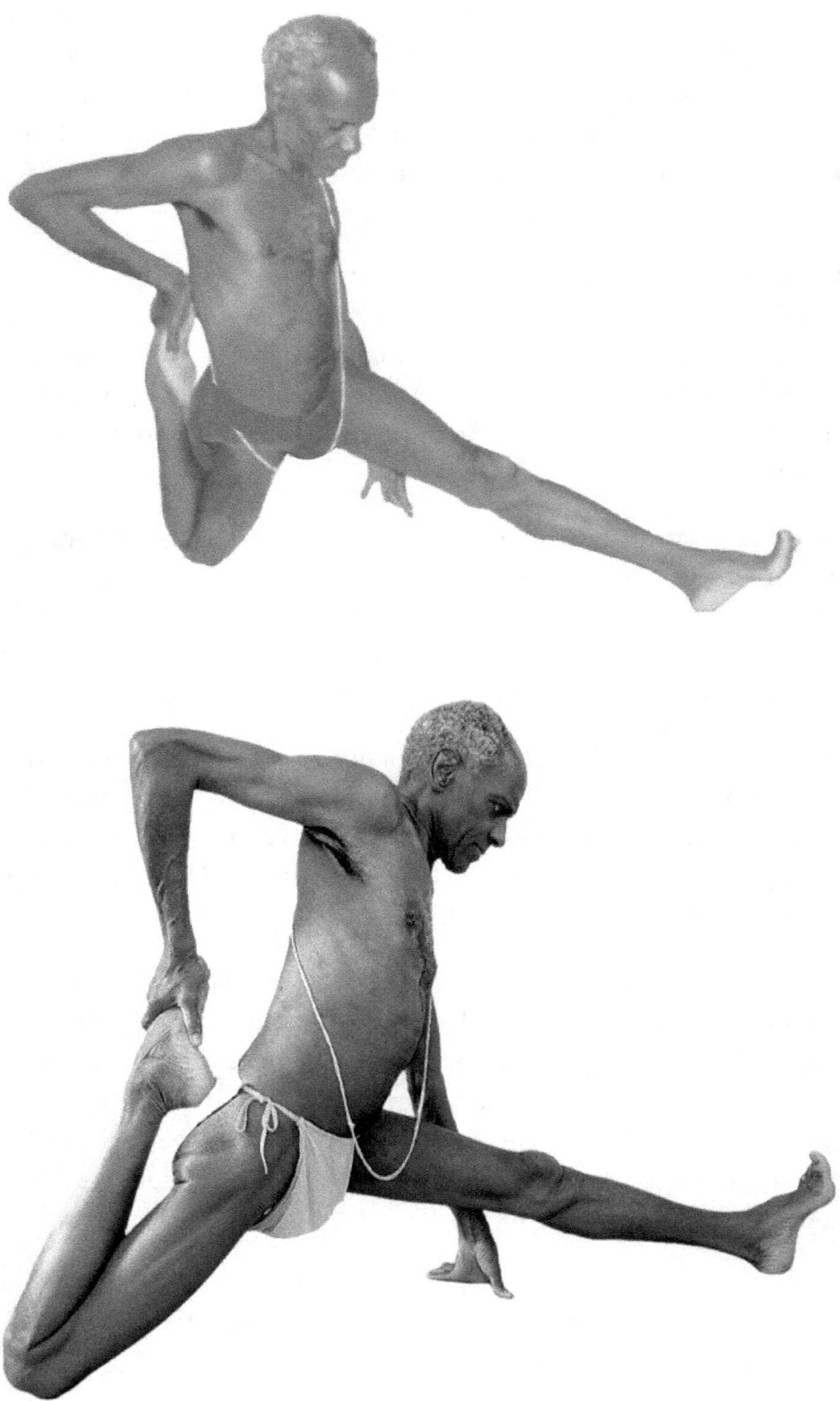

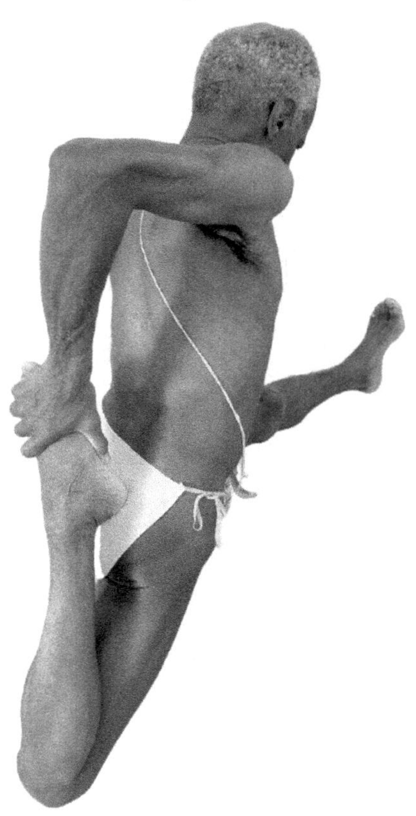

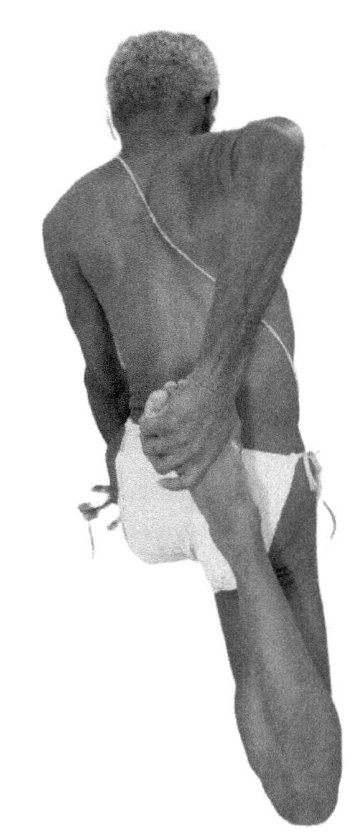

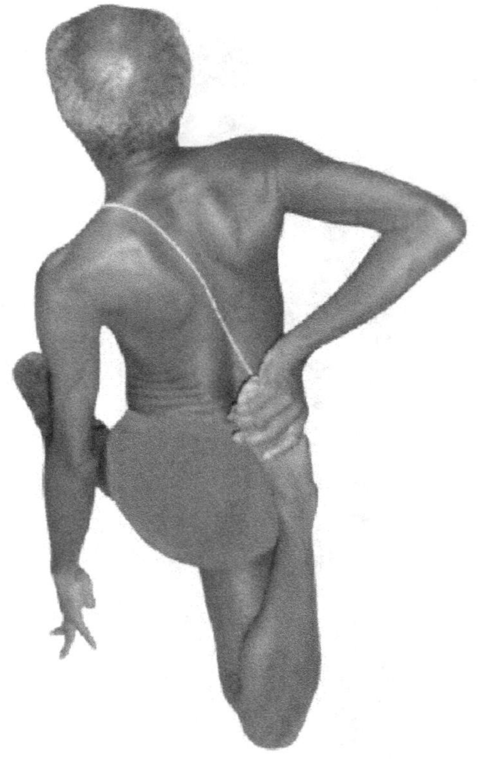

As in the diagrams above, the body is balanced on one knee, one heel and some fingers, two or three. The other hand grips the toes and keeps the sole of that foot close to the back of the body. Once this posture is steadied, the eyelids should be closed. Internal focus should be assumed. There should be observation, checking to know where energy flows, or is arrested.

In the pushed-out foot/leg/thigh, there will be energy flowing from the thighs into the knee. In the lower part of the leg, energy will flow into the ankle complex of bones.

In the other knee which is a contact point with the floor, energy will flow from the thigh into that knee. Observe the diagram.

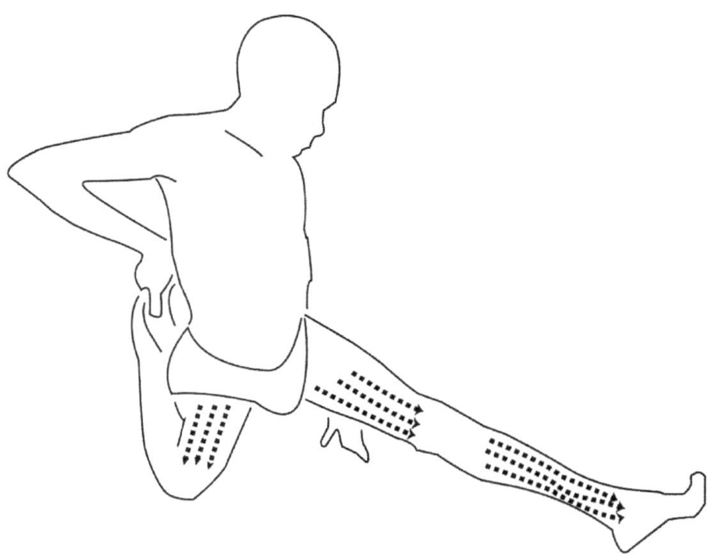

Focus Connection

The *One Knee, one Heel and two Fingers Support* pose, may be done with four fingers for support. The hand used for support, may touch the floor partially or entirely. A cushioned surface for supporting the knee and heel which touch the floor, is useful in reducing the pain of contact, where the body is supported. As soon as the pose is assumed, the yogi should check to be sure that the posture is balanced. The outstretched limb should be inspected from within the body. The check is on the inner condition. How the posture looks physically has no relevance.

The yogi should do a flash check. Then, from within the mind, he should shift attention to the outstretched thigh. The direction of energy in the thigh should be known.

- Is the energy flowing into the pelvic region?
- Is it going into the legs or ankles?

Collecting the energy in the head of the body, the yogi should move into the outstretched limb. If there is resistance, where the yogi cannot do this, or if it happens but the energy jumps back to the head, and does not remain in the thigh, the yogi should consider this. He should account for this behavior.

At some point when this investigation ceases, the yogi should switch so that the outstretched limb is repositioned to make the other limb as the outstretched one. When this switch is made, the yogi should do the observations with the other side of the body. When he is satisfied that enough was done, he should sit on his heels or between his heels or in another posture for relaxation.

The yogi should meditate. He may feel energy falling, like rain over a forest. He should appreciate this falling energy which is a bliss radiating environment. He should absorb it.

Hands on Heels- Camel Pose – Upright Bow Pose

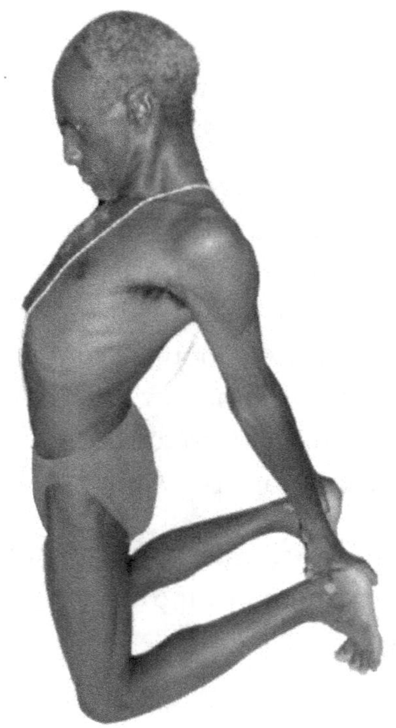

This *Hands on Heels - Camel Pose – Upright Bow* pose, is known as camel posture. It has variations. This example is with the feet up. A common format for this, is with feet flat down. In this example, the hands are on the heels. The toes are pressed forward. There are variations, where the hands make contact with the Achilles tendons. In the photo, the head is pressed forward. In a variation, it may be tilted back. When it is pressed forward, the yogi feels the esophagus. The tracheal is not compressed even though there is tension in the neck and throat.

As soon as this posture is assumed, the yogi should inFocus. Eyelids should be closed to prevent visual distractions. Focus should be in the trunk of the body. There may be a partition line at the waist, such that energy comes up into the trunk, and is dispersed. It loses format when it reached the shoulders. Otherwise, there will be energy which diverges from the waist down through the bucket of glands which are in the pelvis complex. The energy which goes down, will be of short shoots like a two-inch spike of light. The energy which goes up from the waist into the chest, will be like a five inch spike of light.

In this posture, the waist is pressed forward. This causes the abdomen to lift and be drawn to the spine. Where the vertebrae deviate from being centered, where it begins to tilt backwards, a tension is felt.

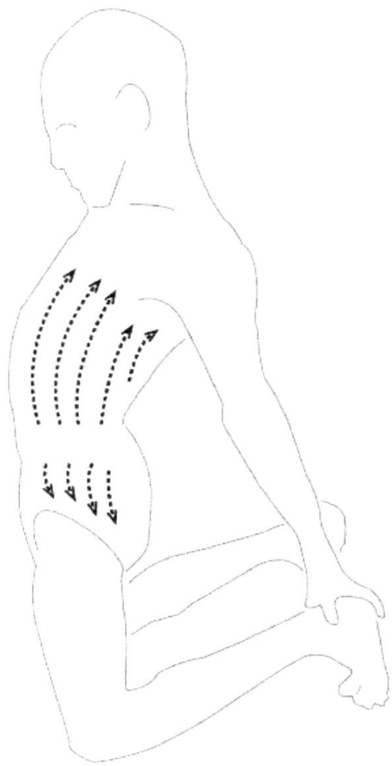

Focus Connection

In the quest for *samadhi* trance absorption states, to make contact with higher planes of existence, and to feel the quality of self, which is beyond soberness in this physical world, a yogi must research various types of contacts and transits. There are two ways to achieve this. One is to wait for happenings which are spontaneous. The other is to put the self in an existential position, which makes it more likely, for it to experience higher dimensions, either through contact with supernatural, and spiritual beings, or to access higher planes.

Patanjali yoga is an aggressive process, for making the psyche of the self more likely to access higher dimensions. That yoga charts and maps methods. Some of these may work for one yogi. Some may not. The system or process has leeway, so that experiences gained, may be charted by student yogis, so that details which are not elaborated in the *Yoga Sutras*, are hinted or divulged.

Keen observations should be made when doing any part of the eight sectioned process, which Patanjali charted. Even when doing *asana* postures, a yogi should be attentive within the psyche. He should note energy movements. He should not be concerned with the external format, as to if it is attractive or impressive. The physical actions during yoga, have a psychic counterpart, which is the factor to hold his investigative interest.

The idea that yoga is gymnastics, is ludicrous. That view is held by those who want to use yoga for body display, and by others who want to ridicule yoga, as being a physical system, which has nothing to do with spirituality.

When doing the *Hands on Heels - Camel Pose – Upright Bow Pose,* the pelvic region is pressed forward fully. The chin is kept close to the body to compress the throat. The head is tilted forward.

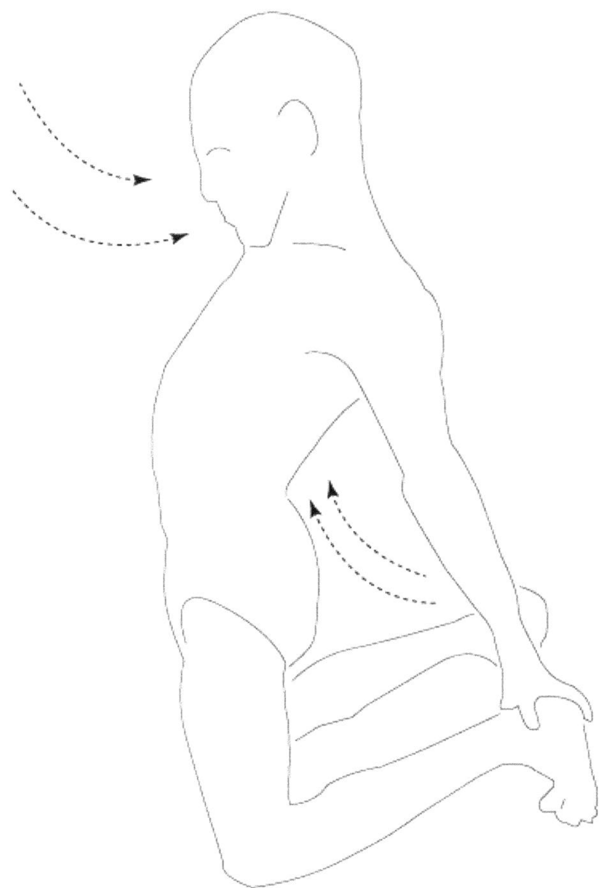

The feet are positioned so that the big toes only are used for support. But there is variation, where the big toes and two or more other toes are used together for support. Whatever is used, should be noted mentally. A yogi is concerned with the internal format. To someone looking at his practice, his external movements and positions may seem to be the achievement. And yet that is not the focus.

A yogi must check the hands which are on the heels. The hands and fingers will be stressed. The spread of energy should be noted. It should be diagramed mentally. It should be realized emotionally. Slowly he should direct his hands to slide to the floor. This is for causing the hands to bear the weight directly to the floor, instead of transferring the weight through the heels and feet. When the hands contact the floor, they should be close to the feet, and should have a fist shape. That allows firmness so that the weight does not pass through any individual finger. It passes through the wrist and then the fingers collectively.

From that position, the yogi should lower the body, so that he sits between the heels. The hands should rest on the thighs. The feet should be flat on the floor. At this point, the yogi should shift into meditation, to discover quiet energies in the psyche. Until it becomes intolerable, he should remain with the buttocks between the heels.

After that posture becomes stressed, the yogi without any rash movements, and keeping the inner focus as an investigation, should sit in any easy pose. He should meditate. Instead of setting a period of time for it, he should leave the duration open.

The ability of the mind to be unsettled, its tendency to not have definite focus, its periodic habit to create thinking schemes, its susceptibility to thought invasions from others, should be patiently noted. If there is any portal which opens to a bliss environment, or to a spiritual being who inspires, that should be experienced. A yogi should wonder about his future, in regards to how long it may take to achieve the divine eye, and portal access to higher worlds.

Stretch Forward / Under-cross Leg

This *Stretch Forward / Under-cross Leg* position, is a variation of the pigeon pose. It focuses on the hip which is connected to the forward knee. The hands are supportive of the chest-abdomen area. A hatha yogi should do this pose with inner concentration on the energies, which run wild in the psyche, when this post is assumed. It should be discovered that many energies in the forward thigh, run towards its corresponding hip joint. When the energies arrive there, they are streamlined. A yogi finds that the energy turns to go upwards into the subtle head.

If this pose is mastered, it will be discovered that during its assumption, there is a loud volume of naad whistling sound in the subtle head. This will saturate the head. The yogi will be induced to focus into it.

In this posture, it is best to close the eyelids. That will decrease the likelihood for the mind to wander to visual objects. Because of the herding of the random energies which this pose causes, a yogi will find that he cannot think during this pose. That itself makes this a valuable posture for aiding in sensual withdrawal and focus, which are known as *pratyahar* and *dharana*.

Hatha yoga or *Asana/Pranayama/Pratyahar/Samyama* yoga is not a waste of time. That holds true if a yogi focuses internally to the mind and feelings of the subtle body. Otherwise, if one does the postures with an intention of making the physical body fit and pretty, one will not derive psychological insight. The key is to explore the subtle body and to upgrade it.

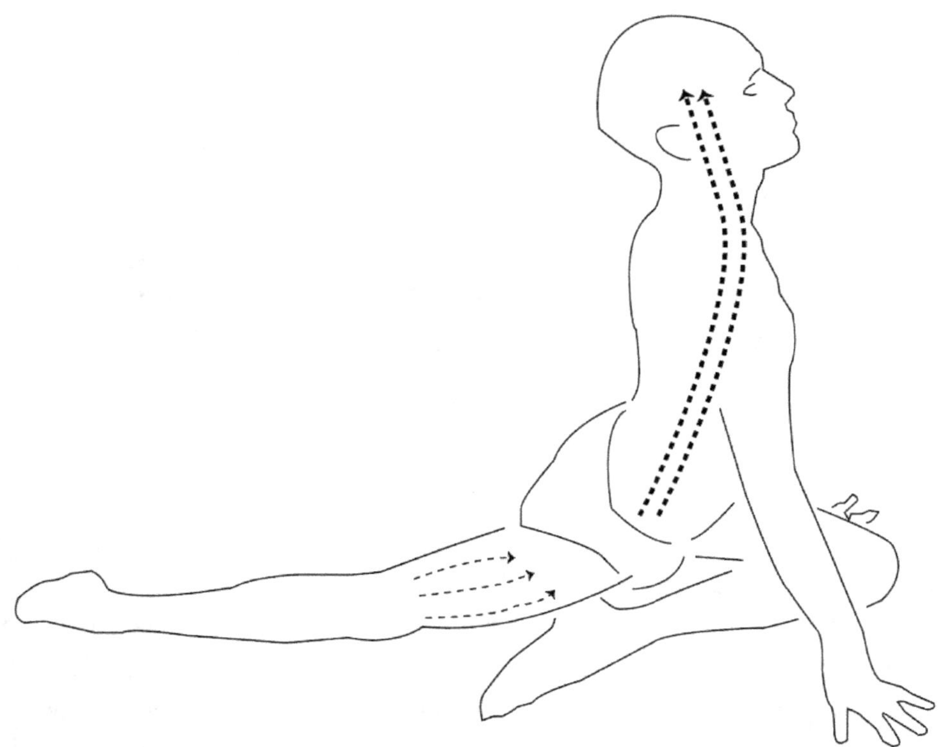

Focus Connection

This *Stretch Forward / Under-cross Leg* posture, is easy for some, but it would be trying for others. It is however valuable when studying the problem of *dharana* or the 6th stage of yoga, that of applying the attention to a higher concentration force or to discover such a force or person. When one is confronted with a blank mind, or a vacant space for a mind, or hollowness for a mind, there arises the problem of how to focus within that situation. If there is an object, focus is easy. The sense of focus is designed to apprehend objects. It may be a tiny or cosmic object. Provided there is some contrast with it, focus can be applied. If to the contrary, the object is present without contrast, or if it is simply not detected by the focus, then to hold the focus somewhere in reference to it, is problematic.

This pose, the *Stretch Forward / Under-cross Leg* posture helps considerably in training the mind how to remain focused when there is no distinct or indicated object. How does one focus when there is nothing for a focus, when the object expected is not present, or does not appear before the viewer.

Some students of *asana* yoga, posture assumption, feel that the pain and stress in postures is undesirable. This is the wrong approach. It lacks the understanding that starting with physical discipline, one can graduate to subtle body mastership. The pains and stress in a posture can help the yogi to discover various areas or zones in the subtle body. Most of all, one can learn to focus within the psyche. That is psychological perception which can be developed if the postures are done with care, with intention to discover the subtle system.

When doing the *Stretch Forward / Under-cross Leg* pose, a yogi should hold the neck perpendicular to the floor. For the limb which is stretched backwards, the thigh, knee, leg and foot touch the floor. For the limb which is forward, the knee and toes touch the floor.

One side is done. The yogi remains in that posture for a time. The other side is done. In each there is intent inner focus, where the yogi tracks the energy which is observed. There may be a confusion of energy at first. This will be such that it is difficult to determine what originates from where, and what is being resolved in some place in the psyche. Particularly in the shoulders and thighs, there may be confusion. The focus will find tensions, because some of it will emit pain sensations.

The yogi should hold the posture steady. If need be, he may reposition a part of it. He could move one hand or some other part of the body. Such shifts should be done quietly without jolting. In that way, the focus is kept constant within the psyche. The examination or mapping should continue as before.

After a time, much confusion will vanish. The yogi should slowly switch to the other side, so that the limb that was in the rear, becomes the one in the forward position. Once assumed, this should be held for focus.

Noting the energy confusion and its distribution, the yogi should compare it to the situation he observed when doing the other side.

- What is the difference?
- Does the application of focus hold better on one side?

In that way a yogi understands the behavior of the mind.

A yogi, after doing either side, should apply focus according to how the confusion of energy is settled. Then, he may shift focus into the hollow space of the eye which is on the side of the forward foot. This hollow may have a spheric edge which is slight and hard to detect. However, it will give the yogi practice, in focusing on what is subtle. This is an ability which he must have to be successful with the three highest stages of the yoga process.

In this pose, when focusing on either side, a yogi can study how tension and pain demand the application of focus. When a pain calls for attention, it instantly gets it. But when the yogi wants to focus into the blank mind, the focus drifts and may be arrested even by a thought sequence.

- Why is this?

Submitting the self when the mind to applies itself to the pain or stress, helps the yogi to develop the ability to focus where there is blankness, hollowness, or scattered random energy, which has no focal point.

Lean Back Folding at Knees

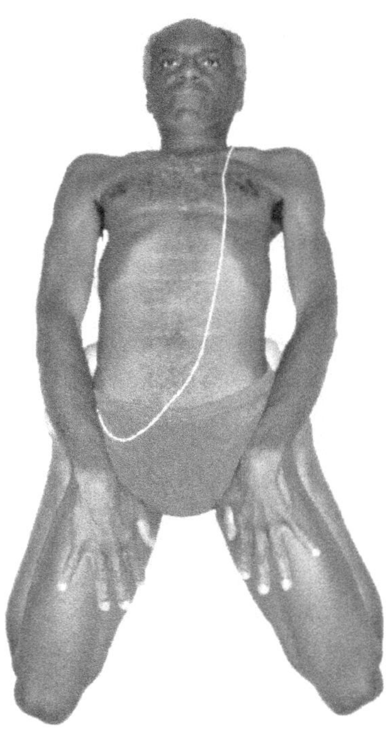

In this *Lean Back Folding at Knees* pose, the scapula lays on the floor, along with the buttocks and the back of the head. The hands may be on the thighs or floor. One remains relaxed in this position. If, however, this posture feels unnatural, one may do it with a pillow between the scapula and the floor, so that the back of the head is on the pillow as well. *Asana* posture is useful in developing inside concern of the psyche. However, an effort should be made to cause the mind to focus internally during various positions. A yogi should release himself/herself from the need to use posture for beauty. If postures are used for developing a beautiful form, it is likely that there will be no progress to the higher stages of yoga, which are *pranayama* breath infusion, *pratyahar* sensual energy withdrawal, *dharana deliberate* inner focus, *dhyana* spontaneous inner focus, and *samadhi* prolonged spontaneous inner focus.

This pose can be used to develop *dharana* which is internal focus with deliberate avoidance of external objects. In this posture the attention of the self is applied internally. Hence, the system of sensual apprehension no longer has interest for things, which are outside the psyche.

A yogi will feel a quivering energy when this posture is assumed. It may be such that at the base of the spine, there is a shimmering pulsation of energy, which radiates through the body, and passes through the neck continuously into the head.

To use this internal focus, one should close the eyelids and mentally go to the base of the spine. Once there, one should trace the energy which is released in this pose. There may be a quivering of subtle power moving through the trunk. This will rapidly move through the trunk and enter the neck. When it passes through the head, it will resonate and quiver, to arrive at the place where the skull meets the floor.

A yogi should focus on that. One may do this pose for a minimum of three minutes.

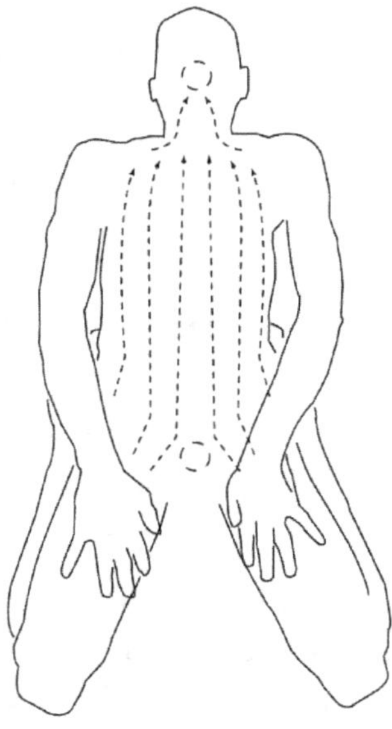

Focus Connection

When doing the *Lean Back Folding at Knees* pose, it is important that no extra stress is felt anywhere. It is best to support any part of the body which makes contact with the floor. These places are the head, scapulas (shoulder blades), buttocks, and thighs. Set up the cushions before assuming the pose. Spend time determining what support is needed. Acquire the cushioning and put it in place.

After assuming the pose, dig deep within the body. If no blindfold is used, be sure to keep the eyelids closed. Focus within the body. Search for and map energies. Check where the pelvic cage meets the abdomen. There may be tension there. On each side three coils of energy may be discovered. These may move through the torso, going upward through the neck, and then enter the head. These may curl toward the jaws and disappear there. This will be a continuous transmission for some time. Eventually this will cease, or it will continue, but the encouragement to be aware of it, may vanish.

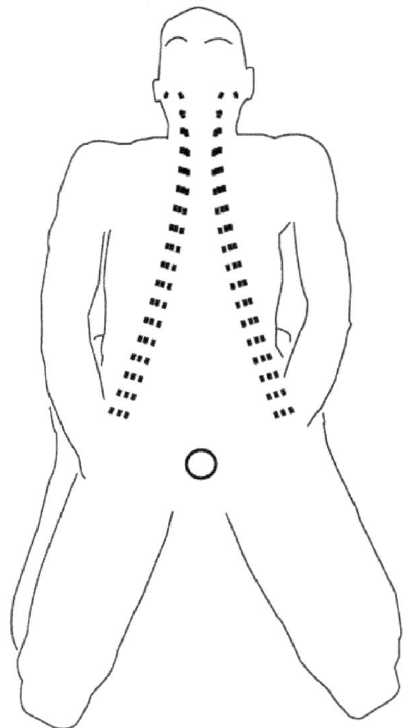

The yogi should raise the torso to sit upright. He may hear naad inner frequency streaming. He should focus to determine its source or location.

On Back – Knees to Chest – Chin Pressed to Throat

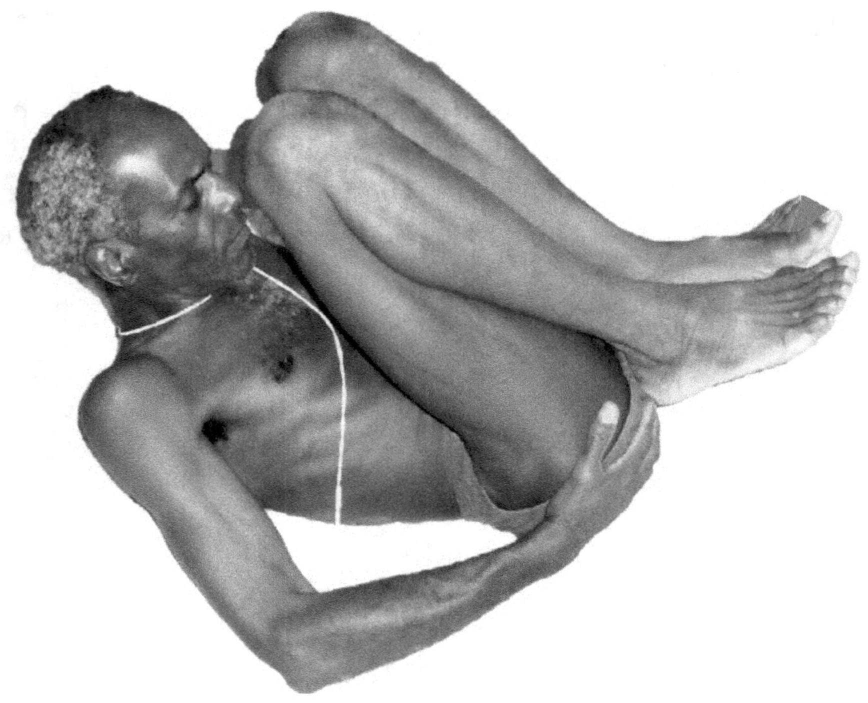

For this *On Back – Knees to Chest – Chin Pressed to Throat* pose, the knees are pulled to the chest. The hands grip the buttocks. This is done while the body is balanced on the back. The toes may or may not be pressed forward. If they are pressed, the yogi should be sure that his attention does not scatter as a result. If it does, he should let the toes assume a relaxed position.

The head is pulled up. The chin is pressed over the Adam's apple (laryngeal prominence). This is an important hold in this posture. This is a throat lock. The knees should be pulled towards the chest and held there. If somehow the knees relax, the yogi should restore them toward the chest. The elbows may or may not touch the floor.

Once this posture is assumed, a yogi should check to be sure that the eyelids are closed. This stops the mind from pursuing visual objects. While pressing the chin inward to the throat, the yogi should be aware of streaming energy which moves through the upper chest. It flows to the vertebrae which are behind the throat. There should be a centralizing position, where the streaming energy enters and disappears. A yogi should focus on this energy which will flow continuously. After a short time, the naad sound may be heard. That is a high-pitched frequency. This is an *asana* posture which takes the yogi to a *dhyana* spontaneous steady inner focus.

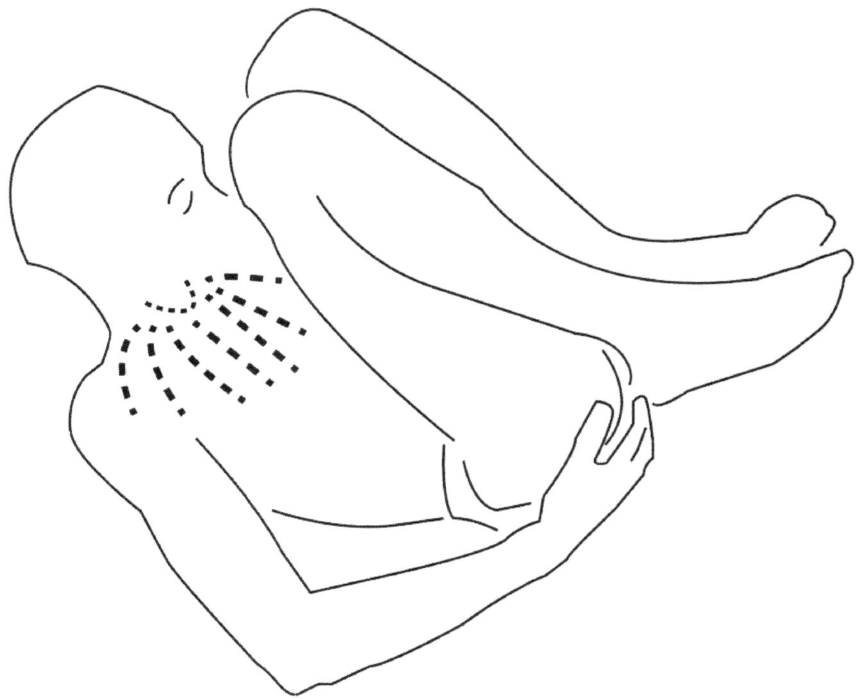

Focus Connection

This *On Back – Knees to Chest – Chin Pressed to Throat* posture, explains to the yogi from within his psyche, what *dhyana*, the 7th aspect of yoga, is. This is a sample of *dhyana*, which is highlighted by there being no application of willpower force, nor does it require focus on a target. The focus happens spontaneously. It relieves the yogi from the task of willpower application, a method which must be applied for the *dharana* 6th stage of yoga, which is generation, and direction of focus within the mind.

The spontaneous focus in this pose, is generated from where there is muscular tension at the back of the base of the skull, where the muscles in the neck connect. Those are the suboccipital muscles. They are put under tension in this pose. The result is that they demand attention which is amply given. The yogi may use this pose to observe this process of *dhyana* spontaneous focus. A yogi should learn how to recognize when that process happens. Many students experience high states of consciousness, for short or long periods, but cannot identify these levels of awareness. Thus, they do not learn how to use some higher states. By studying these positions of consciousness when they naturally occur, or when they occur in certain postures, the student integrates various states.

When in this posture, a yogi feels that he should relax, the head should be rested on the floor. This means that the *dhyana* spontaneous focus in the muscles at the base of the skull, will vanish. Instead, the yogi may feel that the eyes are filled with heat. The spontaneous focus will shift there.

With focus going to the heat in the eyes, the yogi may hear naad inner sound which may be like a whistling frequency. At this time, there will be no thoughts. But the yogi may realize that a thought is displayed. It may be so vague that the yogi cannot read it. It would be like something faded beyond recognition. But then naad inner sound will be heard again. It will be coherent.

That is a *dhyana* focus but on sound, with no tension, nor muscular energy release. Some thought may arise but it will fade. It will have no displaying power. Inner sound will broadcast continuously.

Inverse Wheel Pose

This *Inverse Wheel Pose* is exceptional, for gaining an understanding about the compact psychological energy in the subtle body. This pose should be done on a surface which has traction. It is necessary that once the feet and hands are placed and the body is elevated, that the limbs do not shift. If one senses a shift, one should slowly lower the body. Then, one should reposition the feet and hands.

Once the hands and feet are in place, one should raise the body gradually. When one reaches the maximum in pushing the trunk, one should stop and hold steady. If there is uncertainty, one should lower the body. Then do the posture again.

Once this practice is mastered, one should get the trunk up, steady the posture, and then focus within the physical and subtle bodies, noting the energy which traverses in the psyche.

After staying up in a steady hold, one should with closed or opened eyelids, focus within the body to discover the traversing energy. When one feels that one should lower the body, one should slowly (not rapidly and not with jerks) lower it. When the trunk is on the floor and without moving the hands or feet, the yogi should focus within the detect the shimmering energies.

One may feel that one should gasp for air. This is because in this posture, when the trunk of the body is elevated, the heart is compressed. It yields less blood flow. To normalize the system, the heart will increase its pumping rate, and conversely the lungs will gasp for air. A yogi should note this.

During this *Inverse Wheel Pose,* the thighs will release energy. It will also reconfigure the way it handles blood distribution. When the yogi realizes that the system needs more air, he should increase the intake. That should be remedied when the trunk is lowered and is relaxed.

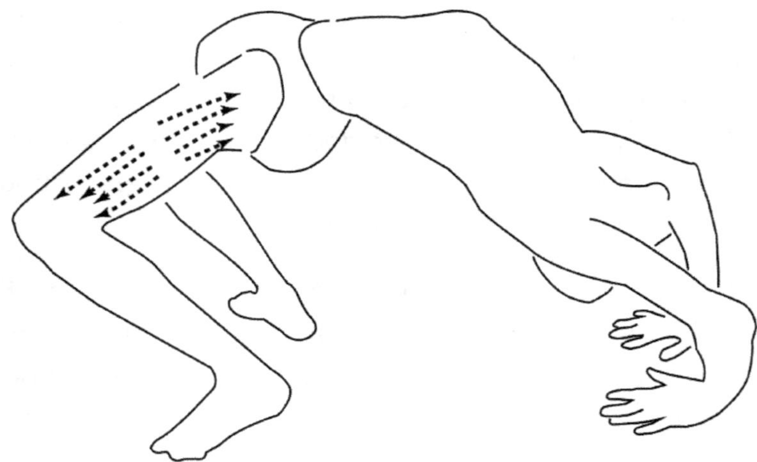

Focus Connection

The *Inverse Wheel Pose* is difficult. It should not be forced. One may or may not master it. The ability to do it does not guarantee success in *asana* postures. The inability to assume it, does not stamp one as a failure at yoga practice. A yogi should know that the genetic design of the body received by the parents, carry limitations. One should do the best, but should not expect that every posture can be perfected with any physical body.

To do the I*nverse Wheel Pose*, one should lay on the back of the body. Then, one should calm the mind and think about the objective. While lying on the back, one should bring the feet near the buttocks. The hands should be positioned near the shoulders. Mentally one should check this.

When one is confident that the feet and palms are positioned on the floor, one should check for slippage. If it seems that the floor is slippery, one should either rise and install a rug or mat, or go to a floor which has no slippage. With the hands and feet positioned, the yogi should check the entire body and reposition it if needs be.

At first one should raise the buttocks. Then one should be attentive within the body. One should listen inside the psyche, checking the mental condition of the entire body. With the buttocks elevated, one should check the feet to determine if they should be pulled closer to the buttocks. The yogi should make any other adjustments to the feet or hands. Slowly, one should begin rising the rest of the body. This will cause the arms and forearms to be stressed. This is done at a slow pace. If it seems that one cannot assume the full pose when lifting the body, one should stop, and hold the position.

Hold the body in the partial or full position. It should be done with care, so as not to strain tendons nor muscles, and not to cause other injury. Inner checking of the condition of the body is necessary. One should not allow the mind to lose concern for the body. Due to the potential for damaging the body, rash movements are prohibited.

Once the yogi reaches as far up as is safe for his body, he should stop. With the mind internalized, he should hold that pose either in a partial or full format. He should hold it as long as he can tolerate. Then slowly he should lower the body. Once the body is lowered, where the back is lowered to the floor, he should check to see if the stress in the body was relieved.

Feeling that the tensions ceased, he should check for other energy movements. A yogi may notice that the rate of breathing increased. He should have a positive attitude towards the lifeForce for doing this. Appreciation for the lifeForce, which commits many involuntary actions for the maintenance of the physical and subtle body, is a correct attitude.

Foot Out- Foot In – with Palms Support

This *Foot Out - Foot In – with Palms Support* is an easy posture. From a squatting position, one foot is pushed out. The weight of the body is shifted to the toes of the foot which remains in the squatting posture. Both hands are set on the floor. The yogi presses forward slightly.

The yogi closes the eyelids. He checks within the subtle body and the physical system, to detect and track energy. There may be movements which are similar to cramps. These should be in the wrists, hands, and fingers. A check should be made to be sure that the chin is pulled to the throat. The eyelids should be closed. The focus should be where the energy accumulates, or runs to some other parts of the psyche.

This is not a difficult posture, but it causes the yogi to feel energy moving through the forearms, and becoming intense in the wrist. This intensity will move towards the intersection of the fingers and the wrists. Some energy from the fingers will be blocked. It will be confronted by energy coming down the forearms into the wrist. After a short time, even for fifteen seconds, the yogi may hear inner sound, naad. This will be a ringing sound which persists. A yogi can skip out of this posture by slowly pulling back the out-stretched foot. Then he should squat with arms over the knees. He may meditate in that posture for a time. Naad resonance, way be predominant.

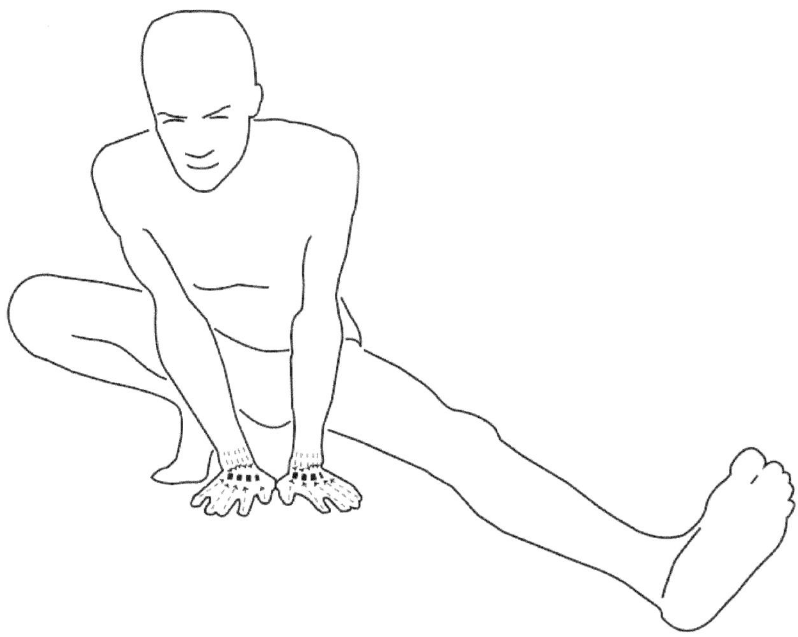

After a short time, even for fifteen seconds, the yogi may hear inner sound, naad. This will be a ringing sound which persists. A yogi can slip out of this posture by slowly pulling back the out-stretched foot. Then he should squat with arms over the knees. He may meditate in that posture. Naad resonance will be predominant.

Focus Connection

This *Foot Out - Foot In - with Palms Support,* is relatively easy for anyone. If, however, there is discomfort, the yogi may use cushions under the stretched heel or weight bearing toes or the hands. In this posture the foot which is held under the buttocks is the main weight absorption area. The stretched out foot carries no weight. However, it helps somewhat to keep the body in balance. The weight bearing foot has the heel as the contact with the buttocks.

The hands are flat on the floor but carry no weight. They assist in keeping the body balanced. After being in this posture for a time, there may be a slight shivering at the elbows and under the shoulders. When this is checked within the body, it will emanate a confusion of energy which is not focused, but which is haphazard and forms a zone of confusion.

The yogi, when checking here and there in the psyche, may notice that there is spontaneous focus, where the buttocks meet the heel. No effort is required to focus there. Instead, the focus is held there by the energy which is at the contact of the buttocks, and the heel of that retracted foot.

When checking to map the energy, a yogi may notice that there is no specific point. Instead, there is a zone in which the shivering occurs. This is observed in detail to get some understanding about the spontaneous *dhyana* focus when there is no dot or point location nor object upon which to focus.

- How does a yogi hold focus within the psyche towards a zone or area?

Doing this posture and staying in it for some time, gives practice in zone observation process. This accelerates progress for meditation.

Front Hold Shins Rooster

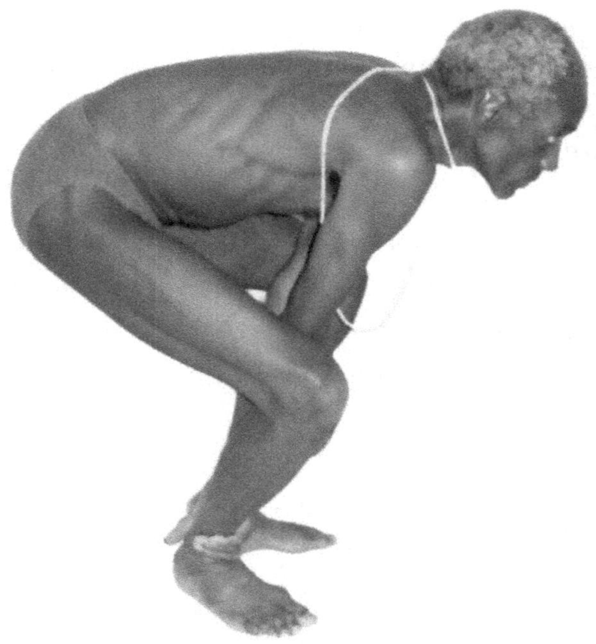

This is the *Front Hold Shins Rooster* pose. Alternately, the shins may be held with the thumbs holding the front from the outside while the first finger *(not little finger)* compresses the Achilles tendon.

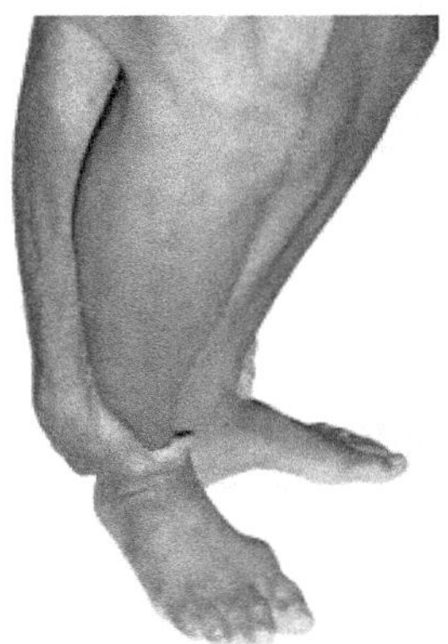

The yogi should be sure that the spine is as parallel to the ground as his body can tolerate.

This pose may cause kundalini to rise suddenly. Hence, a yogi should apply the locks before coming out of this pose. If *bhastrika,* or *kapalabhati, pranayama* breath infusion is done in this pose, a yogi should take care that the reverse neck lock is used, while doing the breath infusion. However as soon as the infusion is finished, the forward neck lock with the chin pressing towards the throat should be applied. The anus lock should be checked to be sure that it is applied. Perineum should be pulled as well. Abdomen should be pulled to the spine.

The yogi should stand with the locks, even with the abdomen retracted. With great care, with the mind-focus being applied, the yogi should slowly move into a sitting position. There is the likelihood that the kundalini will take control of the body, in which case it may fall to the ground. Hence, the floor should be padded.

It takes some years to master this pose while doing breath infusion. In fact, I recommend that while doing this, one should have someone stand near the body, where that person is sturdy enough to hold the body, to prevent it from falling.

After doing this pose, a yogi may sit in the lotus posture. He should be focused in the spine and head, to check the whereabouts of the physio-psychic energy. Naad resonance which is a continuous ringing sound, may be part of the focusing objective.

The fear of the kundalini lifeForce rising, must be taken into account. This happens because of a lack of regular inner focus. For instance, sometimes when someone stands, there is a rush of energy through the torso into the neck and head. A yogi should be attentive to that. In any example, when circumstantially, one has to pass urine and cannot do so because of being in a location which is not suitable, there develops a discomfort energy. As soon as one sees a toilet or urinal, one becomes anxious to use it. There may be an electric sensation in the ureter relief valve.

Again, when one releases the urine, there may be an increase in the electric sensation, where it may be spread into the shoulders and arms. This is kundalini but we do not make to effort to study and regulate it. Again, during sexual arousal, and during sexual discharge, there are sharp darting currents which spreads from the genitals to other parts of the body. This also is kundalini.

- What effort does one make to study this?

Kundalini is in the body functioning as an involuntary force, which one may monitor and manage to some degree. For the most part it is an independent electric generator. The purpose of *pranayama* is to get into an existential position, to study and best manage this force. That is kundalini yoga.

A yogi should abandon the tendency to use posture practice (*asana*) to form an attractive physical body. He should also not be obsessed to use postures to improve and maintain the health of the body. If one keeps the physical format and the healthy condition in mind while doing postures, one will lose sight of the spiritual benefits which may be derived. What will happen is that one will fail or succeed at making the body handsome or pretty. That will not give one supernatural vision. It is the subtle body which is the target. Hence during *asana,* whatever tension or relief, one experiences, should be processed by the mind in terms of what it facilitates or hinders in the psyche, the subtle body.

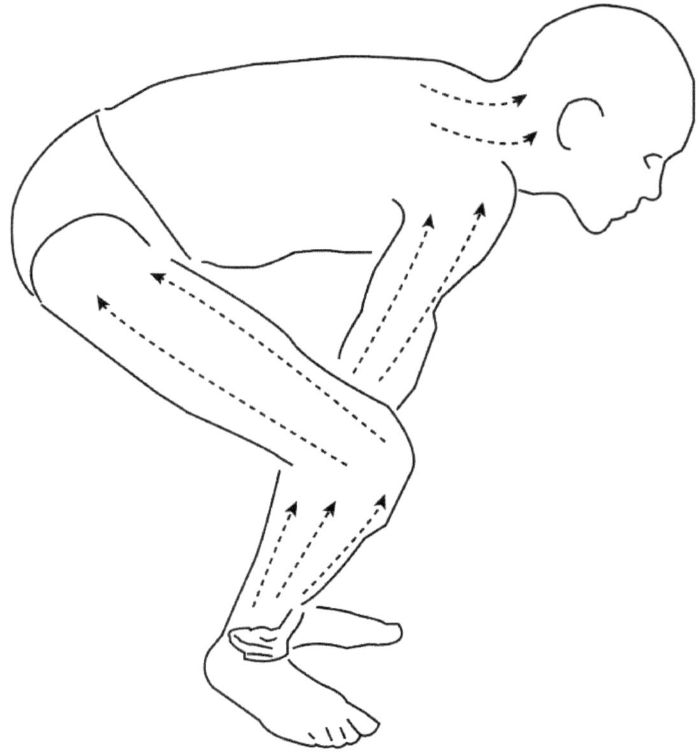

Focus Connection

That posture, *Front Hold Shins Rooster,* has stress which requires awareness in the feet, ankles, legs, thighs, hands, wrists, forearms and arms. These areas exhibit nervousness. They may twitch when the nerves react to the position.

When the yogi can no longer hold this, he should, without losing inner vigilance, connect the fists to the floor. Then, the buttocks should be slowly lowered. In that position, he should keep the head tilted back as far as possible.

He should focus on the back of the head, the area where the neck meets the skull. He should lower the buttocks but keep the focus where the skull meets the back of the neck. A yogi may experience an attractive blankness at this place. He should focus there and experience a meditative state, where the focus is easy to observe. He should appreciate this blank space. Focusing there, causes the mind to appreciate spontaneous clearness.

On Back Grab Toes

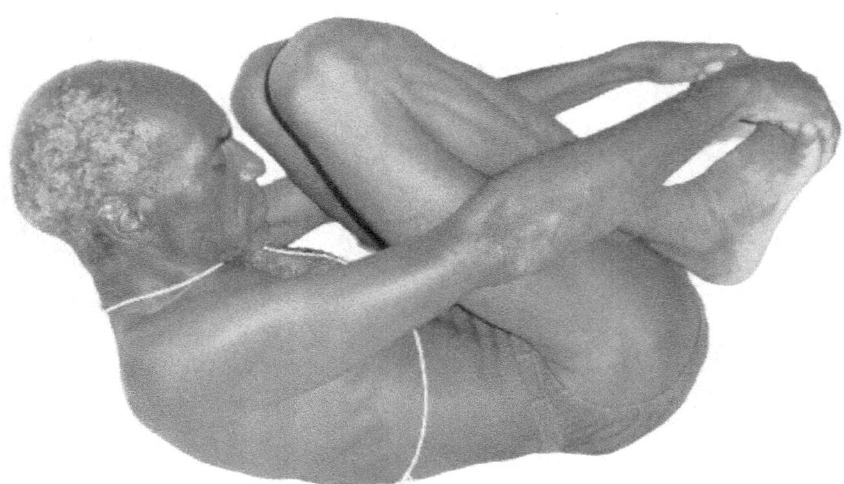

In that *On Back Grab Toes* pose, the yogi grabs the toes with the hands. He raises the head and presses the chin to the throat. The toes are grabbed from the outside. He checks to be sure that the head is pulled up as far as possible. The chin is pressed on the throat. The back is curved inwards.

When this is done, the eyelids are closed. Inner focus is applied, so that there is no interest in anything physical, which is outside the body. The yogi should be sure that the head is raised as much as it could be. He should press the chin to the throat.

He should hold the pose and shift focus to locate the energies which attract his attention. Whatever happens due to the pose should be the focus for the meditation. If need be, he should slowly do a count of numbers. If he can, he should focus on the scattering of energy, or the random spread of it, or flashes, or streaks of it. He may hear sounds or throbs. Whatever it is, he should focus on it. Since these occurrences will happen with no effort to make them occur, this is a *dhyana* spontaneous occurrence.

After a time, after some seconds or minutes, the yogi should relax the body from the pose. This should be done slowly. Then the yogi should remain in a reclined easy stress-less pose. In that he should note any events. He should focus. If there is inner sound, he should be attentive to it. This could evolve into *samadhi* which is prolong spontaneous focus.

In this pose, being on the back and grabbing the toes, there may be a formation of energy in the area of the Adam's apple in the throat. This may be two strands, like two passengers who use bodies of light. These will go through the eyes and into the brain. This will be like a screaming energy which speaks aloud.

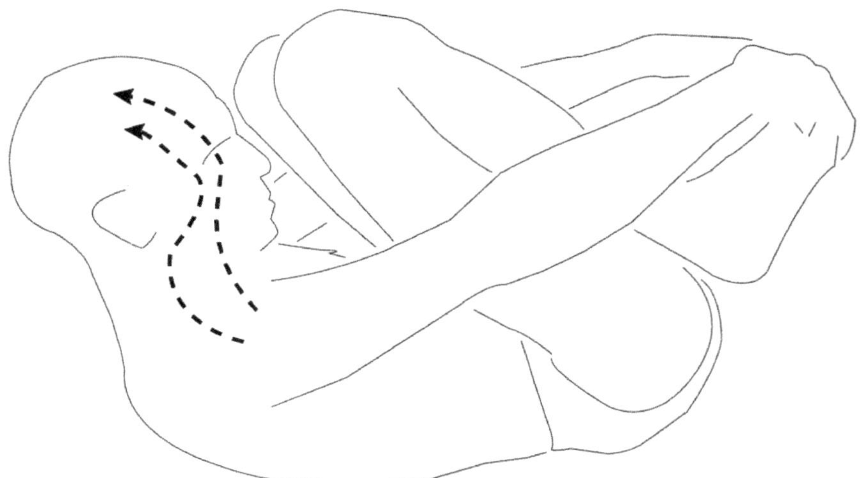

Yogeshwarananda suggested the composition of this book. He wanted to give hints on how *asana* postures are part of the first steps to higher yoga. His idea is that if one does the postures with the correct focus, one will in time gain an inner understanding of what *dhyana* and *samadhi* are. Patanjali listed *dharana* deliberate focus, with *dhyana* spontaneous inner focus, and *samadhi prolonged* spontaneous absorption, as being a conjoint practice which he termed as *samyama,* the complete restraint of access to lower reality.

For *dharana* one uses a defined focus. That has a downside, because the focus selected may be an abstract reality, which one fails to grasp because of it being so subtle, that it does not arise during the effort.

But when doing *asana,* one should not imagine a focus. There is no need for that. Instead, one will find that according to the particular pose the body assumes, there is a spontaneous focus. Since the subtle body is superimposed in the physical one, a pose which the physical system does, happens simultaneously for the subtle body. Any tension or shift which is experienced in the physical system, has a parallel experience in the subtle form.

Hence one will do *dhyana* spontaneous focus on that place in the psyche, where there is tension or shift of energy, because of the pose. One does not have to imagine nor wait for a spontaneous focus.

While if one sits to meditate, and causes the self to have a deliberate focus, that focus may not hold. If, however, one does an *asana* posture, and focuses internally on the stress point, or shift area, which one becomes aware of, one will go into a *dhyana spontaneous absorption,* and will not have to do a *pratyahar* sensual energy withdrawal, or *dharana* deliberate forced focus.

This gives a hop from *asana* posture to *dhyana* meditation. One requirement is there however, which is isolation of the yogi. He needs isolation. He should be in an environment where there is no interference from other persons.

Focus Connection

That *On Back Grab Toes* posture results in holding the breath, as if one cannot breathe. In fact, due to the crunching of the lower abdomen, the diaphragm is restricted. It cannot expand as it may. As soon as he assumes this pose, a yogi will notice this breath restriction. There will be a signal in the mind, that the automatic in and out action of air, needs assistance from the coreSelf. The yogi will have to assist the inhale/exhale operation.

The yogi should focus on completing the operation. He should appreciate that normally, this rhythmic system occurs spontaneously, with little or no input from the coreSelf.

- What system executes this vital infusing and venting engine?

The yogi focuses on assisting this breath exchange. He should notice that his focus is somewhat fragmented, as if it is broken in bits. One part is concerned with holding the toes. Another part checks on the position of the thighs. Yet another part checks to know if the head and neck are pulled forward. Then again, the breath is checked. That is a demand in this pose, such that anytime, the mind does not focus on anything else, it focuses on keeping the breath operation in motion.

There is some discomfort doing this pose. This is because the spine is curled with the neck situated in a taut curve, with the chin held close to the throat. The yogi will notice that the breath does not go to the base chakra. In fact, it does not reach the reproductive zone. It reaches as far as the navel where it collects breath energy which begins in the nostrils and travels to the back of the body, to the navel area. Here is a diagram.

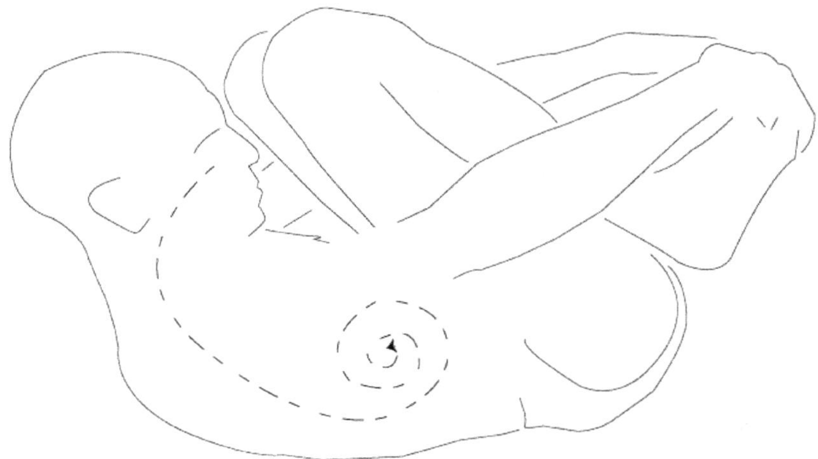

After meditating there in the center of the torso behind the navel, the yogi will realize a dark-grey blank space. He will see that this space does not stretch to the reproductive area nor the base.

After a time, it will be necessary to relax. The head should be slowly lowered to the floor. The hands should release the toes. The hands should hold the shins. The thighs should be relaxed. With this easement, the yogi should de-stress. The mind should release itself from duties, such that only the involuntary system operates. Remaining like this for a while, it is likely that the yogin will astral project.

He may have detailed perception of micro-forms which are tiny but vivid. This is a type of divine eye perception. This is so subtle that if it happens, the yogi may have no idea that he uses it.

Lean Back on Elbows

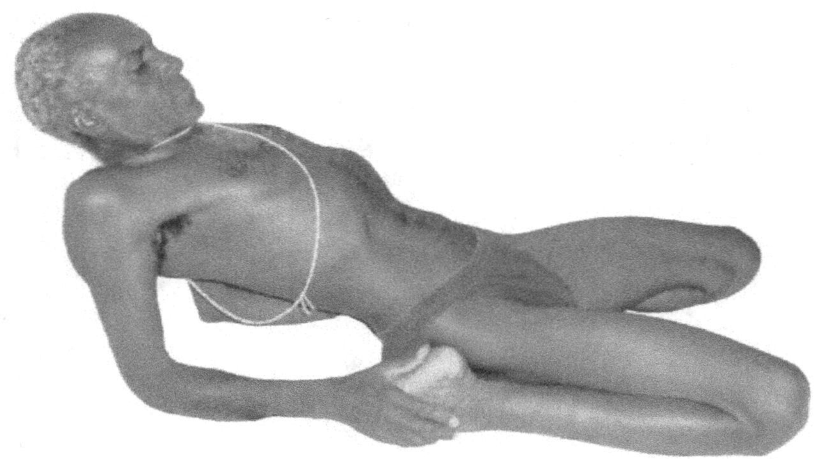

Ideally, for this *Lean Back on Elbows* pose, one should first sit on the floor between the feet. Then one should lean on the elbows. The hands should be on the feet with the thumbs on the soles. The abdomen will fall back to the spine in this pose. It will not be tense however. The head will be up with the chin pressed to the throat. The head will tilt forward slightly.

Once this posture is assumed, a yogi should raise the buttocks slightly from the floor. He should then close the eyelids and focus within the body to detect and observe the course of energy. The yogi should check to be sure that the anus is pulled up. The buttocks should be taut.

With that, the yogi should focus within the body. There should be a tightness in the thighs. This energy will run into the thigh bone, the femur. If focus is maintained, this energy will seem to be a round pipe which emanates light. It is as if there were two rods of light, each in each thigh.

After keeping the buttock lifted slightly from the floor, the yogi will feel as if the buttocks are on the floor or that it should be rested there. The yogi checks to be sure that the buttocks are relaxed on the floor. The chest and head will be full of random energy. There may be naad resonance in the head. No thoughts will be present but there may be ideas about this posture. These will be incomplete thoughts which begin and then fizz out. What will be present which replaces the ideas, is a sense of observation along with random energy, and a whistling sound in the head.

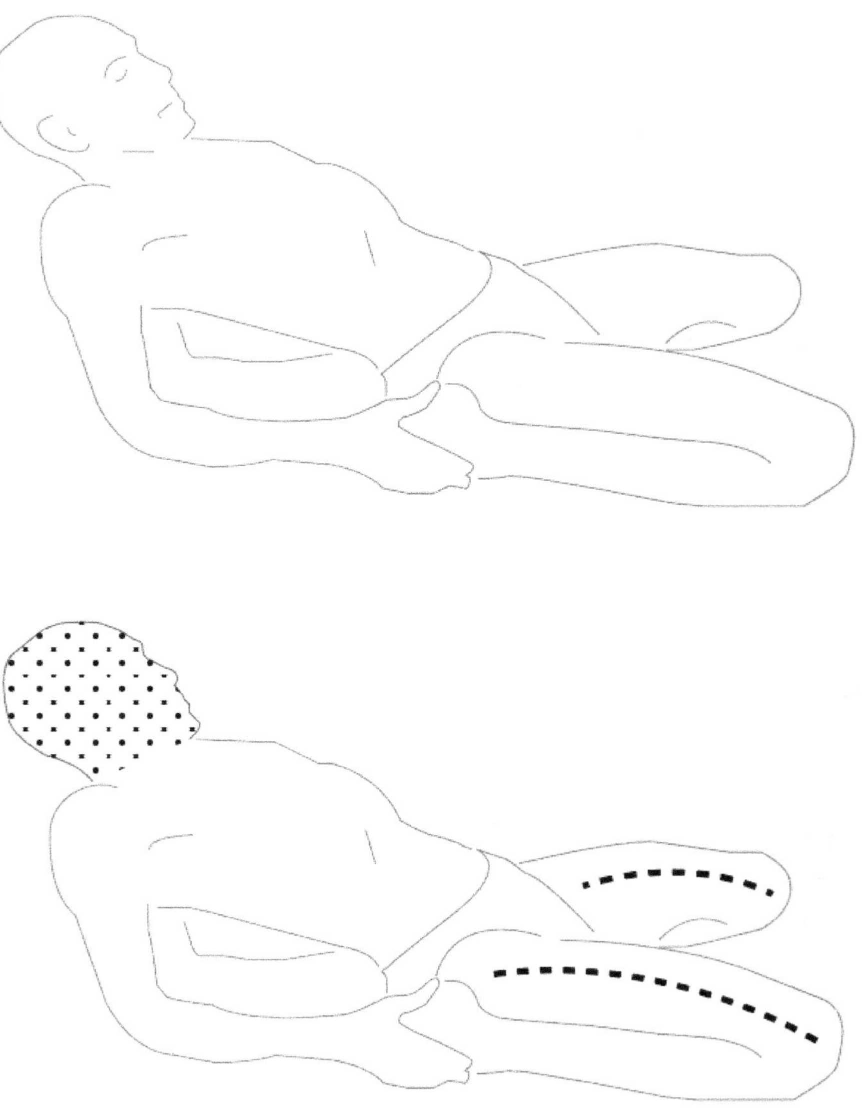

Focus Connection

When assuming the *Lean Back on Elbows* posture, if the yogi relaxes, there may be no striking energy moving, nor compelling focuses, which are due to stress or physical strain. A yogi who is at ease in this pose, should hear inner sound, naad resonance, in one ear or the other, on the left or right side of the head. That head area is the mind.

The inner sound, if heard on one side, may then be heard on both sides. Or the side which is heard, will transfer a part of itself to the other side, such that both sides resonate. It will saturate itself in the subtle head. It may be heard in the middle of the head for a time.

Listening to it at ease, with no sharp focus, the yogi should repeat this mantra continuously while hearing naad.

- *Om Namo Shivaya*
  - *Om Namo*

The first line is submission to Shiva.

The second is open submission to any spiritually-elevated persons in the vicinity. Such persons may not be seen by the yogi. There is a slight pause just after saying the second mantra.

A yogi says this mantra without disturbing the naad sound resonance. The mantra and naad are complimentary. While becoming absorbed in naad, and this mantra, a yogi may realize that the declaration of the mantra ceases. The naad resonance ceased as well. They are replaced by a thought sequence. When the yogi realizes this, the disturbing thought will cease. It will act like a robber who was discovered and who ran away.

The inner focus on naad will continue as before, the mantra will be said as before. Then again, the yogi may discover that his focus was arrested by a thought.

Sit between Heels – Lean Back on Forearms

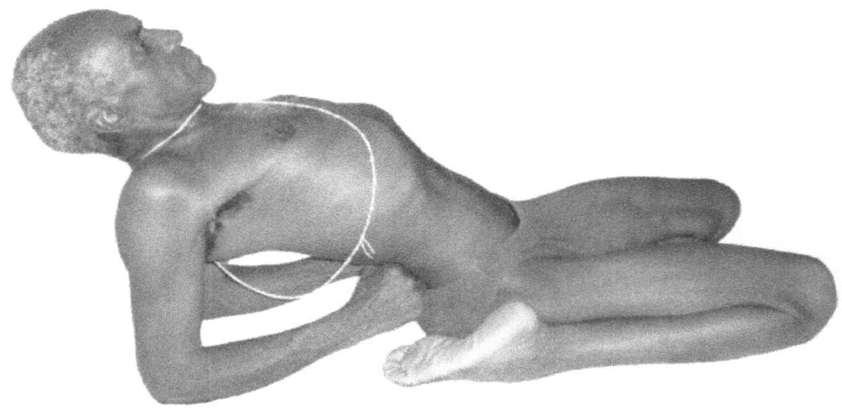

For this *Sit between Heels – Lean Back on Forearms* pose, a yogi should sit between heels. If he cannot do so, this posture should not be done. He should do a preparatory pose in which his thigh muscles stretch and relax. For yoginis, this posture may be impeded by fat in the thighs. A yogini may sit on a cushion so that the buttocks are elevated while the feet remain on the floor. With this the elbows may be cushioned as well.

The ideal position is to sit between the heels. Then lay back on the forearms and elbows. The fists should brace the back torso above the hips. The chin is locked to the throat. The eyelids are closed. Internal focus is applied. This is with a curiosity to know where the energies in the psyche are located. Keep the chin pressed to the throat. Keep the head as far up as possible.

Energy in the torso will slowly be released through the neck into the head. It will be defused slowly while circulating in the head. From time to time, the yogi should check to be sure that the back of the head is raised, and the chin is pressed to the throat. This posture will allow the yogi to train the focusing power to be absorbed within the psyche. This is a *dhyana* spontaneous mental focusing practice. It causes the attention of the coreSelf to develop interest in what occurs in the psyche.

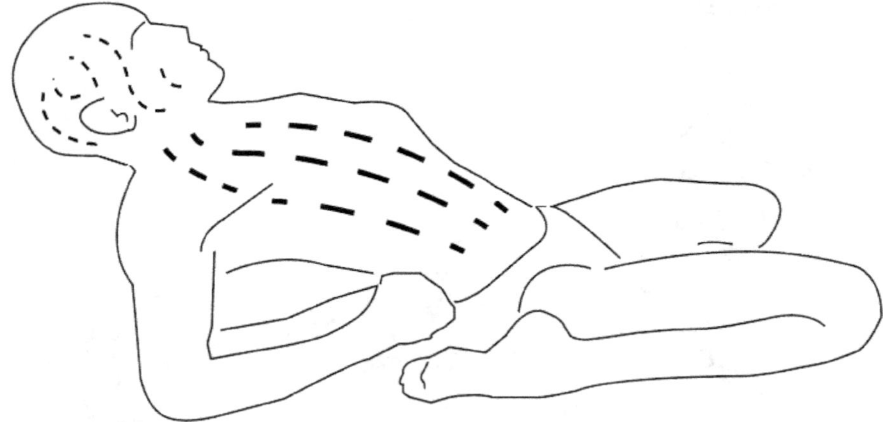

Focus Connection

The *Sit between Heels – Lean Back on Forearms* posture is a relatively easy pose. It could be stressful for persons with large buttocks or whose thighs prevent folding at the knees. When this posture is assumed, the yogi should make a decision for inner focus. Then or prior to that, he may hear inner sound which is like a high pitched scream. The yogi should listen intently. He may realize that the subtle body is forgotten. It may seem that there is no other sound, as if naad resonance is all-penetrating.

When this posture seems tiring, the yogi should slowly bring the torso up, as to sit between the heels. As soon as the body seems stabilized, the yogi should assume the posture again. The fists should support the lower back just above the rear pelvic region.

Again, he will hear naad frequency resonating. He should relax by sitting between the heels. This process of assuming the posture, and relaxing in the sitting position, should be repeated. A yogi should notice how naad sound resonates, with no prompting from the coreSelf. It provides a target and brings the self to itself. That is a *dhyana* spontaneous focus, which evolves into a *samadhi* continuous focus. The self does not have to exert itself, except to make use of the target.

Sit on Heels with Soles together- Leaning back

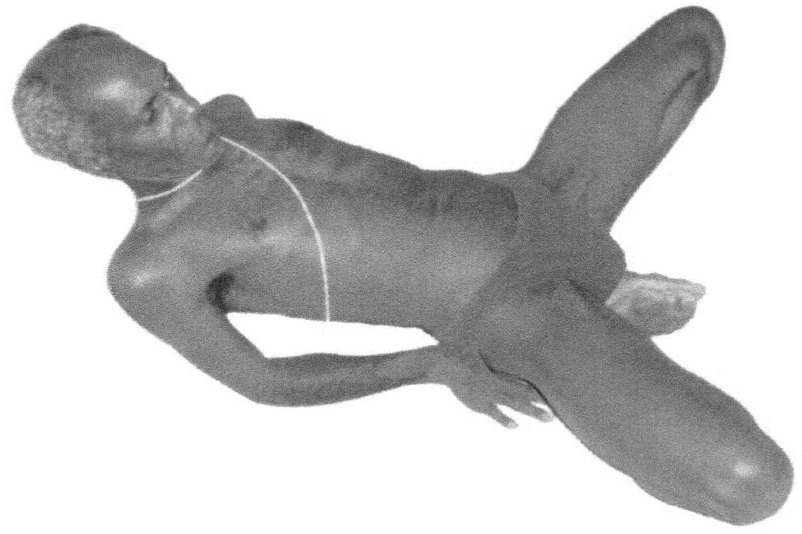

For this *Sit on Heels with Soles together - Leaning back* posture, first sit on heels while soles are held together. Lean back on elbows. The hands may support the lower back. Push the chest up. Apply the chin lock by keeping the head forward while the chin is pressed to the throat.

Close the eyelids and focus, within its feelings. Pull the trunk of the body. Apply pressure on the throat by pressing the chin. The chest should be drawn up as the chin is held down.

Focus on the inside back of the head and neck. Keep this focus. There may be a dropping of energy into the throat. It may feel as if there is a hollow space, which is clear and blank, with random noisy energy falling into the hollow.

Hold the pose. Keep the eyelids closed. A yogi may feel shivering in parts of the body which are below the waist. This may also be in the arms and forearms. Keep the eyelids closed. Focus on the hollow in the throat. Focus on any high-pitched sound which may arise spontaneously.

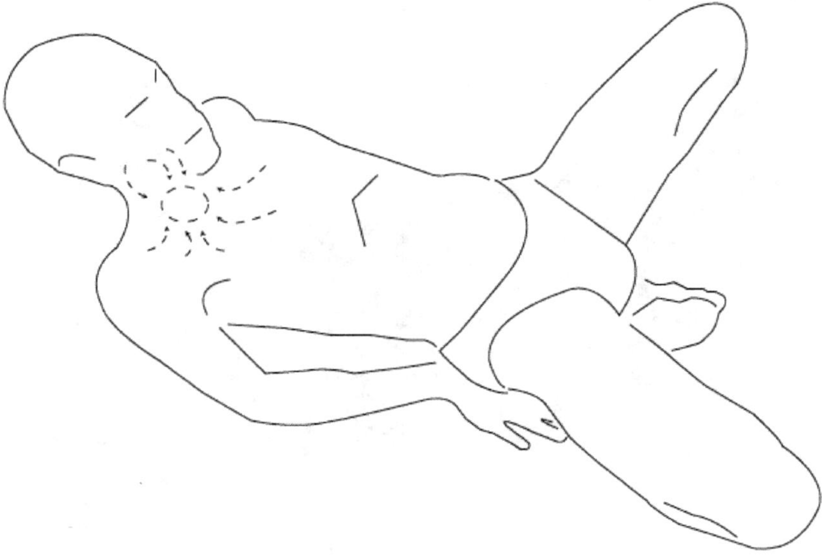

Focus Connection

The *Sit on Heels with Soles together - Leaning back* pose, is done with the buttocks on the sides of the heels. The sides of the soles, the hands, the forearms and elbows make contact with the floor. For a short time, while doing this pose, one may feel a flash energy which is circular. That is located in the thighs where they are connected into the pelvic area.

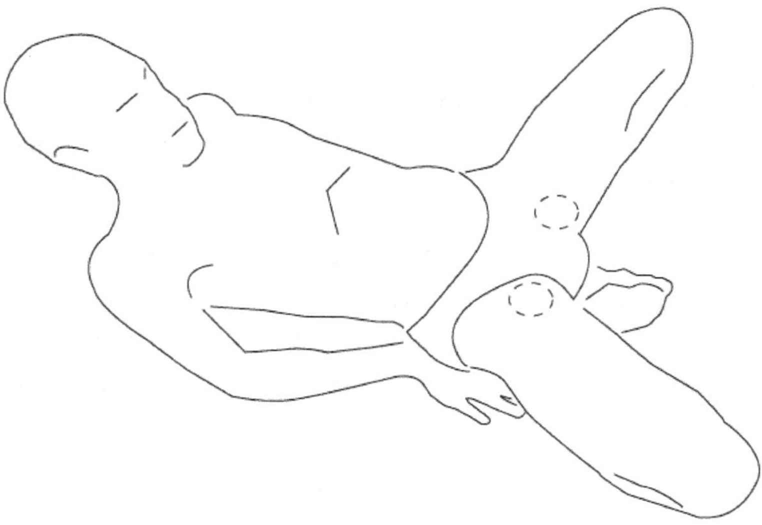

Focusing within the psyche, the yogi should press the chin to the throat. He should listen to an inner sound which may be a screeching resonance. After a time, being in this pose, the thighs may begin a shaking movement. That should be noted. It should be used as a meditation focus. A yogi may experience that this shaking movement causes one not to hear naad frequency. This absorption teaches the yogi how to be focused on vibration. The shaking action of the thighs has the earth's gravitational force as its cause. For the time being, in so far as he is assumed as a physical body, the yogi may study this power of the earth. It regulates every action on earth. To an extent, it manages even psychic behavior.

Tight Lotus with Brace on Palms

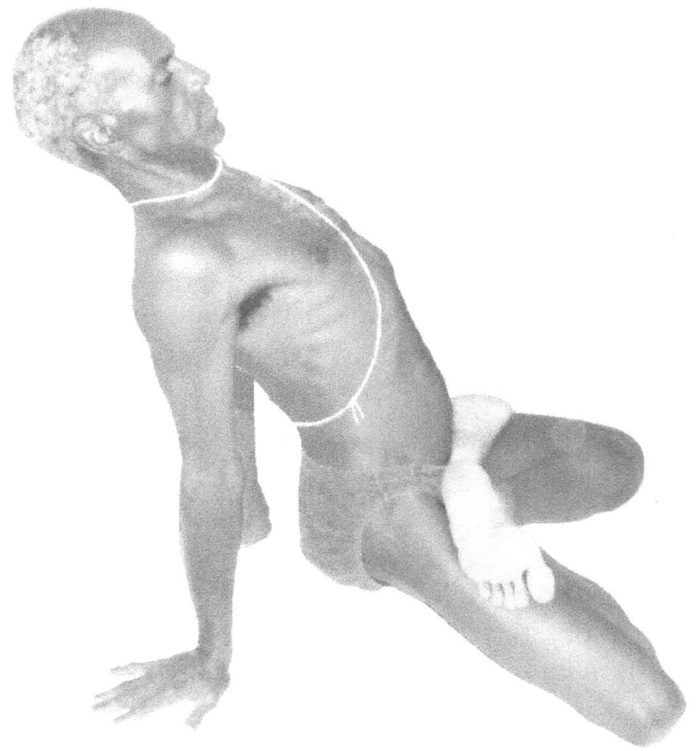

For this *Tight Lotus with Brace on Palms*, the lotus posture is assumed. It should be tight with the spine erect. The yogi should raise the buttocks and resituate it so that it sits squarely on the floor. A check should be made to be sure that the base combination lock is applied. This consists of a three-grip process, where the anus is pulled up, the buttocks are pull to the center of the body, the urinary muscle and the perineum are pulled in and up.

Sitting in this lotus, the palms should be spread on the floor as in the image above. The shoulders should be stretched up so that the abdomen in centered under the rib cage. The neck lock should be applied with the chin pressing to the throat.

With the eyes closed, the yogi should observe the mental and emotional energy. It may be coursing into the face, where it streams inwards from outside the subtle body. This is a *pratyahar* sensual energy natural motion. A yogi may on occasion do *pratyahar* by deliberately retracting the sensual energies. This reverses their flow. However, in this practice, no such effort is applied. In fact, the system itself courses inward. The yogi observes this and becomes absorbed in that event.

Naad sound may be heard at one side or the other, or at the back, or all-surrounding. After a time, this inward streaming will cease. The self will notice that the energy is still, just as there is calm when a storm ceases. This is a *dhyana* seventh (7th) stage. The yogi should remain in the posture, noticing this.

To extend this practice, a yogi should resituate the spine so that it no longer leans back, where it stays upright and there is no muscular application. The hands should rest on the thighs or soles. Then the yogi should notice how the meditative state is prolonged. These observations explain the definition of some stages of yoga which are discussed in the *Yoga Sutras*.

In this posture one can learn the definition of *dhyana* which is the seventh (7th) stage of yoga practice. This may allow a student to define *pratyahar* which is the fifth (5th) stage, sensual energy withdrawal from the quest for sense objects.

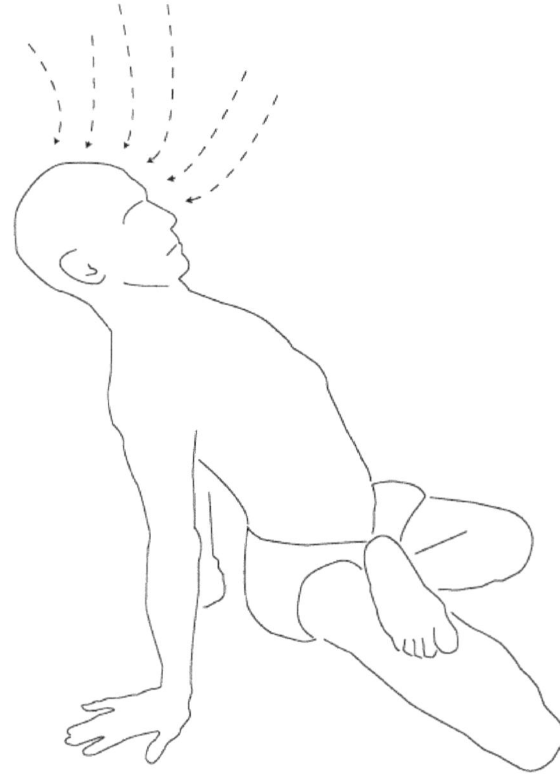

That fifth stage is abstract. The remaining three stages which collectively are known as *samyama,* or the compliant restraint of the pursuing energies of a self, can be understood from the definitions explained by Patanjali. However, to understand the components of internal practice (inselfYoga™) a yogi should learn this, when observing when such states are assumed in the psyche spontaneously.

In certain postures and with certain breath infusion actions, a yogi may experience any of the states. He can study what those states are, and learn how to recognize and benefit, from being observant of them. He may also learn how to induce the psyche to assume those conditions.

Yogeshwarananda is of the view that after many hours of meditation in a silent mind, the yogi will develop the divine eye. Then he can use it according to his natural interest. He must learn how to be in silence, and how to induce the mind to have a silent content.

Focus Connection

The *Tight Lotus with Brace on Palms,* may cause the arousal and release of long lost memories. It produces agreeable ones only. At first when this posture is assumed, and when there is inner focus, with no effort to reach any object outside the physical body, a yogi may hear a pronounced high frequency. It will be to the right or left and somewhat to the back of the head. This sound may be startling. The yogi will know that he did not produce it. He only realized its presence.

As soon as the yogi listens in earnest, it will spread like water which floods dry land. Even though it spreads, the yogi will know that its source point, or source zone, is still prominent.

This posture causes the release of memories from the chest area. These usually arise from the right or left chest, the same side where the high frequency node was located. By this, I had a memory from forty years ago. It was a pleasant memory with details and colors of scenes which were related. After this memory was displayed, another related memory began. In that one there were conversations heard. Some were energy exchanges with other persons, years prior.

Then, some other memories were released from the chest, but these were in a compressed format, where there was no expansion into pictures or sounds. These memories, though released, were not expanded into scenes. There was no hint as to what these comprised in the original events.

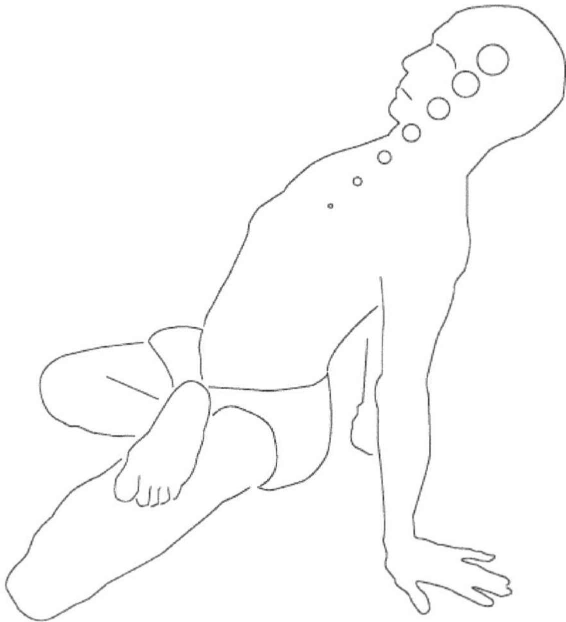

After a time in this pose, there was a pain in the muscles of the arms. It was continuous like the naad sound. It attracted the attention of the core. I sat up with hands on the thighs. This caused the ringing frequency to continue as before. Memories began rising into the head again, except that they remained compressed, and were not illustrated. This was like a light shining in the dark, except that it had no specific color, as the memories remained unrevealed.

One Foot/Leg/Thigh out at 45 Degrees

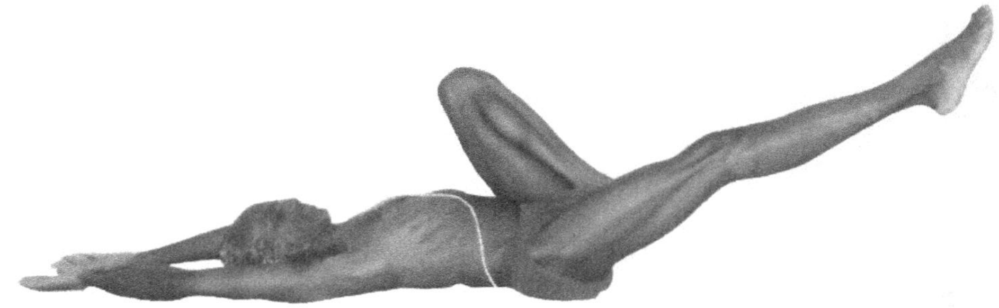

This *One Foot/Leg/Thigh out at 45 Degrees* posture is assumed, with the body on its back, with hands, forearms and arms pushed along the floor away from the body, one knee should be pulled back. The other thigh, leg and foot are stretch forward at about 45 degrees.

As far as possible, the yogi should use a blindfold. No light should reach the eyes. Since the visual sense is so demanding, this is the way to restrict its interest in visual perception of objects, which are outside the body. This increases the inner focus.

In this posture which is a relatively easy pose to hold, one may feel as if there is a hollow area in the eye. It corresponds to the stretch-out lower limb. There may be a space under the corresponding shoulder. Energy in the extending limb may quiver on the inside. If this happens check to consider if the drawn-back thigh, leg, and foot, should be adjusted.

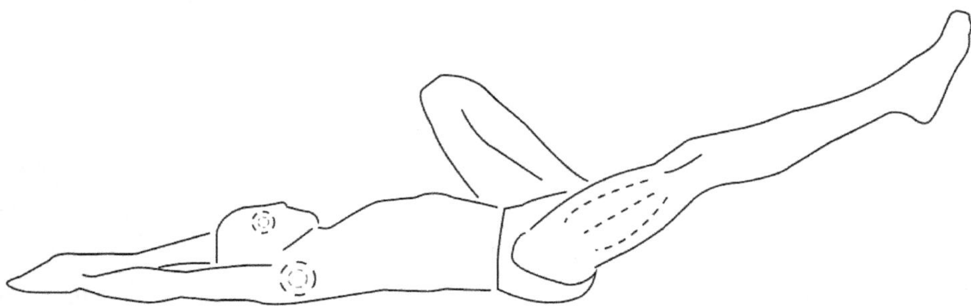

Focus Connection

The *One Foot/Leg/Thigh out at 45 Degrees* pose, may cause some shivering or vibrating. That is due to the extended lower limb. It may also cause a side to side swing which is like the movement of a pendulum. Both effects are due to the gravity of the earth. It is caused by a lack of support for that limb.

When the vibration, shivering, or swinging, can no longer be tolerated, the yogi should retract the extended limb, so that it is positioned like the other in-drawn limb. This will cause the inconvenience to cease.

As soon as the discomfort ceases, the other limb which was first retracted should be extended. Then again, when that extended limb shivers and causes discomfort, it should be retracted. Then with both lower limbs drawn in, with the knees close to the chest, the yogi should check to be sure that his attention checks the inner energy, as to its configuration and alignment.

The yogi may realize that each eye is filled with heat. He should focus on that. He may hear naad resonance, but it may not be compelling. It may demand no attention. It may have an indifferent attitude.

This posture has a shoulders check. The yogi checks on the outstretched arms, forearms and hands. These may cause a tension from the armpits up and through the shoulder. In the neck, he may experience a blank space. That may be like a bubble. As soon as he discovers that, there may be memories from forty years prior. Experiences, which are events of that memory may be seen in the mind space. Some will first appear in the bubble. Those will be flimsy just as a bubble comprises a thin sphere. Like a bubble, those memories will vanish.

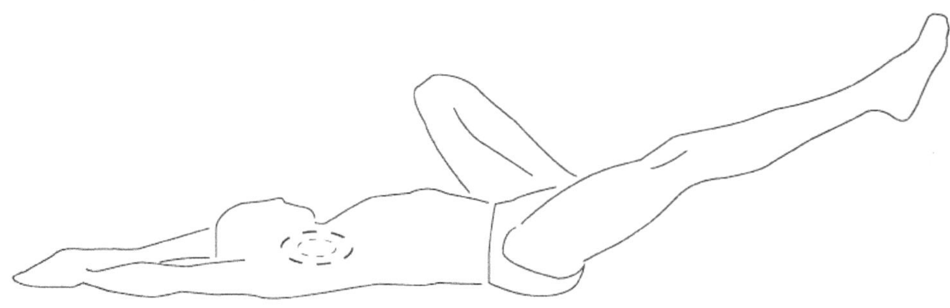

Variation of Bow Pose, *Dhanurasana*

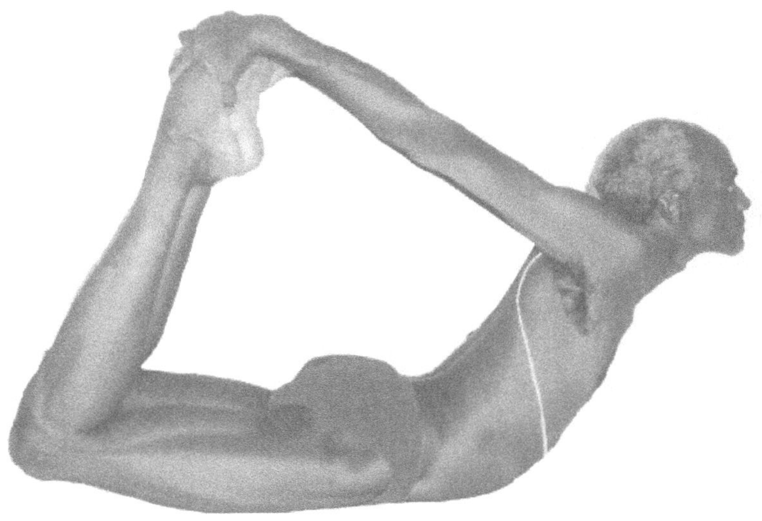

This *Variation of Bow Pose,* is a relaxed version of it. The knees are lifted from the floor but some of the thigh and abdomen remain in contact with it. The toes are grabbed by the corresponding hands. Males should place the genitals so that the testes are not crushed.

With eyelids closed or with a blindfold, the yogi should focus inward. There may be a shivering energy in the back of the neck. Energy in the legs and thighs may course to the corresponding knees. During the inward focus, the yogi may notice that there is a *dhyana* constant inner focus in the body.

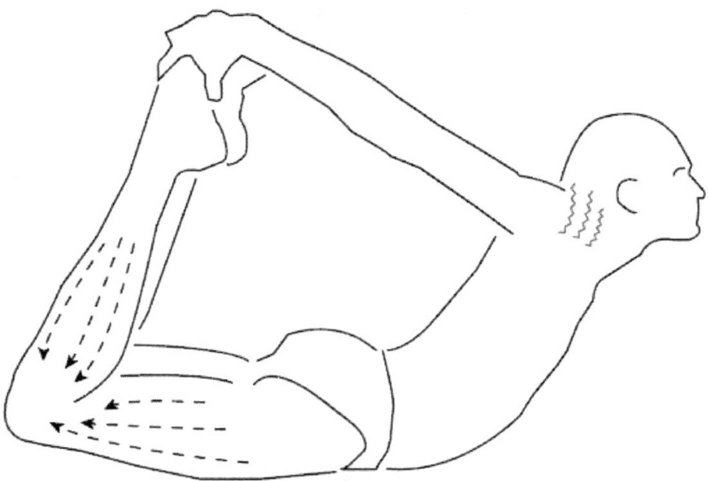

Focus Connection

That *Variation of the Bow Pose, Dhanurasana,* is easy for some and difficult for others. The way the muscles interact and shed energy during the pose, varies from one ascetic to another. When it was assumed for one hold, I noticed that the genitals, had a profile for energy. The rest of the body had none. It was as if there was only a sexual energy complex as a physical object and there was nothing else. The rest of the body disappeared. This did not continue for a long period.

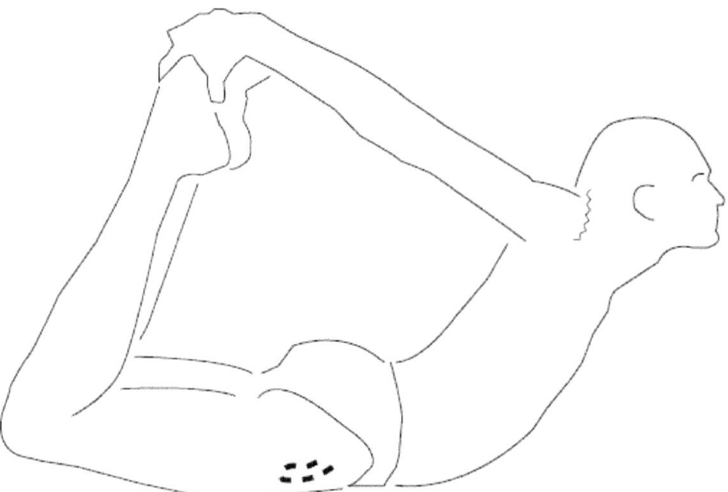

Then, the sex complex disappeared. There was a shift to the thighs where there was an oblong slab of light in each thigh. Then there was in the front center of the abdomen a radiation of light. This continued for a time.

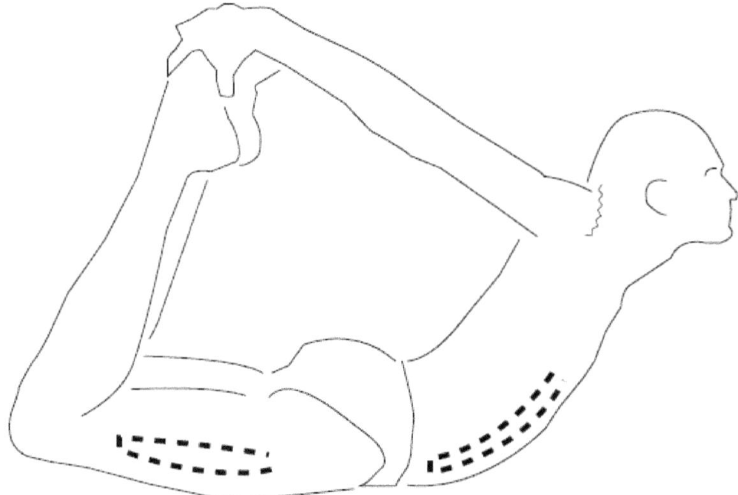

I became aware that the backward neck lock was no longer in place. I applied it. When I did that, the focus of awareness was the back of the neck, with every other place of the psyche losing significance. By this time, I could only hold the pose for a bit longer. While keeping focus in the psyche, I slowly released the posture. Then keeping that inner focus,

I sat on the heels. The hands were gently placed on the thighs. I applied the backward neck lock.

Checking for inner focus, I noticed quiescence. There was no thought, no thinking attempt, no image, no memory illustration nor prompting. There was no event consultation. Feeling this, I assumed the quiescence as a spontaneous free state, and then as a continuous free state. In such a state, a yogi should wait for *chit akash* access or the appearance of a portal.

Foot Clamp by other Thigh

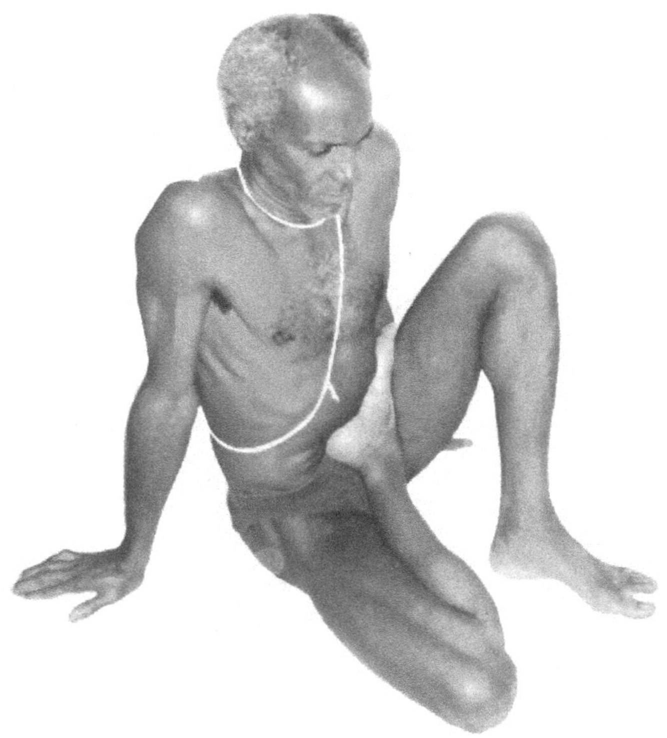

After assuming this *Foot Clamp by other Thigh* posture, a yogi should check to be sure that the positions are balanced. Shifts and adjustments should be made. Bring the body to order. For instance, a decision should be made, regarding where the upright foot should be. If it is placed close to the thigh, there will be adjustments made with the buttocks. Likewise, if the foot on the floor is positioned, as it is in the image above, the buttocks will be in another position on the floor.

A yogi should check to be sure that the hands are at the proper position on the floor. Once the hands, buttocks, and foot on the floor, are properly placed, the yogi should check the other foot, which is not on the floor. That other foot is clamped between the other thigh and torso.

With inner focus, the yogi may notice energy moving through the arms into the neck and lower jaws. There should be energy moving up, through the back of the neck. When this is observed, one may notice naad resonance which will be like a screeching frequency. From time to time, there may be blankness in the head. The yogi may hesitate when this happens. He may realize that this is a *dhyana* spontaneous inner focus, which he should absorb.

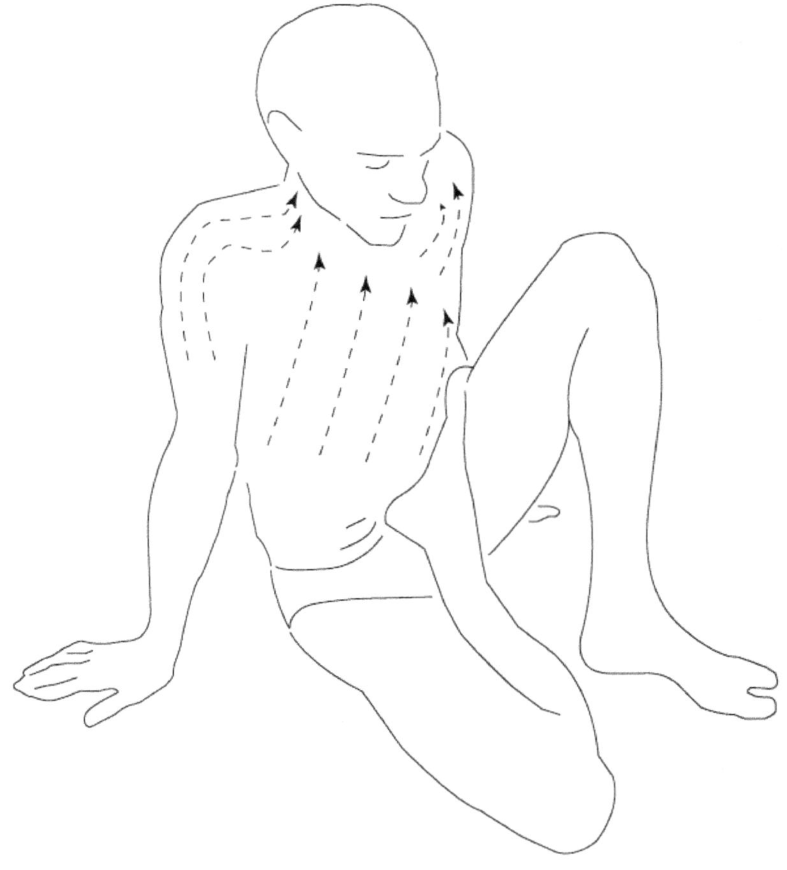

Remember that in doing a posture, the focus is internal. It is not concerned with the health of the body, nor with its beautiful appearance, nor with weight reduction. The focus is psychological, having to do with sorting the subtle body from the physical one, and studying what will happen regarding where one will be, when the physical system is no longer accessible.

For meditation, one needs inner focus. When that is steady, when that is natural, when one sits to meditate, then absorption happens. It may happen as directed by the yogi, where he wants to achieve a certain focus. It may happen otherwise, where the yogi discovers the psyche in a favorable state. For that he merely continues with the naturally occurring mental condition. If this lasts for a long time, it is called *samadhi or* the complete enlightened (*dhi*) state of mind.

Asanas or postures, when done for the purpose of yoga, shows the yogi how to become absorbed in various parts inside the body. A particular pose will cause a certain tension or relaxation. That will happen during the posture. Then the yogi does not have to exert a mental force for the absorption to be initiated or continued. The pose itself causes the absorption. The yogi joins the focus and, in that way, helps to train the mind to be in *dhyana* which is spontaneous higher focus. This diverts the mind away from its sense hunting procedure, which keeps the self externally occupied, with what is outside the physical body.

Focus Connection

The *Foot Clamp by other Thigh* posture is somewhat difficult, especially if one has bulging thighs which is due to muscle configuration or fat placement. The foot which is placed on the floor, should be adjusted to get the correct position. With the eyelids closed; while focusing within the psyche, the yogi should set the position, where he gets the feeling for maximum placement.

In the knee which is on the floor, a blank space may be felt. When this happens, the tensions elsewhere will disappear. The yogi should enter that blank space. He should remain there for a time. He should ponder.

There are two triangular configurations.

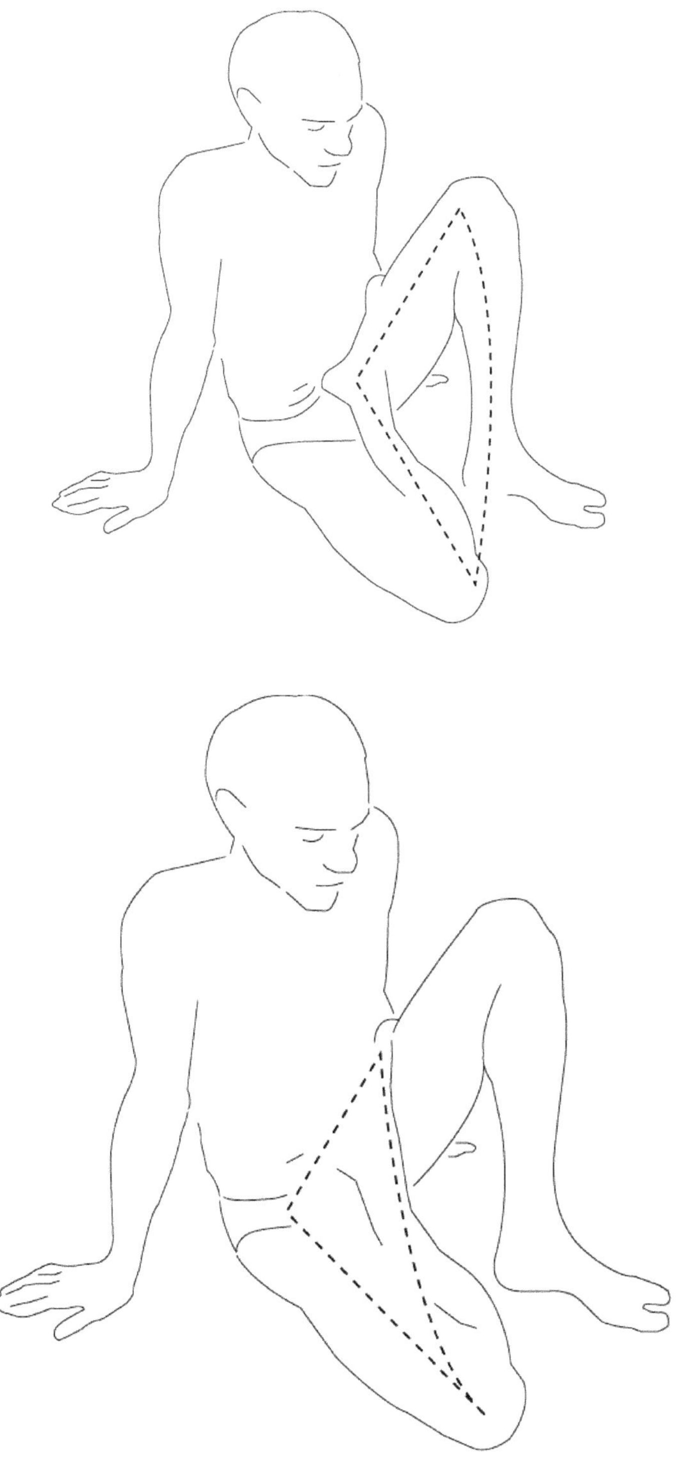

The yogi should be absorbed in these. One may feel as if it is one joint energy in three corners but with one special linking place. The yogi should be emerged in this.

On the lower knee, the one which touches the floor, there will be a running current which will be from the corresponding toes to that knee. This will be flushed with feelings. Any practice which gives a string, or strings, of feelings, is important in the development of *dhyana* spontaneous focusing. Focus on feelings must be practiced.

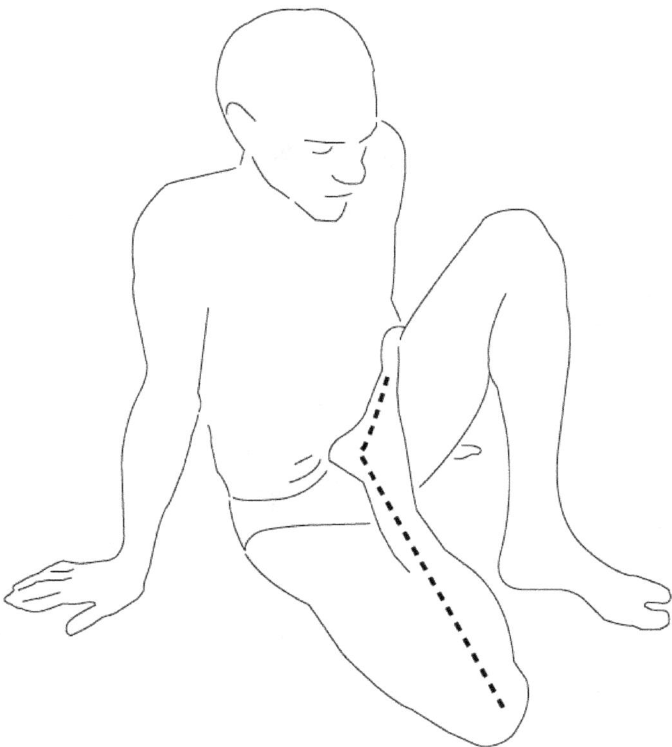

During this posture, one may hear naad sound blasting, and with demand for attention. The resonance may override the tensions in the limbs. The yogi should take the opportunity to study the *samadhi* continuous freely-occurring focus or target.

On Back Grab Soles

This *On Back Grab Soles* posture, may be studied to give different inner absorptions. It would depend on the level of advancement of the yogi, and on his/her holding the posture, and focusing while doing so.

Even though this posture contains and spreads the pubic area, its focus in not that zone. Particularly in females, this posture diverges the pubic face. It spreads the sexual apparatus. But the sexual organs are not the focus in this posture. This shows that even though physically a particular part of the body may be tensed or relaxed in one posture, that area may not be the target. A yogi should check this by keeping the mental focus, and the emotional sensual interest, in the body.

This posture is done on the back of the body. The head is raised from the floor. The knees and thighs are brought to the chest. From the outside, the hands grab the soles of the feet. The nose is brought to the toes. The knees are positioned under the arms by the elbows.

While in this posture, one will notice that there is shortness of breath. A full breath cannot be inhaled. This is due to compression of the lungs. The diaphragm cannot flex as it normally does.

There may be a stab of energy in the neck, where it feels as if an energy in the neck forms into a tube. The color of it is silverish-white. Once the yogi does this, and perceives the focusing energy which occurs, he may hear naad sound which may cross from the vicinity of one ear to the other.

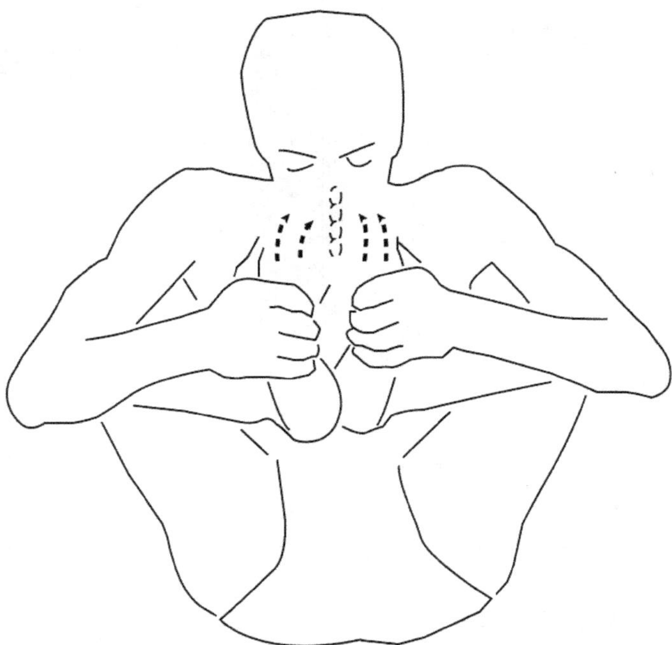

Focus Connection

This *On Back Grab Soles* position, can be difficult for some. A yogi who cannot do it, may adapt the body into a partial format of this pose. When this is done, the situation is that of holding the body's weight on the curved spine. The yogi should keep his attention inside the body. He should track to determine how the weight is distributed. There will be a central place which supports the body and keeps the balance, so that it does not tilt to the right, nor left, and does not rock the body up nor down.

The neck should be positioned so that the chin is pressed to the throat. This will cause tension strands in the back of the neck. The yogi should focus on these. He should apply his attention to determine the length of the strands. He sees how they are electrified. These may be like metal wires which convey electricity. The yogi should track these flashes which run through nerves in the neck.

A yogi may experience that when his attention to applied to the neck, when it senses the currents, its application of focus there, converts from *dharana* deliberate focus to *dhyana* spontaneous focus. This experience is a partial demonstration of *samyama* sequential development, which has its lowest aspect as *dharana* deliberate focus, its median one as *dhyana* spontaneous focus, and finally evolves into *samadhi* prolonged automatic focus.

Dharana concerns the yogi's directive instruction. *Dhyana* is a spontaneous condition. *Samadhi* is one which is both spontaneous and continuous. Each aspect may occur with the yogi's directive trigger. When they occur spontaneously, that is the most desired occurrence.

During the focus on the neck, a yogi may suddenly realize that naad resonance blazes. It may do so loudly. The yogi may understand that it did that all along, but he was unaware of it. He may then switch to hearing naad, to being emerged in it. But then he may switch to the focus within the neck. This may repeatedly occur. He hears naad and is emerged in it, and then he is aware of currents in the neck. Then again, this back and forth happens.

After some time, the yogi may bring his head to the floor. He should do this without interfering with the energy in the psyche. When the head is rested in this way, the yogi will notice that the currents in the neck disappear. Naad may be heard then as a total saturation of the psyche. Inside the head and outside the head, he may hear naad resonance. It may be loud, blasting. It may penetrate everything.

With the head rested and naad blaring, the yogi may decide to remain in that relaxed condition. The focus then will be naad inner sound. This will crash through the psyche, like needles passing through a fabric.

After a time, the yogi should release the feet. The feet should be brought to rest on the floor. The hands should rest on each side of the body with the palms up. There should be no sudden movements, no jerks. The yogi should hold to inner sound which absorbs his focus. He should check for feelings. He should find some here or there, and should focus accordingly. Then he should refocus on the loud inner sounds. Then again, he should look for feelings and focus on them. This is a practice. It is instructive so that the yogi learns to recognize how to become absorbed, how to target aspects of the psyche, and how to remain absorbed.

Soles Together Grab Shins Do Partial Squat

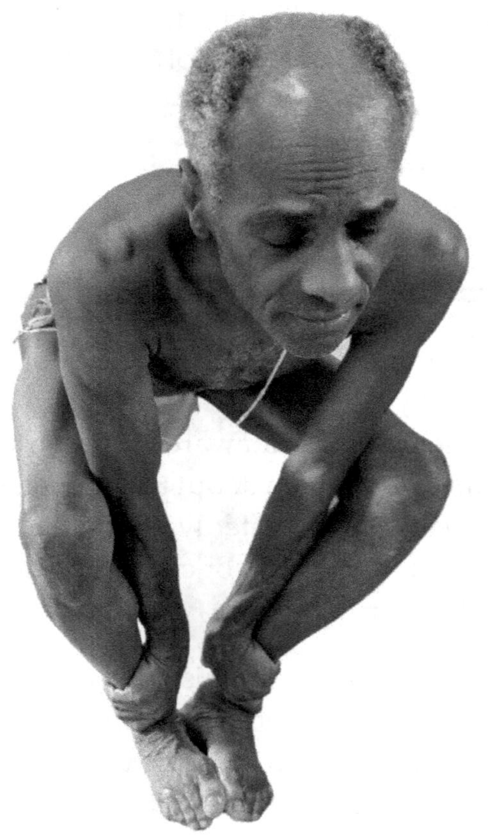

This *Soles Together Grab Shins Do Partial Squat* posture, begins by standing with the soles together. According to the construction of the physical body which was adapted from the parents, some yogis cannot bring the soles fully together. Some toes may touch while sitting on a floor but the heels may remain apart.

With the soles fully or partially together, squat forward while grabbing the shins. The hands should grab the shins. The body should squat forward with the spine parallel to the floor. The yogi should steady the posture. There may be nervousness or shivering. The eyes should be kept open. That will assist in balancing the body on the outer edges of the soles.

Initially, this posture may be done with much nervousness and shivering. Over time, that will decrease. When one resumes an easy pose, after doing this posture, one may discover that the breathing pace is accelerated, as if the lungs crave air.

In this posture there may be a spontaneous focus on the ankles and shins. The mind will focus there with no exertion by the willpower. This is a *dhyana* involuntary absorption which gives the yogi perception in the body at the shins and ankles.

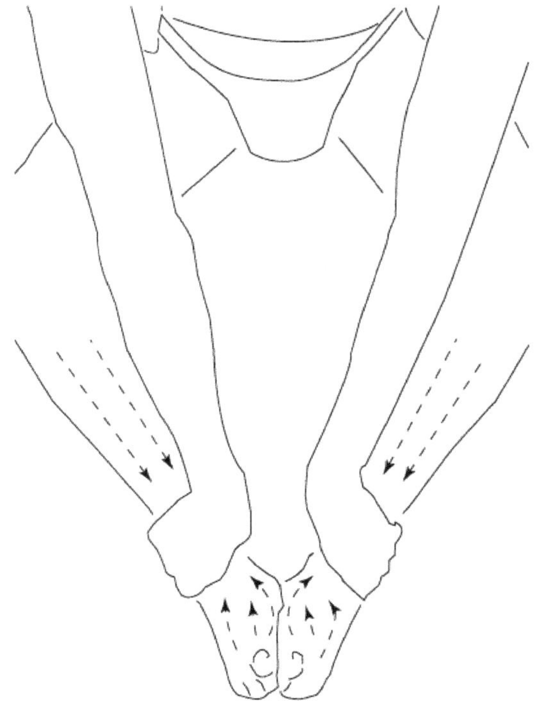

Focus Connection

The *Soles Together Grab Shins do Partial Squat,* is a feature posture for measuring the curvature of the spine, and checking to see if the nerves which respond to balance, function with stability. As a body ages, its balance perspective deteriorates. This means, that a yogi in an elderly condition, cannot expect the same stability, which he noticed when the body was youthful.

It is interesting how so many persons who mistake *asana* posture as the complete process of yoga, do not study the internal condition. However, there are many parts of yoga which cannot be figured or discovered by every student. This means that one must be shown how to act, or one must be inspired by someone, who either discovered a process, or who was shown it by another yogi. While doing this book, which was inspired by Yogeshwarananda, I noticed many details about inner absorption, which I experienced before, but which I did not give the proper significance. One may have a tool but be unaware of its usefulness. One may have a human body and not figure its value. Someone else who has more hints, may alert one if one is open to advice.

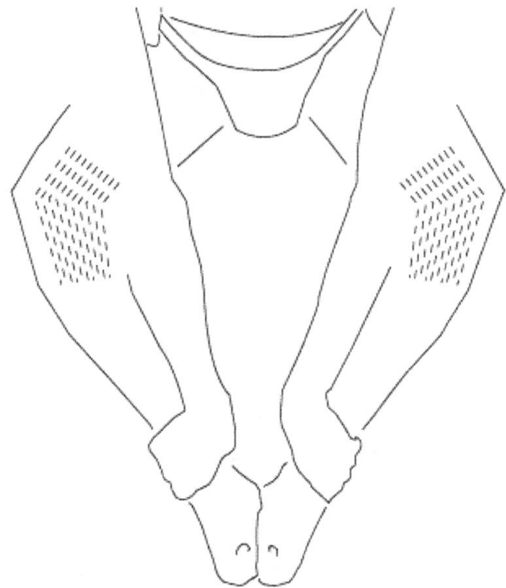

Due to weakness where the knees and legs connect, a yogi may be discouraged from doing the *Soles Together Grab Shins do Partial Squat* pose. For such a yogi, he may do this for short periods. Then he may squat and study the energy distribution.

After squatting and noticing that the system normalized, and the traumatic weakness ceased, the yogi should stand, but without losing hold of the configuration of energy. Standing, he should have the hands on the hips. The thumb should be in the back. The four fingers should be in the front. With the eyelids closed or using a blindfold, the yogi should check to notice if some weakness is felt. He should note if an imbalance is present.

This practice should cease if there is weakness or imbalance. Otherwise, if the unwanted feelings cease for the most part, the yogi should again do the *Soles Together Grab Shins do Partial Squat* pose. In it, the yogi should be vigilant to notice the configuration of energy. He should not be alarmed if there is discomfort. Rather, he should mentally note it. He should map it and make a description.

As soon as the weakness in the knees and legs is experienced, he should prepare to map it. He should not panic. Instead, he should slowly assume a squatting position. He should hold that squat for a time, then slowly he should assume an easy pose. In that easy pose, he should realize that the commotion of energy vanished. There would be nothing to focus on except blankness in an open space. That would be similar to a cloudless sky at dusk, at the time when birds roost. It will be like looking to the east, when there is no sun as a singular dominant object. A yogi should become absorbed in that blankness.

Lean Back between Heels

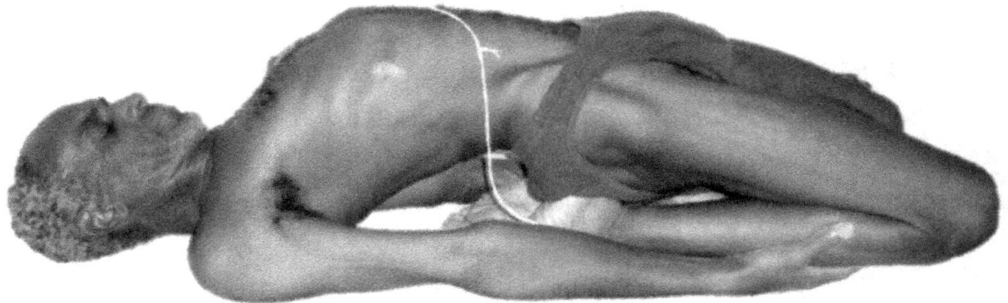

Every posture has variations. Before practicing several, be sure to have a cautious attitude. Muscles, tendons, arteries, veins, nerves, and other tissue may be torn, stretched, crimped, squeezed, or popped. There could be injury. By being patient, not being in a hurry, not being careless, being attentive within the body, a yogi could avoid regrets for injuries which happen during practice.

It is sensible to study anatomy diagrams. The energy in the psyche is mental, sensual, and emotional. By keeping the eyes closed during practice, there is a likelihood that a yogi will develop sensitivity to understand the psychological movements.

In the *Lean Back between Heels* posture, one should rest on the heels or do so between the heels. If one is between the heels, the buttocks may rest on the floor. However, if the thighs are not formed to allow sitting between the heels with the buttocks on the floor, one can use a cushion to relieve strain. The padding will be under the buttocks to support the body.

Ideally, a yogi may sit between the heels, while the buttocks are on the floor. Then he should lean backwards and recline with the head and upper back touching the floor.

He may grab the legs. There may be energy darts in the thighs. These may go toward the tailbone of the spine. There may be darts from the lower trunk to the tailbone.

Alternately, due to stress in the knees, thighs, back and neck, there may be a confusion of energy. The yogi should observe this chaos. He should wait for it to become organized. No mental effort should be made to streamline or discipline that energy. It will organize itself in due course.

This is a *samyama* meditation practice. Eventually the energy will assume a focusing format. Then the yogi should observe that. It is likely that the two lower chakras will be activated. These are the base and sex complex chakras. A yogi should focus on it. He should notice that he does not have to make an effort. The energy assumed that focusing format by itself. The chaos ceased. This will give the yogi some idea about *samyama* absorption concerning the two highest stages of yoga, namely *dhyana* spontaneous absorption and *samadhi* continuous and spontaneous inside focus.

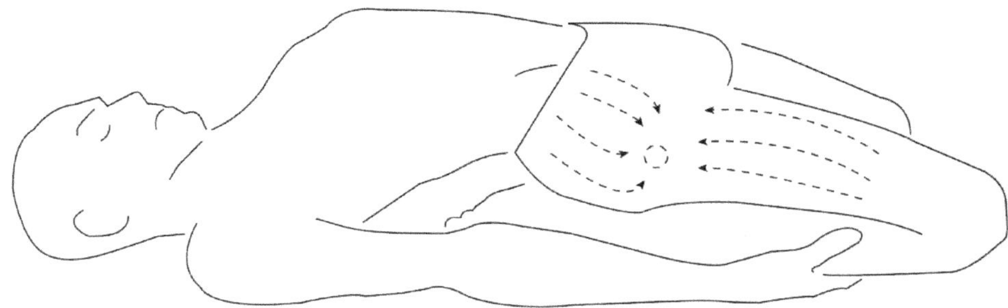

Focus Connection

If it is done with the buttock sitting on the heels, this *Lean Back between Heels* is a dangerous posture. That causes severe stress on the thighs and spine. A yogi must use caution. This should be done step by step, so that there is no sudden action, nor drastic tilt, which the yogi cannot reverse easily nor without injury.

Internal vigilance is required in any pose assumed. That is how a yogi can gage what happens on the physical or astral sides of the psyche. In this pose the feet, legs and head touch the floor. The buttocks are elevated above the heels. The spine and neck floats, but the head makes contact with the floor.

There are variations of this. Those should be done with care, either with no supervision or with help from a more advanced yogin. When this pose is assumed, there will be vibrations in the lower torso. That is a scattering of psychological energy. Some feel that only the head issues such energy, but every living part of the body also emits mento-emotional signals. If a yogi is attentive, he will realize that from head to toe, there is psychological energy. Whatever happens to impair the distribution of that power, affects the head area. Hence it is efficient if one secures the energy in every area.

When doing this pose, if the yogi finds that it is intolerable, he may ease the body by lowering the buttock between the heels. Those who cannot do this or who can do it with increasing stress, should sit up. That should be done carefully, with full application of attention within the body.

When the body is eased between the heels, and if the yogi can hold that pose easily with no injury, there may be a fine mist of energy in an oval shape at each thigh inset, the place where the thighs are near the genitals. Remaining in that position for a time, the yogi may realize that there is a netted covering of energy over the feet, legs, thigh and lower torso up to the waist.

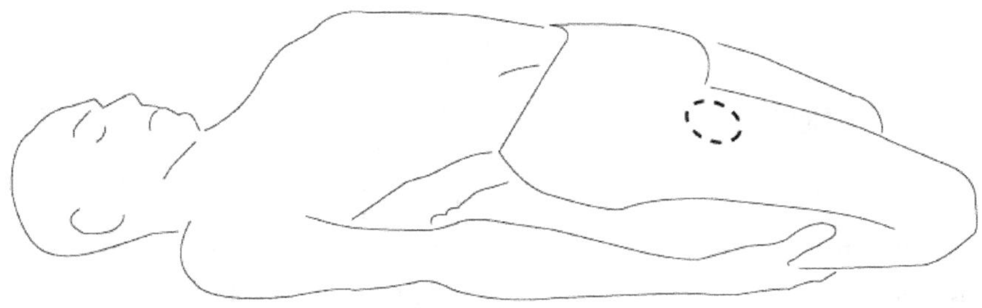

Step Forward – Fingers Support

In this *Step Forward – Fingers Support* posture, the forward foot, the fingers and palms, the knee which is behind, and the toes, and dorsum area (top of foot) which is behind, touch the floor. The foot which is forward is positioned under its vertical leg. That vertical position is the reference for this pose. That leg is perpendicular to the floor.

The chin is tilted up as much as it can be. The top part of the chest is lifted to draw the waist into a contraction where the muscles of the chest remain drawn up and taut. The yogi should press the fingers to the floor. That pertains to eight fingers. The thumbs are flared.

When this pose is steady, the yogi should do inner focus, to observe where and how, the energy courses through the body. It may be felt in the inner thigh of the limb which is stretched backward. At that inner thigh there may be a resonating energy, which shimmers.

It may feel like a series of electric currents flashing. These may rattle like springs which vibrate. A yogi should focus. He should use this convergence of energy, to do an absorption meditation at the zone, where one thigh, the one which is backward, connects to the pelvic area.

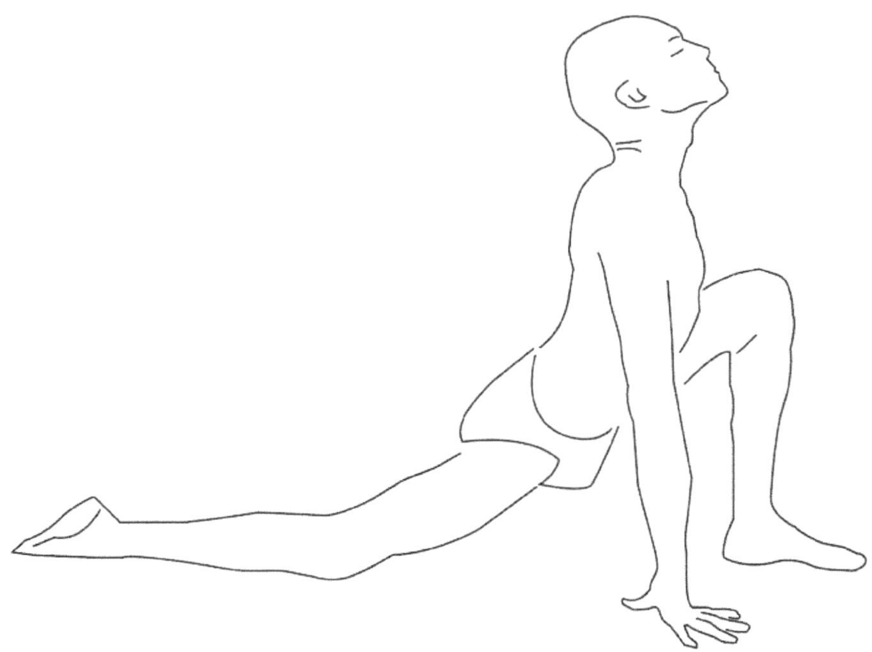

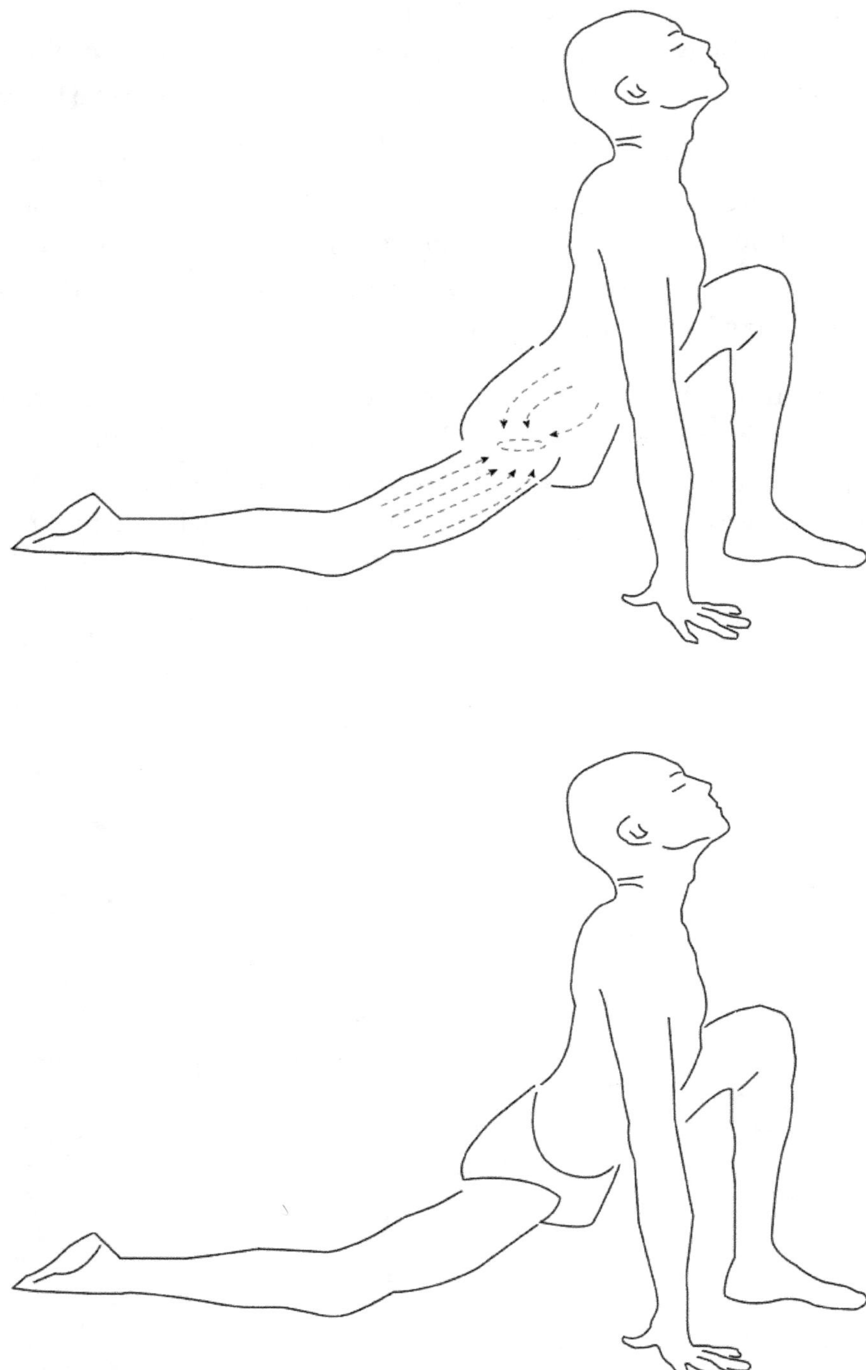

Focus Connection

This *Step Forward – Fingers Support* posture is not difficult. However, it may be a task for some yogis. One may adapt this to accommodate a similar pose, or a variation of it. The forward foot is planted firmly on the floor. The rear foot is stretched back with the leg making contact with the floor. The sole of the backward foot faces upward. The fingers of each hand assist to convey the weight of the body to the floor. Because the fingers are under tension, a yogi gets a message within the psyche, that the fingers vent tension though the palms of the hand.

When blood from the heart, courses through the arms, forearms and palms, that is used in the fingers for energizing cells. However, the same plasma becomes polluted, and requires conveyance to the lung. In the lungs, that blood is energized. If, however, blood is used by the fingers and that blood does not course back to the lungs, via the heart, the cells of the hand will utter a pain feeling. A yogi should do breath infusion to increase the quantity of energized blood, which flows through the body.

Care should be taken to assist this system of energized blood distribution, especially in relation to fingers and toes, which are the extremities. Healthy actions for the physical body are healthy actions for the subtle form as well.

When one does this *Step Forward – Fingers Support* posture, one side should be done, then the other side should be done. Each has a portion. The first is to step forward into position. Then one waits until that is intolerable. Then one rocks back to get relief.

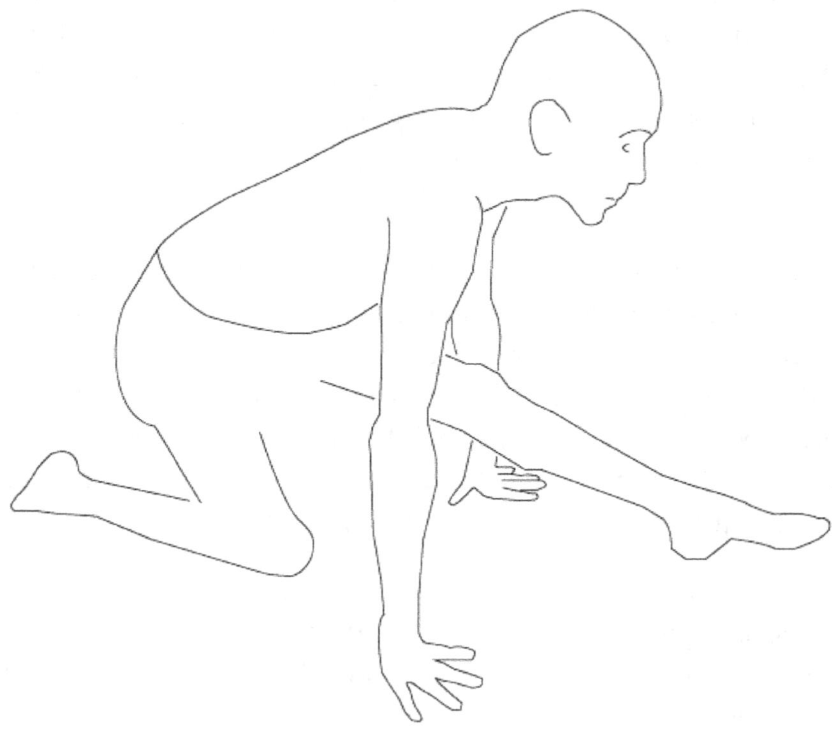

During this pose, one should map and be involved in the energy configuration. Then one should relax from it.

One should change which foot steps forward. Then, one should rock back, when that other side of this posture is assumed. When the second action is completed, one should complete the poses on each side again.

When a yogi completes both sides several times, he ceases. He sits where he is, in an easy pose.

Then he will observe an even spread of energy through the body. He should meditate and be absorbed with this energy. This is a *samadhi* practice to develop a mento-emotional energy stability, a relaxation of *chittavritti* mental and emotional disturbance.

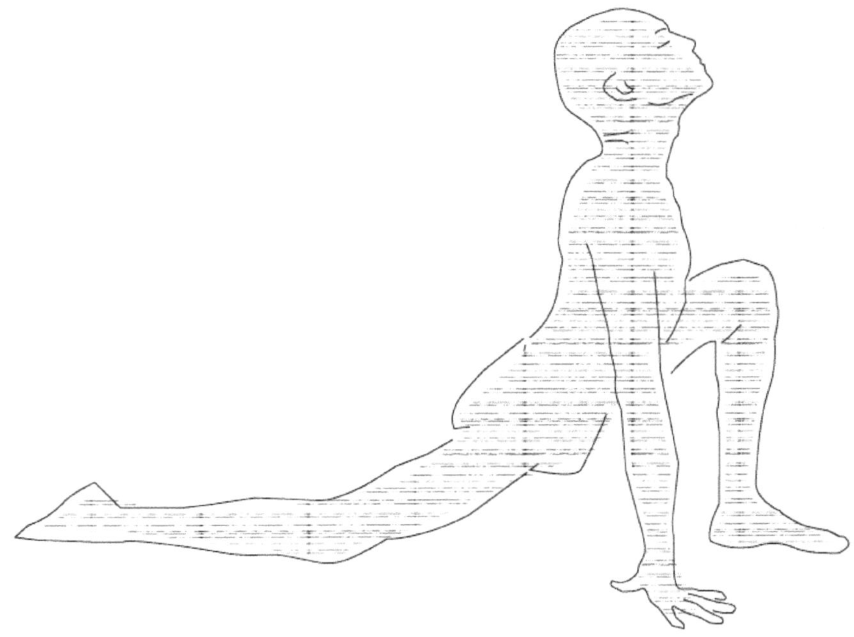

Body over Neck

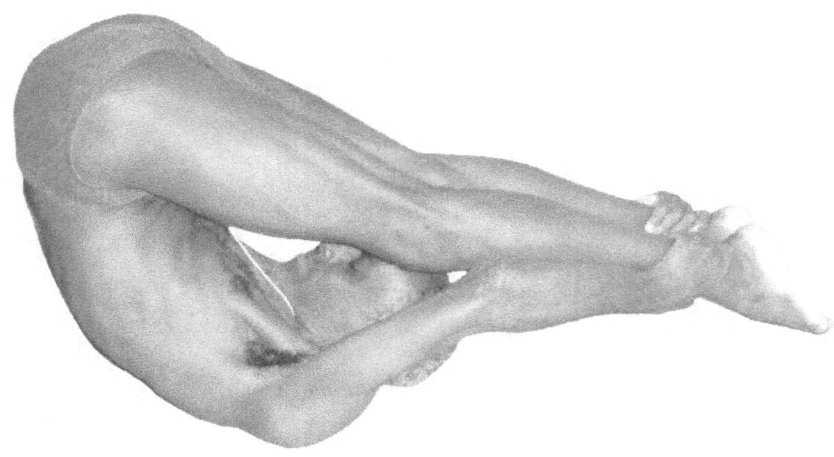

For this *Body over Neck* posture, a yogi puts the knees over the head. After laying on the back, one grabs the shins from the outside. One pulls the toes over the head to the floor. The neck and shoulder blades remain in contact with the floor. This posture is held while focusing within the body, to observe energy movements and alignments.

The natural focus is the central neck. A yogi may feel energy converging in the neck bones. This is nerve energy. Naad sound may be heard. The yogi should become absorbed in it. For this pose, naad is the audial object.

When relaxing out of this posture, the yogi should stay for some minutes in any position where there is a relaxation energy, and where with the naad sound is prominent. This pose is wonderful for training the mind to be absorbed in naad, and to be interested internally within the physical body, within the subtle body, and in any psychic portals which would give access to the yogi.

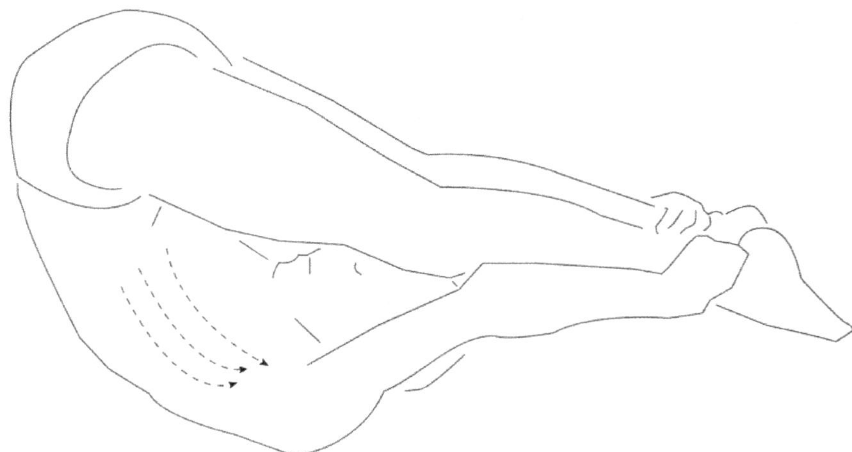

Focus Connection

The *Body over Neck* pose should be done cautiously with minute internal observations. Enter this posture slowly. Undo this posture in a timely manner. In its maximum hold, the feet when held by the hands are positioned so that the toes touch the floor. This will cause the knees to rest on the forehead. The minimal posture is with the feet floating above the floor, while the knees do not touch the forehead.

Because the bottom of the diaphragm is blocked, this posture has a crisis. There will be interruption of air intake. A yogi may use this posture to research the value of air.

- What would happen if the body lost access to air?

In this, there are many energy alerts but the one which will be the priority, has to do with air intake. The involuntary breath procurement system is suspended in this pose. The yogi will find that he is made aware that air is difficult to obtain.

- Will the subtle body peel away from the physical one if the procurement of air ceases?

Rear Thigh Stretch

This *Rear Thigh Stretch* posture has variations. In most the objective is the rear thigh stretch. The hands on the side of the body, which has the thigh stretched to the back, carry most of the weight. Some weight is borne by the heel of the foot which is stretch forward. A yogi should not be in a hurry to assume a posture. Patience is required. Inner focus should be applied. The yogi is attentive to the stretch of ligaments, tendons, muscles, organs, and regions.

In the image above, the rear thigh is tensioned further by using the hand from the other side to press the foot towards the buttocks. This should be done attentively, so that the focusing energy takes note of the tension and energy accumulation.

Before focusing fully in this pose, check to be sure that the forward foot is as far forward as it can be. Push it forward carefully. Check to be sure that the weight of the body is on the palm of the hand, which is on the floor, and which is the main support. Check the rear foot to be sure that it is pulled towards the buttocks.

In this posture, one should close the eyelids, or wear a blindfold. Focus within the psyche. Discover where energy courses, accumulates, or shifts. A yogi notices a current of energy where the thigh bone (femur) connects to the hip. See the sketch.

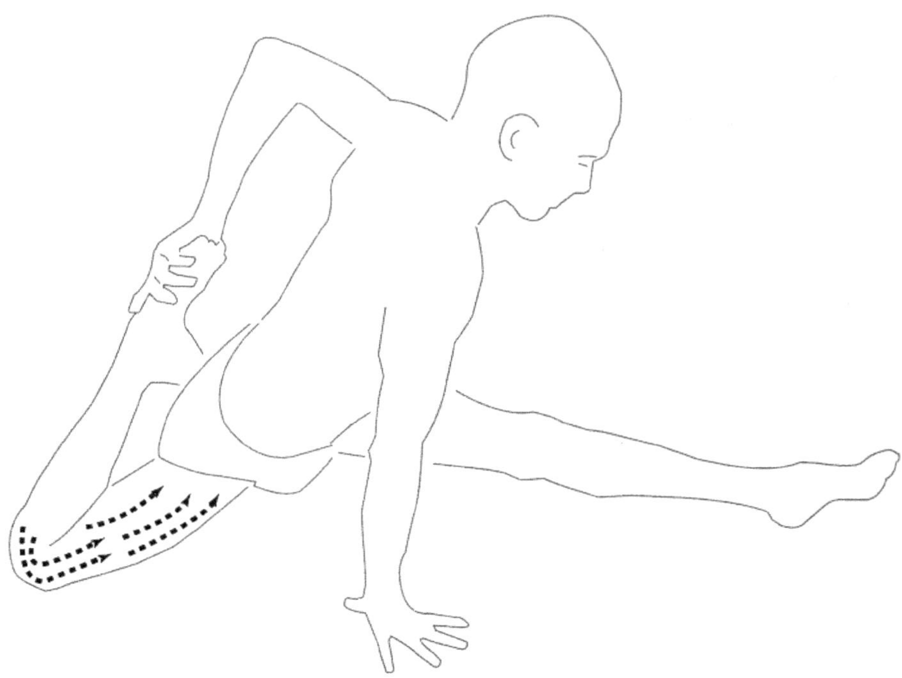

When the energy dissipates into the hip, the focus will shift to the thigh. Then it will again follow the energy to the hips, where it will become invisible. But it will rise through the trunk of the body and disappear in the head.

A question arises regarding the need for this information. The purpose of this book is to comply with a request of Yogeshwarananda. He wrote a book, which was titled, *First Steps to Higher Yoga*. In that text many postures are illustrated. Advise is given with each pose. The need for this publication surfaced, when Yogeshwarananda discussed, that most persons who learn *asana* postures, do that for reasons other than establishing a foothold in higher yoga, which culminates in the development of the divine eye.

This volume describes the subtle effects of postures. This is about using positions to develop the skill of *dhyana* spontaneous inside focus. The postures are physical but the focus is psychic. The focus is not health and beauty of the physical body. It is not that the focus described will be the same for each yogi, who does the particular pose. Each yogi may discover a different focus while doing the same posture.

Focus Connection

The *Rear Thigh Stretch* is strenuous. It is so, even for persons who have loose joints and relaxed muscles. The pressure control points are the knees, and inner thighs. The controller for gaging the tensions is the hand which holds the opposing foot to the buttocks. That hand regulates the tolerance, that the yogi can endure.

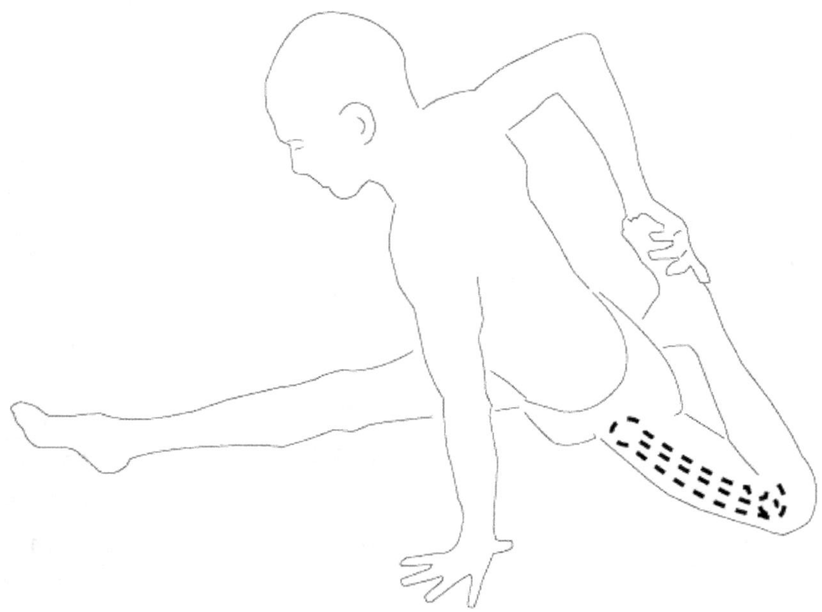

This posture exposes the attention focus. As soon as the hand pulls the opposing foot to the buttocks, there is an alarm message which is declared. As this occurs, the yogi gets an inner warning to cease the tension. If he listens to the message, he may discover that there are two directions of travel. Alternately, it may be so confused that the yogi cannot sort it.

One set of messages run from the inner thigh to the knee. The other set runs from the knee to the inner thigh. These clash in the thigh and flash in the brain to produce an unclear communication. A yogi may halt his general attention and focus on these messages. However, the jumble of signals may not be sorted. He may decide on an action even though he lacks clarity.

When translated to language, the messages will generally read as this.

- *This is happening.*
- *This should be checked.*
- *This should cease.*

Knowing this, the yogi may attempt to decipher the signals which produced these three messages, but he may be unable to do it. That is due to the jumble of energy, which is a confusion, when the foot is pulled tightly to the buttocks.

When a yogi ceases this *Rear Thigh Stretch* for one side of the body, he should complete the same for the other side. This is done by switching so that the foot which was pulled to the buttocks is used as the outstretched one. The converse is done for everything else.

The yogi should do so. Then slowly, he should assume an easy pose. For instance, he may sit on the heels with his palms on the thighs. Then he should meditate. It is likely that he will hear a loud screeching sound. He may realize that the breath rhythm normalized. It became silent and effortless. He should study its quiescent attitude. He will benefit from its lack of anxiety.

Press one Sole and one Thigh

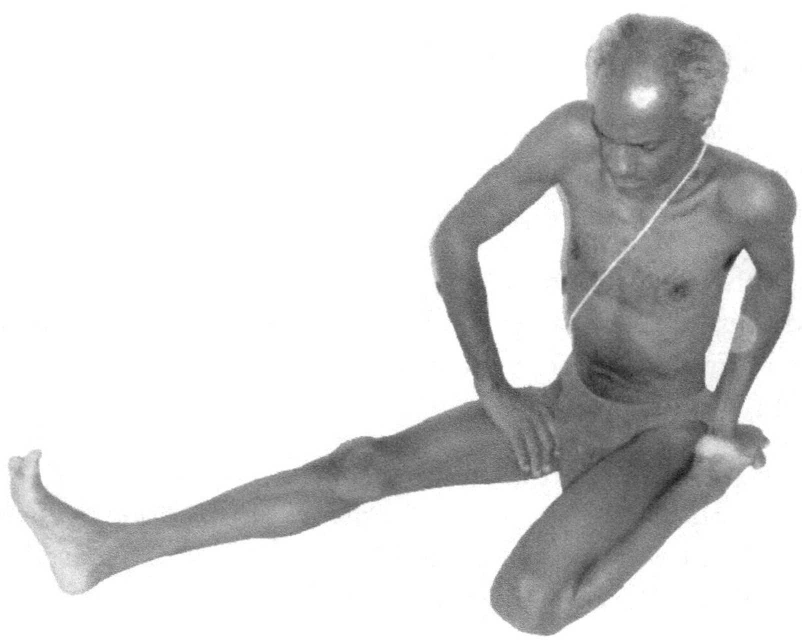

This *Press one Sole and one Thigh* posture is relatively easy. However, if one has much fat tissue or if one is muscular, it may be painful to assume this, with the buttocks on the floor while one leg is turned back.

If this is difficult, use a cushion. While in this posture push both elbows. One hand should grip the inner top side of the stretched limb. The other hand should rest on the sole of the foot, which sits by the side of its hip. The chin should be pressed to the throat. The spine should be erect.

To prohibit the mind from pursuing external objects, close the eyelids or use a blindfold. Focus within the subtle body. One may notice a screeching inner sound, naad resonance. This may be loud. Link the focus to it. Notice that it is spontaneous. Be attentive. It may be heard everywhere in the head. It may be heard in a specific area. This attention to naad will give the yogi some understanding about *samadhi* which is the highest of the eight processes of yoga. *Samadhi means* that one is effortlessly absorbed in a higher reality and for a duration, for more than some moments. One does not have to exert a focusing objective. Naad serves as that.

During this absorption one may be aware of rushing energy in various zones. For instance, there may be a dart of energy from the throat to the head. This may be only for three or four inches when estimated mentally. There may be a dart of energy from the throat to one shoulder and to the other. This will run through the central shoulder region and the central neck. Be sure to maintain the chin lock by pulling the chin without bending the head forward.

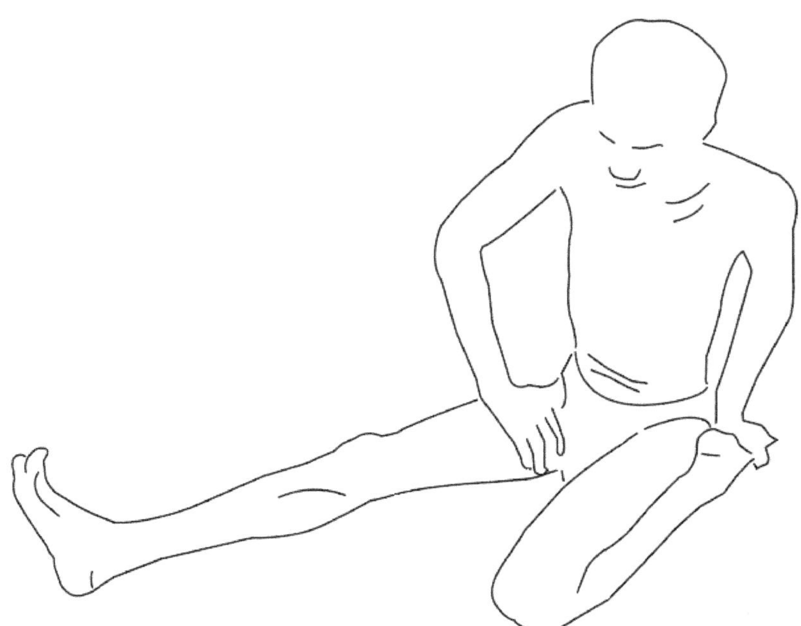

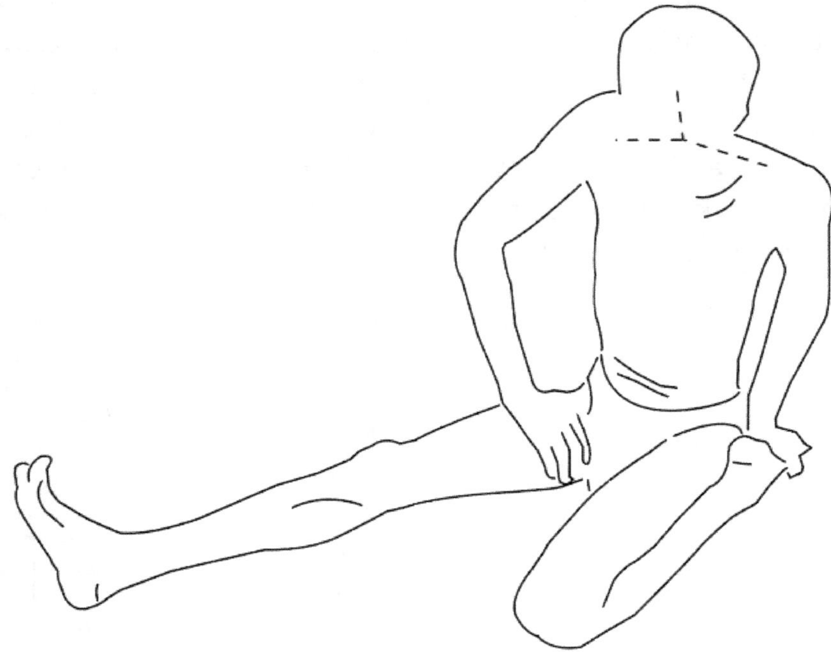

Focus Connection

The *Press one Sole and one Thigh* position is relatively easy to assume. As soon as the yogi attempts to review what it is internally, there may be a split of focus.

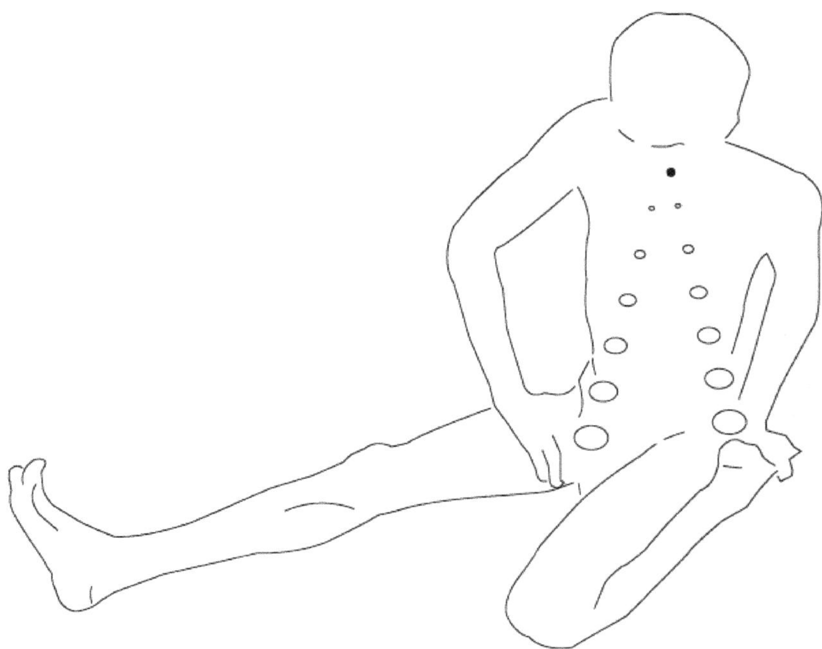

This may have the one beam of focus splitting to investigate the pressure applied to one thigh and the sole of one foot. There may be a slight hesitation, which may result in mental confusion. This is due to a hesitation to split, and a reluctance of the splitting mechanism to do as requested.

The two focusing signals originate in the mid neck. At that place there will be a bubble as the splitting origin. According to the degree of pressure on each side being applied by each hand, there will be a demand for focus. This will not be an equal demand. Instead, it will switch, such that one side may be sixty percent of the focus, while the other is forty percent. It will fluctuate during the posture, as each hand applies pressure and is relieved of pressure. The fluctuation will continue to behave erratically.

After some time, when the pressure relaxes, there may be a reeep sound. It may continue for five minutes. Then, an eeep sound will arise. Then again, the reeep sound will be heard. These sounds will arrest the focusing power, such that the pressure applied by the hand relaxes slightly, because of being deprived of pressure. There may arise a thought, but it will vanish before it is understood. The yogi will not read it. His attempt to know what it communicates, will not be serviced.

Again, there will be the reeep sound. Then after a time, a thought will appear, but it will not be understood. It will be in a compressed state, which is not legible.

Rack on Elbows

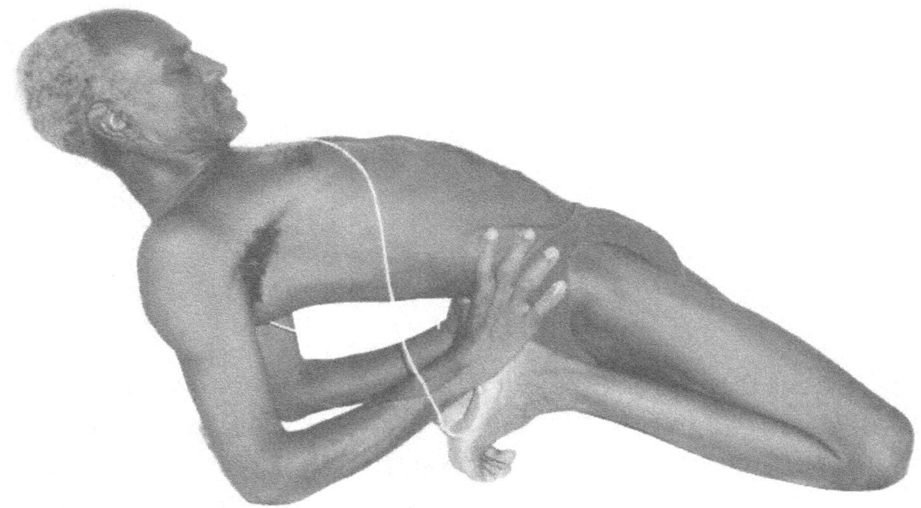

For this *Rack on Elbows* practice, the weight of the body is *racked on the elbows*. The thumbs brace the spine. The fingers are visible on the outside near the waist. The toes are yirked under the foot. Some weight is supported by the legs near the knees.

There are variations of this pose. In one, the buttocks are supported by the heels. In another, the buttocks are between the heels which do not support them. To apply the chin lock, the chin is drawn to the throat.

During the check to discover the actions of the energy in the psyche, a yogi may notice a loud screeching resonance which seems to be all-pervasive. The yogi should be absorbed in that, for the realization that it is a type of *samadhi* continuous energy display, which requires no deliberate focus. Since this sound is scattered in every direction, any focus on it anywhere is sufficient.

Focus Connection

At first when one assumes this *Rack on Elbows,* there is a confusion of energy. This happens because the buttocks are tensioned on the heels. The spine is yirked to create a spring-like tension. Various energies are released, even from the thigh. Because the head is tilted up as far as it will go, the neck and throat remain in an alert. The mind shuffles to find a solution for the energy which is disordered.

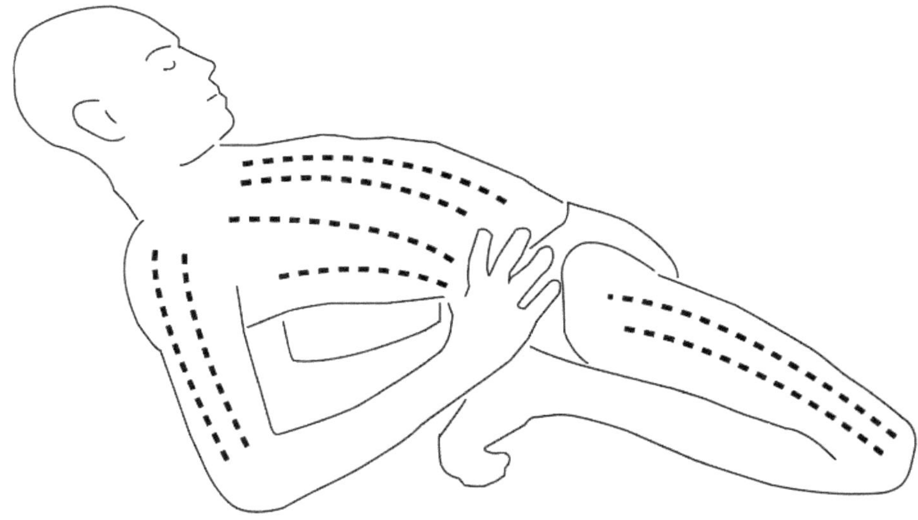

There is an abandonment, where the mind no longer searches for order. Instead, it finds that there is a focusing shimmer of energy in the eyes. This is like mini-needles flashing as they rush pass each other. There are flickers occurring rapidly.

Then the chaos is reduced. There is more order, with the heels expressing a semicircular loop of energy. The big toes echoed a stout holding energy, to support the weight of the body, which comes through the heels.

After a time, the yogi releases this pose. He slowly sits between the heels. The buttocks contact the floor. The hands are placed near the abdomen on the thighs. The body begins to swing. This is a slight swing. It is barely noticeable. The yogi ceases this swing. He again assumes the *Rack on Elbows* posture. He observes how it causes energy release. He notes the confusion, the lack of symmetry.

The yogi again sits between the heels, and gradually places the hands on the thighs. He again swings left to right and right to left. Now he notices that thoughts arrive but do not display. The thoughts are released in the mental chamber as packages of energy, but they do not have the revealing energy. They do not burst into ideas which are coherent, and which required involvement. They are like sealed packages. They appear and disappear, with no idea of their information. This is a blank mind meditation. It has thought energy, but it lacks thought display. It is a special state.

Butterfly Squat – Closed Wings

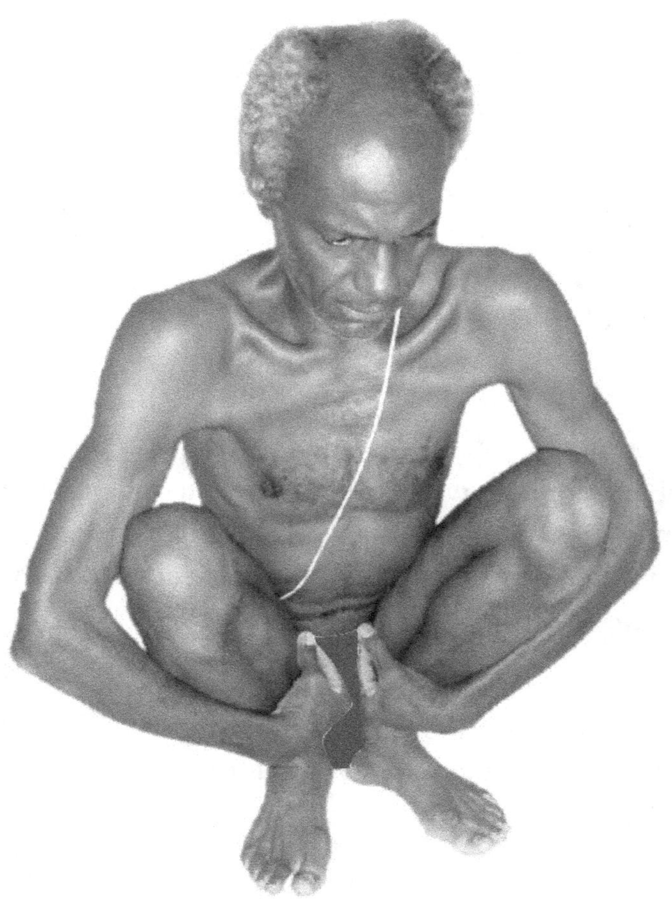

This *Butterfly Squat – Closed Wings* posture, is similar to the format of a butterfly, when it folds its wings, while remaining on a branch. This is a squatting pose, which has variation. If possible, it is done where the weight of the body travels through the shins into the feet. The buttocks rest on the legs just above the ankles. The buttocks do not contact the floor. Only the feet are in contact.

This is easy for some but difficult for others. For instance, if the thighs are large, there may be an imbalance. Then it may be necessary to off-center the body, so that some weight is shifted forward. This is one of the poses which utilize balance.

The chin should be compressed the throat. The balance should be checked so that on the feet, or on the feet and buttocks, one can remain in this posture for minutes. A yogi should close the eyelids or wear a blindfold. Searching for energy within psyche, the yogi should discover any movement or stillness. Sometimes, there may be an energy distribution which is like a sand storm. There may be a pipe-like energy on each side, high in the chest region. A rod in the center of the chest may radiate energy away from the center.

When a yogi becomes absorbed in this way, his understanding of *samadhi* full spontaneous awareness may be experienced in the head, where the energy presses to the nose, from the inside of the subtle body.

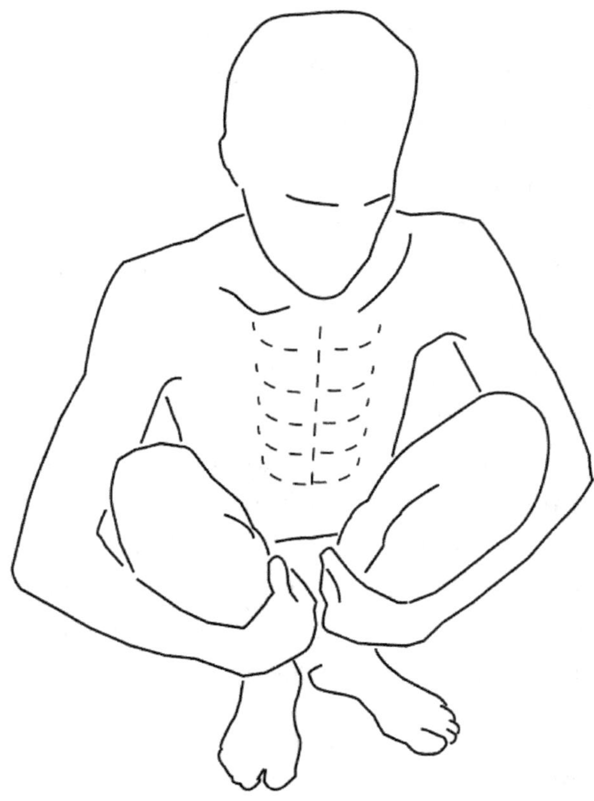

Focus Connection

The *Butterfly Squat – Closed Wings* posture, is easy for those whose thighs allow balance when squatting. When a yogi assumes this pose, it is likely that there will be no strain or stress in the body. If so, naad resonance may be heard at the top back of the head, perhaps, on the right or left or center. The chin should be pressed to the throat.

Keeping the attention in the throat or chin, the yogi may observe that within the neck, there is an open area. This is a psychic opening which runs the length of the neck. It is oblong in shape and is empty. A light may glow there. If the yogi sees no light, he may feel a blank space.

After a time, inner sound, may be heard everywhere. It may be difficult to determine where it is, specifically.

No thoughts may arise but then one may be aware of the lub dub heart rhythm. An attempt should be made to catalog that. It runs for the duration of the life of the body. It does so involuntarily.

- What person or force operates it?

After a time, listening to the vibrations which are a result of the heart's actions, the hands will begin to feel heavy. Even with an effort to hold them in position near the thighs, the hands will drop to the floor. This will happen with the palms up. At that time, with the hands resting on the floor, the focus should shift to the breath. A yogi should notice that it is shallow. The air goes only to the top of the lungs. It has a rhythm but it is not deep. It does not reach even the mid portion of the lungs. A yogi should from within the psyche, look down into the chest to observe that.

Sit Between Heels – Lean Back 45^0

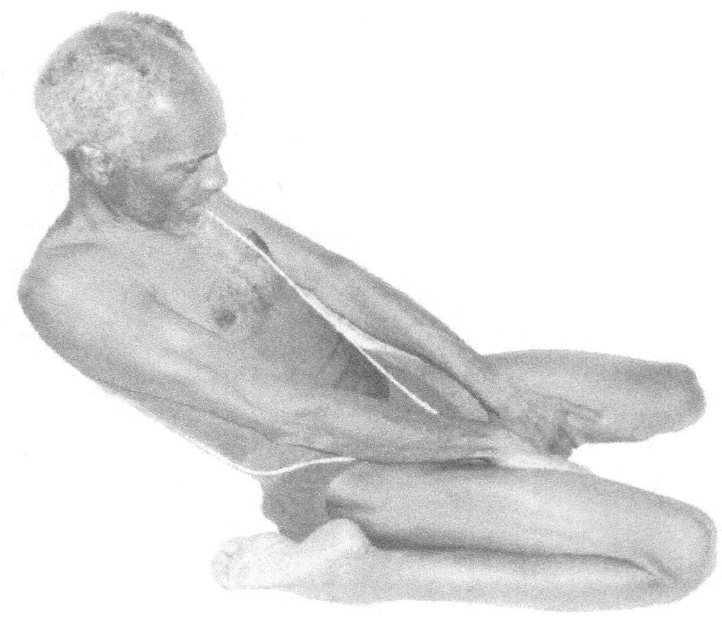

To do this *Sit Between Heels – Lean Back* 45^0 posture, one should sit between the heels. Grip the inside of the thighs, near the genitals. It is best to have the grip area be free of fabric. Fabric may cause the hands to slip. After gripping the thighs, lean back at 45 degrees. Check the chin lock. Be sure that the chin is pressed to the throat. Close the eyelids if there is no blindfold. This will assist the inner focus. It prevents the eyes from seeing external objects, which distract.

Focus into the body, using the throat as a sluice through which vision energy passes. Look through the center of the throat. If nothing is seen, or if only random energy is perceived, continue peering through the center of the throat.

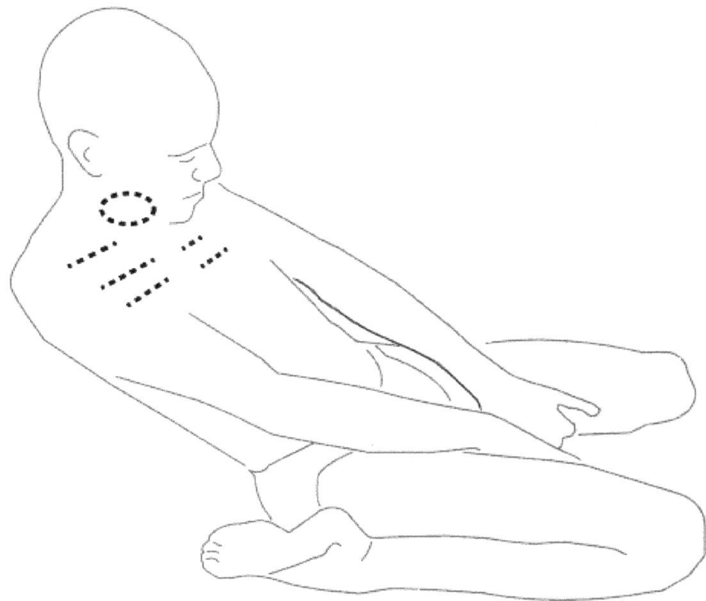

Check the chin lock to be sure that the chin is pressed to the throat. There may be a circular hole in the throat. Energy may pass through this place downward. Check to be sure that the hands maintain the grip of the thighs. One should hear naad resonance somewhere in the head. If that happens, one should become absorbed. This is a naad *samadhi* training. The mind must be trained to appreciate naad high-pitched frequency.

Focus Connection

Inspecting the *Sit Between Heels – Lean Back 45⁰* posture, I found that when this form was assumed, there was spontaneous focus on the tip of the tailbone. I discovered a tiny hole at the lowest end of the spine. This is a hard-to-locate place, which may be used as a focal point during some meditations.

While focusing at the tip of the tailbone, a shivering of the entire trunk began. That became the focus. The perception of the tailbone tip ceased entirely. The focus on the shivering was kept for a time, not for long. To relieve that, the spine was put upright, with the hands on the thighs. The chest was lifted as the spine was pressed forward towards the navel. This relieved the shivering.

Pausing for a time, the yogi should again resume the posture with the *45^0 tilt backward*. This time a search should be made for the pubic spot. This is the center of the second chakra, the reproductive mechanism area. The yogi should search to locate where the tubing from the testes enters under the genitals. In females, the search should be for a single spot, a dot. It is about one inch back in the center of the genitalia.

A check should be made for shivering. If there is any, the yogi should make an effort to arrest it. If he cannot, he should sit up, and place the hands on the thighs. Inner sound should be targeted. The yogi should investigate its origin, regarding its entry into the psyche, and its generator.

- Is it a generated sound?
- Is it spontaneous and perpetual?

Thoughts may arise but these will have no power to open. By becoming aware of these ideas, the awareness itself will cause them to disappear. The yogi should test to see if he has the power to banish the thought packages.

Squat with Fingers Pressed to Floor

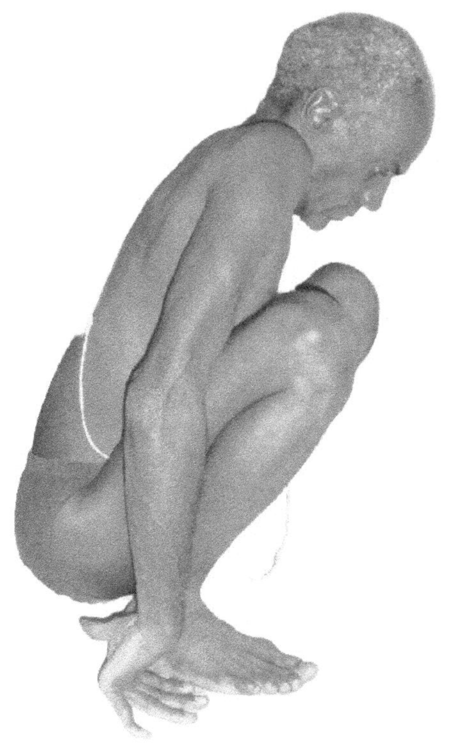

This *Squat with Fingers Pressed to Floor* is an easy posture. If, however, the thighs are bulky, either from taut muscles or from accumulated fat, this posture may not be assumed. One may, however, still do this posture if one leans forward between the thighs. That however may place extra torque on the ankles and feet. That would change the posture, such that the focus within will yield different energy shifts and compilations.

When doing this pose, heels should be apart. For females the spread of the heels may be wider than for males. This accommodates the breasts which should be between the thighs or knees.

One special act is to keep the thumbs off the floor. Only the four fingers should be pressed into the floor. Another special feature is that the palms should make no contact with the floor.

Only the first pad of each finger, the distal phalanx, should be pressed, not the entire finger. The yogi should check for balance. If necessary, the feet should be moved to adjust balance of the body. The fingers should be shifted to cause better balance

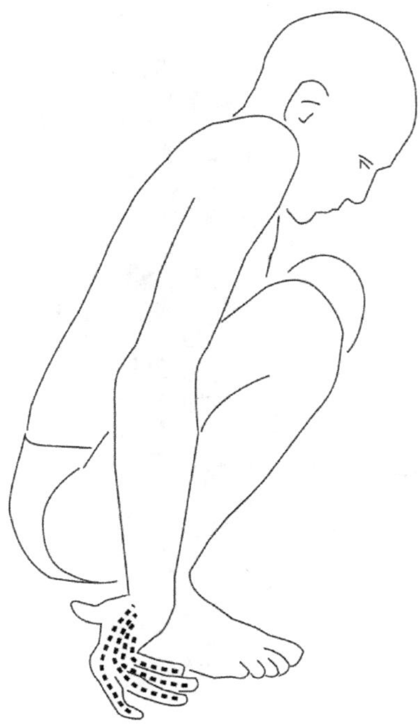

When pressing the fingers to the floor, the yogi should focus within the psyche. With sufficient focus, one should be aware of the pressure. Much is applied, so that an electrical sensation is felt in each segment of each finger.

Naad resonance may be heard. It may surround the observing self. With the focus as described, this posture should be held for a time. Thereafter, the hands should be relaxed. The fingers should be interlocked. They should be twisted one way, then the next, repeatedly. Then again, they should be pressed to the floor with the palms making no contact. Then one should meditate and tune to the screeching sound which resonates in the head.

Focus Connection

The *Squat with Fingers Pressed to Floor* posture, causes an observation regarding split focus. It is to be determined by a yogi if it is possible to simultaneously hold inner focus on two objectives.

- Can the mind be split so that its sensual quest operates pursuing two targets?
- Or is it that the mind cannot do so, that it can only pursue one object, and then another in turn, switching from one to the other?

There is a need to know this when a yogi does *samyama* meditation, particularly when he does *dharana* deliberate focus.

- Can he focus on multiple objects.
- For instance, can he hear naad and keep it in focus, while processing some other objective, like focusing on inner light?

The *Squat with Fingers Pressed to Floor* pose, renders two pressing concerns, which the mind must attend to immediately.

- Which one should be the priority?

The yogi may find that the mind retreats from the fingers through the wrists, forearms and reaches half way up the arms. At that place in both arms, it shuffles its judging ability, to weigh which situation has the most urgency.

If one set of four fingers are being pressed lightly, the mind will rate that one as being of low priority. It will focus on the other hand which has more muscular pressure applied. It will favor relieving that pressure but since the practice requires the application of dual force, it will instead check the other fingers which are lightly pressed.

This will cause the mind to become more confused, in determining if it can hold equal pressure on each set of fingers. In the meantime, the objective of the practice which is to apply maximum pressure on the fingers of both hands, will assert itself. This will cause the self to note that there is a force which is similar to an electric current, which runs from the wrists to the forearms, and arms, and then through the shoulders. These will shoot diagonally across to the neck. From there a current will traverse the third eye chakra.

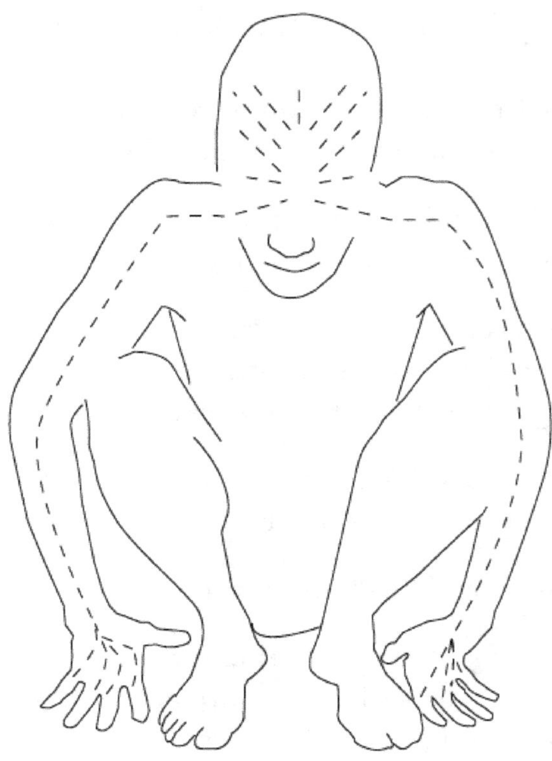

For the self this will solve the problem of the split attention, as that energy converged in the neck, and became unified as one dart of energy upward.

After a time, pressing the fingers, it will be necessary to relieve the tension. The yogi should rest the hands on the feet but without applying pressure. When this happens, in moments, the twinkling energy in the fingers will cease. Then the fingers should be relaxed even more. They should be positioned for the maximum ease. Then the focus will shift to the center of the eyebrows. This focus will cause a *dhyana* spontaneous absorption. The yogi should study this state, and maintain an intention to induce it, during other meditation sessions.

Inverted Wheel Pose-- *Chakrasana* or *Urdhva Dhanurasana*

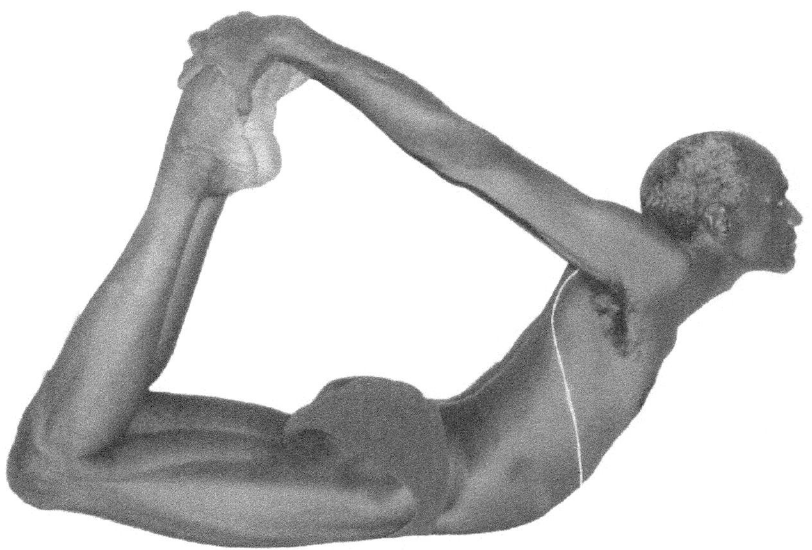

This is an *inverted wheel pose.* The ability to assume this and hold it, is related to the proportions of the limbs of the body. To assume it, lay on the abdomen. Males should be sure to safely position the genitals. No part of it should be located where it can be crushed.

Lay on the abdomen. Push the genitals out of the way. Grab the toes of each corresponding foot. Pull the chest up. Simultaneously, the knees and some of the thighs, will come up.

Hold this pose for a time. The head should be held up. While in this pose, one should feel electric sensations in each arm. By slowly releasing the pose, relax the body. The tensions will disappear.

Repeat the pose. Focus on the confusion of energy. One may notice that the energy is scattered. It is random. There may be shivering in the thighs.

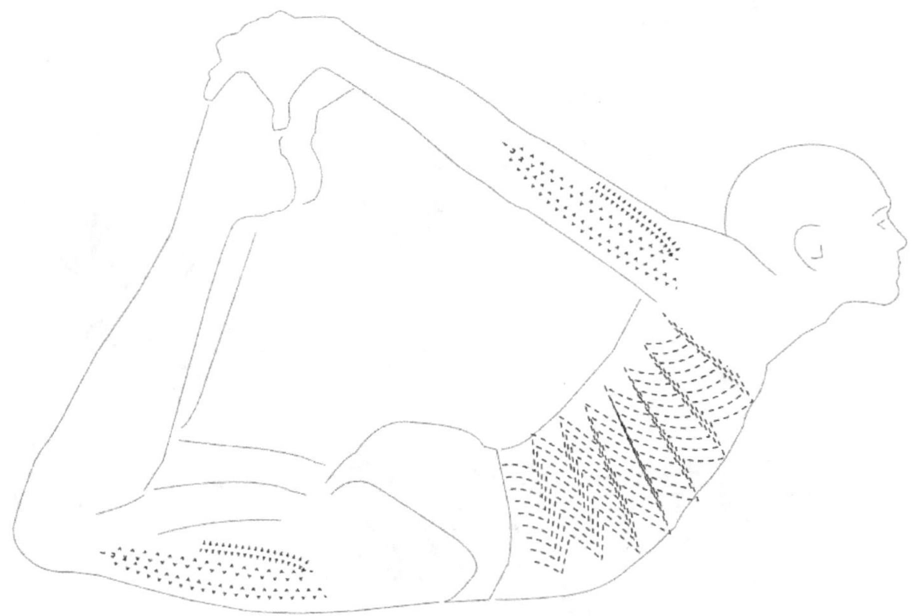

Focus Connection

The *Inverted Wheel* pose can be a difficult one. If so, a yogi may find a way to adjust it. If one cannot do a posture, or if in doing it one causes injury, one should either cease the pose or do it in part. According to the capacity of the infant form, one derived from parents, the body may or may not assume particular forms. Each body received from parents may or may not assume a posture. One should not have the idea that one should perfectly do each pose.

The body which can do the numerous variations of a posture, is the subtle body. In that form there is full flexibility. Hence there is no need to injure the physical form by forcing it to do every possible posture.

When doing the *Inverted Wheel* pose, a yogi should be attentive. That is because it is a form which requires attentiveness and expertise. In the male body, one should be sure that the genitals will not be crushed. One should properly hold the feet with the hands. Then with attention one should pull up.

As soon as one does this, one must hold the feet properly, to arrest the pose and make the body stable. There will be a confusion of energy on each side of the body. Noticing this, one will also notice that the attention looks for, but is unable, to properly catalog the genitals. It will convert into a mental demand like this.

- Where are the genitals?

When that inquiry is made, the genitals will be found as a clod of grey-green energy in the middle of the body. It will seem as if the genitals are opaque and dense. There will be a blankness where the organs are located. Elsewhere in the psyche, there will be tiny sensations. These will be in contrast to the denseness of the genitals. In the middle of the chest, there will be a space which is void. After a time, the yogi will relax the pose. The feet will come to the floor. So will the hands. The yogi may hear the heart beating. This will seem to come from a distance.

The yogi will check to see where the chin is located. This will happen because the breath will be irregular. The yogi should set the chin for convenience of breathing. Still again, there will be discomfort. The yogi should check the hands to be sure that they are relaxed. He should move them to the sides of the head. He should check the neck. It may have pains and tension. He will decide to sit up, so as to relieve the discomfort in the neck, and to resume involuntary breathing.

Squat Forward on Hands

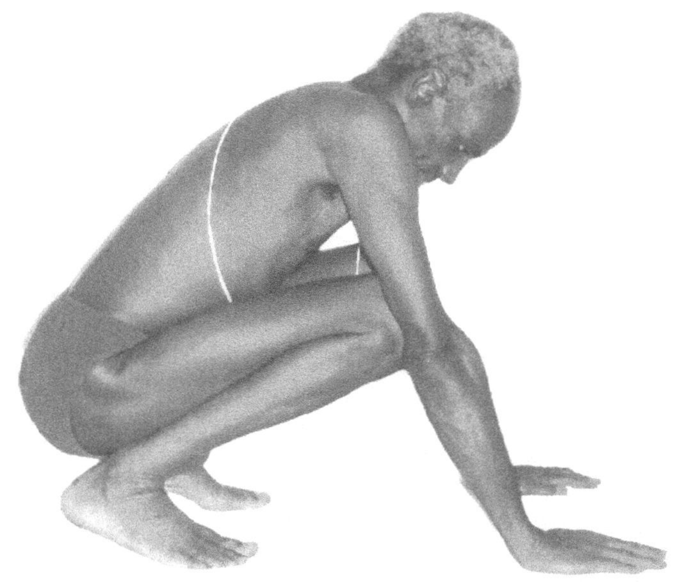

This *Squat Forward on Hands* is an easy pose. Little, if any tension is felt. This has variation, with the elbows outside or inside the knees. For this instance, the elbows are outside. The fingers and palms rest on the floor. The toes and the metatarsal pads touch the floor. The heels, and much of the soles, do not.

A yogi should focus through the neck, chest, and lower trunk. From the upper chest, a coolness may radiate upwards. This may be experienced as a beaming light which has a light-green hue. One may also feel the heart throbbing.

A yogi may focus internally towards the eye sockets or the back of head, where a light may be experienced.

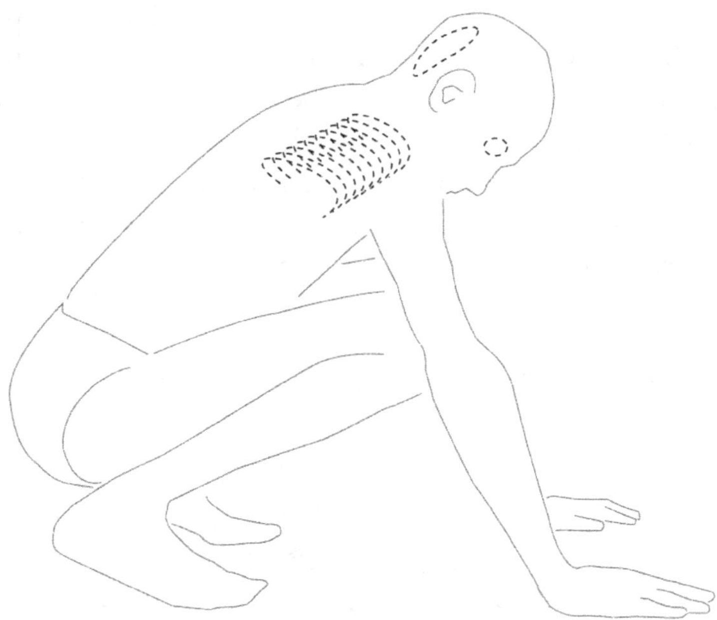

Focus Connection

The *Squat Forward on Hands* pose is relatively ease. Some persons will have some discomfort doing it. In that case, the hands should be set and then reset for the best position. Once that is discovered, the yogi should internalize, forgetting the posture, but focusing internally on the energy, as to how it is scattered through the body.

As soon as he gets some mapping, he should mentally repeat *Om Namo Shivaya*. No physical sound should be heard. Slowly, he should say that mantra while being centralized in the psyche. At some time, while saying that mantra, the yogi should realize that naad inner sound is present. It did not start at the moment it was heard. He will realize that it resonated prior. He should hear it but he should continue to say *Om Namo Shivaya.*

The time will past with these two features interlocking with the yogi's attention. After a while, the yogi will realize that he is engaged with a thought which did not open and was not illustrated. His attention was released from that thought. It was reinstated to saying *Om Namo Shivaya* while hearing naad sound continuously.

That will proceed, the chanting of the Shiva mantra and the hearing of naad, which serves as a continuous background, which is like a raft which carries an object through deep water.

The yogi will at some point, realize that the physical body is tilted forward. That happens because of gravity, which constantly makes a successful or unsuccessful attempt, to change a position which it is dissatisfied with. The yogi should reset the body, and bring the heels to the floor if they are lifted from it. This should be done without disturbing the energy configuration. As someone would be careful with fragile glass, so the yogi would be with this posture. He should neither jerk nor move aggressively, where he would lose the focus, and cause the energy to be change within the psyche.

At some point, the yogi will realize that the breath rhythm was affected negatively. Due to the posture, due to the position of the thighs against the chest, the diaphragm cannot expand sufficiently. Less air was absorbed by it. This caused a deficiency. The yogi should note this, but he should not change the posture, nor make an effort to change the position, nor to breathe deeply.

He should remain in the meditation as is. He should begin saying another mantra. The mantra is *Om Namo Naadaya*. After a time when this mantra is said, the yogi should slowly without jerks, assume an easy pose. In that pose he should mentally say the naad mantra.

Yirk-Back- Camel Posture

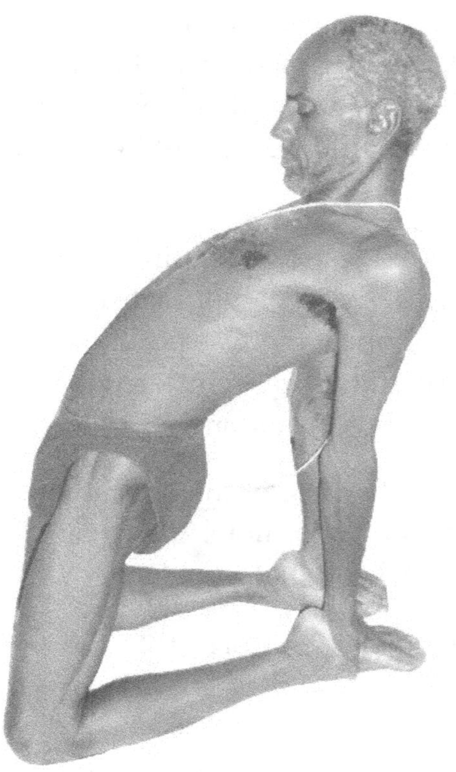

There are several variations of the *camel* pose. Each has tension in a particular part of the body. The support structure is the knees and instep, with the hands, forearms, and arms, and shoulders providing stability.

Depending on where the hands make contact with the soles, the legs or the floor, the distribution of weight will be realized. The head may be forward or pressed backward. A yogi should assume the post, then with eyes closed, he should check to determine where energy settles or shifts.

Periodically when any part of the body relaxes, one should check to be sure, that the waist is pressed forward.

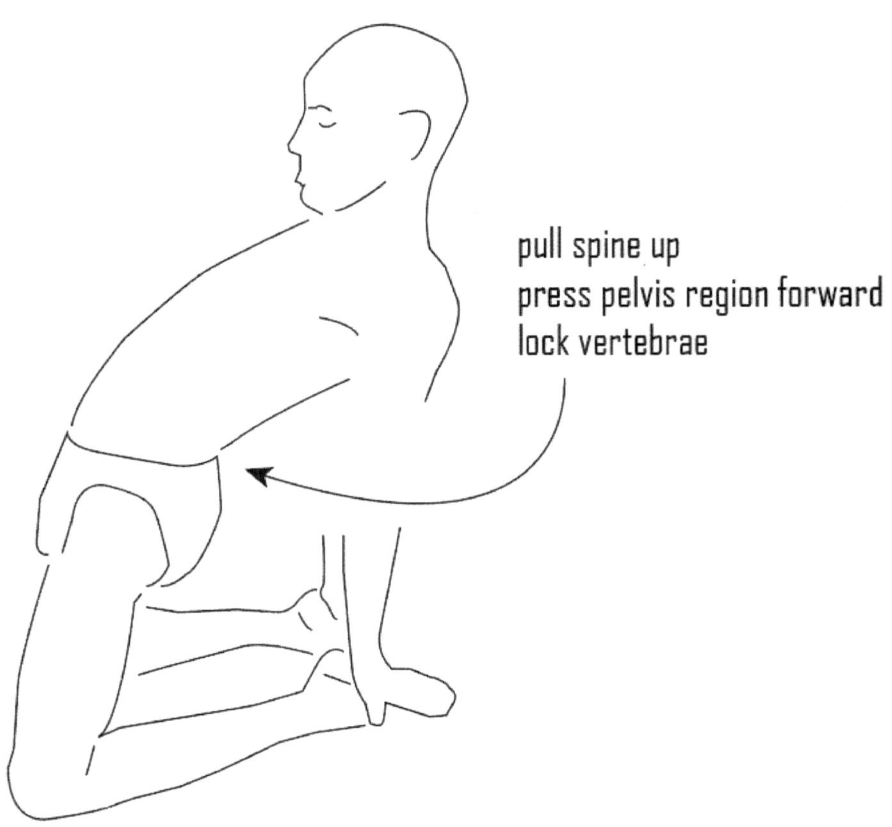

There may be electric sensations moving from the knees to the thighs. One should again press the thighs forward, while keeping the focus in the body, not allowing the mind to drift outside the body, nor to pursue ideas which are from memory.

A yogi may hear naad sound blaring. When coming out of this pose, it should be done slowly with steady inner focus. The yogi should sit on or between the heels. Holding the meditation while sitting on or between the heels, one may become aware, of an oozing energy in the central chest. This will move through the neck where it will dissipate and disappear, as if it is absorbed as it transits through the neck, into the brain. It may be a clear bliss energy.

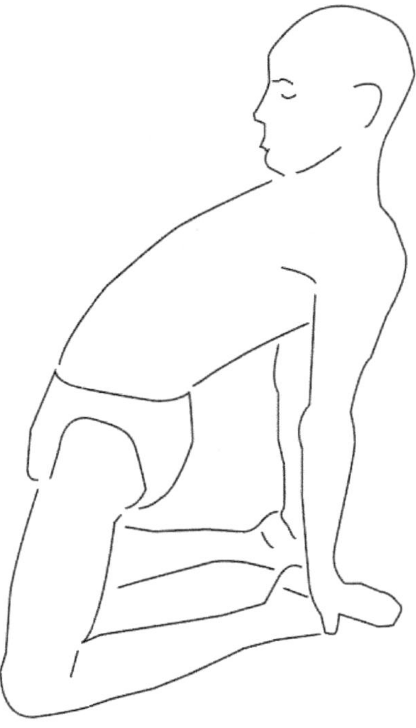

Focus Connection

The *Yirk Back - Camel* posture can be done with variations. These are based on the position of the hands, regarding where they are located either on the soles, heels or Achilles tendons. There is variation as to where the toes are located, as to if they lay flat on the floor with soles facing the sky, or if the feet are vertical to the floor with the toes yirked inward. According to the set position, there will or will not be certain effects. The yogi should map the energy configurations which arise.

When this pose is assumed, the yogi should check within the body to observe the energy. The hands should be checked. The abdomen should be monitored. A final observation of the chin position should be made. It should be pulled towards the throat. It should be held there. This is followed with a spine check, to determine if the spine is pressed forward as much as can be safely tolerated.

Once these muscular attitudes are in order, the yogi may realize that there are two balls of energy, where the thighs pivot into the torso. These balls will be transparent like crystal glass.

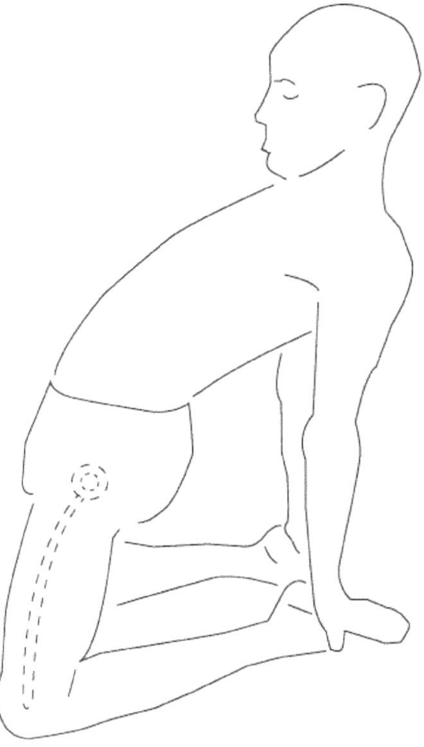

If a shivering begins, the yogi should determine its cause. It may be required to relocate the hands on the soles, heels or Achilles tendons. The chin may need adjustment. The spine may need to be locked by a forward press. Balance of the body in reference to gravity may need to be determined. If the shivering continues, the yogi should lower the torso, to bring the buttocks to the floor. This should be done without jerks, or sudden movements which will disrupt the energy spread.

With the buttocks on the floor, the shivering will cease promptly. The yogi should meditate in that position. He should check to be sure that every part of the body is in order. He should raise the torso again and resume the *Yirk-Back – Camel* posture. He should observe the condition of the energy. He should check every part, to be sure that the energy is matched to, or is dissimilar, to what he experienced before. When this posture becomes intolerable, when there is shivering again, or when he can no longer hold the torso, where he finds that it drops, and does not stay pushed out, he should sit on the heels. He should do so without jerking, bringing the buttocks to the heels slowly, and with observation of the internal feelings, and energy dispersion, or collection. Sitting on the heels, he should have the hands on the thighs with the palms facing up.

After a time, when the energy is quiescent, the yogi should again assume the *Yirk-Back – Camel* pose. Then he should search internally for the tailbone, the very end of the spine. It may be experienced as a sliver of black silk thread which is about a foot in length.

Again, the yogi should carefully lower the buttocks to the heels. This will ease the pressures. The energy will normalize. The yogi should take this as an opportunity to experience quiescence. After a time, he should again assume the *Yirk-Back – Camel* posture. This time, there may be an energy release from the thighs to the bottom of the torso. Some feelings will gradually spread through the torso, which is the lower abdomen area, the middle section and the higher chest region. It may have a dark grey opaque space. Observing this, he should sit between the heels. There he should check the center of the chest for energy movements.

This practice teaches the yogi how to arrest, release or develop focusing regions, which is a skill that is required for doing *samadhi* continuous absorption practice.

On Back – Knees to Shoulders

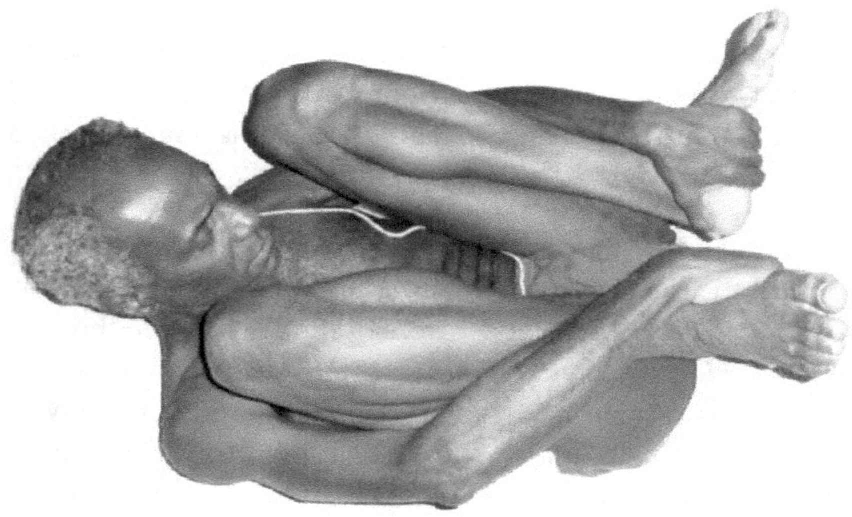

From this *On Back – Knees to Shoulders* posture, from being on the back, curve upward, the knees are brought to the chest. The hands grab the corresponding foot arches from the outside. The head and neck are brought up tightly. The body is tensed.

When this posture is assumed, the yogi should focus through the body. He should be aware of the thighs, legs, feet, arms, and forearms. The head should be raised. The chin should be pressed to the throat. There will be a tension where the neck is connected to the lower back of the skull.

A yogi should notice that there is an effort to breathe, as if the body cannot get sufficient air. This happens because the diaphragm is restricted. One should notice short breaths, as well as the inability to cause the lungs to fully inflate.

Tiny shafts of light may be experienced. These shoot through the chest into the neck, where it is dissipated before it enters the head. While this happens, a yogi should grab the arches more firmly. He may experience some discomfort. This posture makes one realize some chaotic energies.

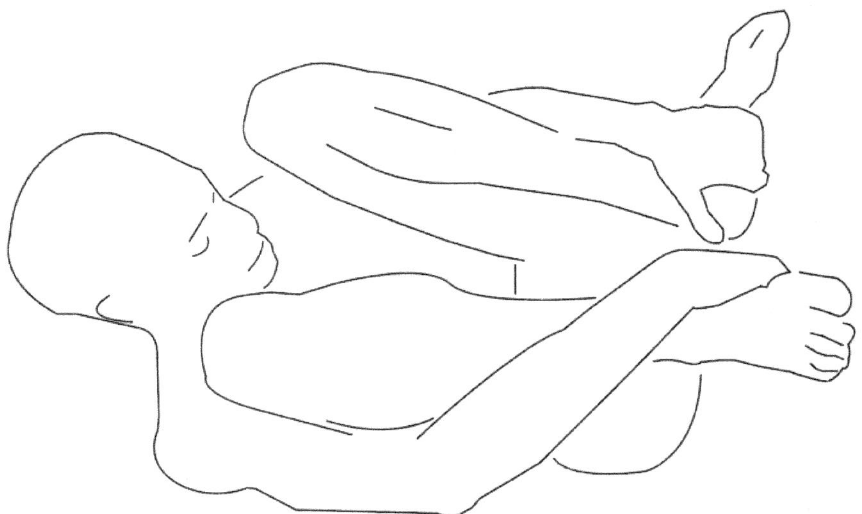

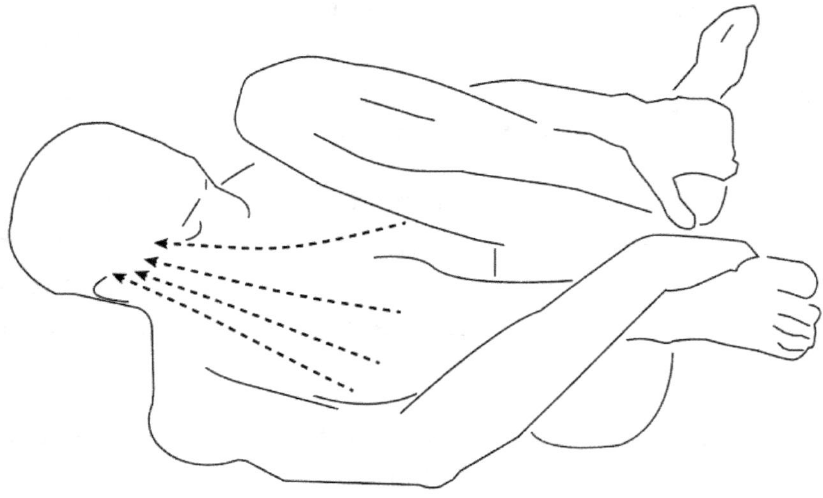

Focus Connection

The *On Back – Knees to Shoulders* posture is relatively easy, except for persons with large thighs. When this posture is assumed, the yogi should check the grip of the hands where it clutches the feet. The final check should be the throat.

- How does the chin lock to the throat?
- Is the back of the neck fully tensioned?

After these checks, the yogi should get an intuition to check the energies in the throat. It may seem that energy from every part of the psyche runs towards the throat, and becomes part of an orbit around the center of the throat. When these energies get near to the throat, they become formatted to be part of a whirlpool. This has a slow downward pull which has the color of a gold-white liquid. When this happens, there may be a memory, or flashback of an event prior.

In the top half of the spine, it is experienced as a sliver of energy, which is like a sliver of granite. The yogi will return to focusing on the whirlpool of energy which is centered on the throat. If the chin is lifted from the throat, this whirlpool will disappear. The throat will lose its centralizing power.

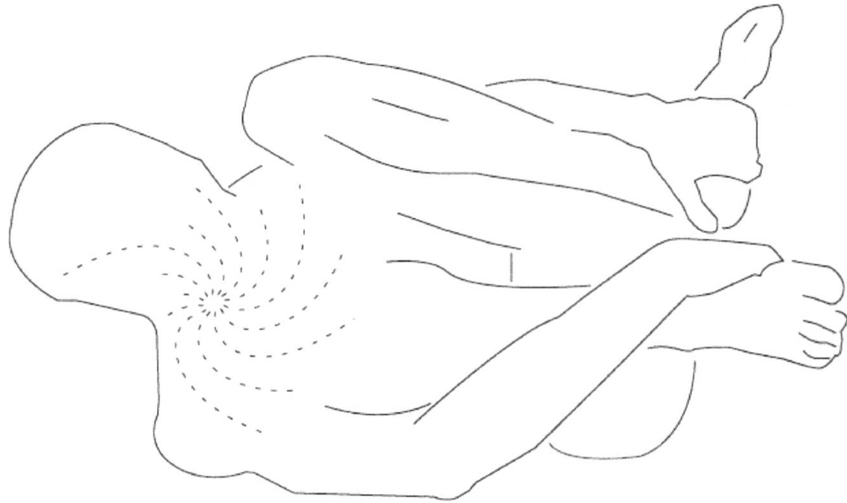

So long as the yogi holds the chin to the throat, and if he loses the focus on the throat, he will realize that there is irregular breathing. The timing of the inhale and exhale will be irregular. Noticing that, he will be inclined to releasing the posture.

That will result in releasing the feet and bringing them to the floor. The hands will of their own accord, seek support from the floor. That may occur with the palms up. That could vary. In that relaxation, the yogi will notice that the breath rhythm resumes. He should stay in this relaxation for a time. Then he should assume the *On Back – Knees to Shoulders* pose, gripping the feet, holding the knees to the chest, and keeping the chin locked to the throat.

Again, he should focus on the throat and check for a whirlpool of energy moving through the vortex of the throat, and dissipating to nowhere. He should keep the posture for as long as he can. Then he should relax the feet and hands, supporting them on the floor. At this time, he may hear the naad sound. He should listen and determine if there are other inner melodies.

He should identify naad location. He should map the resonance as to its volume and intensity. He should challenge the configuration of the psyche, to know the location of inner sound.

- What is its volume?
- Does it have an origin?
- How did it begin?

- What about visual aspects?
- Is there a portal?
- As naad is heard and is spontaneous, is there anything visual in comparison?

On Back- Grab Shins over Head

To assume this *On Back - Grab Shins over Head* posture, lay on back. Bring feet up. Grab shins with corresponding hands. Keep knees straight. There may be a discouraging force which causes the lower limbs to bend at the knees. Apply pressure to straighten the knees. Tolerate the pain. Use it to identify an energy release in the knees and thighs.

The buttocks should be off the floor. The head may or may not be off. To keep the head up, the hands should tightly grip the shins. There will be tension in the legs, thighs, arms, forearms, and hands.

Pull the shins but do not bend the knees. Focus within the body. Notice a puzzle of energy. Some of it will be like tiny electric currents firing steadily.

From below the navel cross-sectionally, there may be nerve feelings. These may feel like twinkles of pain firing into the buttocks and then entering the thighs. A yogi should focus, becoming absorbed in that energy. This will give a mapping of the energy circuit in the thighs, pubic area, and navel zone.

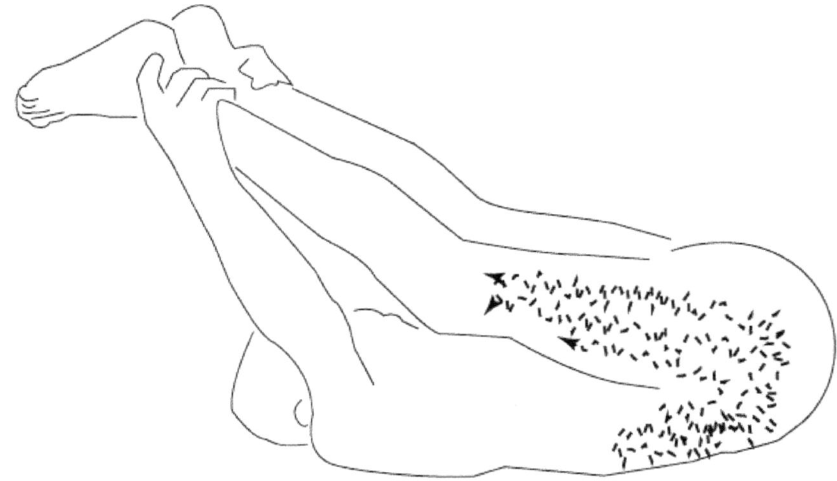

Focus Connection

The *On Back - Grab Shins over Head* posture is relatively ease. It could be difficult for anyone with stiff limbs. The head should remain on the floor, but it could be lifted if one finds that to be tolerable.

There will be sensations in the back of the thighs and buttocks. These will be like threads of glass having a white color. The yogi should focus on that region and notice the flashes in the glass-like threads.

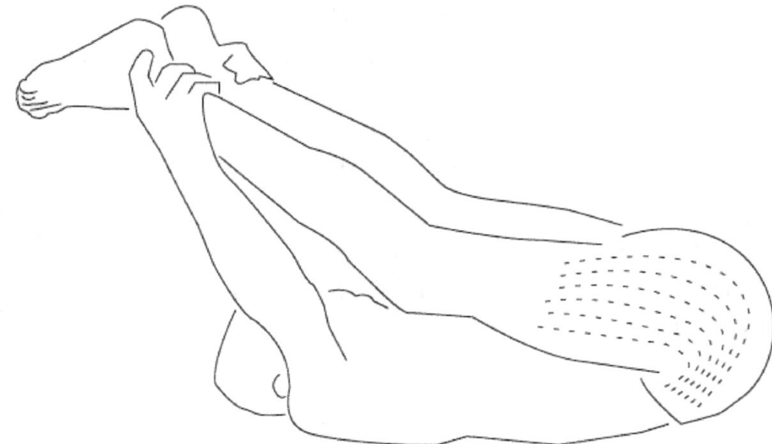

During that focus, there will be thought interruptions. A yogi should notice that these idea packages do not open. They do not burst into mental images or memories. Instead, the packages will appear and then fizz to nothing, with no idea of their contents. These thoughts do not have the power to command and utilize the mind for illustration. Hence the packages, though complete, cannot be known to the coreSelf. This observation is handy for understanding the process of thought compulsion during meditation, where a yogi applies the self to be free from ideas, but somehow, he is unable to banish images and verbal meanings, and is force to leave aside the objective.

- Why is it that in this posture, the thoughts do not open as a compulsory display?

After a time, the yogi should relax the pose. He should release the shins. The feet should be gently brought to the floor. On each side of the body, the hands should be brought to the floor. The yogi should meditate. At first, he should observe the condition of the energy. He should note that all stress vanished He should meditate on that condition, and allow for clarity of consciousness, with no imaging nor thinking.

Again, he should assume the pose. Then again, he should relax.

Triangular Grasp above Knees

This *Triangular Grasp above Knees* posture is not strenuous. Yet, it may be difficult to hold for a time. Stand with heels reasonable apart, and feet spread for placement and balance. Lean over. Grasp above the knees. Here the knees serve as a stop. The hands do not slide down. Press so that the knees remain pushed back.

The head may be tilted back as far as it can go. The elbows should be straight. Close the eyelids or use a blindfold. Keep the attention within the body. Check for energy movements and accumulations.

Listen carefully for a naad screeching sound within the head. If there is one, it may be loud with one shining vortex. Listen for it. Recognize it. Consider its location. While listening, remain in the pose. Periodically hear it. If you lose track, listen and focus into it.

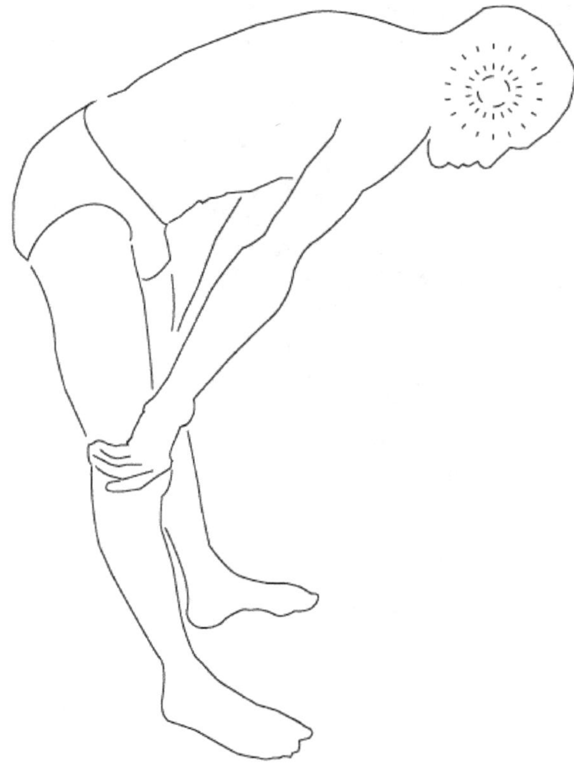

Slowly come out of the pose by assuming a squatting position. Check to hear naad resonance. Study to know if naad sound radiates effortlessly. Check the focusing attention of the coreSelf. Understand if it is tuned to naad and remains absorbed.

- Does it drift?
- What does it drift to?

Study naad's location.

- Is there a core for naad, a psychic location from which it emits its sounding?

Focus Connection

This *Triangular Grasp above Knees* pose, is simple. Most students can do this. The elderly ones may have difficult with balance, and with knee uncertainty. In the elderly years, the knee compound bone structure and alignment, shifts for the worse. This causes a lack of confidence in standing postures, and in actions with the limbs, which cause the knee combination complex to be faulty. Yogis using elderly bodies, have every reason not the trust the knee joint. It may malfunction at any moment, causing injury from a fall or dislocation.

When doing postures in an elderly body, a yogi cannot be careless as if he used a youth's body. He should recognize when a posture may cause bodily situations, for which there will be regret.

For the *Triangular Grasp above Knees* pose, proper balance is required. Even the leaning forward should be done with vigilance. Even the way the neck hangs from the torso should be monitored. Inner attentiveness should be applied. Why? Because it is likely that there may be giddiness, or even fainting, or partial loss of feeling in some part of the body. It is preferred that one should do postures on a padded floor, in a location which has no sharp objects, or edges, which will harm the body. With an elderly body, a yogi should be cautious.

Once the posture is assumed, the balance of the body should be properly determined. The yogi should check that the hands grip the area just above the knees. The feet should be monitored. If the floor is sliddy, a different surface used. There should be steadiness, otherwise the imbalance will negatively affect the pose.

Once the yogi is satisfied that the body is situated, he should internalize to meditate. At first, he should search for the energy distribution. He should map the layout. If he finds that there is shivering, or an undesirable nervous condition, he should slowly move into a squatting position. There, keeping the mind internalized and watching the energy outlay, he should continue the meditation.

After a time, when the psyche is settled, he should rise the body and set it again for the *Triangular Grasp above Knees* pose. If there is an uncertainty in the knees, he should slowly resume the squatting position. He should continue the meditation in that pose.

Either in the *Triangular Grasp above Knees* pose, or while squatting, he should persist in the meditation. He should listen for inner sounds. He should focus, checking inside the eyes.

Sit Between Heels – Lay Back on Elbows

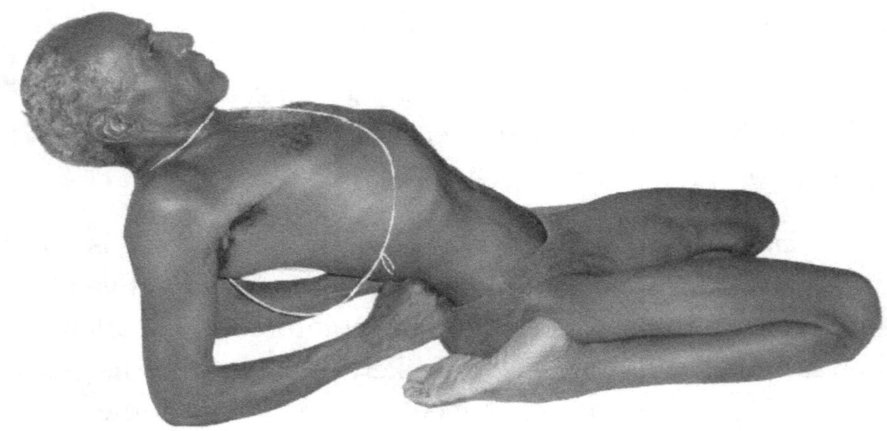

For this *Sit Between Heels – Lay Back on Elbows* pose, if the thighs are slim, it should be easy to sit between the heels. Then the yogi should lay back on the elbows. Make fists. Place them to the area above the hips. There are variations, as for example using the hands to grip the area just above the hips. In one variation, the buttocks are raised, which adds pressure to the elbows.

In this posture, the abdomen naturally draws back. However, if there is bulk in the abdomen which is due to distention and fat accumulation, the abdomen may not retract. The head may assume three positions. One can be that it is all the way back with the chin as high as possible. Another can be that it is connected to the neck as it usually does. Yet another, is that it may be with the chin pressed to the throat. A yogi should practice variations of this pose to determine what energy configuration it causes.

There are many forced configurations, or *kriyas,* when doing the *samyama* process of meditation. These are worth the practice. However, a yogi is required to study the natural energy spreads which occur spontaneously in each posture. This trains the mind to be satisfied with inner focus.

As suggested by Yogeshwarananda, I composed this book to share the methods of using *asana* postures to advance in the two highest levels of yoga, which are *dhyana* spontaneous focus and *samadhi* prolonged effortless focus. This was a secret practice which advanced yogis did not divulge to others. In this book, some methods are shared.

It is interesting that in the history of yoga, the *asana* posture which is the most famous, is the lotus *padmasana* pose. However, if one uses the other poses for meditation, one may discover that each pose renders its own meditation zone, where in a certain part of the subtle body, energies move to align or contrast other energies.

The lotus and some other poses, allow the yogi to lose physical body control without damaging that body, through falls, pulled muscles, crippling cramps and other problems. And yet, the other poses render much understanding about *samyama* meditation.

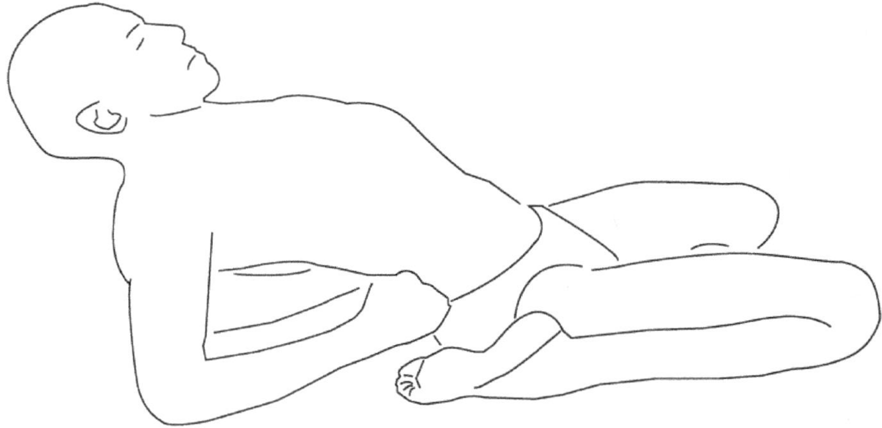

When doing this posture, it is best to do it with the chin pressing to the throat. Raise the chest, as it is pulled to the neck. The rib cage should rise. A yogi should close the eyes or use a blindfold. No visual distractions should occur.

During this pose, when focusing in the body, notice the energy in the chest which rises through the neck, and enters each cheek. On each side, some energy will go under the tongue.

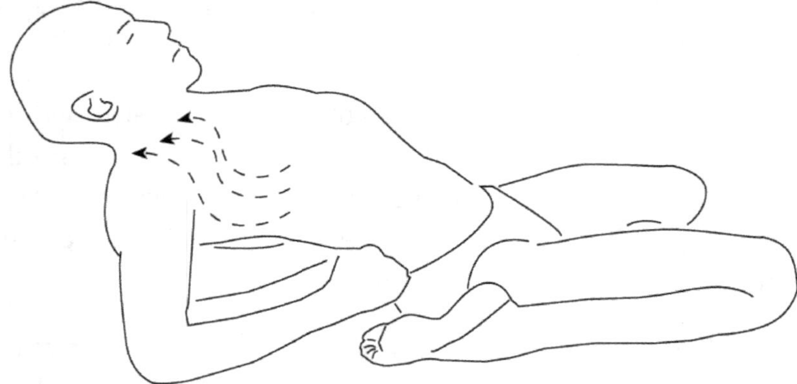

After a time, thinking will cease. One will realize that it did so, when one finds that the mind began a thought sequence as usual. That thought in a series of visual and sound impressions will be weak, so that the self can easily shift to hearing naad resonance.

One will note how thinking ceased. Naad permeated the mind. No idea will be in the mind space. That zone will be satisfied being with no ideas flashing.

A yogi must check to see how he becomes aware of the thoughtless mind, as if he did not know when the mind assumed the thoughtless state. After a time, he realized it. This gives insight into the operation of the thought producing adjunct, the intellect. It is invisible but it is located as its operations.

Focus Connection

The *Sit Between Heels – Lay Back on Elbows* posture, can be strenuous for some students. The places where the fists make contact with the lower back, may express discomfort. A yogi should position the fists to have the least inconvenience. Once this pose is assumed the yogi should check every place in the psyche. He should map the outlay of energies. Some questions arise.

- Why is this here?
- Why is that there?
- What is that inner sound?
- Is the chin pulled to the throat?
- How long can this posture be done?

After a time, when the energies are settled to a greater degree, there may be a misty energy in the lowest part of the abdomen. This may be above the pubic area. When the yogi checks this energy, he may find that his interest in it, switches to an inquiry about the energy in the top back part of the head. There he will realize that naad resonance is present.

The yogi should listen for a time, for until he feels that he should relax the body. Then he should slowly sit upright between the heels. The hands should be put on the hips or the thighs. He should keep the chin to the throat with the neck upright. He should press the waist forward. He should listen for inner sound. It may be here or there.

Tight Lotus Yirk Back

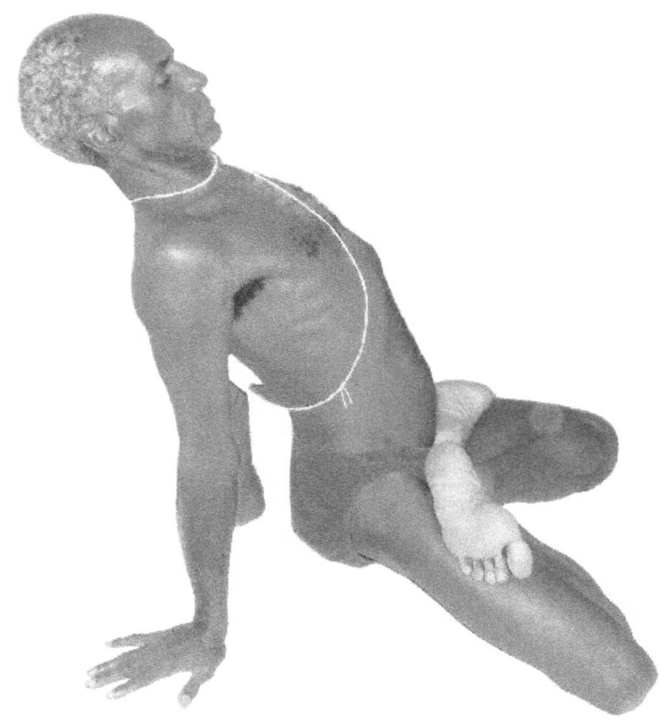

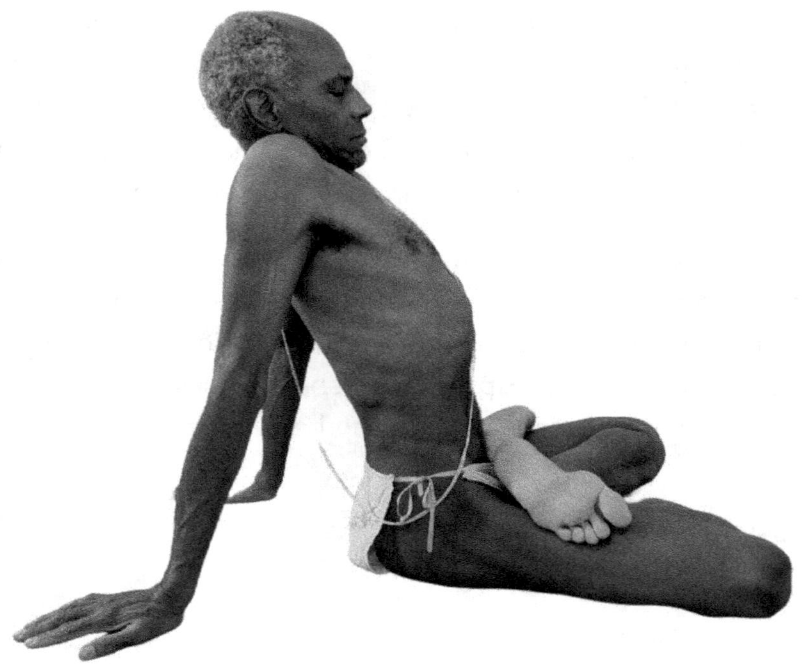

This *Tight Lotus Yirk Back* posture is a lotus pose variation. It is best practiced with a body which has limber thigh muscles, and which can easily assume the lotus *padmasana* pose. First the yogi should assume a tight lotus. It should be such that the soles of the feet face the sky. At first the yogi should sit with the spine being perpendicular to the floor.

After this is set, the hands should be placed on the floor. The chest is lifted. The chin should be pressed toward the throat. There should be energy moving upward to the elbows and shoulders. Naad resonance should be heard.

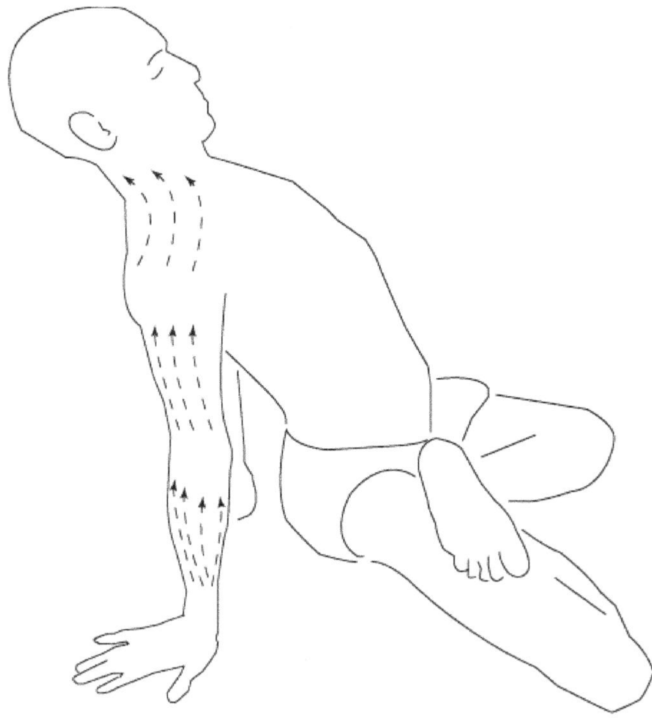

This posture may be done with the chin pressing to the throat, or with the head pressed back all the way. Hearing the naad sound blaring, a yogi will notice that thoughts do not arise, or that ideation occurs infrequently

Focus Connection

The *Tight Lotus Yirk Back* has variations. One is with the head tilted back fully. This is the reverse neck lock. When the chin is pulled to the throat, that is the chin lock.

When doing the chin lock, the head may not be tilted but should be upright between the shoulders. For the reverse neck lock however, the head is tilted all the way back. It is held there while focusing within the psyche.

In the *Tight Lotus Yirk Back* pose when the reverse lock neck is used, there may be a focus through the face. When this happens, the yogi should follow the focus out of the face. The alert should be to determine if the attention energy can follow the rays, which protrude beyond the face, or if the attention cannot leave the face, but the rays keep streaming independently. This is a practice with *dharana* deliberate focus, and *dhyana* spontaneous absorption, happening simultaneously.

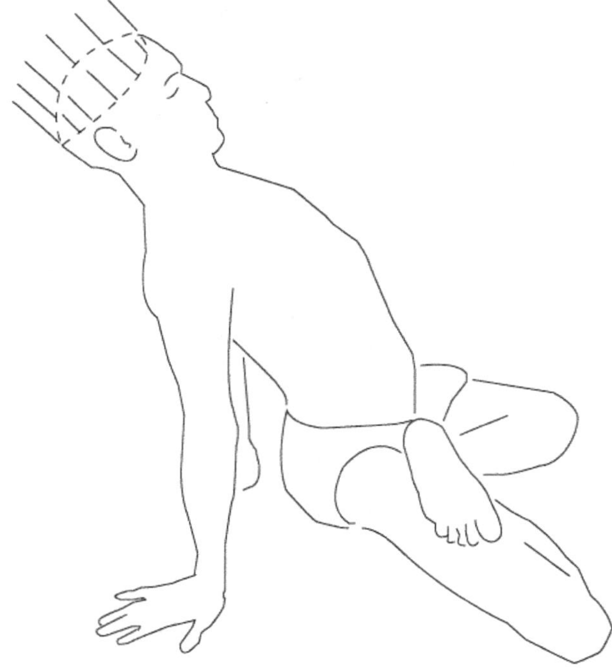

After some time, the yogi should relax the body. He should check to know if the head is tilted. He may or may not reset the neck. He should decide to focus on naad resonance. He may remain like this for some time.

On Back with One Foot Out

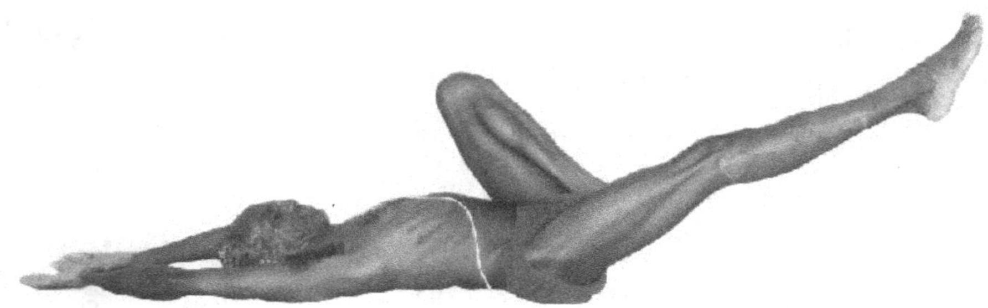

The *On Back with One Foot Out* posture is strenuous. It is a tax on the nerves which passes through the extended lower limb. A yogi can begin this by reclining on the back of the body. Then he may retract one knee to the chest. The higher limbs consisting of the arms, forearms, and hands, should be extended away from the body. Keeping that one knee retracted toward the chest, the other limb consisting of the thigh, leg, and foot, should be extended and held at forty-five degrees (45^0). That limb should be held out. If, however, it cannot be tolerated, it can be raised to a position where the discomforting feelings cease.

The more the extended foot is lowered, the more discomfort one may feel. It depends on the shape of the body, and on its muscle and nerve outlay. Once the yogi is in this posture, he should focus internally, to determine which energy is located here or there, and what is the configuration of the feelings within the psyche.

The hands should be on the floor. That should be the situation for the buttocks as well. The middle of the back may be raised from the floor. In most cases, a human assuming this position, will not have the entire back touching the floor. In the case of most humans, rarely will the mid-back make contact.

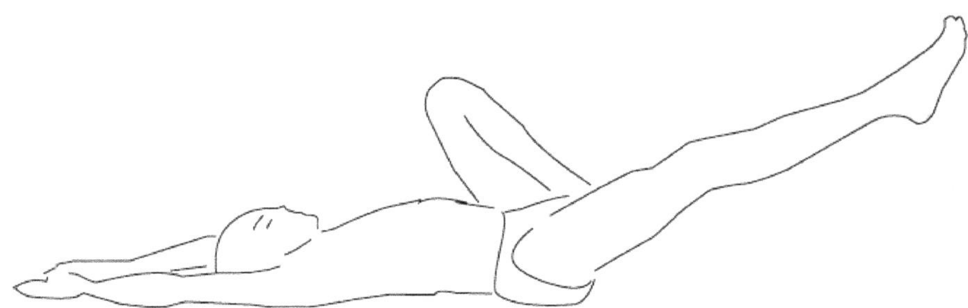

When this posture is assumed, patience is required to hold it for any length of time, even for a short duration. There may be quivering or shivering of the extended limb. This is due to the weight distribution on the hip complex of muscles. A yogi should hold steady and be inwardly focus on the shivering energy which is released or contained.

When the quivering becomes intolerable, a relaxed posture for the extended limb should be adopted. Either the extended limb should be brought in toward the body with the knee collapsed and pulled towards the chest, as the other limb is, or the extended limb should be brought to the floor, while the contracted limb remains as it is.

Once this is done, and it should be done slowly, the yogi should focus on the energies in the psyche. He should check and note what energies shift. At this time, inner focus on the subtle body should be applied. There should be a quiescence of the energy, a full relaxation.

After a time, when the psyche is settled in that meditation, the yogi should do the posture again. He should observe the shivering. It may develop from one zone to another as labeled below.

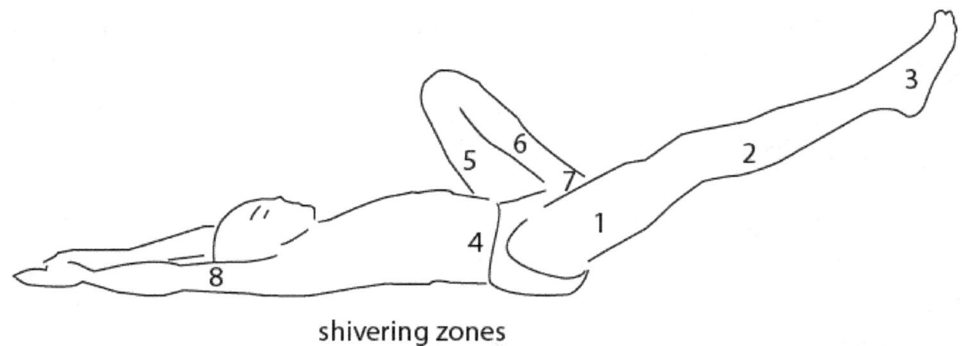

shivering zones

Focus Connection

The *On Back with One Foot Out* posture, may stress the arms and forearms more than any other part of the body. The arms and forearms may float while the shoulders and hands make contact with the floor. When assuming this posture, one knee is pulled to the chest. The other lower limb is pushed out at about 45^0. That extended limb should be positioned at the easiest angle, where it will have the least stress. When the posture becomes unbearable, the yogi should slowly pull the raised limb in. Once both knees are in a similar position, the yogi should make an energy search. He should map the stress areas, adjust the lower limbs and the higher ones, to ease the stress.

There may be areas in the hands, wrist, forearms, arms, and shoulders, which should be repositioned. That should be done but with care so that the energy configuration does not change considerably. When the body is repositioned, the yogi should slowly stretch the other lower limb. That should be done slowly and with focus, without disturbing the energy which was set before.

In this pose, with either of the lower limbs extended, it may happen, that the yogi has visual flickers, where spontaneously images from memory, flicker, one after the other, in a sequence, at a rate where it seems that there is a continuity. These will be memory items which were stored in the mind of the yogi. Some of it may be coherent. Some may be transparent where it is not distinct. Some may be haphazard. It will cause shifts of focus, where the yogi loses contact with the meditation objective.

The yogi will notice that even though he wants to arrest it, so that it does not produce scenes in the mind, the memories grab and operate the image display equipment. This informs the yogi, that he must develop the power to stop this involuntary mechanism, from interrupting the meditation objectives. The yogi becomes determined to question a teacher about this. The student may apply methods which reform the memory illustration equipment. This concerns the control of Nature's technology.

Grab Soles while on Curved Back

That *grab-the-soles* posture was illustrated before. This is an energy variation. On another day, this same posture may have different energy movements and absorptions.

To assume this, lie on back. Grab the feet from the outside. Bring the knees toward chest. Raise the head as far as possible. Press the chin to the throat. Check the rate of breath. Notice that the inhale capacity of lungs is reduced. That is due to diaphragm restriction. The shortness of breath is due to the crunched diaphragm.

Relax the body. Assume this pose again. Mentally, peer through the body. To prohibit making contact with objects outside the body, do this with closed eyelids or be blindfolded.

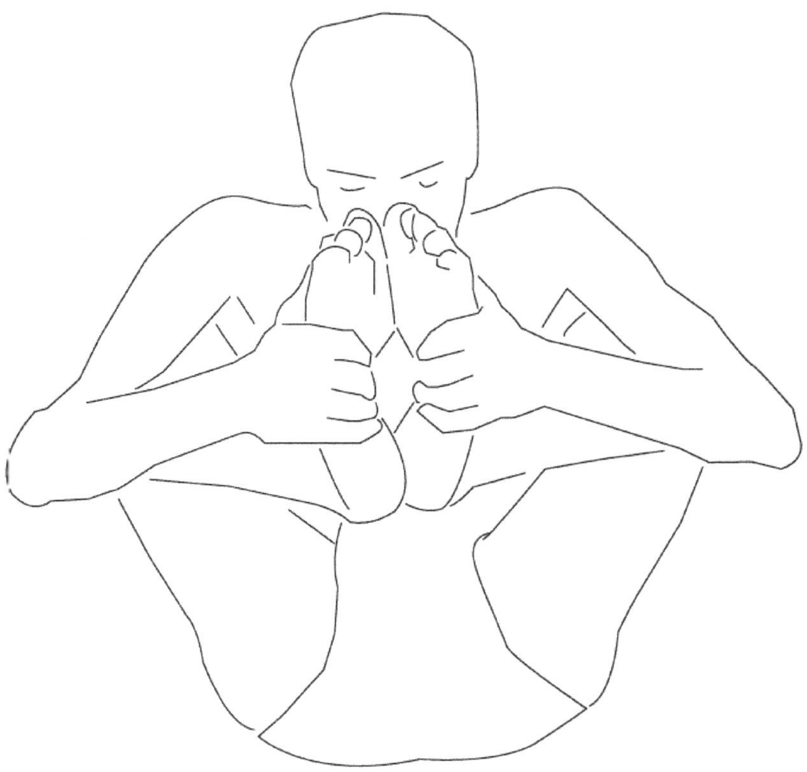

While peering in the body, notice energy accumulations or tensions. As the chin is pressed to the throat, notice any energy movement or formation. A yogi may perceive a hole in the throat. He may see strings of electric energy in the muscles of the arms. This will be like a mild electric shock from the back of the neck to the forehead. There may be energy in the form of a tube which is energized from energy in the neck and throat.

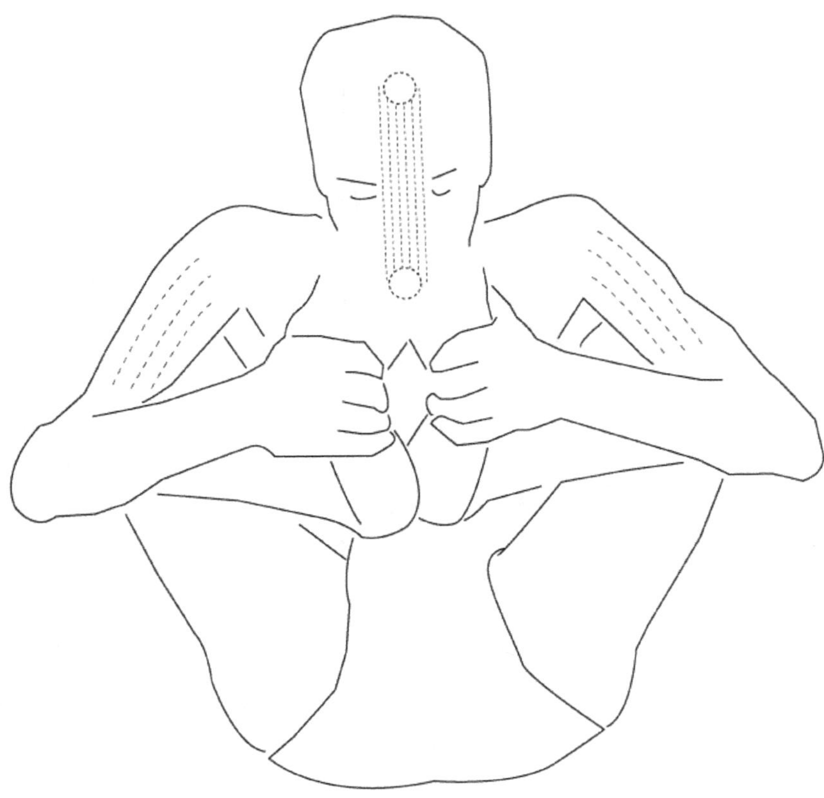

Focus Connection

The *Grab Soles while on Curved Back* pose is easy for some yogis. Persons with large thighs, and inflexible ankles or knees, may find it to be inconvenient. When this posture is assumed, there is a hollow in the pelvic cage. Physically, this pelvis area is fenced with curved bones which outskirt the buttock and lower front of the torso.

When attempting the focus in this pose, there may be an unusual energy layout. At first getting into the torso will be difficult. It may seem that one should remain outside of it. Efforts to get through the neck may fail.

A yogi may realize that there is a hole which is positioned over the pelvic region, where the sexual organ is centered. There may be a hollow space behind that hole. From there a circle of energy will emanate. It may come from within the pelvic area, and emerge from it through the sexual region. An oval-shaped region will be there. A circle is within the perimeter of the oval.

From the inside, the yogi should focus on the hollow area.

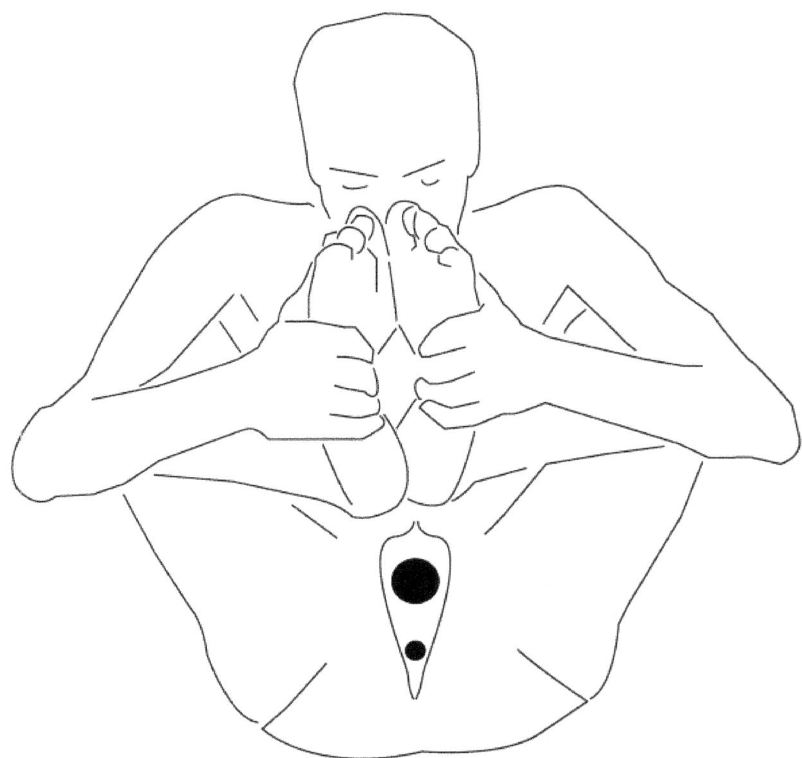

After a time, this posture will cause fatigue. The neck may move. The yogi should again press the chin to the throat. He should check to be sure that the hands still grip the feet. If he can hold this pose no longer, he should relax the head by resting it on the floor. Then, he should release the feet. He should place the feet on the floor near the buttocks. The hands, with palms up, should rest on the floor near the body. In that easy pose, the yogi should account for the energy in the psyche.

After a time relaxing, the yogi should resume the pose. He should check the energy again. If he was aware of the oval and circle before, he should check to see if it appeared again. Otherwise, he should do the pose and investigate its new format.

Lower Limbs at Right Angle to the Body

For this *Lower Limbs at Right Angle to the Body* posture, one should lie on the back, then raise the lower limbs, consisting of the feet, legs, and thighs. The hands should interlock behind the buttocks. The head should be raised. The neck should be locked forward, with the tongue pushed out of the mouth.

The chin should be pressed to the throat. The yogi should focus internally. He may be aware of energy in the neck rushing to the lower back part of the head, where the neck connects to the skull.

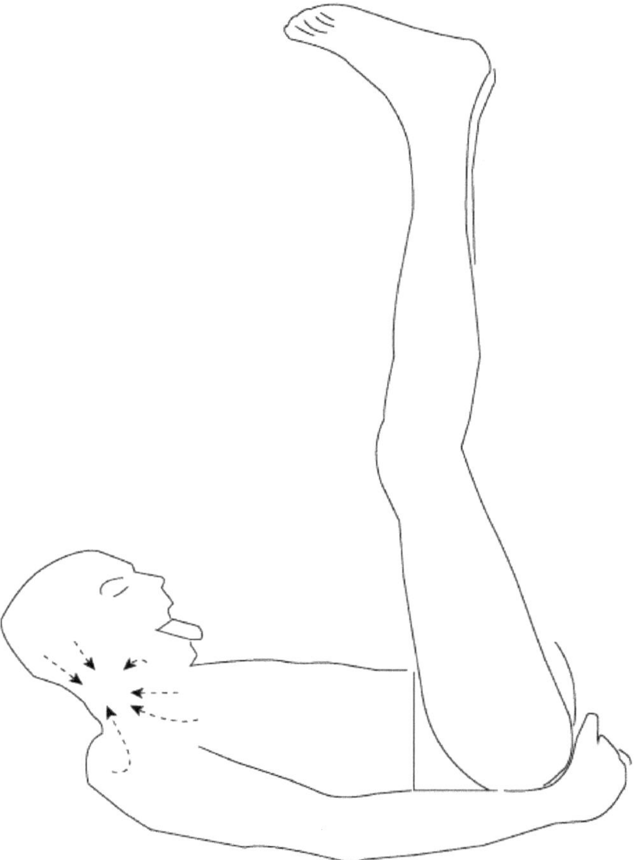

A loud naad sound may be heard after being in this pose for a minute or more. When this is heard, the yogi should focus on it, while keeping the neck pressed forward. After a bit when one can no longer hold this position, one should rest the head on the floor for about 30 seconds. Do this by counting mentally from one to thirty. Raise the head and lock it forward.

Reach naad resonance. That is a *dhyana*, seventh stage of yoga practice. By doing this, one will train the mind to appreciate the absorption, rather than to pursue physical sense objects, and their reflections, which occur in the mind.

Focus Connection

The *Lower Limbs at Right Angle to the Body* posture, is easy to form. The fingers of each hand may or may not interlock with that of the other. The difficulty is to raise the head and press the chin to the throat. This produces some tendon stretching and tightening. It may be a discomfort.

A yogi should be sure to push the tongue as far as possible. When there is a lack of tolerance for this pose, the student should slowly lower the head to the floor. A check should be made within the psyche to discover how the energy is aligned. Soon after, the feet should be lowered to the floor near the buttocks. Remaining in that relaxed position for a time, the yogi should again raise the lower limbs. He should check to determine if the chin compression is applied.

In this pose, a check should be made for thoughts. If any are found, an investigation should be made, as to the resistance of the coreSelf towards the ideas, or images, which arise. The questions to be figured are.

- What triggered the thought?
- Why is it not flimsy?
- Who does it concern?

The yogi should check to determine if any ideas, which are developed in the mind, remain in display after they were illustrated.

- Can the coreSelf banish that?
- Are the ideas heavy like a concrete structure?

This posture causes the diaphragm to be restricted. Even though that may go unnoticed initially, a yogi should realize it after a time. There may be shivering in the center of the chest. The yogi should again lower the feet to the floor. He should relax there.

Squat with One Foot Out at 45^0

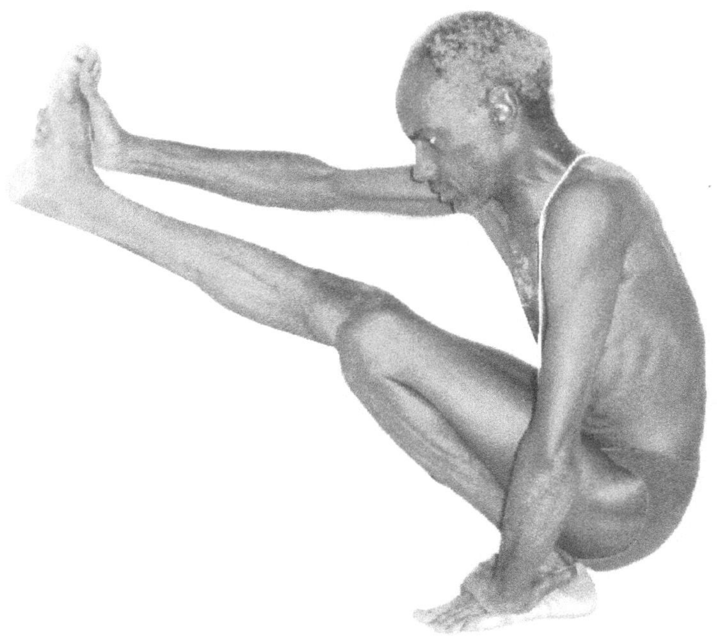

This *Squat with One Foot Out at* 45^0, is based on balance during the squatting position. It begins with a squat. One hand holds the instep of a corresponding foot from the outside. The other hand grasps the other foot from the outside. That other foot is outstretched, with the knee locked out. See the image above.

This is a balance posture. There can be shivering in the body. There may be unsteadiness, and even collapse of the posture. If that happens, the yogi should practice squatting for a time. That is squatting with the buttocks above the floor, where only the feet are in contact with the floor. When this is done, the focus should be on the balancing force exerted on the body.

When some balance becomes possible, when there is less shivering and unsteadiness, the yogi should do the full posture. He may do it with variations. For instance, instead of having the outstretched foot at forty-five degrees (45^0), he may have it outstretched where it runs parallel to the floor. In any way, the buttocks should not touch the floor.

This posture requires no blindfold. In fact, the eyelids should be opened in a blank stare. This will give assistance for balancing the body.

When this posture is maintained for a time, when the body is accustomed to it, a yogi may focus internally, but even then, the focus will be on the center of balance. There is a query.

- Where is the center of balance in this position?

During some practice, energy will be felt in the thigh, leg, and foot of the squatted limb (not the outstretched one). That may be like a smothering log which is red hot in the center. A yogi should investigate that energy.

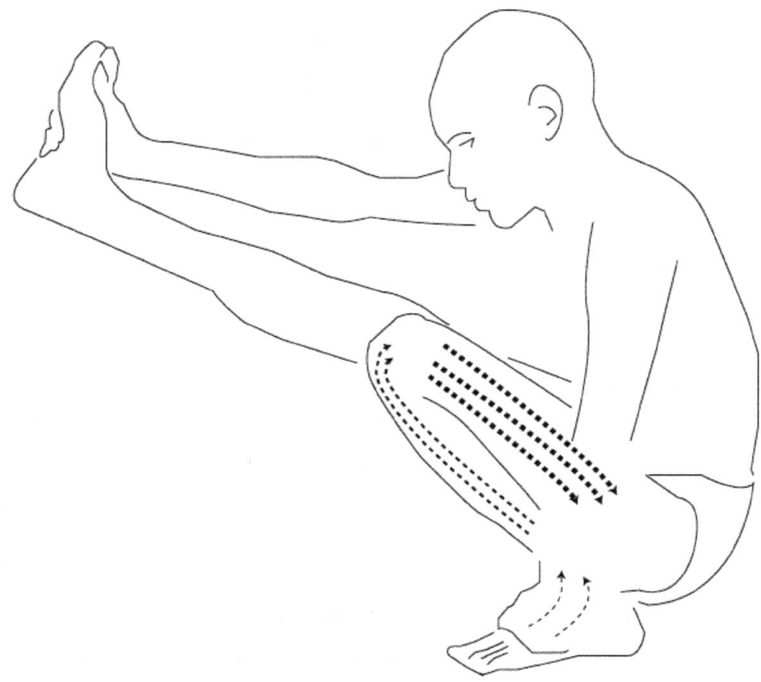

Focus Connection

The *Squat with One Foot Out at 45^0* pose, involves balance from side to side and from front to back. Some persons may find the pose to be awkward. The entire body is required to balance on one foot. As an aid, if it is necessary, the one foot for balance may get assistance from the base of the hand, which makes contact with the floor.

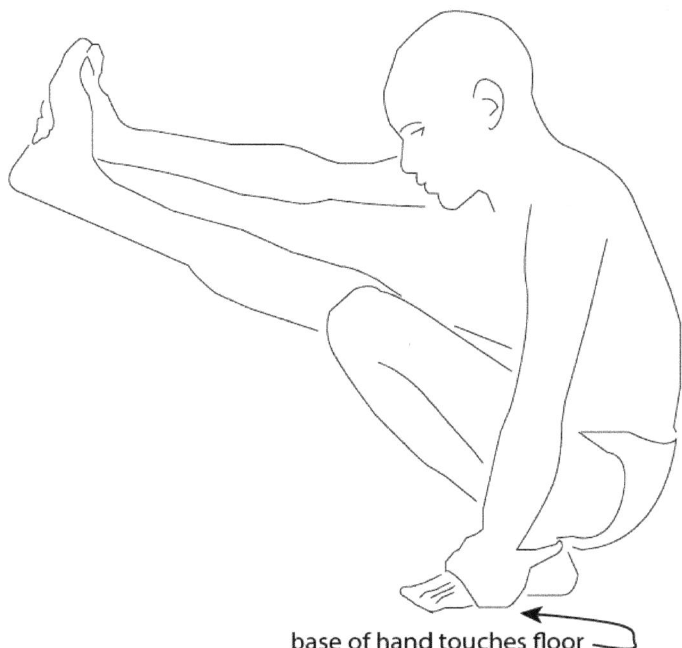

If when attempting this pose on one side, one experiences severe imbalance, where one cannot hold the higher foot even for a moment, one may switch to attempt the position using the other hand.

The weight of the body should descend, through the body to the bottom of the torso, and then travel until it is held by the foot, which rests on the floor, and by a little support from the base of the hand, which holds the foot which is set for balance.

After doing this on one side, then doing it on the other, with the opposing parts of the body, the yogi will get the feeling that he should cease. He should slowly begin positioning the body to assume an easy pose. It should be one in which the spine is upright. In that pose the neck should be in the backward neck lock. Then the chest should be lifted. Then he should check for inner movements of energy. He should meditate to map the psychological situation.

Dreaded Womb Turn Posture

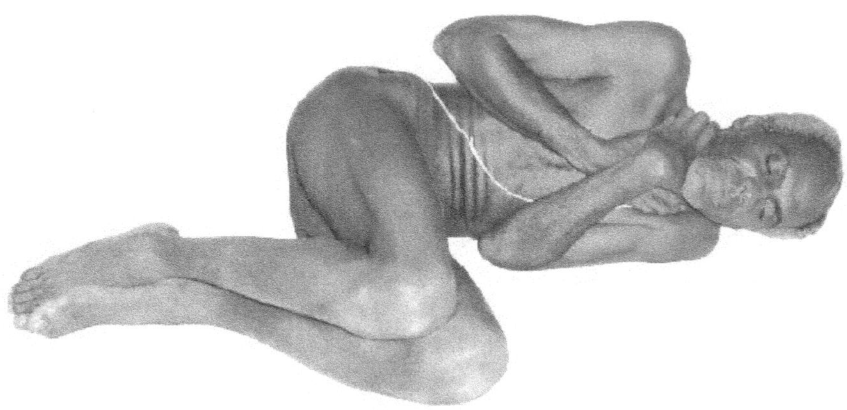

This *Dreaded Womb Turn* position is one of the postures which is useful for studying the condition one was in, when one was ejected through the mother's sexual passage. If someone, a fetus, is unable to escape through the tubing, either the mother's body will die or her abdomen will be cut so that the infant can be removed. In either case, this is a danger point in the process of taking birth as the son or daughter of a woman.

To be a child, one must first be a single sperm. That is a tiny life form which swam through the mother's passage. However, when it grows in the uterus, it becomes bigger than the passage through which it entered. Hence that passage must be stretched.

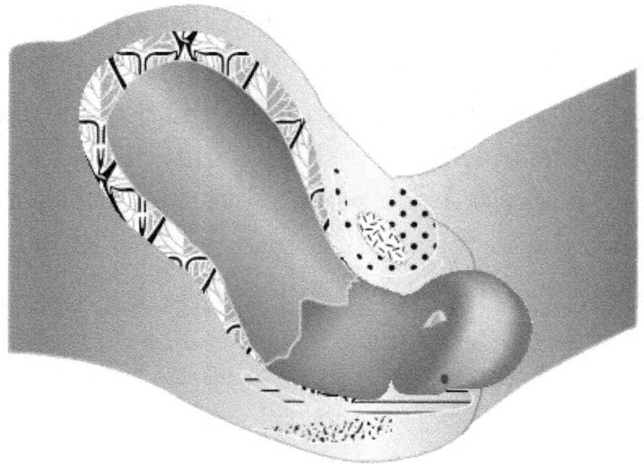

To facilitate the exit, the fetus must be positioned with head downwards on the opening. Doing this posture, gives one some idea of the discomfort and uncertainty, which one would experience, when the fetal body turns downward.

When doing this pose, there is no pressure on the throat. The hands rest there but they do not squeeze the neck. The chin is pressed mildly on the hands. The ear does not rest on the shoulder. One should internalize to consider what it would be like, when the time for parturition is triggered, where one is pressed out. Even though one went into the birth canal as a mere microscopic sperm, one grew in size, such that the infant body felt as if it was one's identity. In meditating in this posture, one can realize what it was like to wait for Nature to begin, process and conclude a baby.

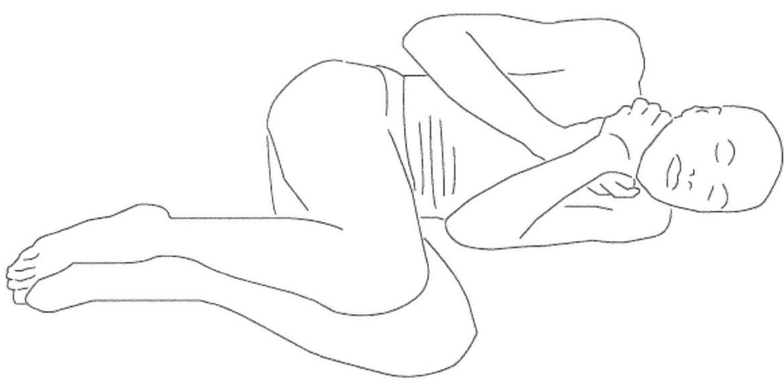

Focus Connection

The *Dreaded Womb Turn Posture* is easy. A pillow support may be used. It is preferred that there be no such support, however. This is suggested because this pose mimics the embryonic development in which there is no other support but a liquid (the amniotic fluid). In this pose, a yogi should consider the situation which was his, before he assumed the identity as a formatted human being.

The yogi should try one side, then the other. He should do this to see if he prefers to be this way, or that way. He should consider if subconsciously, while in the mother's body, he spent most of the time (approximately nine months) in the preferred position.

- What was it like?

He had no impulsive need to process air though the lungs. He lived feeding on someone else's blood, that of the mother.

There are many questions which should be contemplated about developing in the mother's body.

- Can one turn in the womb?
- Must one remain still with a blank mind and with nothing to consider?
- Is one's only pillow, one's shoulder?
- Can one apply attention to anything while in the womb?
- Is there vision while in the womb?
- Does one become frightened?
- Can one smell odors which are in the water which surrounds one in the womb?
- Can one feel or have touching sensations?
- How is time considered when one is in the mother's body?
- Can one detect sunlight or electric illumination?

People inform someone that for the most, he or she spent approximately nine months in the body of the mother.

- How did one gage time when one was in the womb?
- Can one commit suicide when one is in the womb?
- Is there any way one can express displeasure, when one is in the womb?

Those are some of the questions that one can consider about being an embryo.

Hands Pressure Down on Sole and Outstretched Thigh

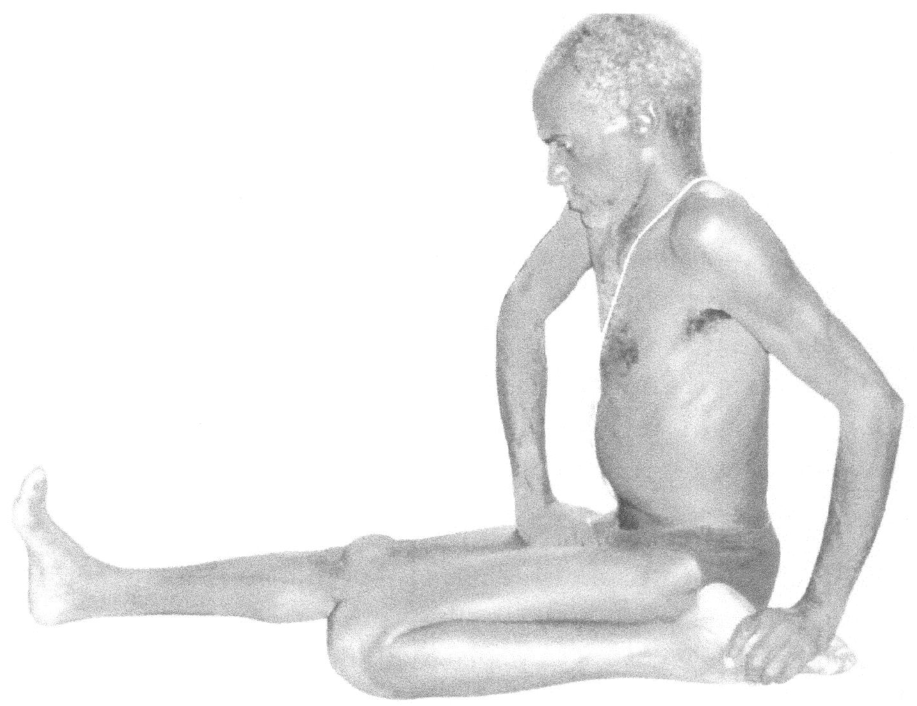

This *Hands Pressure Down on Sole and Outstretched Thigh* pose was listed before. It is easy for persons who have little muscle stress or fat accumulation in the thighs. There are variations. One can use a cushion under the buttocks if that causes less discomfort. This posture was presented before.

Both hands are pushed down. The outstretched thigh is compressed down by the corresponding hand with the elbow facing outward. As in the diagram, the central sole of the back foot is pushed with the corresponding hand. The toes of the outstretched foot are pulled back. That foot is upright vertically (at 90^0). This posture is not strained. No muscles or tendons are stressed.

Once the pose is assumed, the yogi should close the eyelids and focus. There should be the awareness of inner sound. There will be the sense of self, and a high-pitched sound. The self will be in the resonance which should be to the left, right, back, front, up or down, or in every direction. The chin should be checked to be sure that it is pulled back to the throat. The head is upright, neither leaning forward nor being lifted backward.

The yogi should check the energy distribution. He should be aware of a high-pitched sound. At this point, the yogi should begin counting mentally. He should count slowly from 1, until he reaches 120, which is approximately two minutes. Then he should again begin with 1 and continue until he reaches 120. While doing this, he should be sure to keep everything in order, where he remains aware of naad resonance throughout.

This is a study of *dhyana* spontaneous focus on naad resonance with *dharana* slight effort to maintain the count. This focus will teach the mind to meditate using *samyama,* which is the three higher stages of yoga as one progressive technique. In this case, the practice would lead to *samadhi*. For this to happen, the count from 1 to 120 would have to be made repeatedly, for at least ten minutes or more.

Otherwise, the benefit will be that the mind learns how to use the *dharana* deliberate focus and the *dhyana* spontaneous focus, which was provided by the naad resonance with no effort from the yogi, except that he maintained the counting practice, with no thought interruption, and no memory assaults which distract the focus.

Focus Connection

The *Hands Pressure Down on Sole and Outstretched Thigh* pose, is easy to assume. For senior people, whose joints are tight, it may be strenuous. A yogi should do one side, then the other. A pressure is applied downward from the shoulder and elbows.

When the yogi feels that he did this pose, he should check within the body to be sure that his spine is erect. The buttocks should be under the torso but the spinal column should be vertical in reference to the floor. The yogi should listen for inner sounds, particularly the naad resonance which is a high pitched frequency.

After this there should be meditation on naad, with some interest to check for the energy outlay. The yogi should locate and map, how the energy is patterned. While doing this, an interest in naad should be maintained. A yogi may notice that energy transfers from the thigh with the leg curled back, to the thigh with the foot stretched out.

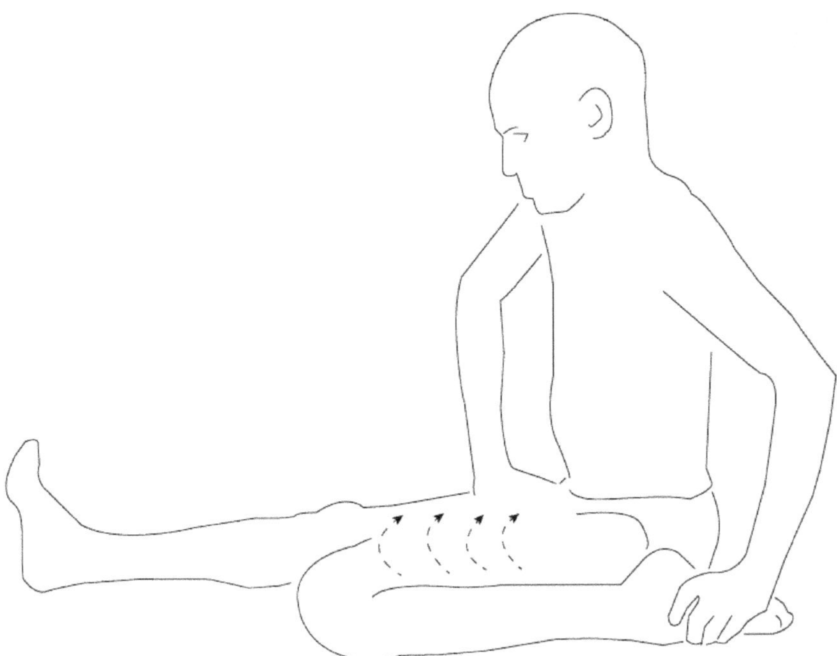

There may be energy interference, when assuming this pose. Thoughts with overpowering force, may be displayed in the mind. When the yogi makes the effort to remove them, he may discover that they have an effective resistance. He may wonder why this occurs.

Such investigations may lead to the conclusion that thoughts which were created with an attachment energy, and thoughts which carry an urgency energy, have the power to overcome the independence of the coreSelf. A yogi must sort the situations. He should discover the cause of a mental dominance. Even though naad may be present, even though the yogi may focus on naad, and be in definite contact with it, still some thoughts may be erected into images, and other sensual displays, forcing the yogi to observe them.

After a time in this pose, the yogi should ease out of the posture. He should do so without disturbing the energy configuration. When he assumes an easy pose, he should continue the meditation, observing if he can maintain contact with inner sound, and if he could suppress thoughts which arise in the mind.

Partial Squat – Grip Feet and Insteps

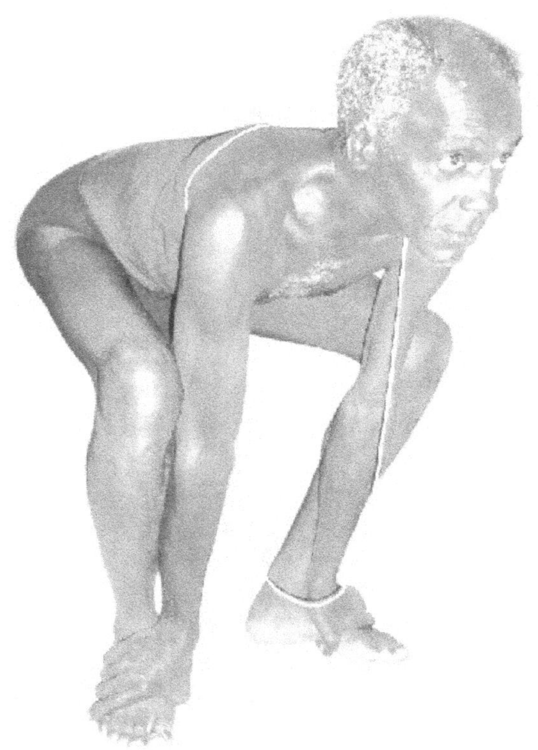

This *Partial Squat – Grip Feet and Insteps* is a master posture. In 1973 I received this from Prem Kaur, a disciple of Yogi Bhajan. Soon after, this pose disappeared from the face of the earth. The reason for that is simple. It is dangerous, especially if one does it, and surcharges the physical body with *bhastrika pranayama* breath infusion.

- Should one do this pose?

One should do it on a padded floor where there are no sharp objects, where if the body falls, it will not be damaged, due to hitting a sharp object or hard material.

If one does this and does no breath infusion, it is hardly likely that the body will fall to the floor. It is possible. This is why this posture should be done only after a yogi mastered the locks (*bandhas*) in the body, and the mind lock in the subtle head, along with vigilant tracking of energy movements.

The danger of the body falling to the ground, is due to the fact that for the most part, the kundalini lifeForce controls the operations. The rational objective self does not. It participates in the control and maintenance of the body, but it does not operate the involuntary functions.

If a man hears a gunshot and instinctively runs from the sound, that action is usually done by the lifeForce. It is not the rational self which operates that. It is an instinct of survival. Many actions happen because the lifeForce operates necessary functions. If for some reason those operations are not performed by the lifeForce, the rational objective self may not substitute a command. This means that the body will be left to itself, with no direction on how to remain in a posture.

Even if the yogi does no breath infusion, even then, if he/she assumes this posture, or a variation of it, it is likely that assuming the posture, will cause no energy shifts, but coming out of it may cause a sudden rush of energy, which overpowers the directive intellect, causing a sudden collapse of the body. It may happen with a jerk before the collapse, or with several jerking actions.

Hence, as a matter of caution, those students who did not master bodily locks and the mind lock, should not do this posture. The teacher, if he is present, should be a person who mastered kundalini arrest, and who has subtle perception, where he can see, what happens in the mind of the student. The teacher should have vision to see the rapid movement of energy in the student's psyche.

If the student cannot apply the locks, because of losing command connection of the physical system, the teacher should call for locks, and hold the body from falling.

To assume this pose, the yogi must get the spine to be as parallel as possible with the floor. The spine should be horizonal. If this is not possible, the spine should be angled upward, but the spine should not be curved.

If, however, this cannot be done and the spine must be curved, due to the design of the vertebrae, then it should be as little of a curve as is possible.

In the diagrams above, the hands hold the feet with the thumbs on the inside. This is a variation. It can be done with the fingers dripping the insteps, or with the finger gripping the Achilles tendons, with the thumbs in the front of the lower legs. Yogi Bhajan instructed that the fingers should squeeze the Achilles tendons. This action interrupts an electric current which passes through the tendons. It causes the accumulation of kundalini lifeForce energy, which makes it likely to arouse the kundalini.

The head should be tilted backward. This is the reverse neck lock, which chokes some electric currents which pass through the neck into the brain. When coming out of this pose, patience is necessary. Sudden actions of release should not be done. Gradually, after checking to be sure that the neck lock is applied, with the forward neck lock, with the chin locked to the throat, one must also check to be sure that the anus is contacted. One should check to know that the sex lock and urinary muscle is pulled. One should know that the abdomen retreated under the rib cage.

One can slowly come out of this pose but with the eyelids closed so as not to focus on physical objects. The mind lock should be on, either to be applying an inward pull through the third eye chakra, or the crown chakra, or to the coreSelf in the center of the subtle head.

For student yogis, standing immediately after this pose is prohibited. In fact, one should slowly drop the buttock to a full squat. Then slowly, after checking mentally, one should release the locks. If one stands, it is likely that there will be a sudden rush of kundalini. One may be unable to control it, due to loss of grip on the locks, or due to carelessness in inner observation of the energy flows. Then the body will fall. It may even fall and assume spasms or jerks for some seconds, with no idea by the yogi that it happened.

Why? Because his coreSelf was disconnected from its observational position in relation to the perception equipment. Shortly after, the student will resume awareness of the body. He will find the body in a position which he/she does not recall. The body may be damaged if it made contact with a sharp or hard object. This is why the precautions should be taken when assuming this pose.

If when holding this pose, there is discomfort, or swaying of the body, or an imbalance in the subtle one, with feelings skipping, the yogi should slowly lower the buttocks to de-elevate the squat. Once that lowering occurs, the energy movements may cease. The yogi should focus inwardly to be sure that the psychological energies are settled. They return to their particular places, and no longer are shifty.

Then again, closing the eyelids, the yogis should assume that posture. He should focus on the inner state, which for a moment or for a time, will be like a windless atmosphere, a stilled place.

Focusing into the lower part of the body, in the vicinity of the spine, the yogi may observe electric sensations which are mild, which are not jolting.

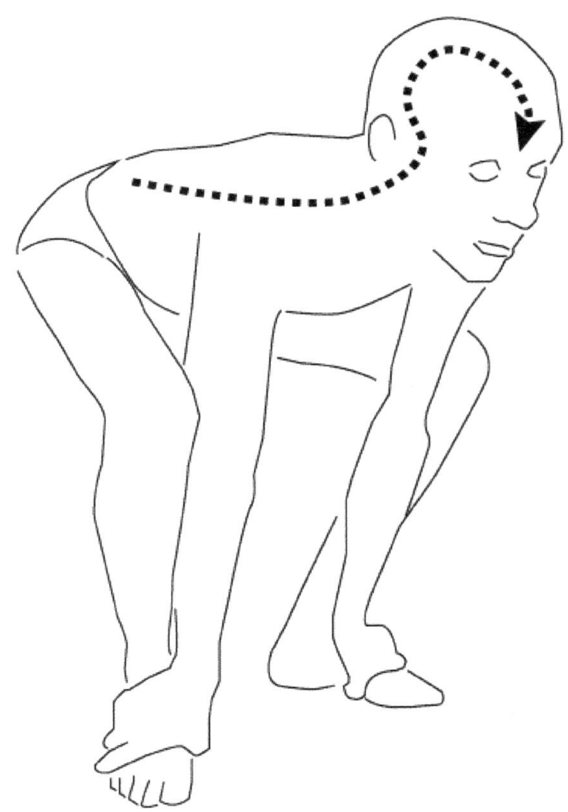

Again, the yogi should lower the buttocks and remain in the lowered squat. The hands should release the feet and be placed flat on the floor.

Then the yogi may hear naad high-pitched frequency which is mild, which is not compulsive and demanding.

Focus Connection

The *Partial Squat – Grip Feet and Insteps* posture, is a balance-alignment pose. It is strenuous for some yogis. Some can only persist with it for some seconds, less than a minute. Those with enlarged thighs may not assume this pose. These may squat while holding the insteps. However, if the buttocks are enlarged, it may be impossible to even squat and grip the instep with the thumbs.

This pose may be so demanding, that one may not hear inner sound. This pose could illustrate internally to the yogi, that the posture may affect how the attention is distributed, and how special objects like inner sound, could, or could not, be grasped by the coreSelf.

One may assume this pose with these visual actions.

- eyelids closed with inner vision not focusing on anything outside the psyche
- eyelids open with vision energy not focused but blaring
- eyelids closed with vision energy pouring though the subtle eyes

In this pose, the knee may press the elbows. This steadies the body. It helps to support the weight which is above the knee complex of bones. It reduces shivering and nervousness.

After a time, when this posture becomes untenable, the yogi should relax the buttocks downward. That will provide relief. The hands should remain on the feet. The yogi should check the energy distribution, in the knees and elbows. He may notice that energy oozes from the inner elbows. Meditation should be done while monitoring this. When he is satisfied that the body is relaxed, he should raise the buttocks into the position again. Then he should note what occurs.

- How long can the yogi hold this pose?

All-Fours Variation

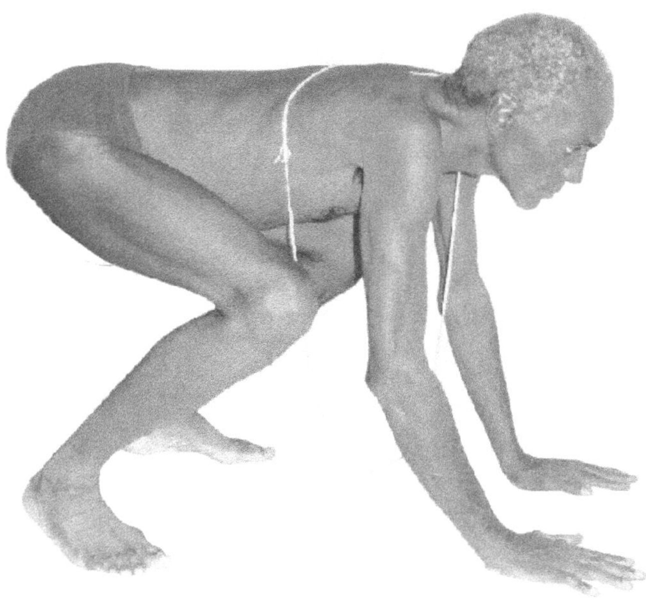

This *All-Fours Variation,* is with hands and feet in contact with the floor. The key feature is to keep the spine horizontal. The head should be tilted back as far as possible. Someone may do this with the heels in contact with the floor. Someone else may have to raise the heels while the rest of the sole remains in contact with the floor.

There may be a tension behind the lower legs, in the lower forearms, and in the thighs, where they meet the torso. There may be a shivering in the knees and thighs. As soon as that is felt, one should count to fifteen. Then squat by lowering the buttocks. In that position, focus through into the body.

While doing this, the eyelids should be closed. Take note of released energy which runs to specific areas and locations. The value of this observation is that the mind is trained to observe and utilize the energy flows. One notices that even with no deliberate focus (*dharana*), still the psyche assumes a meditative state, and maintains that during a specific position.

In this posture however, a yogi will notice that when he relaxes out of it, the energy which was emitted, returns to the place from which it emerged. This is like when water falls from a high place to a lake. Then somehow whatever left the high location, returns to it by a mysterious reverse action. Of course, nature does not allow that in the physical existence, but it happens when doing certain postures, which cause energy movements out of a zone or location. When the yogi relaxes from that pose, he notices that the released energy which travelled to another zone, returns to its original location.

Hence that relaxed pose gives the yogi the opportunity to observe an absorption state, which is specific to a particular posture. In time, the yogi will develop an appreciation, for the cooperation of the mind, during those meditative states.t

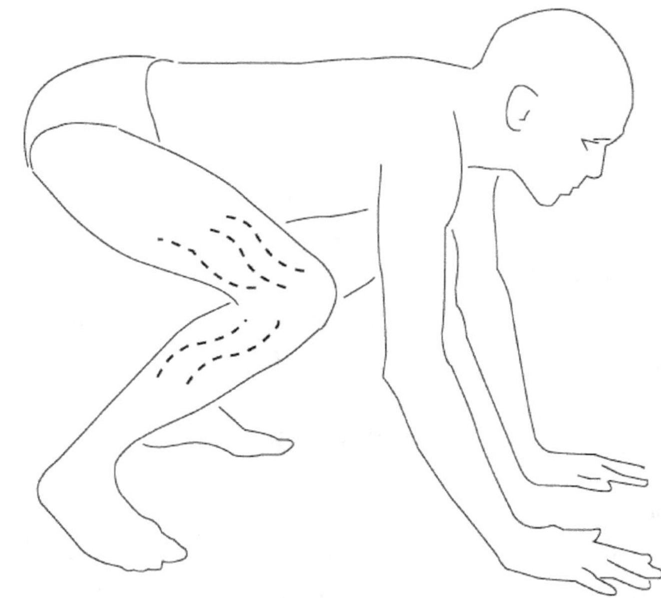

Focus Connection

The *All-Fours Variation* targets balance in reference to gravity. A human body is not designed for this pose. Rather, one may observe that it is used by monkeys, baboons and the like. It is useful for scampering through trees, and for sprints to escape from predators. When a yogi does this pose, even if he is supple in joints, still there may be micro-shivering.

A yogi may do this for a short time. Then, he may move the torso into a squatting posture. He should remain in that pose for a time. While in that position, he should investigate to determine the energy distribution. In the muscles of the arms and forearms, energies may be released. This will seem like droplets or mist, dispersing slowly, carrying a pearl-like substance.

As soon as the yogi feels satisfied that the tensions cease in the squatting posture, he should assume the *All-Fours Variation* again. Then, he should again observe its energy distribution. Holding the pose and mapping its layout, he should tolerate it for a time. Again, he should lower the buttocks and squat to relax the system. The internal state should be observed, inspected and noted.

Squat with Fingers Down

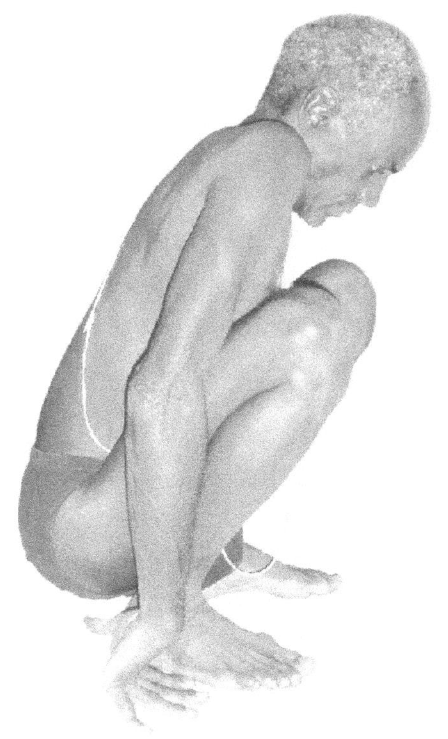

This *Squat with Fingers Down* is a simple posture, a squatting variation. The fingers are pressed but the thumb and palm do not touch the floor. The pressed fingers are pressured by pressing forcefully. There is no tension in any other part of the body.

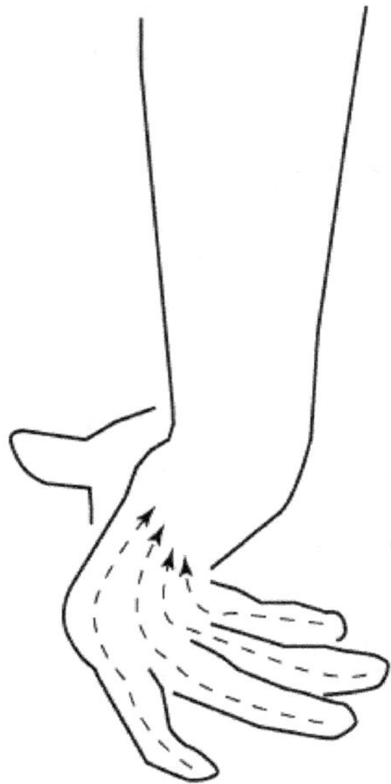

The physical tension in the physical hand is the result of a subtle electric tension. The yogi is more concerned with these subtle movements. Where the pressure in the fingers migrate to the wrists, a mint-like feeling is present. In the wrists, this energy is misted and then dissipated. The yogi should check the chin to be sure that it is pressed to the throat.

One should hold the pressure for a time, until it feels that one should cease. Then one should release the pressure, but remain squatting with the hands free of the pressing tension. The fingers should be interlocked, and should be swiveled back and forth, one hand against the other, back, and forth. When the electric sensations in the joints cease, the hands should be relaxed.

The yogi should focus through the trunk. He should check the trunk, arms and forearms. There should be energy percolating through those regions. When this energy is quieted, there should be a shift, where energy from the trunk moves into the head. This is a mist energy. It will slowly move to the coreSelf in the head of the subtle body.

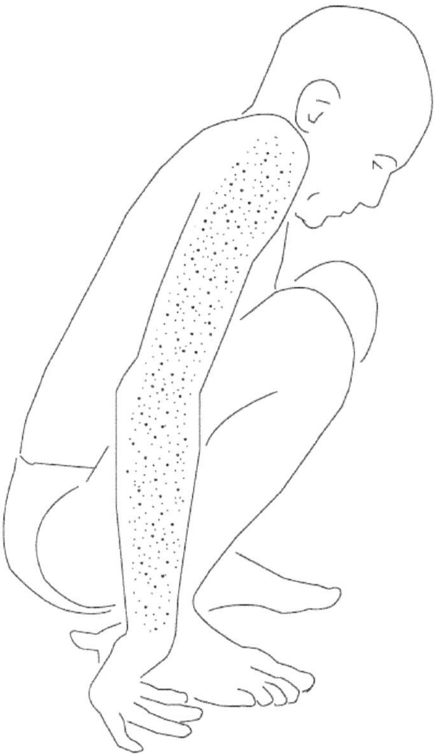

Focus Connection

The *Squat with Fingers Down* is an easy posture. And yet, it awakens the nervous system and brain. The nerves and tendons in the fingers demand attention. At first there are energy jitters in the finger joints and tendons. These send nerve messages to the brain. They report a crisis in the hands.

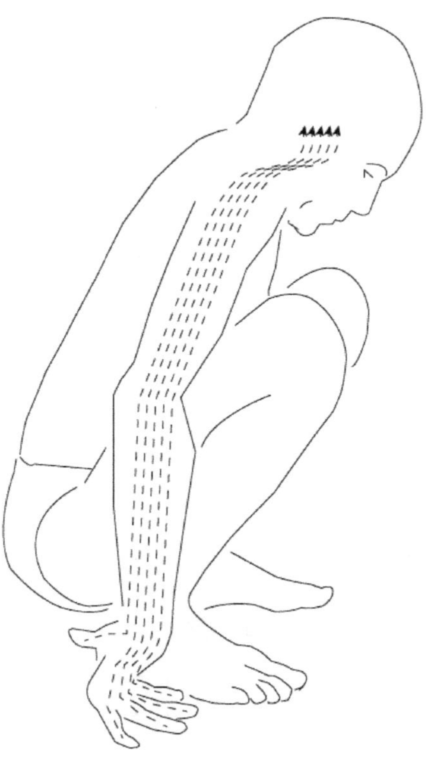

There is a flow from the shoulders to the fingers. As well as one from the fingers through the shoulders into the brain. There will be an urge to move the fingers. The yogi should perceive that information but should not change the position. He should hold the fingers under the tension of pressing them to the floor.

While this happens, the yogi should check to be sure that the four fingers of each hand are under pressure. The thumbs make no contact. They are not under tension. While doing this, the yogi may become aware of a thought development. That will be a mild display with no emergency energy being emitted. The yogi should notice that the thought force operates to be displayed, but it does not have a compelling force. However, even though it is mild, it still develops. The yogi makes no effort to stop the display.

Looking to see what the thought is, as displayed images, the yogi will notice that it is hardly visible. It fades. There are no crisp edges to it. Its form cannot be seen clearly. It is like a thin cloud which has edges which dissolve into the sky. It has very little insistence power.

A yogi should study this, to understand that a strong alert, from somewhere in the psyche, may cause thought displays to be imperceptible. By some involuntary force, these muted displays happen. They are not legible neither as messages nor images.

Sit on Heels with Tilt-Back Spine

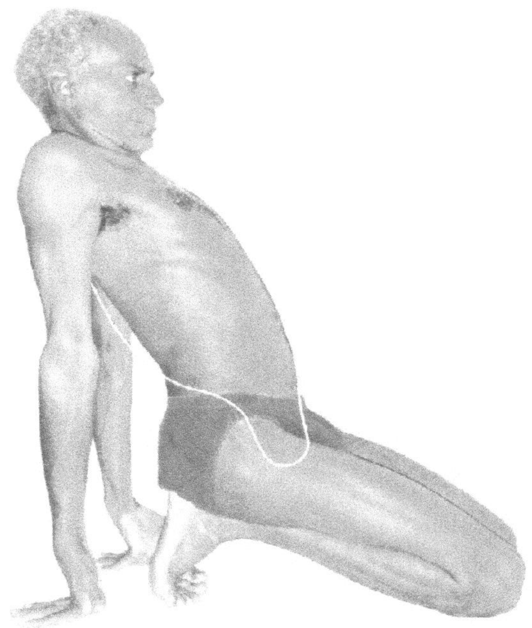

This *Sit on Heels with Tilt-Back Spine* posture has fingers (not palms), curled toes, and knees in contact with the floor. The yogi first sits on the heels but with the toes curled. The knees remain in contact with the floor. The palms do not touch the floor. A tightness is felt in the soles of the feet.

The spine is tilted back somewhat, just enough to maintain taut fingers, with the palms near but not touching the floor. The chin is kept down, pressed to the throat. Pressure is applied to the fingers which are under a high tension.

After a time, a shimmering energy will twinkle in the fingers. This will be released continually into the palms, where it will dissipate. The yogi should focus on the palms. He should observe internally how energy radiates from the fingers, and is collected in the palms. After a time, after he can no longer maintain the posture, he should release the fingers. The hands should be over the head. There the fingers should be interlocked, and swiveled back and forth, to release the cramp feelings. As soon as those feelings subside, the hands should be relaxed on the thigh.

The yogi should resume the *Sit on Heels with Tilt Back Spine* posture. He should look down through the body to recognize any energy movement. In the lowest part of the back, there may be a release of energy which is like a misty atmosphere with a bliss aspect. This energy will transfer to the vertebrae in the neck.

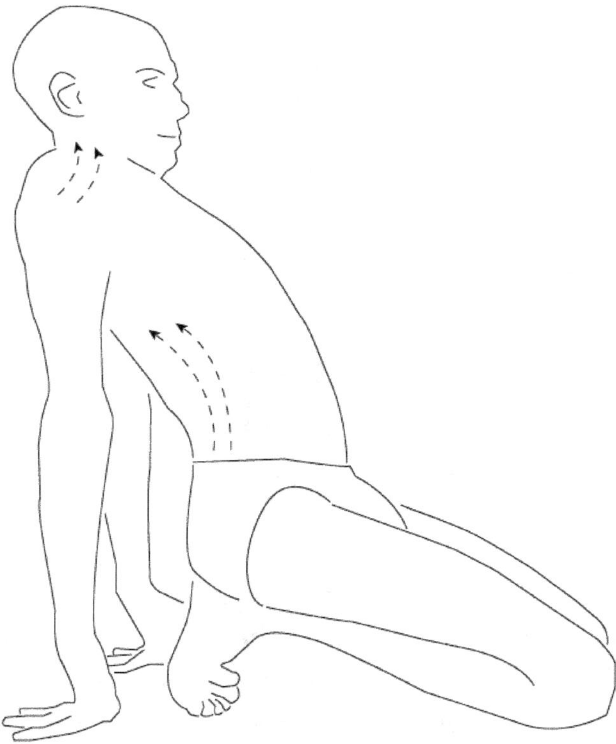

There may also be a sudden awareness of naad high-pitched frequency being sounded in the head. It may be on the right side in the back or somewhere else. It could be all surrounding, with or without a node.

Focus Connection

The *Sit on Heels with Tilt-Back Spine* is overall, a relatively simple pose. If there is stress in the four fingers of each hand, which contacts the floor, a cushion or block may be used to elevate the fingers. Women may find that their breasts are pressed forward by the rib cage. It may be necessary to reposition the mammary glands.

In this pose with the fingers pressed to the floor, there will be currents running from the fingers, through the wrists, forearm and arms. This will be experienced as a collective of moving energy, which travels through the shoulders, and then disappears. Just as one may separate one strand of wire in a multi-stranded cable, a yogi should attempt to sort the single currents in the collective.

After a time, the toes will cry out. The yogi should straighten the toes. He should move them from the curled position. This will cause relaxation. The cry which was expressed, will cease. The yogi may compare this relaxed condition to the one with the toes under tension. He will find that now with the relief applied, the toes emit a dulling energy.

In that posture, he should sit to meditate. He should again apply tension on the fingers but it will not feel as it did previously. It will not be as compelling for focus.

Ape Decision Posture

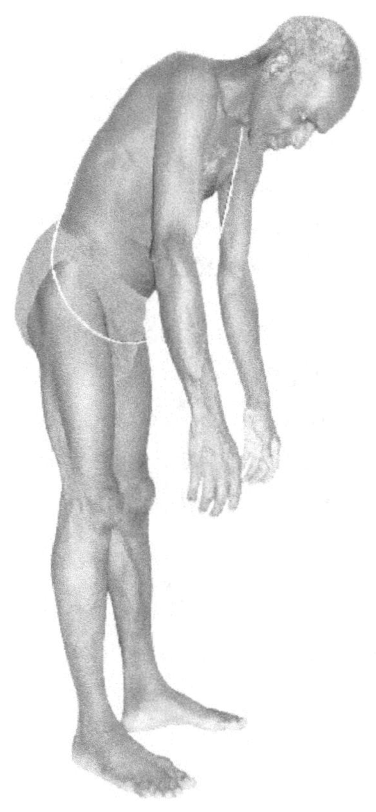

This *Ape Decision Posture* pose, is where one becomes located, so that he can make the decision, to convert from the ape specie. There is a general mammal category which has many four-legged formats. However, the monkey, lemurs and apes are regarded as primates, a special set of mammals. It has to do with walking upright, or walking on all-fours, or switching between two or four legs for movement.

A yogi should study the body profile of the ape-format.

- How does it influence the aspirations and objectives of the coreSelf which uses that configuration?

To do this posture, one should stand with feet reasonably apart, with just enough space to keep a firm balance. One should then lean over slightly. Let the arms hang forward with no muscle contraction. The head should hang accordingly. One should relax in this pose. One should close the eyelids and retreat within the psyche.

Focus through the central trunk. Eventually there will be a curl of energy from the lumbar area of the buttocks. This will be revealed in the psyche to be a curled energy which terminates in the central throat area.

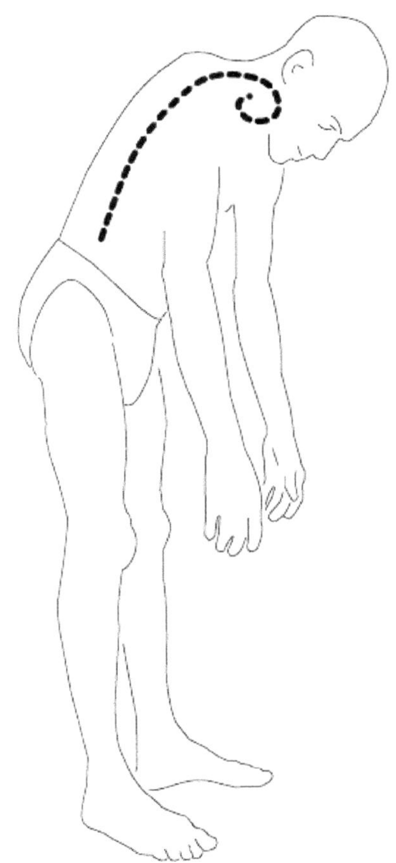

When one comes out of this pose, one remains standing but the back straightens. Then, assuming the human standing posture, there will be a switch, where the curled energy from the lumbar area, goes straight up through the spine into the head. Instead of curling in the throat and ending there, it will go up and through back of the skull. It will diverge forward to the center of the eyebrows.

Instead of looking downward, and having to make an effort to raise the head and eyes to look forward, the forward scan will be natural and spontaneous. There may be a button shaped one inch squirt of energy, spinning in and out at the third eye chakra between the eyebrows.

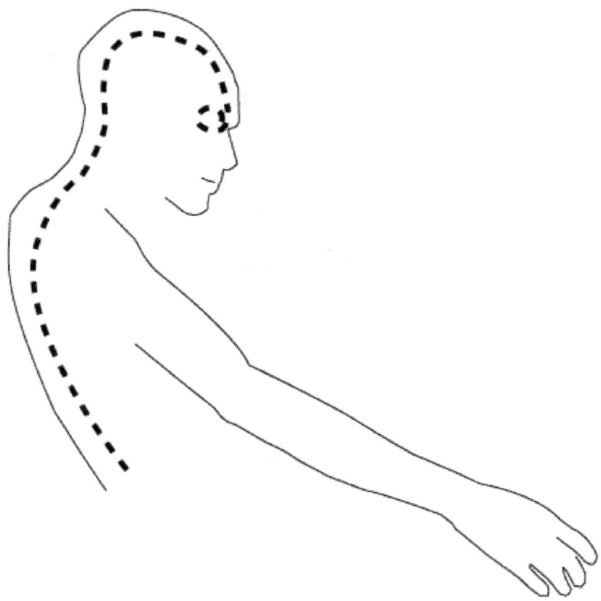

Focus Connection

The *Ape Decision Pose* gives the yogi some understanding of the importance of the human standing posture. If the human being was slouched over, even with the same brain, there would be a negative mood.

In this pose, one can sense, that there is a resistance to the evolutionary development from monkey to human. There is a reluctance to this shift. Physically, it means a blockage to having an upright spine. Lastly, the curve at the shoulders and neck, is difficult to transform.

Even though the individual is a psychological reality, still that psychic something has to contend with the biological attitude, which it uses in particular species. A monkey may conceive of walking upright, and shedding its four limb mobility, but it cannot put that into practice permanently.

A yogi can assume several positions which are natural for other species. In these positions, he can get some idea of the demeanor, he would use in those other lifeForms.

Lotus Over

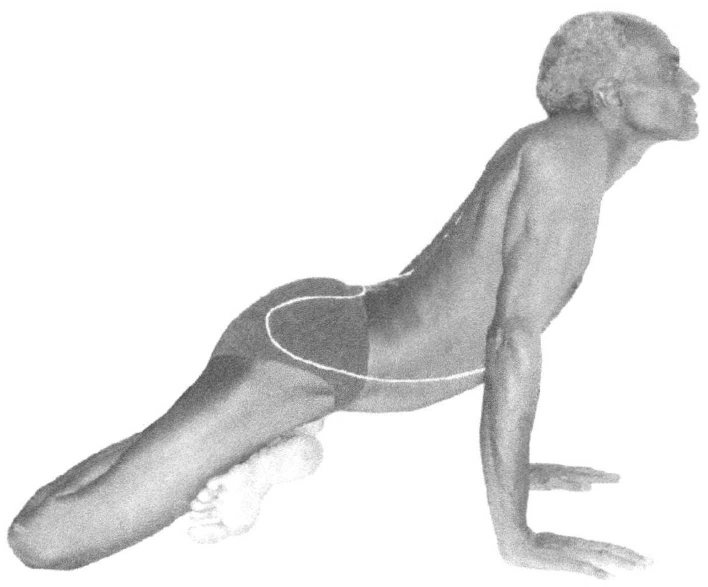

This *Lotus Over* pose, has the lotus posture as its basic requirement. It works wonders for the vertebrae of the physical body. The small of the back, where it bends the most when one leans back, is a pressure sensitive region. If this part has discomfort and pain, it will be difficult to do other postures in which the spine is involved.

To assume this pose, the yogi should first make the *padmasana* lotus pose. He should take care to be sure that the spine is perpendicular to the floor. With that he should lean forward on the knees. The weight of the body will be on the thigh-knee area and on the palms. The head will be tilted up for the reverse neck lock. For that the head is tilted back as far as it will go. The chin is raised to the maximum.

In this posture, there should be full in-the-body focus. An electric sensation may be felt in the thigh and lumbar areas. Electric energy may surge through the thigh. It will flash into the trunk.

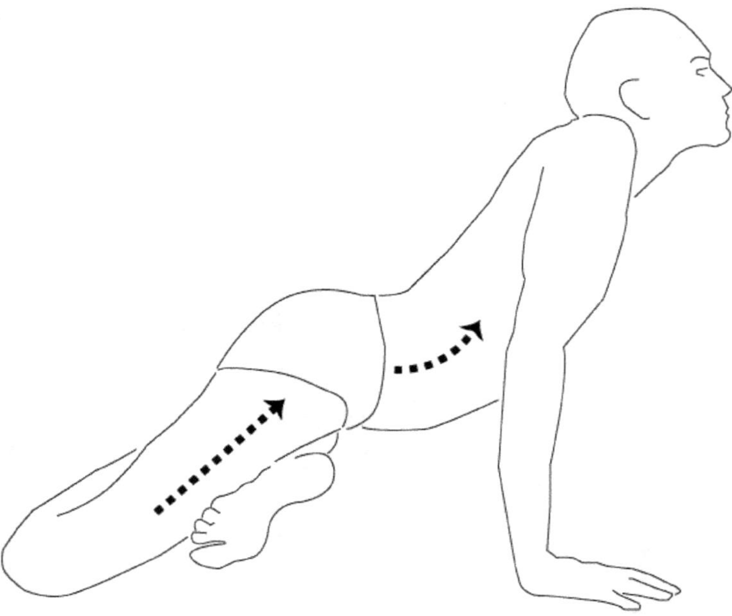

When the yogi feels that he should relax, he should slowly take the body out of it. This should be done with no sudden movements nor jerks. With full attention, and slowly, he should resume sitting in lotus. If convenient, the yogi may assume an *all-four* posture and may remain in that for a time, until the energy shimmers to a standstill. In the all-four posture, using the palms and the knees, the yogi may hear the naad resonance. It may be more distinct in a specific area, as for example in the back of the head, or to the right, or left, or below.

There should be energy feelings everywhere in the subtle body, with no stressed areas, and no focusing except for the scattering of charged energy in every part.

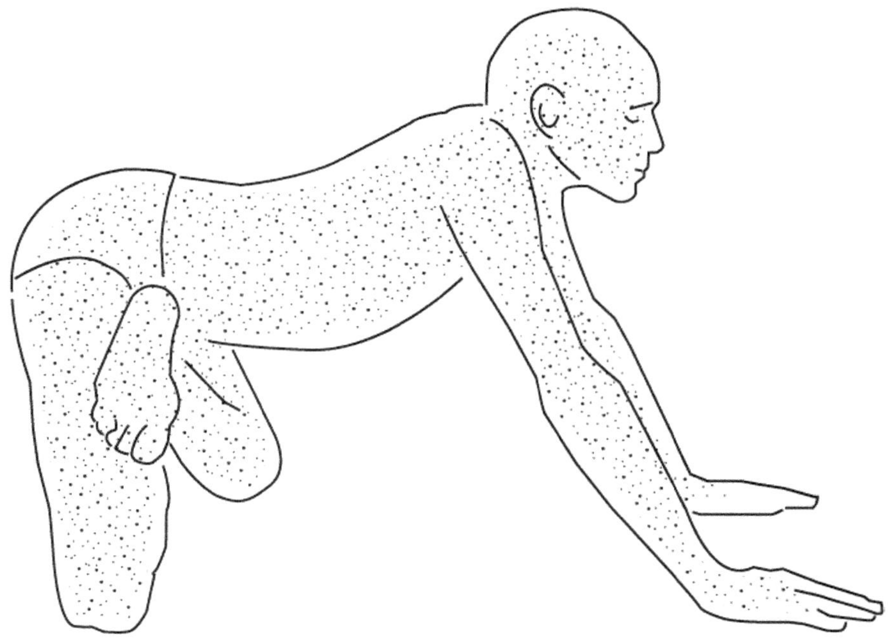

Focus Connection

The *Lotus Over* position requires the use of the lotus interlocking legs posture. A yogi who cannot do the lotus, should avoid this pose. This posture is also used for spinal corrective actions when the spine develops a hunch back, or slouched back curvature. It may take time for the body to develop this. It may take years. In some cases, it cannot be corrected because the biological profile changed permanently.

In this *Lotus Over* pose, the yogi remains in the posture for as long as he can tolerate. While doing this he focuses internally to check for energy movements. The neck position should be noted. If possible, the backward neck lock should be applied. This involves tilting the chin up as far as it can go.

After the yogi has the posture stabilized, he should check for the energy positions. One may feel as is the sky falls through the face. One may hear inner sound. This may blare in the back top of the head. When the posture becomes intolerable, the yogi should slowly move back, until he sits in the lotus pose. Then he may remain sitting upright. Or he may rest his elbows on the thighs. The palms should be upward. Remaining like this for a time, he should analyze the energy.

Again, he should resume the *Lotus Over* pose. He should do this slowly step by step. When it is completed, he should again consider the energies. After a time, when the pose becomes tiring, he should sit in the lotus, doing so without disturbing the energy format for the *Lotus Over* pose. Thoughts may develop. He may lose objectivity. He may discover that he is caught in the progression of a thought, which has a sequence of events, like a story being told. He finds that he is in a flow of observation of a sequence of thoughts. He has no control of it. He does not supervise it. Like a sail boat which is handled by the wind, he is maneuvered by it

Sometimes a thought is constructed from memory events only. Sometimes, it is constructed by memory, and by newly created scenes, which blend into the memory events, but which are not from the past. The yogi observes his lack of control of the display of memories.

Out-stretched Forward Limb with Other Folded at Knee

For this *Out-stretched Forward Limb with Other Folded at Knee* posture, one limb (foot, leg and thigh) is pushed forward. The opposing hand is used for support. The other foot, leg and thigh is pushed backward and

folded at the knee. Using the corresponding hand, reach back with the opposing hand to grab the rear foot.

Once this position is assumed, checks should be made to be sure that the fingers of the supportive hand are positioned to bear some weight. The forward heel is pressed forward, to be sure that it as far away as the body can tolerate, and with no strain on tendons, muscles, or joints.

The rear knee which bears some weight is pushed back. It may be readjusted to be sure that it is in the optimum position. There will be tension here and there. By the back knee, in the thighbone, the yogi may experience electric currents going through the thigh. These currents may disappear at the mid-thigh.

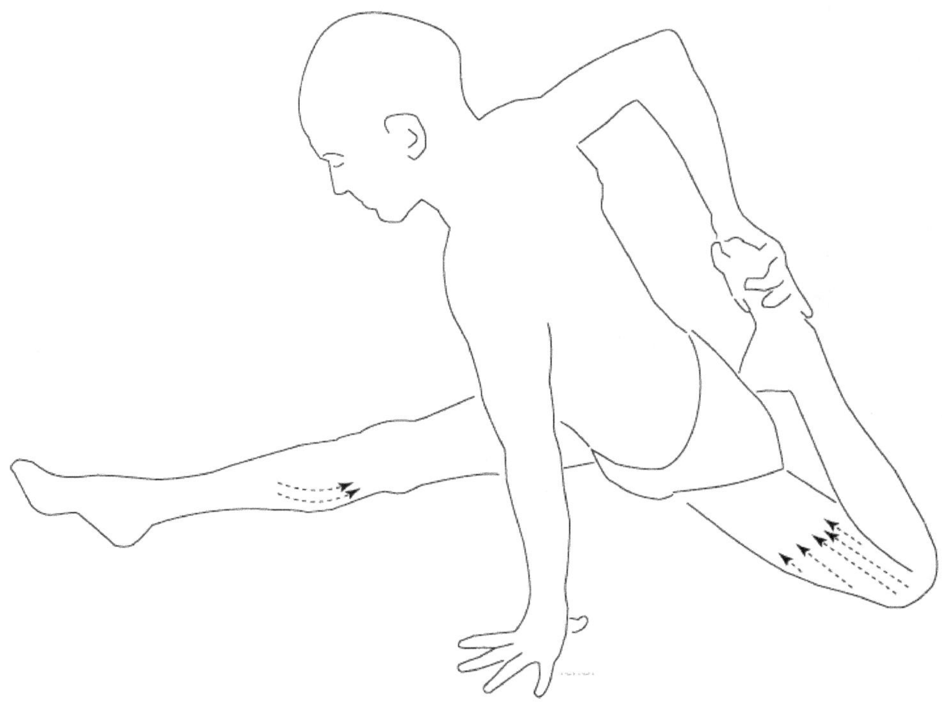

In the front leg by the calf there may be electric energy, which radiates but does not travel out of the area. Hold this pose for a time. Focus within to make contact with any area where energy moves, accumulates, or is dispersed. When the tensions feel unbearable, one should slowly come out of the posture to reach a relaxed position. In that pose, one should peer through the subtle body, to track any jitters. When these cease, one should assume an easier posture, and continue peering within the subtle body, focusing inside the psyche. One should realize a silence in the chamber of the psyche. There may be naad blare. A yogi should connect the attention with naad. He may enter a *samadhi* effortless focus saturation.

Focus Connection

The *Out-stretched Forward Limb with Other Folded at Knee* is a tension posture. Due to muscular tightness and joint malfunction, some yogis cannot assume this pose. Even for yogis who can easily do it, there should be caution. It is a fact that, when an easy pose is assumed in a careless way, it may cause injury.

In this pose there will be tension in the thigh, which has the knee to the floor. If necessary, that knee should be cushioned. The hand which is used to support the body will be stressed. A yogi should note how these pressure points in the body, demand the use of the coreSelf's attention. The demand is so great, that there are no thought appearances and no conscious or subconscious giving away of attention energy to an idea. A yogi should study these psychological events. They usually occur with no notation of their operations. It is a lesson about the confiscation of attention. It gives hints of how a yogi may command the attention, to complete focusing targets during meditation.

After a time in this pose, the yogi will be forced to relax. Both hands will be placed on the floor. The body will relax. The yogi will shift into a pose which will give relief. Again, the yogi will resume this pose. At this time, he may hear naad sound. There may be no thoughts. The mood of the inner mind may be one with no ideas, flashing. However, the tension from the pose will resume. The yogi may tolerate that for a time. Then he should go into an easy pose. There, with no muscular or tendon distress, he should listen to inner sound. A decision should be made, either to intently focus on the inner frequency sound, or to hear it with no intent to focus. Naad will blare, but the yogi will exert no interest to focus intently on it. He will hear it with no willpower exertion being applied.

Up, On Crimped Toes

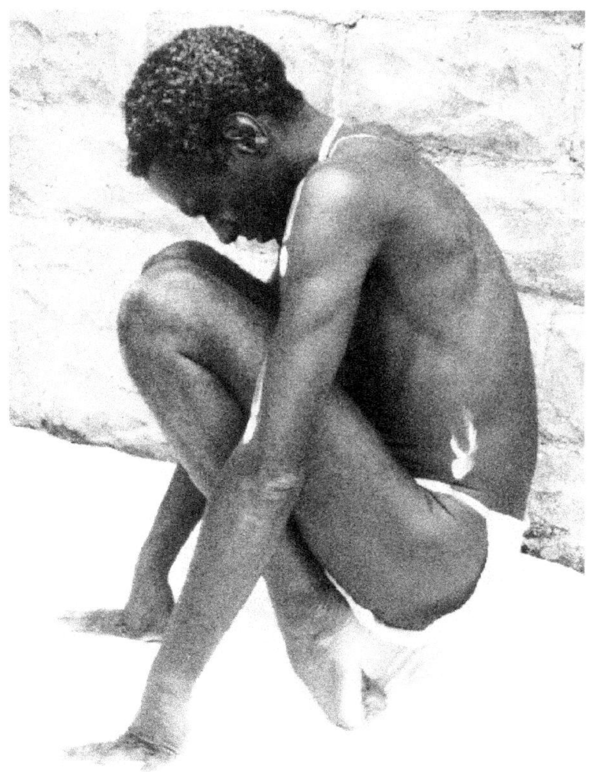

For this *Up, On Crimped Toes,* one should sit on heels. With fingers flat on the floor, one should raise the knees, until the weight of the body shifts to the toes and hands. Being careful and attentive, one should shift the weight so that it runs through the toes which are pressed in a curled position. The buttocks may rest on the heels. The toes will be pressured by the weight of the body.

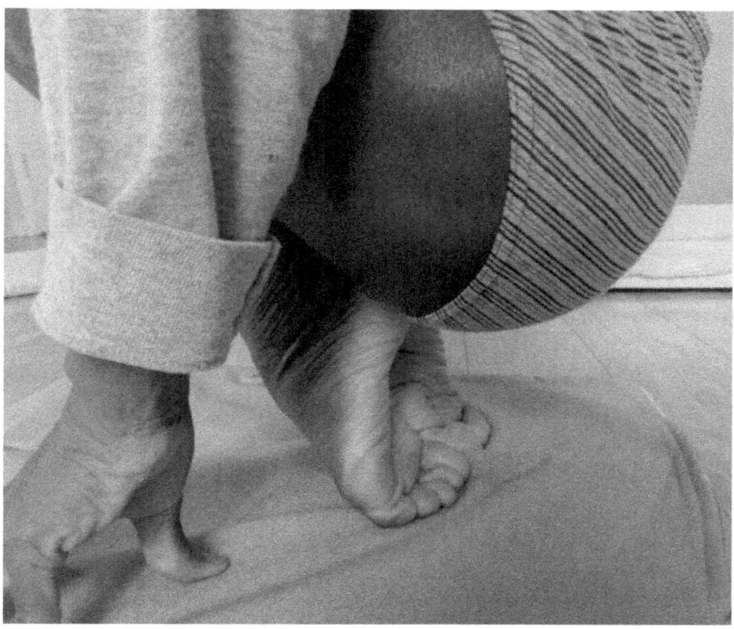

A yogi should remain in this posture for a time. He should hear naad, a whistling sound.

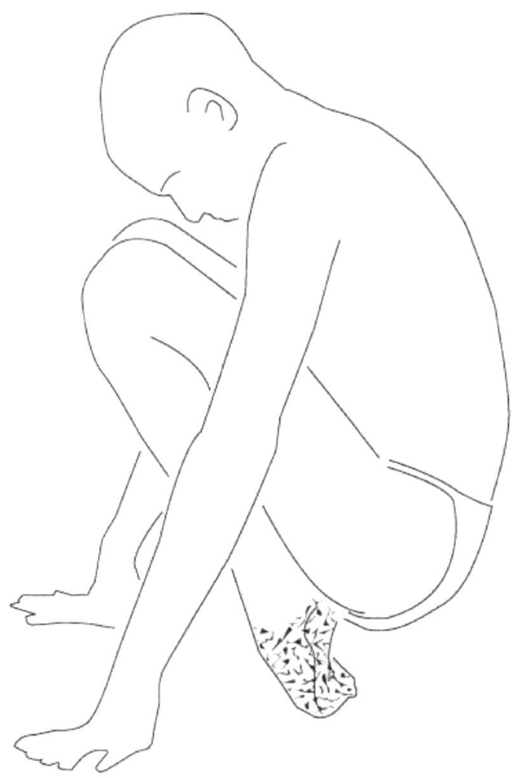

Focus Connection

The *Up, On Crimped Toes* posture, causes the weight of the body to travel through the toes into the floor. This causes severe stress, which may be experienced as pain. The hands assist for support. The yogi becomes aware of several strings of pain, flaring in the bones and tendons of the toes. This pose should not be done on a slippery floor. The fingers which help in support, should not slide. If the pose feels that it should be respositioned, a yogi should slightly move either the feet or hands, to allow balance and weight adjustment.

In this posture, once it is stabilized, and the yogi feels that he can maintain it in a balanced position, he should examine its energy distribution. When doing this, he may notice that thinking ceased entirely. Inner sound will be heard. The attention focus will be either on the toes or on the inner sound, or it may be aware of either. No thoughts will be exposed in the mindspace.

Sometimes however, a thought will attempt to show itself. It will be unsuccessful. That thought will have energy to attempt to reveal itself, but it will have no energy to sustain its illustration. The attention will be absorbed by the pressure in the toes.

After a time, a yogi will relax from this position. He should do this slowly so that there is no jerk nor sudden movement, so that he maintains the inner focus and can tract energy. He should slowly lower the body so that he sits on the heels. His hands should be on the thighs. The inner sound should blare. His sight power should blare but his eyelids should be closed, or he should already have a blindfold. The inner vision, being open, should be felt. He should be aware of what happened to the energy which was stressed in the toes.

- Did it vanish because the weight of the body was no longer passing through the toe area?

After meditating for a time, the yogi will feel the necessity to relax. He should slowly move into an easy pose. Then he should intensify inner focus. He should experience a shift in inner sound, where its frequency changes. He should be aware of a new resonance. He should note its saturation.

In relation to this *Up, On Crimped Toes* pose, Yogeshwarananda mentioned that a yogi who sits in a cavern, or dugout in the earth, should be monitored by another ascetic. This is because there may be need for the sitting yogi's body to be excavated. There may be an earthquake. The walls or roof of the dugout may cave in or collapse. There may be a flood. A natural mishap may occur. If the watcher yogi is alert, he can rescue the body of the one who is in the dugout.

For some yogis, hours of meditation in a dugout may be required. If the body enters a trance, it may not react rapidly if there is a crisis. Hence the responsibility for the body should be taken by another yogi who is physically active.

Sometimes, hours of meditation are required for a yogi. He may do this under the earth, where the vibrations from the sun and atmosphere does not cross into his mind space. This serves to purge his psyche of previous impressions which continually flash in the mind.

If one is in the earth, some thought energy will leave the psyche. That will free the yogi from being subjected to endless thinking displays.

Some yogis have a fear of low places or of heights. These tendencies are carried over from mishaps in previous lives. As for instance, a yogi whose body was killed by a fall from a cliff, may carry a fear of high places. Meditating in a low place in the earth, could cause that fear energy to leave the psyche. After several days staying in meditation in the earth, a yogi will find that thoughts which are kept in the memory chambers, come to the surface. These pop up one by one, or in groups. They are released from the psyche into the psychic environment.

Sit between Heels – Pressure Fingers

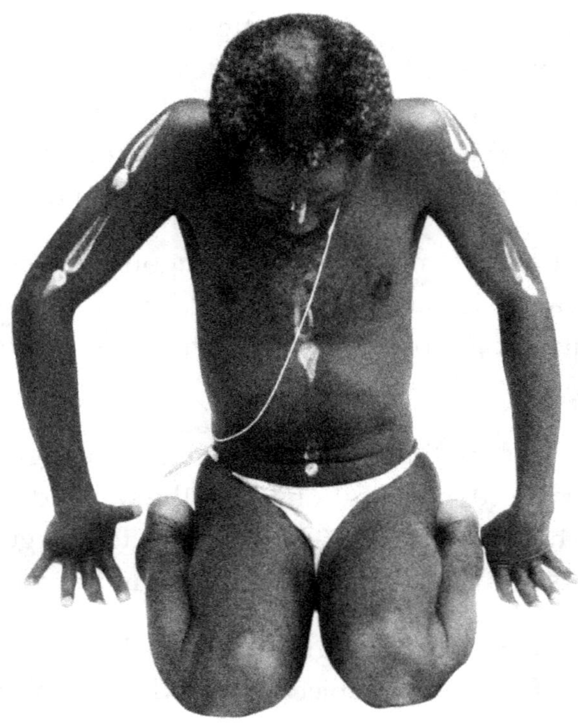

This *Sit between Heels – Pressure Fingers* is an easy posture, if the thigh muscles are not tense, in this position. The yogi sits between the heels with the feet facing backward. There should be little tension in the knees.

The spine should be erect. The fingers should be pressed to the floor. The thumbs should make no contact. The palms also, should make no contact. A constant pressure is applied to the fingers, but the palms and thumbs remain aloof.

There will be needle-like spikes of energy in the fingers, especially in the finger-joints. It will twinkle and sparkle with electric energy. After a time, the energy which is released from the pressured fingers will escape from the joints. It will travel through the forearms and arms into the shoulders. After it accumulates, it will run through the shoulders into the neck.

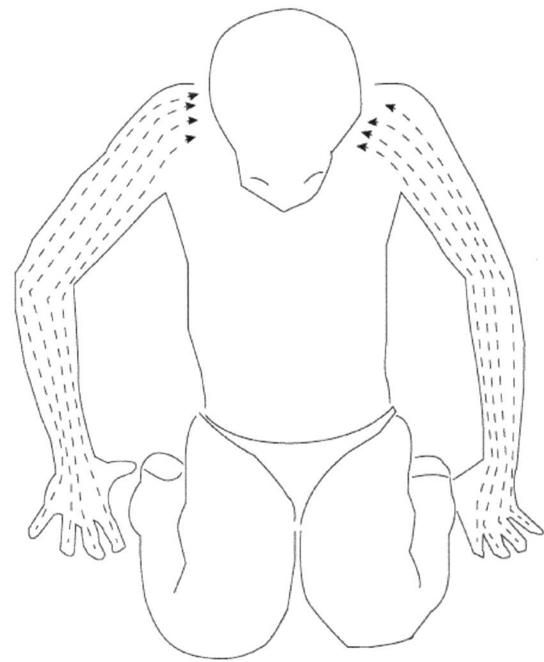

When this energy in the neck subsides, the yogi should release the pressure on the fingers. He should place each hand on its corresponding thigh. This should be with the palms facing the sky. That will cause the mind to relax. The yogi may hear naad resonance. It may be heard in one direction or another. It may be in the back of the head. The yogi should become absorbed in this energy which is both a sound and a force.

Still sitting between the heels, the yogi should become aware of subtle movements. The physical body will remain as it is, but the subtle one may attempt to move. It may actually move. It may flip. A loud naad sound may be heard in the head. Remaining absorbed in that sound, the yogi will train the mind to appreciate the state of having no mental impressions or demands. This is a *dhyana-samadhi* practice which assists in the quest for the divine eye development.

Focus Connection

Provided that the yogi can sit between the heels, or can sit with buttocks elevated between the heels or even sit on a chair which has room on each side to press the fingers, the *Sit between Heels – Pressure Fingers* posture is easy to assume. This is a *samadhi* practice. Males should be sure that the testes are not squeezed.

The focus in this posture concerns the shoulders and fingers, particularly the fingers. The eight fingers are pressed to the flood. The thumbs float. The palms are kept off the surface. Only the four fingers of each hand experience the downward pressure.

Due to the pressure exerted, there will be a frosty release energy emanating. The yogi should be absorbed in that sensation. This is a *samadhi*. A yogi should train his mind in recognizing, mapping and indulging in the sensation. During that, he should note that there are no thoughts or that if thoughts arise, they do not expand a full display in the mind. This leaves the mind in a *samadhi* absorption. Over and over, the yogi should be mentally and emotionally, involved in this.

Hands Up by Ears

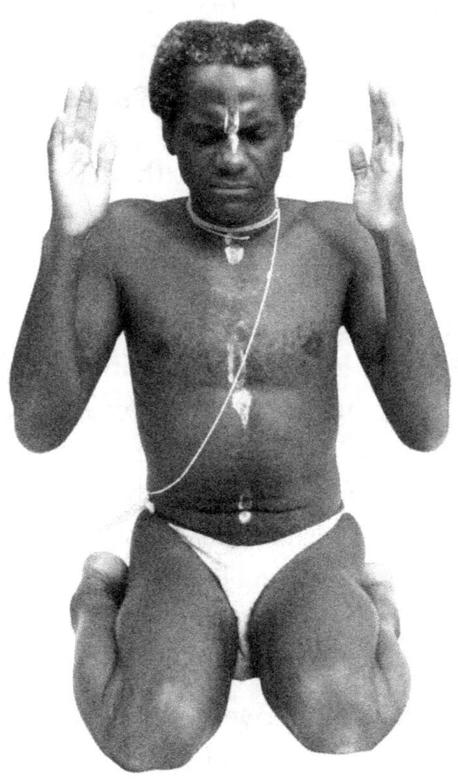

Many *asana* postures, concern a stretch and/or contraction. There are some however which have only relaxation. This *Hands Up by Ears* pose is primarily involved in being relaxed. Even so, someone may have a body which does not relax, in this pose. For that person, this posture may not yield the results mentioned. In each case of every yogi, specific postures may yield familiar or strange results. The importance is the introspective observation, while doing a pose.

In the *Hands Up by Ears* pose shown above, the key relaxation is the *sitting between the heels*. If a yogi sits like this and experiences stress, stiffness, and discomfort, this pose should be done with the buttocks raised on a cushion. That eases the muscles in the thighs and knees.

After sitting in this pose for a time, one may feel tiny shivering energy in forearms and arms, near the elbows. Again, after a longer period, one may feel shivering energy in the mid torso below the rib cage. The yogi should focus on this.

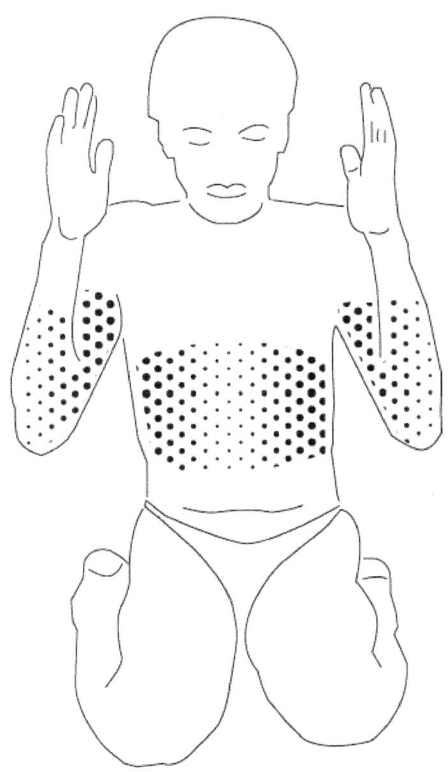

After a time, the raised forearms may disappear, whereby even the arms, and hands fade. When this happens, the yogi should place the hands on the thighs. Do this without jolting or jerking.

Meditate. Remain so for a time. If when doing this, one becomes aware of the body with the head drooped, slowly without interruption, reposition the head. Slowly shift the neck into the correct position. If this happens again, one should cease this posture, or repeat it after standing, and then sitting between the heels again. Any adjustments should be slowly assumed.

Focus Connection

This *Hands Up by Ears* posture may cause the mind to be attentive to inner sounds. It will do so for someone who is accustomed to hearing naad resonance. The position of the hands by the ears, causes the mind to shift interest to the ears-regions of the head. This will, more than likely, cause the person to listen for external or internal ssounds.

There are hardly any tension points in this pose. The mind will not be in a hurry to either figure tension areas, or to express interest in a point, or location which demands it. This will give the yogi a mild focus attitude. In it, thoughts may arise, but these may be impressions, which are not expanded enough to be understood coherently.

The coreSelf will have very little sense of itself, and may not know that it is involved in the roll out of a thought energy. While this happens, the yogi may feel some swing from one elbow on one side of the body, to the other on the other side of the body. The attention will shift back and forth. The yogi may decide to stop this pendulum-like action. He will then refocus on naad resonance. By then, the feeling to relax the body, to assume an easier posture, may assert itself.

The yogi can move the body into a comfortable pose. It should be one in which the inner format of energies is not lost. He keeps the focus. In the easy pose, he hears naad resonance clearly. He becomes attuned.

Over on Two Hands

For this *Over on Two Hands* posture, the yogi must sit on one foot, which is turned, so that the yogi sits on the heel. The image which follows shows the rear view with the foot turned under the buttocks.

Once the yogi sits on the turned foot (90^0 to the leg), he should place the hands flat on the floor on either side of each knee but with the elbows out. The head and neck should be positioned in alignment with the trunk of the body.

The yogi should press the trunk down but the back should not be arched. There should be no intention to make the head curve down. The only part which should come down is the trunk of the body. This should be done without curving the back. The yogi should hold this posture. Energy will be released from the trunk, throat, and head. Inner sound may be heard. It may blare through the psyche. The yogi should stay down until he can no longer maintain the pose. Then without jerks, he should slowly release this pose by allowing the stressed trunk to move into the upright position. Sitting like this, he should become absorbed in naad resonance.

Some postures are single positions. Many postures however are dual. The yogi does one side. Then releases that. Then does the other side of the body. Each side should be done with care and with observational stability. The focus of the feelings released and arranged, are known to the yogi. His focus should be inserted into the energy released in every pose.

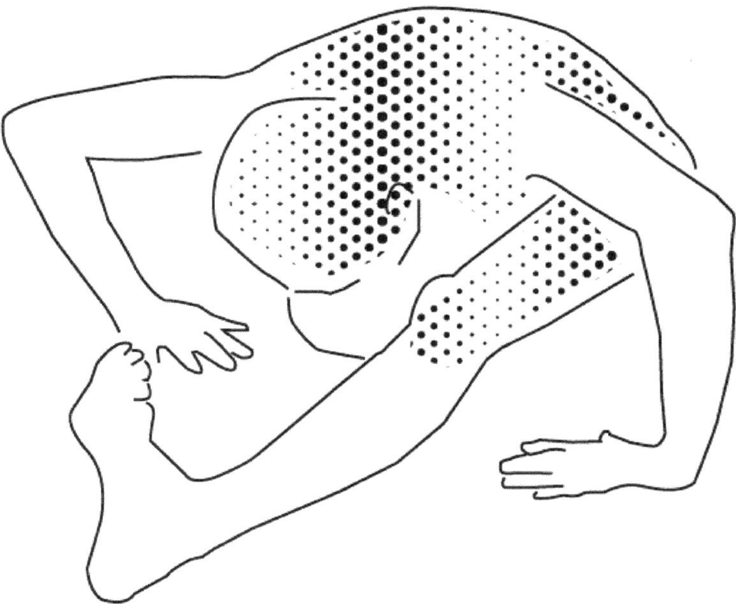

Focus Connection

When doing this *Over on Two Hands* posture, the yogi should be sure to keep the head up. He should not curve the back. The head should not make contact with either knee. The entire spine should be brought down. The pivot is the waist, with the head and spine acting as the folding part. A yogi may feel cramp-like electric sensations in the calf of the outstretched foot. That tension will rush to the back of the corresponding thigh.

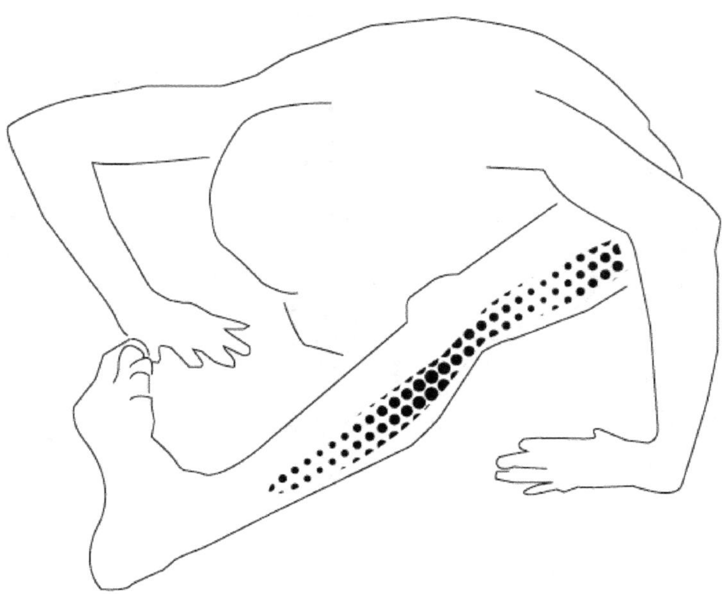

When this happens, thoughts will pass like the shadows of clouds on a windy day. Those thoughts will not be seen. Their contents will not be revealed to the yogi. None of their ideas will be illustrated in the mind. This will help the yogi to understand that unless a thought is developed and illustrated, the coreSelf may have no idea of its content. The self relies on memories emerging, developing and illustrating. Otherwise, the packages of information will be unknown. A yogi should ponder this to understand how the adjuncts interact with, serve, or undermine, the authority of the self.

In this *Over on Two Hands* posture there may be a grid formation across the back of the body. When a yogi feels this, he should focus on it to map its territory. It will hold his attention, teaching him how to do *dharana* deliberate focus and *dhyana* spontaneous holding of the attention to an area, zone or point.

When the body tires in this pose, when it can no longer be held, the yogi should observe the area of tension which makes it impossible to hold this position any longer. Then, the yogi should slowly bring the trunk to sit upright. The lower limbs should be left as they are. The arms should be adjusted just enough to keep the spine upright. In that position, the yogi will get relief as that would be an easier pose in which much stress will disappear.

In that upright pose, when it is first assumed, there may be energy sparkling in the armpits. The energy in the head may seem scattered. This is caused by the release of the posture, so that energy which was barricaded at the waist, rushes upward. It invades the head and causes a scattering which soon disappears.

When the yogi resumes the *Over on Two Hands* posture, he may feel two stream of energy rushing through the arms into the center of the spine. These streams will clash and disappear.

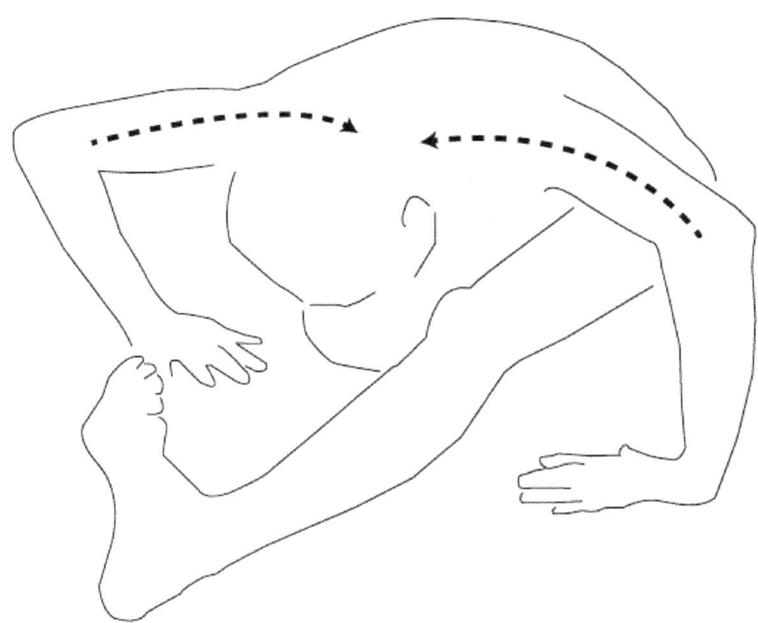

Yirk Back – Palms on Floor

For this *Yirk Back – Palms on Floor* posture, the yogi should be upright on the knees. Then slowly, he should hold the heels and allow the hands to slide to the floor. The hands with fingers should be flat on the floor, but with the wrists touching the feet. The toes should be curled towards the knees. This will cause stress in the muscles and tendons in the hands, forearms, and arms. The torso should be lifted as far as possible.

The head should be tilted forward. The chin should be pressed toward the throat. Eyelids should be closed, or a blindfold should be used, to retain visual interest in the psyche. A check should be made to be sure that the weight on the hands, which passes through the wrists, is conveyed through the palms into the floor.

The yogi should the check internally to determine where energies shift. There may be tension in every part of the psyche, as if there is confusion. The yogi may not determine where the energy is configured. This is because of the stress in the hands, forearms, and arms. This may be experienced as chaotic energy. The yogi may feel a crisis in the arms, forearms, and hands. That force will make an effort to go through the shoulders but it may be unable to do so. The yogi should focus into the wrists, forearms, and arms. After a time, a short time, it will seem that the energy in the wrists, forearms and arms dissipated as a random energy which is felt throughout the subtle body.

As a high screeching frequency, naad sound may be heard. It may seem that the waist of the body attempted to be relaxed, where it cannot hold itself into the maximum up-position. Then the yogi should slowly bring down the torso. He may sit on the heels or sit between the heels. There should be no jerking actions. He should put the hands on the thighs. He should meditate. In the meditation, he should find energy which is stilled. He should focus into it.

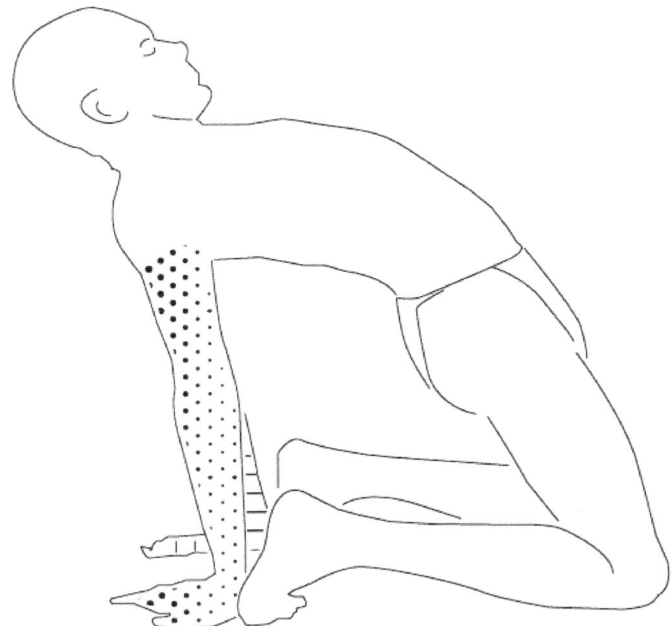

Focus Connection

The *Yirk Back – Palms on Floor* posture is assumed with the wrists touching the bottom of the feet near the toes. After leaning back, the hands cup the heels. The hands then slide down the soles of the feet, until the hands are flat on the floor, with the wrists touching the feet. This causes some tension in the wrists. A yogi is vigilant in this posture. With the eyelids closed or with a blindfold, he spontaneously focuses through the arms, forearms and wrists. This is for tracking some weight of the body as it transits to the floor.

There may be a slight rocking action which feels as if it is up and down. The yogi should stabilize this. It requires the gathering of the focusing power which is scattered in the psyche.

A yogi should study this energy movement. It gives information about the sixth stage of yoga, that of *dharana* deliberate focus. That process is natural in this pose, because the body tries to collapse, but it is held in position by the yogi. To hold it, he must focus. That is encouraged in this pose where to hold the focus is natural and can be studied.

After a time, it will be necessary to ease from this posture. The yogi should do so slowly by lowering the buttocks. He should let the body rest there. To study the energies which relaxed, where no sign of stress is present in the arms, forearms, wrists and hands, he should internalize his awareness.

After a time, when the body is fully relaxed, the yogi should resume the *Yirk Back – Palms on Floor* pose. There will be pain in the upper limbs, the arms, forearms, wrists and hands. At this time, due to knowing this outlay from assuming the pose before, he may analyze the pain to check for the focusing force. He may notice that this power hears, sees and feels some tiny thread-like energies which move in the pain. These currents are bio-electrical energy. They operate the nerves which run through the body from the fingers to the brain.

After a time, again, the yogi will find it necessary to ease from this pose. He will ease the buttocks down to the heels or even between the heels, onto the floor. In an easy pose, he should check the release of tensions. He will meditate to observe what is natural, as contrasted to when he held the pose with tension, which was demanding of his focus.

On Back – Knees Pulled to Floor

The *On Back – Knees Pulled to Floor* position, happens with the curved back as support for the body. It is held in place by the hands, which pull the soles down from the inside. The knees may touch the floor. That depends on the stretch ability of the thigh muscles and knees. The fingers grip the bottom of the feet from the inside. The hands pull the knees to the floor. The head is tilted up as far as the neck will allow.

The yogi should check to determine where energy compiles or scatters. From within the head, the back of the neck, where it connects to the skull, should be observed. If there is confusion of energy, the yogi should pull up the head, press the chin to the throat and wait for clarity.

After this pose is held for a time, it should be gradually released. A relaxed pose should be assumed. The yogi holds that easy pose and meditates. The neck's tautness and its resultant stress will vanish. There will be quietness. The yogi should remain in that state, allowing the system of energies to be in quiescence. This habituates the mind to being in a stress-free, activity-free state.

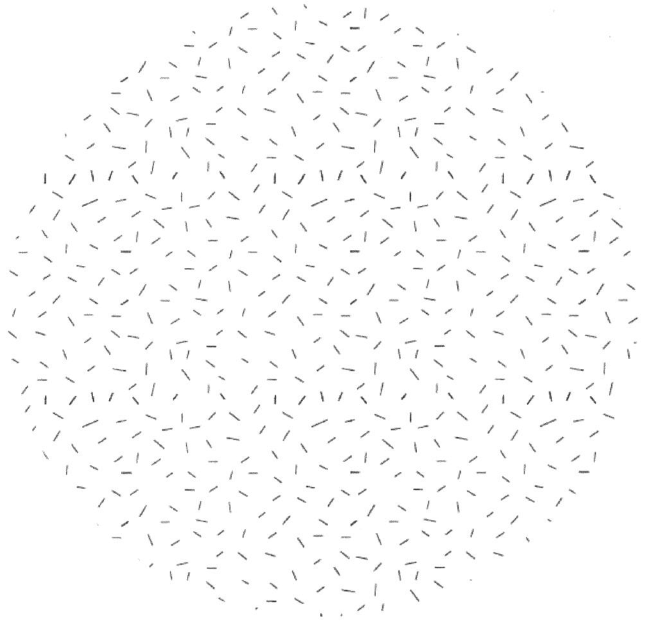

Focus Connection

The *On Back – Knees Pulled to Floor* posture is somewhat difficult. It may not be possible if the yogi has enlarged thighs. It is required that the head be tilted up so that the chin is pressed to the throat. The fingers pull the feet until the knees make contact with the floor. This tenses the body in a lock situation.

If this pose is not done regularly, a yogi will find that when he does it, he realizes that the tendons and muscles tightened. After assuming the post several times over a period of days or week, the body may become flexible, making it possible to do the pose easily.

Even so, usually, there is a strain in the top of the thighs and in the knees. This will disappear after regularly assuming the pose. Then there may be an easy flow of energy through the thighs, and then through the bones of the thighs.

The yogi should get relief from this pose. To do so he should slowly release the hands from the feet. He should release the forward neck lock, allowing the head to rest on the floor. The muscles in the neck, which connect to the back of the skull, should be relaxed.

After relaxing the body, when the yogi feels that he should assume the posture again, he should repeat it. This time it should be easier. He should hold his attention to the back top of the neck, where it connects to the base of the brain. There may be a *samadhi* state assumed. A yogi should check that state. He should note the *samadhi* arrest of his will power and interest energy.

Wheel Pose Setting

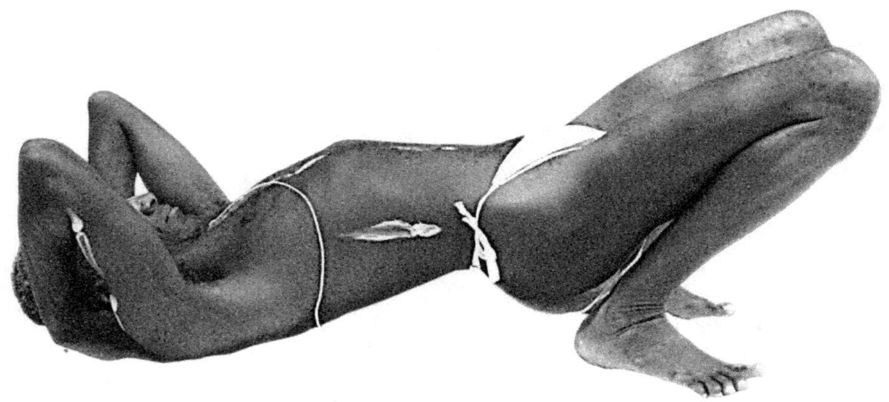

The *wheel pose* has many variations. For this there should be no assistance in raising the body. If one takes assistance, there is the likelihood of causing injury, especially to the spine. Some persons cannot lift the body from this position but if help is given, it becomes possible, except that such help may not take in account, that the vertebrae may be damaged, or a muscle, or tendon may be torn.

Every posture has limits, which set how far one should exert parts of the body. If one is not aware of the limits, the likelihood is injury. There are many risks taken when doing gymnastics and sports. These actions should not be assumed when doing yoga. For instance, when doing the wheel pose which is shown below, the yogi should first lay on the back. Then he/she should draw the feet to the buttocks and draw the palms to the neck. Once this is done, an attempt should be made to gradually raise the body, so that only the feet and hands are the support.

If one attempts to do this, and finds that one cannot, one should complete the attempt by raising the body as far as possible. Then one should hold the body there, and should not try to complete the pose, by pushing all the way up. This partial attempt is satisfactory. One should practice to do it day after day. After a time, one may push up and hold for longer periods. This is how one uses the limits of the body to practice the positions.

If otherwise, one gets the feeling that one should take assistance, by letting someone lift the body, as one pushes up, it is likely, that one will have injury. This may be a severe injury which may or may not heal. A yogi should refrain from this assistance. He/She should instead push to the limit, step by step, over a long or short period of time, which depends on what the body can achieve. It depends on the type of body one got from the parents, as to which postures one can easily assume.

Each person does not have an intuition, which gives instant insight, into the limit of each pose. This means that one may require a teacher, to define the limit. If, however, there is no teacher, one is left to teach oneself. Therefore, caution should be the rule.

The image above is one variation of the wheel pose. In that form, the limit for this particular body is reached. If the yogi elevated more, he would damage the spine, and may even rupture tendons, muscles, and nerves in the body. He risks slipping. His hands and feet are required to hold and not slip. If the body does, there is the likelihood for serious injury.

If a yogi does a certain posture and then ceases to do it for a time, it is normal, then when he resumes it, he will find that he cannot do it, or he cannot do it to its final format. He may have to practice daily for weeks, months, or years, to resume his expertise. This happens because of many factors like loss of elasticity of tendons, muscles, or blood vessels, stiffening of joints, aging of the body, and other factors like dietary excess.

There should be a non-slip surface when doing this pose. If the hands or feet slide during this posture, there is the likelihood of injury. This wheel pose is excellent for toning the vertebrae, and the muscle strands which holds the spine together. However, if precautions are not taken, this pose may cause mishaps. It should be understood that one physical body may do a posture proficiently, while another may do it sloppily.

The feeling that everybody should do every pose, overlooks the fact that there are variations in the production of the infants, in the formative stages, in the parents' forms. Being able to do every form perfectly is no indication of advancement in yoga. This is due to the fact, that yoga has eight sectors. *Asana* posture is one of the stages. Mastering that alone will not secure the complete course.

My opinion is that one should take no assistance when doing this pose. If one takes assistance, one is likely to bypass the limit for one's body. That will result in injury. If the limit for oneself is that one cannot do this posture, then that is the situation which one should accept, due to the limit of the body one got from the parents.

When doing this pose, one should first lay on the back. Then draw the feet near to the buttocks. Move the hands near to the neck. With the hands and feet positioned, one should attempt to elevate the body. If one is unable to, one should repeat the attempt several times. Relax the body downwards several times, if that is all one can do. Consider that as a complete practice of this pose.

Every time one comes down, one should reset the hands and feet. Then try again to raise the body. This effort depends mainly on the hands, forearms, arms, and shoulders. When you attempt this, and do not complete the action of elevating the body, or if you do so partially or fully, then stay up as long as you can, even if it is for seconds only. Then slowly come down to rest the body on its back.

Notice if there is shortness of breath. That is likely because the lungs and diaphragm are restricted and constrained in this posture. Allow the body to reset its breath rhythm.

After making the effort several times or even once, the yogi, should assume an easy pose. Then he should focus within the body for energy movements. There may be naad resonance which may sound like cracking ice. Or it may be a screeching frequency. Be absorbed in that.

Focus Connection

If a yogi fails to safely do the *Wheel Pose Setting* posture, he should do the initial parts of it in steps. Holding the body in each approaching pose, he should focus within the psyche to map the movement of energies which arise from each stage.

The first part of this pose is the laying on the back and drawing the feet as close as possible to the buttocks, while the hands are set under the shoulders. At this point, the yogi should check the internal energies. Then he should adjust the body so that the buttocks are on the heels. This is done by putting the Achilles tendon under the buttocks which are raised slightly.

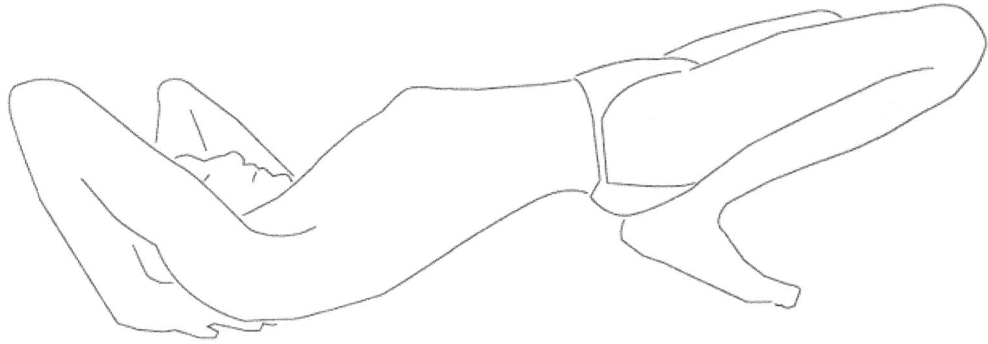

hands under shoulders

buttocks on Achilles tendon

This posture should be done on a non-slip surface. That will secure the body from accidental injury. It allows the yogi to better gage the limit of his flexibility. A yogi should not be idealistic, but should do as much as he can, with respect to his stretching limits. If getting the buttocks on the Achilles tendon is as far as one can do, then this practice stops here, with the yogi meditating to see what the energy does, and how it is arrayed.

There are many muscles, tendons and organs in the trunk of the body and elsewhere. Any of these may be damaged if the yogi is careless, or inattentive. Such injury is unwanted.

The second stage, if the yogi can do it safely, consists of pushing up the arms. This should be done slowly, while internally gaging the limits. If when doing this, there are internal warnings about the possibility of injury, the yogi should cease the lift.

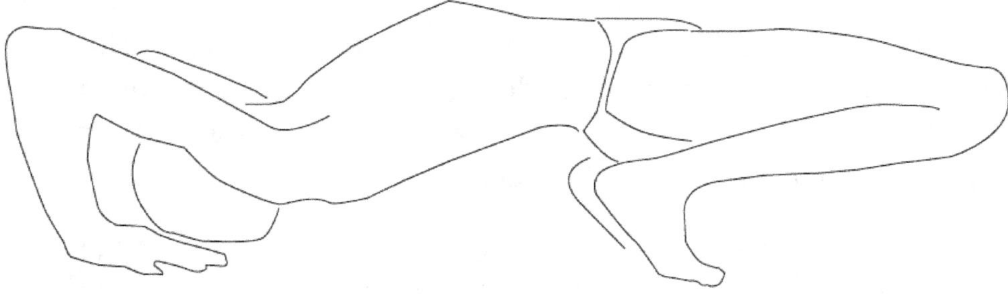

shoulders pushed up
head raise above floor

The next stage is to hold the raised shoulders. Then raise the trunk of the body, where the buttocks are no longer supported by any part of the legs, nor by the heels. A yogi should do this and check to be sure that nothing will be stretched or shifted.

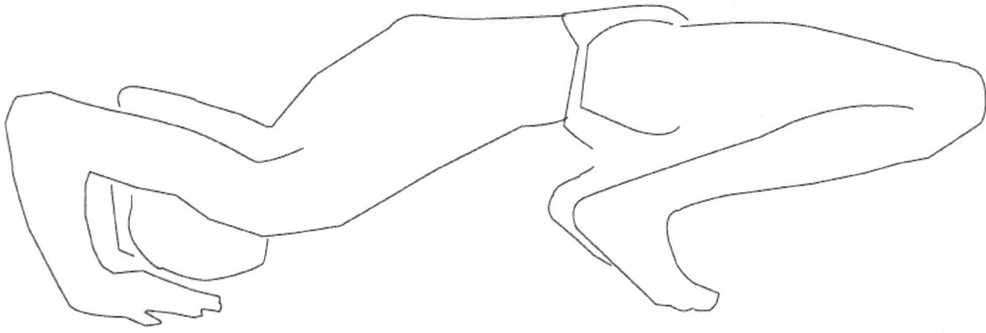

slowly raise buttocks and trunk

He should hold this posture while making a decision about holding it, or pushing the body up further. In this, as it is held attentively, the yogi may feel that the eyes are flushed with blood. He should examine this state to notice if this is a spontaneous and continuous focus. He can align to it, to learn about meditative states.

Back Over Celibate

Many poses are alternate, where one foot, for instance the left limb, is stretched, while the right one stays in an unstretched position. Then the alternate posture is done where the right limb is stretched while the left on stays unstretched.

In most cases, one side of the body may be more supple than the other. When doing that easier side, one will endure less tension. I advise students that when doing alternate poses, begin with the less supple side. Some yogis are of the opinion that each side should be just as fluid as the other. My view is that this is not likely.

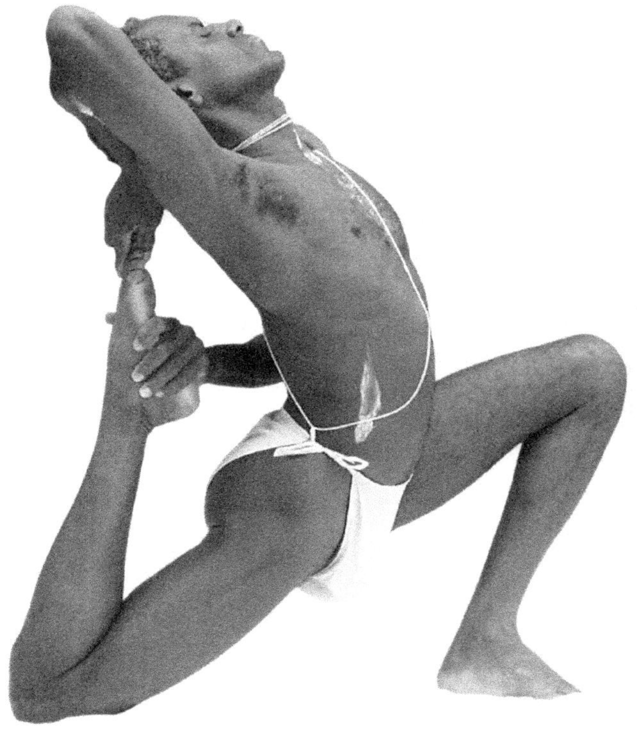

This *Back Over Celibate* pose is an alternate posture. The reverse is done after one side is completed. This is a celibacy discipline. It is best done if the yogi begins the practice, before the body was five years of age. At that time, it is likely to affect the sexual energy formulation in the body. If a yogi began doing this posture before puberty, it is likely that the body itself will be disinclined to pursue sexual interests. It is likely that it will not be eager for sexual targets.

If, however, a yogi begins doing this posture after puberty, he will get some celibate inclination, but it will be partial only. That however is beneficial. This posture involves arching the spine like setting a bow when an arrow is shot from it.

As Nature would have it, a species is required to reproduce. Hence each body develops sexual interest. The critique about this is that in the adult stage, the sexual interest, may dominate the movements of the form. This may cause a preoccupation with sexual quest. That in turn, may foreshadow the research about the duration of the physical system. This lack of interest in the mystery of death, may cause carelessness, which will put someone at a disadvantage.

Nature has a situation of birth, development for sexual participation, sexual expression, elderly condition, and death. However, birth and death are difficult to understand. Due to lack of intellectual development of the birthed infant body, it cannot understand its condition, nor the history of the environment which surrounds its body.

There is death. Due to the termination of faculties over time or abruptly, one does not have the opportunity to study the death process. A living healthy body hardly gives one the ability to analyze death. This means that if one becomes preoccupied only with reproduction, and with the sexual interest which is allied to it, one will be disinclined to investigate death.

This pose concerns arching the body. It should be done carefully. There should be no jerks. The hand which reaches over the shoulder should grab the corresponding foot. If the fingers of that hand cannot do so, this posture cannot be done, until there is more stretching in the thigh, torso, and shoulder. The yogi can try the alternate side. The other hand may reach and hold its corresponding foot.

This is an advance posture. If one fails to do it, one should not be disappointed. In that case, one should practice to arch the back, with the foot gripped with the alternate hand, but without the corresponding hang reaching over the shoulder.

Achieving this posture is a feat. However, focusing within the body to operate the energy releases, which have to do with celibacy, is a special achievement. Due to the bow-like stretching of the arched spine, and due to the tension in the inner thighs, energy from many parts of the body, which usually are released during sexual intercourse, leave the thighs and pubic area of the body, during this pose.

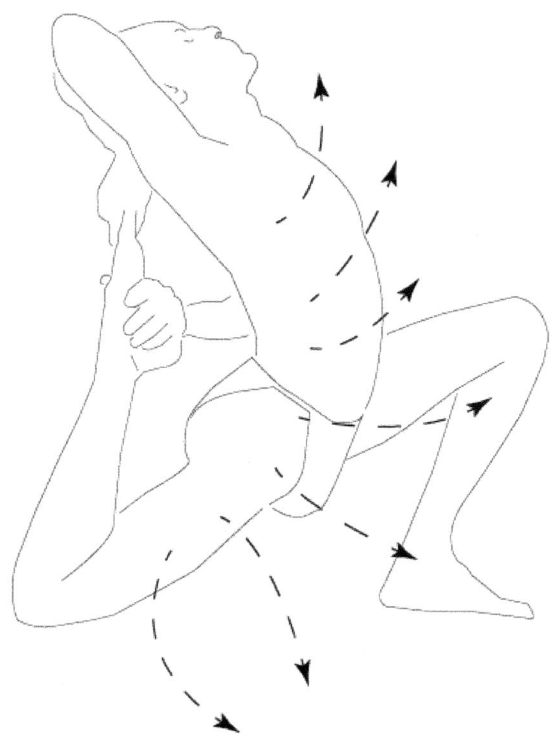

One may or may not understand this focus. Many gymnasts who do this posture in its ideal format, do not know how to direct the inner energies to achieve celibacy. This means that one can master a pose, and have no idea about its use for celibacy. This pose can be done in its proficiency. Still there may be full interest in reproduction and/or sexual expression.

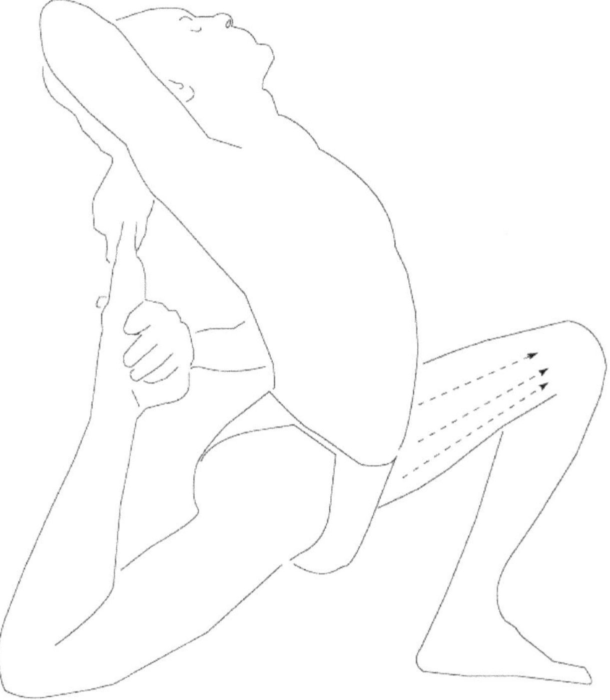

In that diagram, there is energy leaving the forward thigh. That energy targets the knee which is locked into a position which facilitates the rear thigh and the pubic area. Because of the energy which shines from the area where the forward thigh bone connects under the hip, a yogi will notice that energy darts to the knee. A slight rocking action up and down on the torso, will cause the yogi to feel/see this energy. When the yogi withdraws from this posture, the energy which ran to the knee, will itself divert through the thigh into the pelvis joint, where the thigh meets the trunk.

The rear thigh releases energy differently. See this diagram.

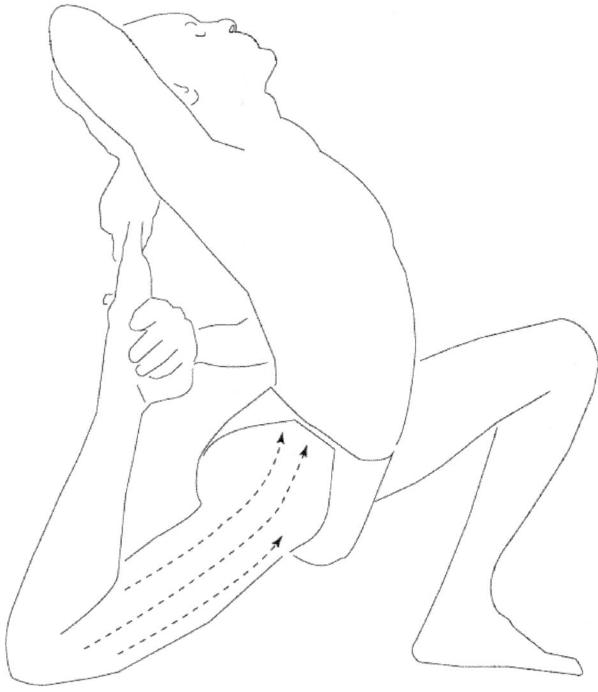

Because of the bow tension, the rear thigh is under a different pressure. The energy in it, runs away from the knee joint into the thigh and into the pelvis area of the same side. Pressing forward causes more release from the thigh. It should be done with care with no injury. Energy will enter the pelvis area and then jump into the lower trunk. That will be captured where the bow stretch is centered. A yogi should stop movements to be sure that the hands clutch the rear foot. He should hold this position, and check within the psyche for energy transitions, and sexual energy shattering. See this diagram.

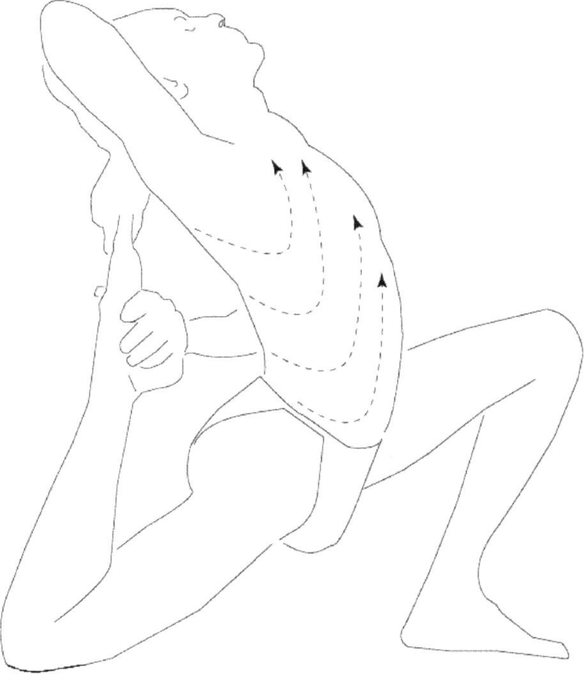

When this position is settled, energy from the thighs will stabilize. The focus will shift into the trunk, where from the arched spine, the nerves and tendons release themselves upward. At first the energy will diverge outwards away from the body. Due to the bow pressure, the energy will diverge upward into the stretched abdomen and chest.

When the pose is set with energies below the neck being stabilized, feelings in the shoulders and front top of the chest, will move into the neck. This means that the reproductive energy that was stored in the pubic zone, was fragmented and relocated, up through the physical and subtle bodies. This decreased the sexual interest. This makes it easy to engage as a sexually-neutral yogi.

Someone who cannot do the bow pose, may do preparatory poses which gradually over time, may allow that person to make his/her current physical body, assume the position. In general, however if the body is in its adult version, but cannot do the bow pose, it will not assume it. This is because of genetic constitution of the body.

Here is a partial posture which can be done, and which will give access to some benefits of doing the full bow pose.

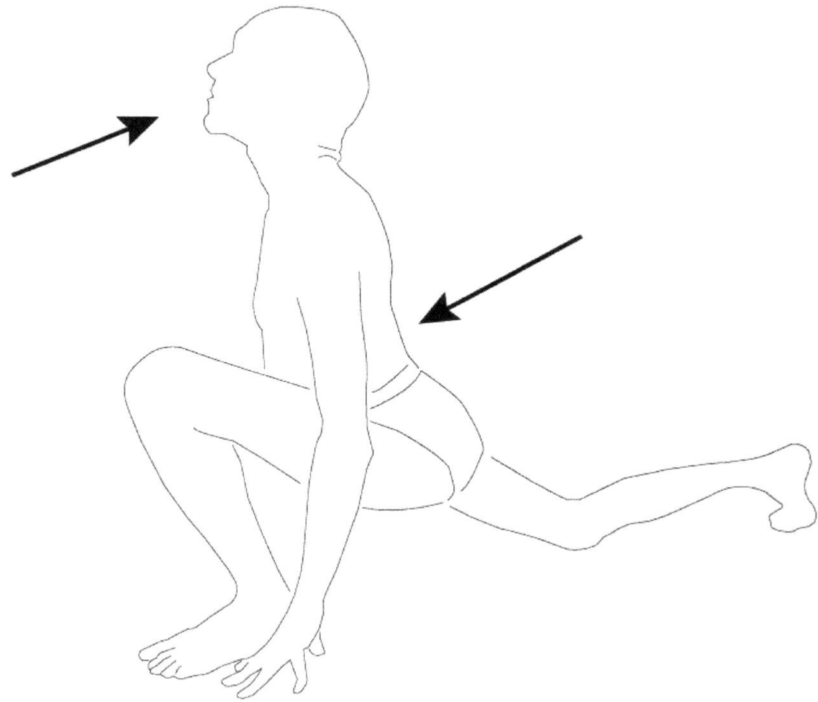

The arrows show where one should apply pressure to the body. Tilt the head back as far as possible. Without over-stretching or over-tensioning, the spine should be pushed forward, as much as one can tolerate. One should hold this pose and shift the forward knee forward. This will cause the corresponding hip to be lowered slightly.

There will be tension where the thighs meet the body, but the stress and focus will be on the thigh of the forward limb. The knee of the foot which is to the rear, may or may not touch the floor. The foot of that rear limb will touch the floor, either with curled toes or the flat foot with toes lying flat.

This is an alternate posture. One side is done. Then, the yogi does the converse. He should note that one side is easier to assume than the other. In that case, when he does this practice again, he should begin with the more difficult side. The easy side should be done as the last of the alternate postures.

This below is another preparation for the bow pose. This is where the yogi applies a stress to the trunk of the body, so that it is pressed forward like the arched part of a bow,

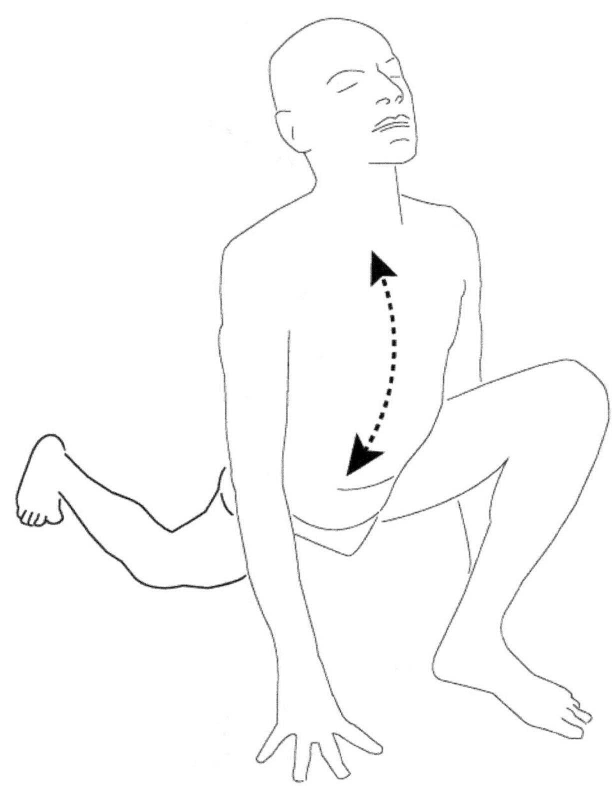

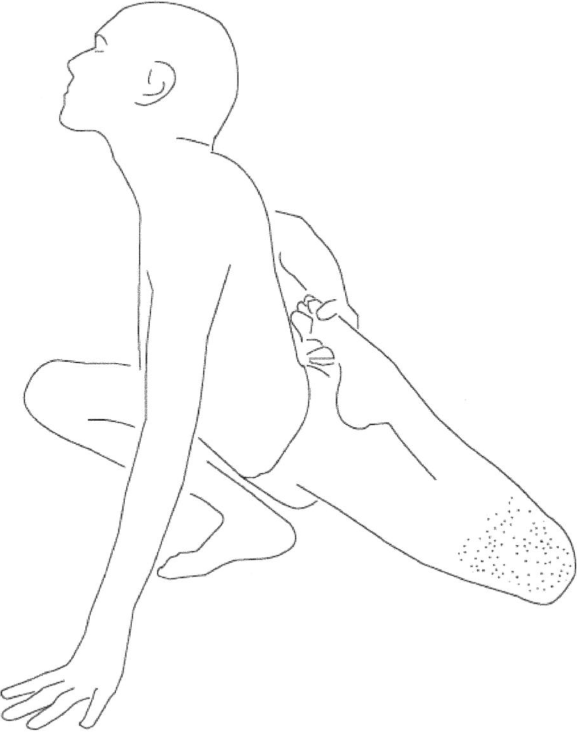

That above is another variation of the bow pose. The focus is on the thigh and spine. The thigh being stretched is the rear one. The primary tendons and muscles of this focus, is where the thigh connects to the rear knee. When this is done, there is release of energy from where the thigh and knee connect. This energy will dart upward through the thigh. The format of the energy will be like strings of psychic electricity. The yogi should pull the rear foot to the body. He should press to create a tension in the lower hip, the pelvis complex.

When this is done to satisfaction, the focus of the practice changes. The yogi should press forward on the front foot. This will cause an adjustment of the rear knee. There may be an urge to shift the forward foot. This shift should be done without upsetting any other part of the body.

Where the rear thigh is connected to the pelvis area, one may feel three tough tendons. This may be an electrical flash. Inner vision which is subjective, may cause this to be experienced as a strand of white energy, which vanishes in the middle of the thigh.

The yogi should raise the chin, and press the head back as far as possible. To some extent, a yogi is self-trained. Physical assistance from an advanced ascetic should be subsidized with psychic assistance. With that there will be occasions when a yogi is inspired by the practice itself. Ideas of posture will flash into the mind of the yogi. He will do postures which he was not shown by any physical or psychic teacher. Some practice which becomes evident in the mind, may be from astral yogis, from whose psyches, those processes emerged.

Focus Connection

When practicing the *Back Over Celibate* posture, a yogi who was proficient, may discover that due to the aging condition of the body, he can no longer assume that position. In fact, this may happen for other postures as well. As the body ages certain irreversible transformations occur. That will be noted by a yogi. Then, he must make an agreement with Nature to accept the inabilities.

The way for this, is to do a variation of a difficult posture, which was mastered prior, but which can no longer be done, due to muscle, tendon, bone and nerve adjustments, which Nature imposes on the body. For instance, this particular, *Back Over Celibate* pose was achieved by this teacher. Then at a certain time, for some years after the body was at about sixty-five years of age, the writer found that its final form could not be assumed.

In consultation with Yogeshwarananda, some stops in the assumption of the posture were revealed. Three such stops will be illustrated. Each should be considered to be a completed posture, rather than having the idea, that these are part of a posture, or that each is a part of the process of completing the posture. As they are, with no idea that these may be developed into any other posture, these should be regarded as completed positions. It means that each is a posture in its own right. Mentally, a yogi should have that idea of these forms as completed postures.

Here is the first of the three. Regard this first one as a posture, which is itself a complete yoga form, which is developed further.

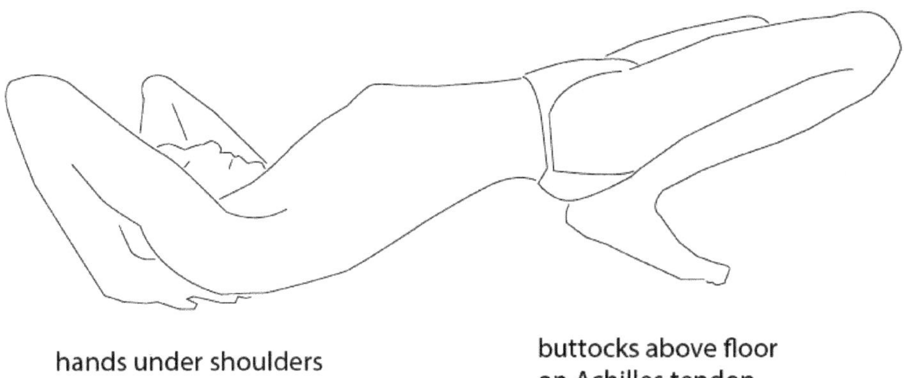

In that first of the three variations, the hands are under the shoulder. The buttocks however are above the floor, and are on the Achilles tendons. The yogi should be content doing this much. He should assume this and meditate to determine its energy outlays.

Now we can consider another posture, the second of the three variations. Again, the yogi should assume this posture but only if his body can safely hold itself in that position. In that situation, the head is slightly lifted from the floor. The buttocks are above the floor but they are in contact with the Achilles tendons.

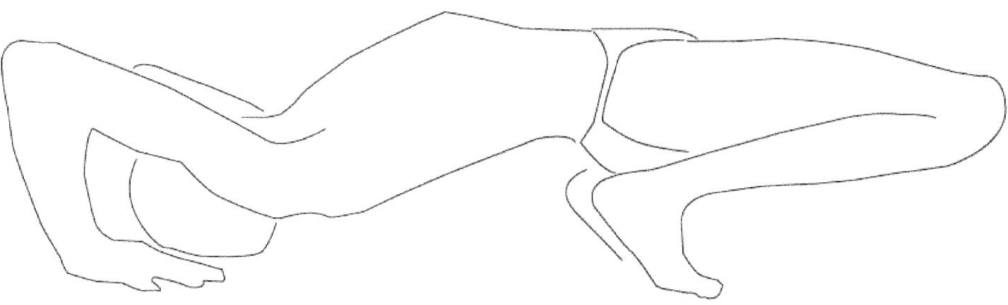

Being satisfied to assume this posture, considering it to be a final form, the yogi should meditate to map what happens in the subtle body. He should examine every part of the psyche. There should be no anxiety about not assuming the final form.

In the third posture, the yogi should raise the shoulders, head and buttock such that the head is above the floor. The shoulders are raised somewhat. The buttocks are raised further above the Achilles tendon. In that posture, the yogi should meditate. He should perceive the energies which are in motion, and the ones which are immobile, but are present.

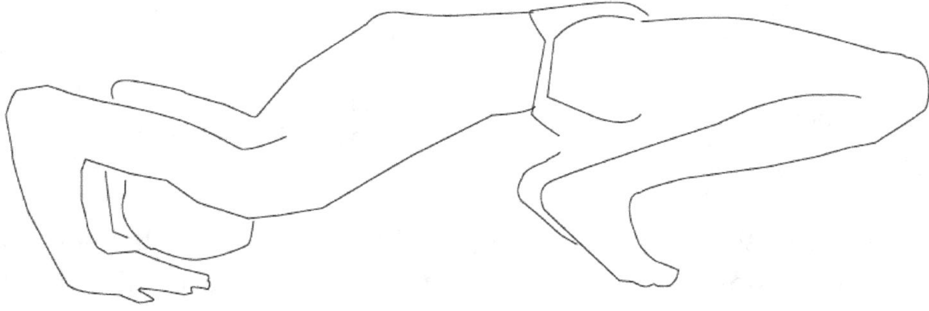

slowly raise buttocks and trunk

Bow / Two-Hand Stretch

That *Bow / Two-Hand Stretch* is a variation of the bow pose, with adaptations made over a period of several years. This took so long, because the design of this body from the parents, was not suited to some *asana* postures in their final forms. Some poses will never be perfected with this body. That is due to natural limitations.

The lower hand which uses its thumb to hold the rear foot, does so with the least grip. The upper hand is over its shoulder. It touches the lower hand. Both knees touch the floor

When one sees this image, there should be questions.

- Where is the inner focus during this pose?
- What energy is released?
- Did the yogi know what happened during the assumption of this position?
- Is the focus too complex to sort?
- What are the limits for safety of the body?

The lower hand touches both the upper hand and the foot. The spine is pressed forward. Due to that action, energy from the torso radiates through the arched trunk.

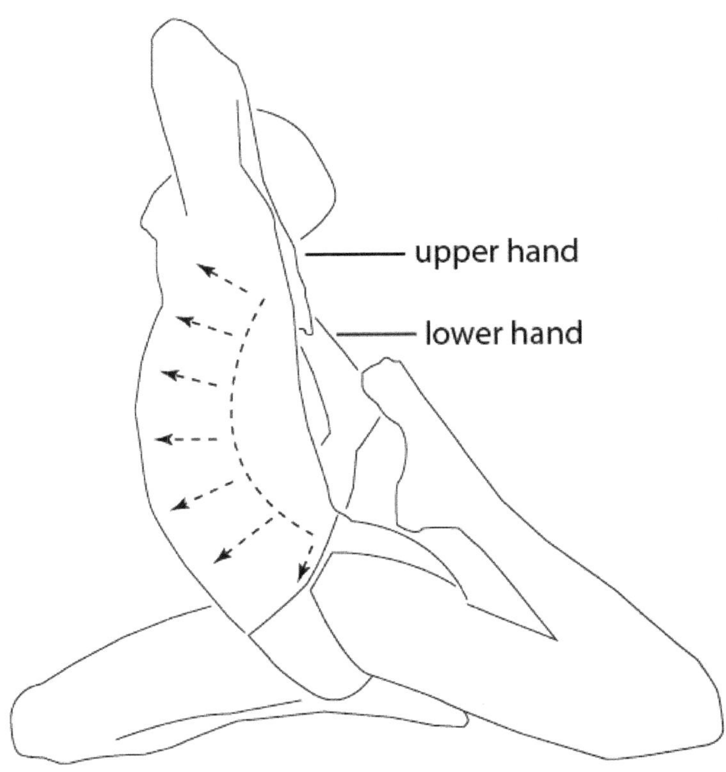

Focus Connection

The *Bow / Two-Hand Stretch* is a celibate posture. It does not yield the celibate potential if it is done without *pranayama* breath infusion. Someone may do this proficiently, and become more involved in sexual expression. That is because the posture may release much sexual energy in the physical and subtle systems, but not allow the person to redirect the released energy. It may cause release, and then it may reformat the energy for increased sexual interest.

Breath infusion should be done during, and immediately after doing this pose. Then the released sexual energy would be surcharged with fresh air, and be directed away from the sexual machinery.

In this posture, the initial achievement is for a hand to grab the opposing foot from the back. After that, the yogi should check to be sure that the legs and knees are positioned firmly, and will accommodate the balance of the body.

As soon as the yogi is certain that every part is positioned firmly, he should put the free hand over its shoulder. That hand should hold a finger, fingers or the hand which is in the back by the head. It may be that the hand is grabbed or some fingers, or just a single finger. This should be held. Then again, the yogi should check for steadiness.

There may be trembling and shivering. If that is unbearable, the yogi should release the pose. He should do so gradually, and with care, so as not to cause injury.

If at any time during this posture, the yogi finds that there is trembling and shivering, he should analyze, to determine if he can hold the pose safely. If he is uncertain, he should slowly release the pose. While doing this, his attention should be inside the psyche. If possible, he should determine the cause for the instability.

It could be that during this pose, there is uncertainty in the thigh, especially at the place where the knee contacts the floor. The yogi may need a cushion under the knee.

There may be a release of energy in the armpit, where the arm and shoulder meet. Arm muscles may shiver. The hand should hold the other hand. If there is insufficient reach, some fingers may grip only some fingers of the other hand. One finger may somehow contact and grip another. Even with a single finger from each hand, there may be sufficient grip to hold this pose. The movements should be deliberate and slow, both in making contact, or in releasing the hold.

If a yogi cannot do a posture, he should do the portions of it which he can safely assume. That is sufficient. The forward foot placement is important in the balance used during this pose. The forward foot should be put in the optimum position to afford as much balance as it can bear. The yogi should shift the forward foot to set it for maximum weight distribution.

When the yogi relaxes the body out of this pose, he should sit on the heels and check the energy reassignment which occurs. Much of the energy will retreat from the places it penetrated during the pose. A yogi should note that behavior.

Examine the posture which is after this paragraph. One shows the front posture. The other shows it from the rear. This posture can be used if the yogi cannot do the *Bow / Two-Hand Stretch* pose. If this can be done easily, this will be a final posture, in which the meditation is practiced. Notice that the forward foot is under the palm of the corresponding hand, while the other hand is placed on the floor. From the back, one can see that the rear foot is as far back as possible. With eyelids closed, or with a blindfold on the face, the yogi should focus within to track the energies.

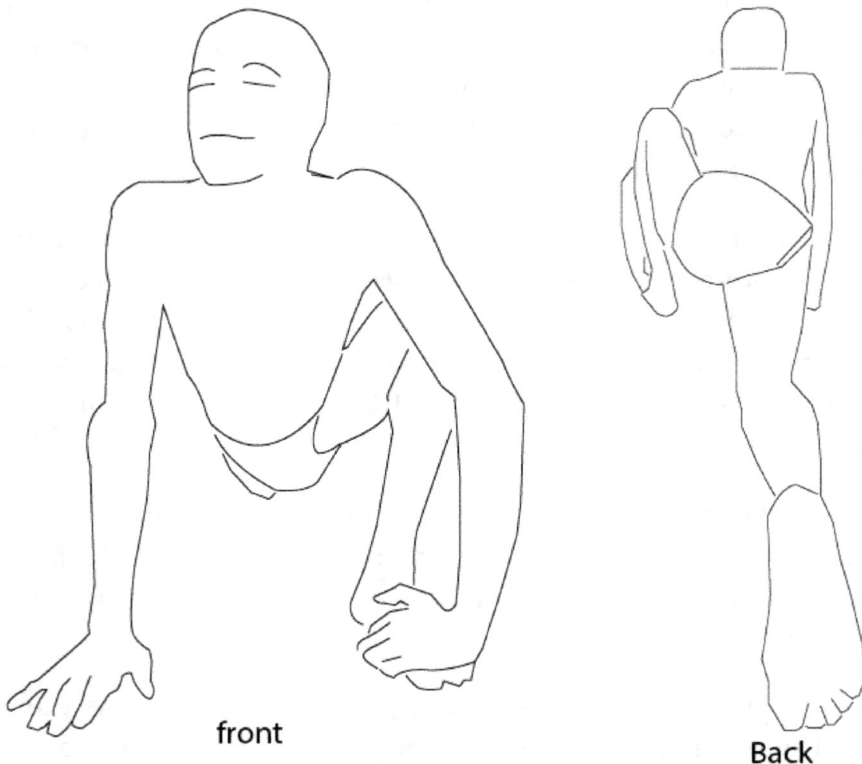

Check the posture, which is after this paragraph. That is more strenuous. In that, one hand is used for weight support. The other pulls the opposite foot from the back. This can be a strenuous. A yogi who can do this, should regard it as a final form.

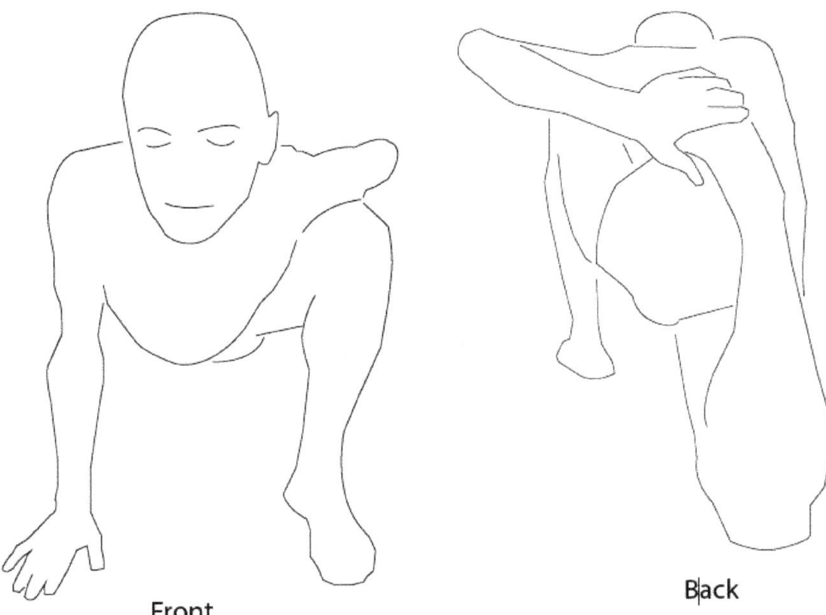

The gist is to use the forward foot for balancing. Be sure that the forward hand and the rear foot are placed for the best stability. The knee which is folded should be positioned properly. Take care. Be attentive when doing this.

Standing – Hips Pressed

For this *Standing – Hips Pressed,* stand with feet apart, set for steadiness. Press hands on each corresponding hip. Press the hip bones. Pull up abdomen. Pull back abdomen. Retract abdomen contents under rib cage. Press chin to throat without tilting the head.

Close eyelids if there is no blindfold. Apply focus through the body. Go down with focus as if descending in an elevator. Reach the bottom of the trunk. Pull the anus lock and the perineum areas.

Find the central trunk. There may be energy going there. This may be like liquid going into a pipe. After a short time, naad resonance may beam in the psyche.

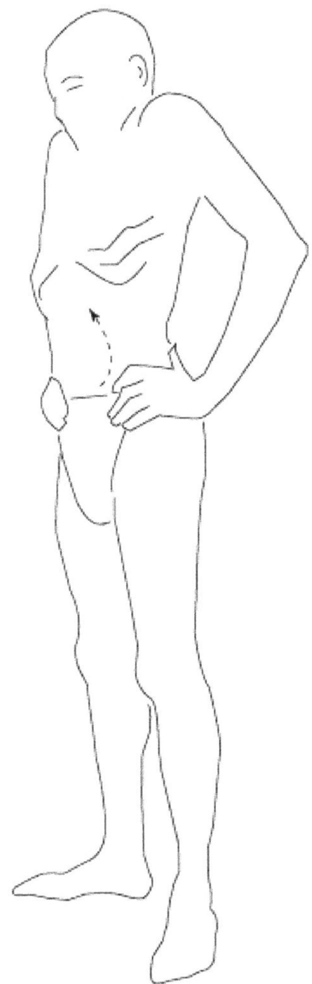

Focus Connection

Doing the *Standing – Hips Pressed* posture, is relatively easy. In the advanced stage, it is more complicated due to the locks which may be applied, and the energy tracking which is controlled.

While the eyelids are closed and inner focus is applied, checks should be made mentally. The chest should be raised. The position of the chin should be checked. It should be pressed to the throat, except that the head should not be tilted forward. With the chest raised, the chin compressed inward, and the neck erect, the yogi should feel a hollow which is like a bowl.

The trunk complex should be lifted with the urinary, sex and anal situations pulled up. The hands should press the hips. The yogi should check to be sure that the compressions and locks are amply applied.

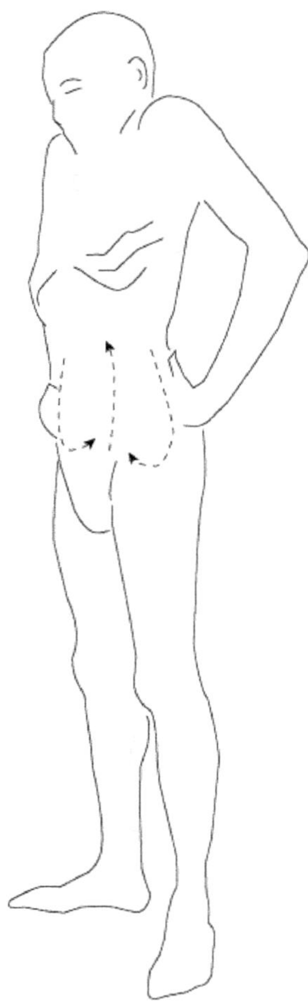

When this standing posture can no longer be held, the yogi should slowly sit on a chair. The spine should remain erect. The hands should relax on the thighs. The yogi should meditate to explore the energies.

Standing Squat

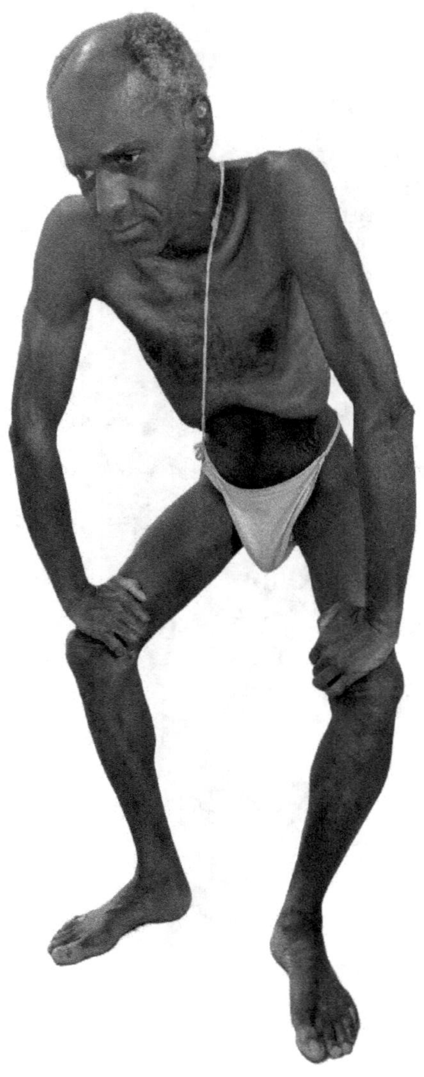

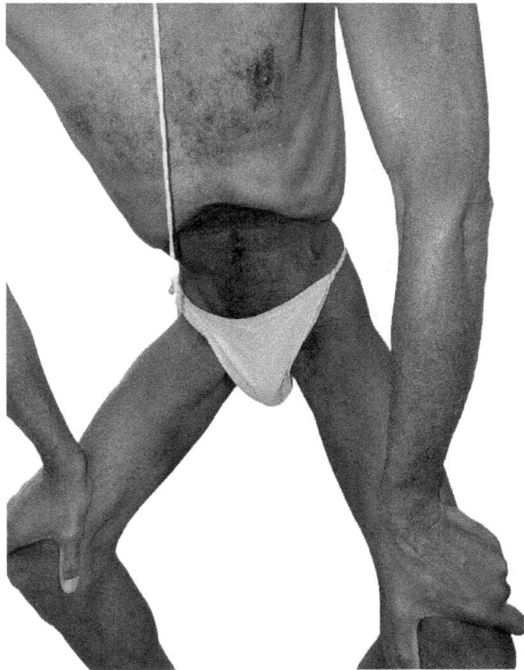

This is a *standing squat*. It is an easy posture which requires that the feet be set apart to accomplish balance. Stand. Position feet wide apart for steady balance. Lower buttocks by bending at knees. Place hands on thighs near knees. The elbows should be arched. Check the focus of the self. Be sure that the lower abdomen is pulled. Focus through the body. The yogi should use a blindfold or close the eyelids. This is to prevent the mind from pursuing visuals outside the body.

There should be no muscular tension. If there is any, make an effort to relax that part of the body. Check on the breath rhythm. After every three cycles of breathing, exhale through the mouth and inhale through the nostrils. That exhale should be a slow long push of air, part by part, until the lungs have no more air to discharge. Then breathe normally for three breaths. Then do the exhale through the mouth again.

After doing this for four or more cycles, stand. Put hands on hips. Meditate while standing. Check on the status of the energy in the psyche. Make a mental note about the condition of the energy, about its scattering or focusing.

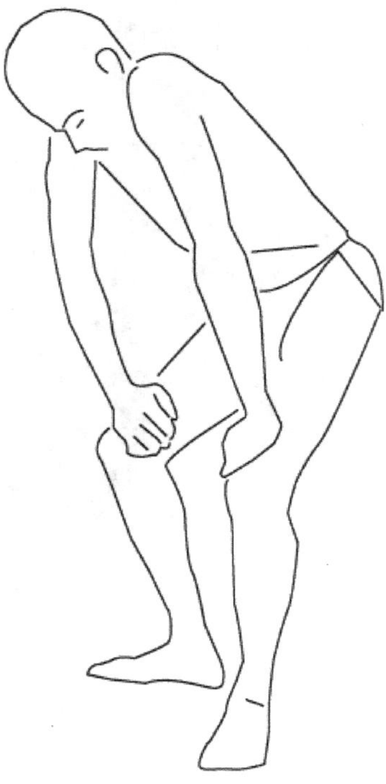

Focus Connection

Even though, the *Standing Squat* posture is simple. Its inner format is complicated. At first there may be tensions in the shoulders where the arms are pivoted into the shoulder bones. Some other locations may be sensitive. It may be such that the yogi has to investigate to isolate the tensions.

Even though there may be pain in this posture, it may be difficult to pin the source of it. A yogi, even one who practiced *asana* postures, may find this posture to be challenging. Some postures produce direct and obvious tensions, and focus-demanding locations in the body, and psyche. This one may not. Instead, it may produce a confusion so that the yogi must patiently search, to identify and sort the layouts.

After a time in this pose, the yogi should relax. It may be that the hands slide on the thighs, or the feet feel uncertain. Then the yogi should relax in some way which eases the tension. He should assume a posture or even sit, but in a slow way, without disturbing the array. He should note if the format changes.

If for instance, the yogi sits on the floor, between the heels, he should check in the psyche, to map how the energy became rearranged. There may be a rocking motion from front to back, but not from side to side. This may be so slight as to be hard to notice. After this relaxation is finished, the yogi should stand. If the floor is slippery, he should move to a gripping surface. If his hands slide on the thighs, he should dampen the palms to increase their grip.

With that he should again focus within as he holds the *Standing Squat*. He should check every part of the body to ascertain the energy format. Again, he should relax while keeping focus within the psyche.

Headstand Partial

The *headstand* is a famous posture. Many famous *asana* yogis demonstrated this form of up-turning the human body. It was recommended for numerous ailments. It has a legendary but questionable reputation as a health-fix for many diseases. The mystery of it!

I admit that even though when I first began doing the headstand, with this physical body, I aspired to master it, still I did not regularly do it.

Why? Due to the fact, that I did not get a benefit from it, which justified continuing it. There are however, two realizations concerning the physical body which I culled from the headstand.

- muscles in the neck support the head
- sense of balance can be cultivated

The muscles in the neck support the head. As soon as the body is upturned, where the weight of the body is supported by the head, one realizes that the neck is what transits the weight of the skull and brains. Since Nature designed the neck to support only the weight of the head, the assumption of a headstand, where the majority weight must transit through the neck, will be a strain on the neck.

When doing the headstand, the question of balance in reference to gravity, must be figured. This causes a yogi who does the headstand, to consider how to set the hands, forearms, and arms, to assist the head in maintaining balance. If the yogi cannot stabilize the body during the headstand, it will fall in one way or the other, according to the pull of gravity.

There are many ways to do the headstand. Each of these have the head as the central support. The hands, forearms and arms may be positioned in various places in reference to the head. I suggest that once the head, arms, forearms, and hands are set, the yogi should slowly lift the feet from the floor. He should stabilize the body by remaining with the feet close to the floor, but not touching the surface. When the body is stabilized there, move the feet higher. Stabilize it. Move the feet further up. Stabilize it. If there is imbalance, keep the feet there. Do not raise them again until the body is stabilized. Remain in the position where the instability was felt. Lower the feet slowly until they touch the floor.

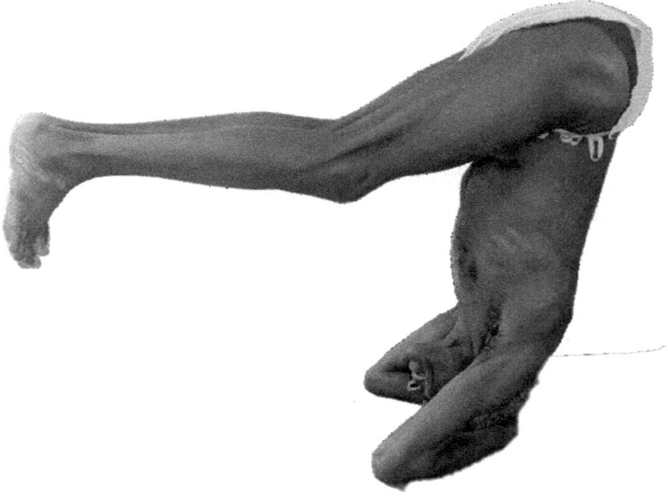

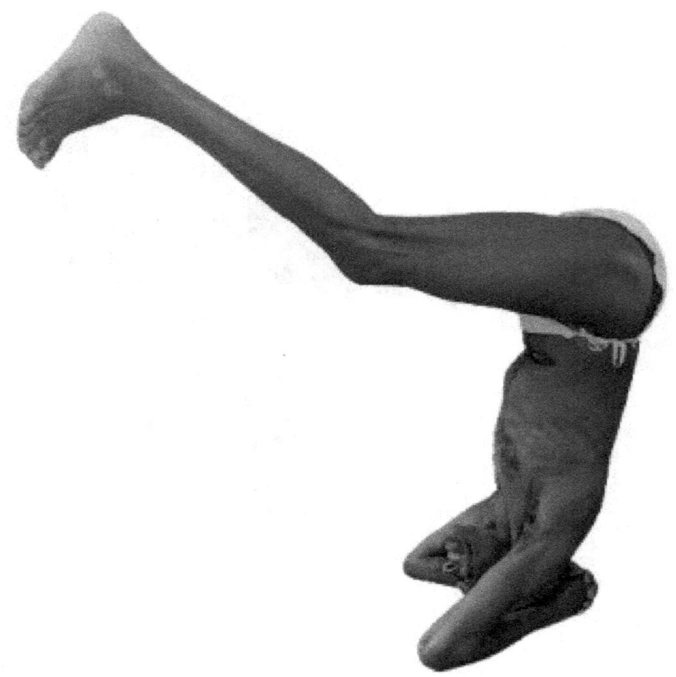

For the next session of practice, begin at the lowest position, with the feet lifted from the floor. Raise them in increments, until reaching where you cannot hold the stability. Come down slowly, very slowly. Do this day after day, so that stability is acquired in every lift position before lifting higher. When coming out of the headstand, always come out gradually, not suddenly.

During the practice of headstand, make no sudden movements. Observe what happens in the body, regarding the muscles and tendons stretching. By going through each stage slowly and being attentive, one avoids injury.

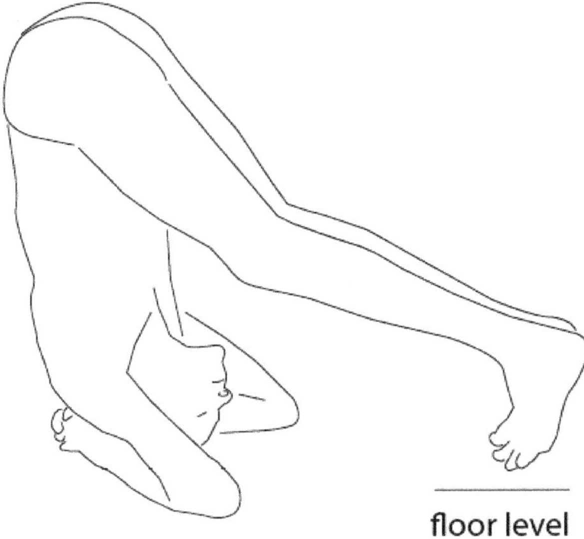

The partial headstand may be done with the feet being only two inches from the floor. The headstand does not have to be with the legs straight up. Notice that the hands are supportive of the head even though the hands are interlocked. The forearms assist, as well as the arms, to bear some weight of the body. The neck participates as the main weight bearing contact.

Some *asana* yogis demonstrated the headstand with the lower limbs in *padmasana* lotus posture. That however does not change the weight bearing duties of the neck, arms, forearms, and hands. A yogi should be careful that his practice does not become like that of a gymnast.

Focus Connection

The *Head Stand Partial,* described above, is a posture which requires stability, muscle control and inner focus. Each stage of it, should be considered as a completed pose. A yogi should not feel that the final form of this pose or any pose for that matter, is the only posture which will yield inner estimation. Each stage of lifting the body, is itself a practice, with specific benefits, which may or may not be present in the final position.

A series of nine (9) stages are illustrated below. At the first, the yogi should pause and investigate the spread of energies. There are many situations for the hands when doing the head stand. Each yields a particular energy spread. The yogi should note the spread that is perceived, while remaining in one or the other lift positions. As it is illustrated below, examine the first step in one variation. In that posture, the hands support is the clasped hands which are placed cupping the head.

A yogi remains in this pose for a time, before proceeding to lift the body. There is no strain. There may be a smattering of light flashing from the head and chest. Provided the yogi is focused internally, this will be noticed. He should accept the experience. He should have no anxiety as to the source of the psychic motion. After a time, a short period, he should decide to assume the next action. This *Head Stand Partial 1* should be regarded as a complete posture.

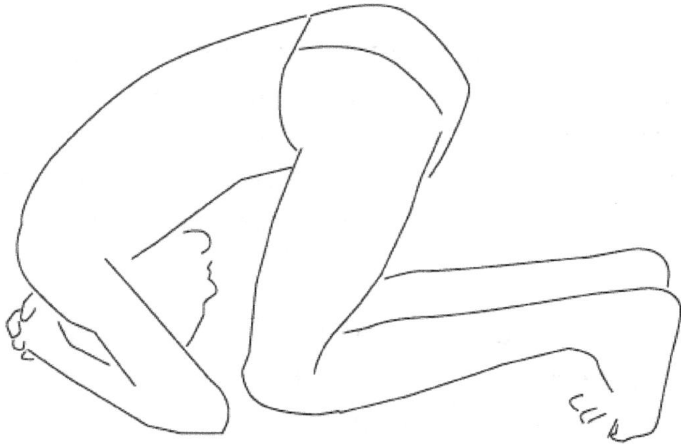

Head Stand Partial 1

The second position is illustrated below. It is the *Head Stand Partial 2,* The yogi begins at the first posture and remains in that for a time, then he pushes the knees up.

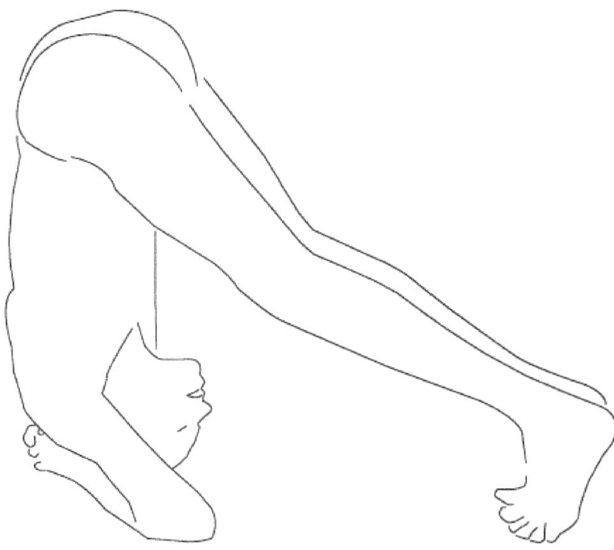

Head Stand Partial 2

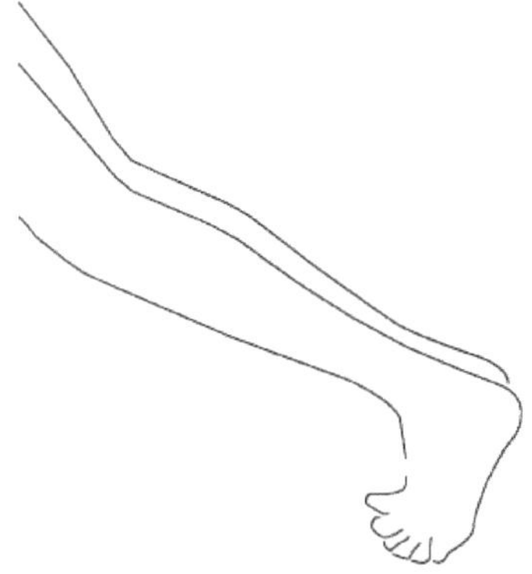

The toes remain in place. The buttocks and spine adjust as the knees straighten. That posture may be strenuous. It depends on the tightness of certain muscles and tendons. Yogis with bodies which have much fatty tissue, may strain in this posture. For such ascetics, this may be the final phase of this pose.

Once this posture is assumed, the yogi should study it internally. He checks every part of the psyche to determine the energy spread, and study what it reveals, about the linking of each energy zone. There will be weight transfer through the feet. The spine will express a spreading deposit which goes downward.

Look at the following diagram.

Head Stand Partial 4

In the *Head Stand Partial 4,* the yogi should tilt the body backward. The toes get some relief. In turn, this increases the pressure which pulls the weight through the trunk. The neck is prepared to accept the weight of the feet, legs, thighs and trunk.

There is an intermediate posture which is a slow moving one. Examine the posture below.

Head Stand Partial 3

When doing this, there is a walking action, to bring the spine to an upright position. Many students are hasty to performing the walking action. In some bodies when this is done, because of the proportions of the limbs, the person cannot walk to an upright position. Thus, some persons make a sudden jerk to get the trunk to be upright. However, that is not recommended. It shatters the observational benefit one gets from making no sudden movements. Any part of the *Head Stand Partial* pose should be done, with neither jerks nor sudden movements.

Look at the walking up movements of the toes.

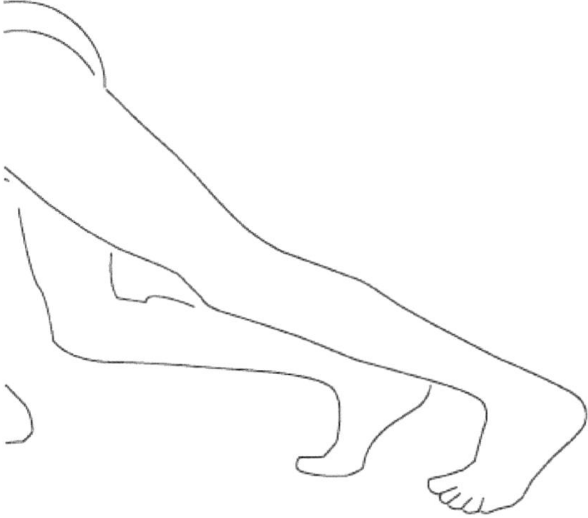

In slow motion, one foot after the other, the yogi should walk so that the feet get closer and closer to the head. There will come a point where one's attention will shift to the spine. This is because the weight of the body will require the toes to be lifted from the floor. This will require attention to set the body in a balanced situation, with the lower limbs hanging from the torso, where the limbs carry no weight, where all weight is borne by the trunk.

That situation with the lower limbs hanging from the torso, is illustrated as *Head Stand Partial 4*. Observe that the trunk of the body is tilted back slightly. This is required because it allows the weight to pass through the spine and neck. There is no weight passing through any part of the foot to the floor.

Head Stand Partial 4

In doing that Head Stand Partial 4 posture, the yogi will remain in it for a time. This requires stability and focus. Many students do not remain in this pose. Instead, they pass through this pose rapidly. They find it difficult to tolerate the hanging of the lower limbs. The recommendation is however, that one should remain in this pose, treating it as a final posture. This is both a transit pose, in a sequence of doing the Head Stand, and it is a pose by itself.

In this pose there may be shivering of the lower torso, the buttocks and thighs. This is a gravity stabilization posture. The yogi's full attention is required to hold this. He should use this pose to study the *dhyana* spontaneous focus which occurs. He should be absorbed in it. It is a final pose. There is advancement to be made in the study of trance state in this pose. A yogi should not be hasty to bypass nor to neglect the study of the energy situations in this pose. This is a final pose!

The next in the sequence of these partial or final poses, concerns raising the lower limbs to be parallel to the floor. The weight of the elevated limbs hangs from the lower torso. The spine is tilted slightly. That offsets the hanging weight. This causes some shivering in the torso. The yogi must be attentive to be sure that the body does not fall. This is a final position where the lower limbs hang at ninety degrees (90^0) from the torso. The hands must bear responsibility for the centering of the body.

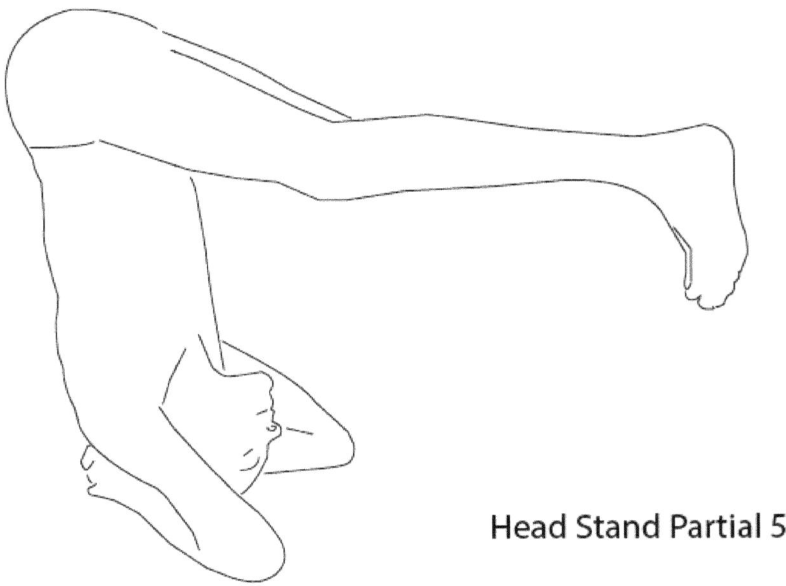

Head Stand Partial 5

The *Head Stand Partial 5* pose, has manifold benefits. It displays a *samadhi* spontaneous state for meditative absorption. A yogi can learn *samadhi* by studying the energy outlay in this pose. Examine it. Check the energy where the thighs are connected to the buttocks. Check the neck's attitude. Carefully analyze it.

In the next posture, the *Head Stand Partial 6,* while on the way down from the highest part of the head stand, the yogi would stop for meditative contemplation. Instead of being excited to relax from the posture, he will use the opportunity to stop and examine the situations, which each part of the posture entrails.

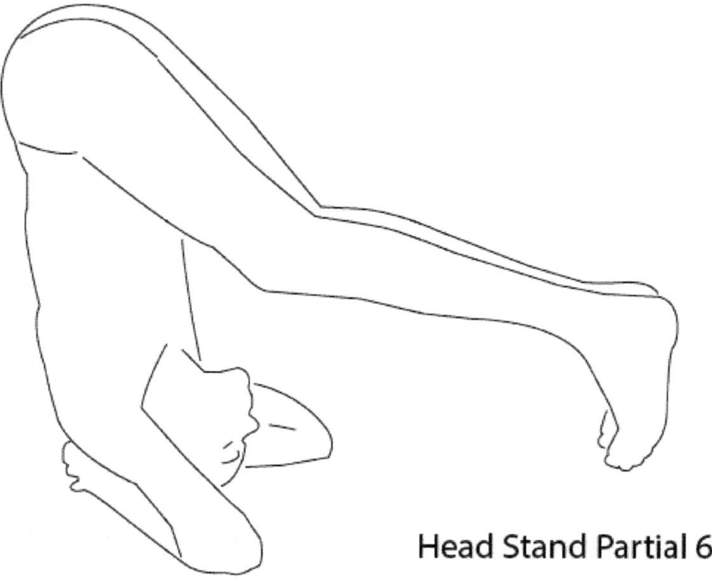

Head Stand Partial 6

The first confrontation he will have, is the need to unfold the posture. There will be a need to lower the feet to the floor. The neck and shoulders will cry for relief. Patience is required to convince the body to stop the descent, and bear the anxiety which is present.

In the next posture, the *Head Stand Partial 7,* the feet make contact with the floor.

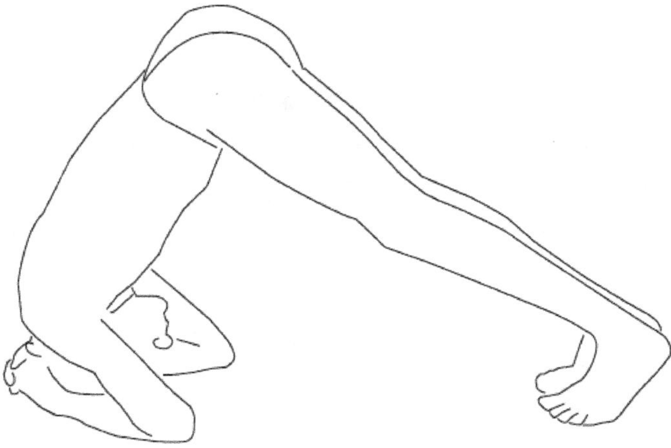

Head Stand Partial 7

This will provide some relief. The yogi should observe from within the psyche, how various energy configurations scatter and disappear, while some reorganize with other formats to create new patterns. Energy runs from the torso and neck into the thighs. The knees propose relief. The knees realize that tension runs through them in both directions. They send nerve messages about that crisis.

When he tries to meditate in this posture, he does not recognize the formations. He must study them and map their situations. This is different to how this posture operates on the way up in the headstand.

In the next posture, *Head Stand Partial 8,* there is a slight difference.

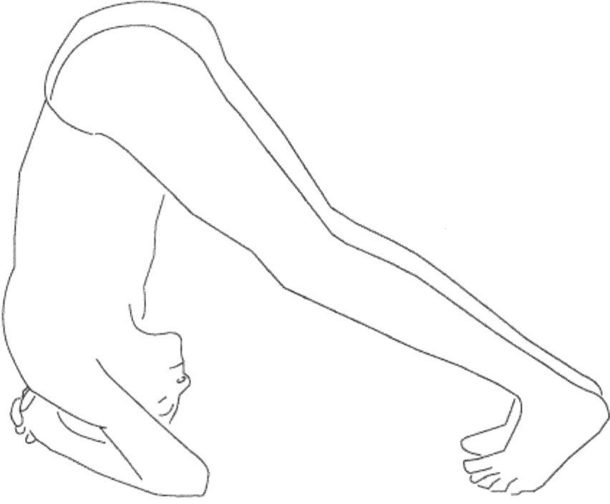

Head Stand Partial 8

This posture is not identical to *Head Stand Partial 7.* The difference is that there is a slight relaxation of the knees. The knees bend slightly. Keeping the knees tensioned which means tensioning the thighs and legs, requires special focus. By relaxing the knees even slightly, the focus energy must rearrange itself. Some of it converges into the knees. Some other part, spreads from it. The attentive yogi should map this.

The final posture for inspection is the total relaxation of the knees. This is shown in the *Head Stand Partial 9,* below.

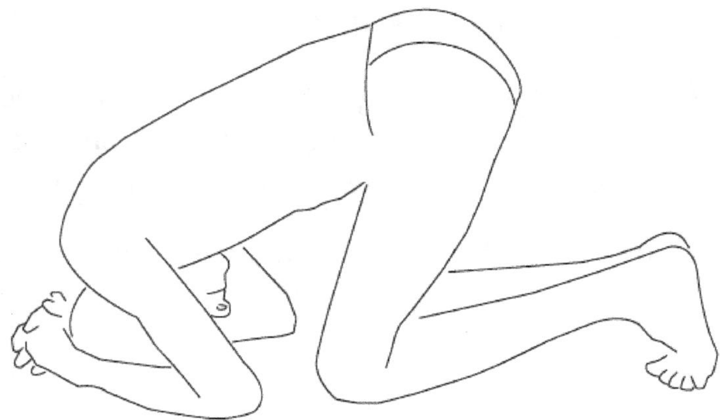

Head Stand Partial 9

The yogi should remain in that position for a time. This is a meditation posture which yields a lightshow of flashing energies moving here and there in the psyche. Eventually the configuration will be one of stillness. The yogi can sit on the heels and enter an absorption.

135-degree Balance Headstand

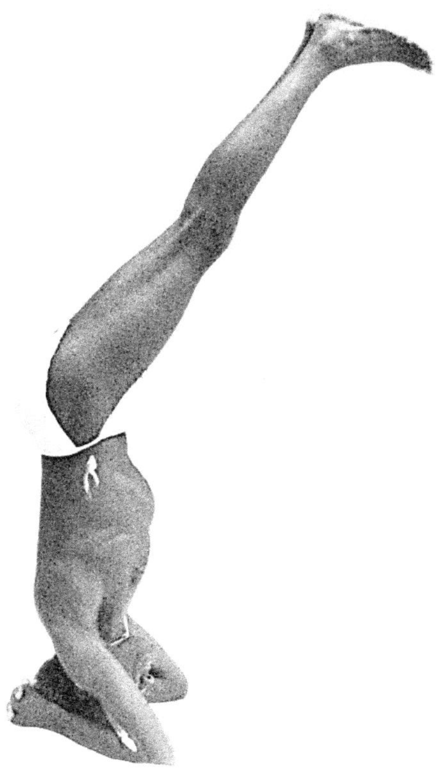

For this *135-degree Balance Headstand* posture, the yogi should focus on balancing the body on the skull, neck, clasped-fingers, and forearms. Each step of the way in raising the lower limbs (feet, legs, and thighs) should be accomplished from one balanced position to a higher balanced position. One should not move to a higher position, if a lower one is not steadied. It may take days, weeks, or months, before one can do a steady vertical lift. This depends on the genetic situation of one's body.

The next diagram shows the shaded area which is stabilized. The yogi gets to this situation with the lower limbs slanted. He steadied this posture for a time. Then he lowers the lower limbs slowly with no sudden actions. All the while, he keeps the balance and controlls the limbs for a slow descend. This practice continues daily until the body remains steady, so steady that he is confident to raise the lower limbs higher, or to raise them steadily to a full vertical position.

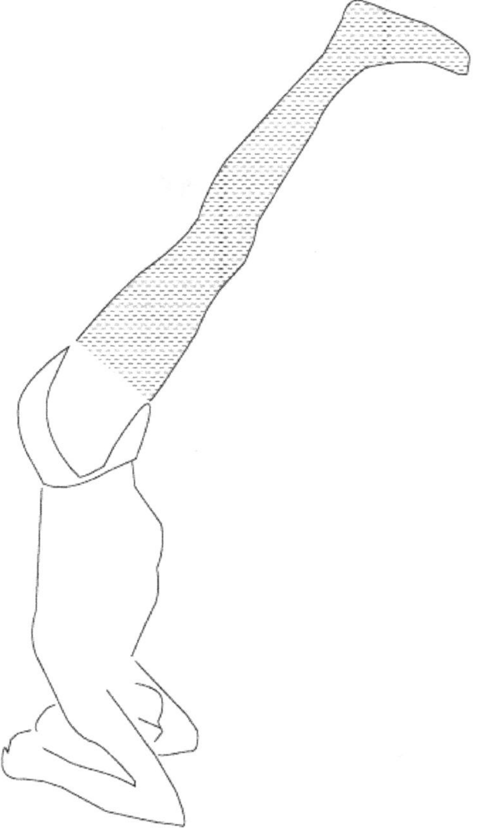

Focus Connection

The *135-degree Balance Headstand* has the previous feature pose, which is the *Head Stand Partial,* as its precursor. I showed *five stops* on the way up to the 90-*degree Headstand* with *four stops* on the way down. With this *135-degree Balance Headstand,* there will be *six stops* on the way up and *five* on the way down.

The yogi should regard this *135-degree Balance Headstand* as a final form. Each position on the way up, and while descending, should be the target of focus and meditative investigation. A yogi should exercise patience during these positions.

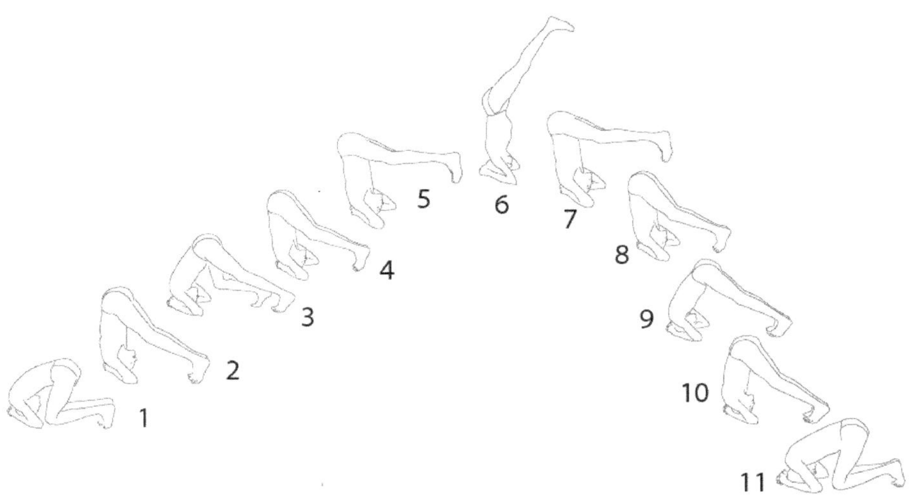

Over Hang Headstand

This *Over Hang Headstand* posture, is a variation of the headstand, but with a counter balance, where the weight of the body is on either side of the center of gravity. The forward headstand with the thighs, legs, and feet, spread out fully is principled on the basis of keeping the weight forward of the center of gravity. In this posture above and the one below, some weight is rearward to the center of gravity.

Until one masters the front centering, one should refrain from this front and rear application. This requires more focus. Until it becomes stabilized, and the appropriate muscles assume their responsibilities to keep the balance, one should practice only, the front-of-center balancing.

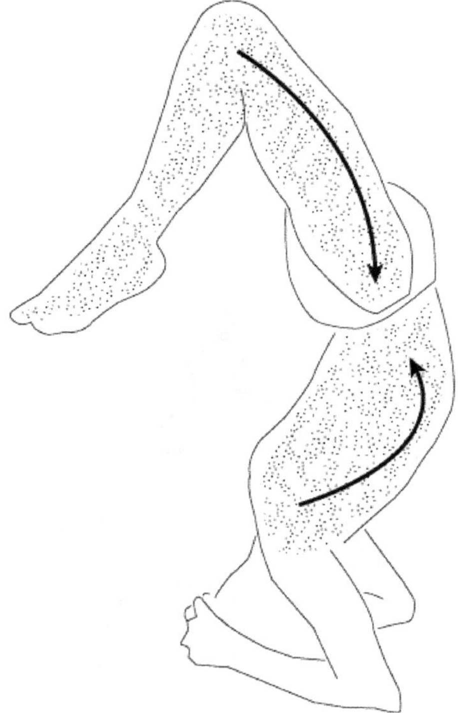

Focus Connection

The *Over Hang Headstand* is a final posture. As explained, any of the headstand postures have sub-positions which are assumed while attempting the final form of the posture, and also while de-positioning from it. Every stage may be regarded as a final form. When the yogi pauses in any position before or after assuming the topmost pose, he may regard that posture as a final form. He may remain in that posture and map its energy array.

Whenever the yogi decides to only use the topmost posture, he should assume the various positions deliberately with full attention to whatever stage his body is in. No rash actions should be made.

In the *Over Hang Headstand*, as soon as it is assumed, there may be a perception in the center of the spine. That is a hollow space which is lit with a hazy smoke or which is clear with a light which is similar to daylight. That will be in the *sushumna nadi* central spine passage. It is like a hollow pipe.

The breath rhythm should be observed. Even though breathing may be short and insufficient, the yogi may be unaware of that situation. Sporadically, for a split-second he may be conscious of it. However, he will not be inspired to correct it. When the feet and thighs hang back, dangling over the waist, the abdomen will protrude forward. This will serve to balance the body. Provided that the yogi, is attentive within the psyche, there may be very little, if any shivering.

There may be electric mini-darts flying in the shoulders. These will disappear if they fly close to the neck, or if they jump into the chest. A yogi may be confident that he can do this *Over Hang Headstand*. Still, care should be taken to regard the preliminary lifts as final postures.

Lotus Posture Classic

The *lotus posture classic,* is perhaps the most famous of the poses used for the practice of yoga. The look of it, gives one the idea of meditation as a contained consciousness program. Shiva and Buddha are reputed for sitting in this posture for days on end, meditating and either staying in or reaching enlightenment.

This is however a difficult posture for the majority of yogis. There are partial formats of this pose. The easiest is known as the *easy pose*. In that pose there is no interlocking of the legs.

For the classic format of the easy pose, someone should have supple thigh and leg, muscles and tendons, otherwise ligaments, tissues, tendons, and muscles, even the bones, may be stressed to the point of injury. One should realize that the assumption of this posture does not necessarily mean that a yogi is proficient in meditation. Ideal poses of the physical body do not necessarily correlate with psychological achievements.

The converse is true, where someone may be advanced in psychological techniques and be sloppy in assuming physical positions. For that matter it can be misleading to the yogi himself/herself and to others who view him/her as well.

In the lotus pose, I did *pratyahar* mentally. I did not do meditation as it is defined by Patanjali as *samyama,* which is the flow of interest to something sublime, either deliberately or spontaneously. Hence the pose with the soles of the feet showing upwards does not explain what I did on the psychological plane.

If when doing the lotus posture, the yogi has pains and distractions in the physical body, that posture damages the effort. He would be distracted by the pains. Even if he has the power to ignore them, they will cause interruptions during the meditation.

Another damaging feature is the construction of the spine, which may require great concentration to keep an upright position. If the spine is braced with a cushion, that may allow the yogi more latitude to meditate or even to do *pratyahar* sensual energy withdrawal.

The issue is that postures in their final or partial formats, may not indicate the meditation level of the yogi. One yogi may be reclined comfortably somewhere, and be in a higher state of meditation, than someone who is in a perfect lotus posture. It is best that a yogi considers the practice of *asana* postures as a method in its own right. He should consider meditation as being a system which uses specific easy *asana* poses, where the focus of the mind will not shift to the physical body during meditation.

Keep in mind that as far as Patanjali was concerned, *asana* posture is the third stage of yoga, a process all by itself. Meditation he listed as *samyama* which is a sequel process of *dharana* focus, *dhyana* spontaneous focus and *samadhi* continuous freely-occurring focus. There is also *pratyahar* sensual energy restraint which he listed as the fifth process. Even that should be done in an easy pose, unless there is a specific internal retraction, which is practiced best even with a strenuous posture.

The lotus posture is troublesome for anyone whose tendons and muscles are tense in that pose. For that matter the lotus pose may irritate someone who has hip stiffness and pelvic aches. If that is the case, the yogi should use other positions.

Once a student alerted me that he found a method of stretching his lower limbs. In six months, he projected that he would do a perfect lotus posture. After the stipulated time, he was no better. His body was still taut. This suggests that it takes time to change a muscular structure. There is also the risk of injury if one overstretches beyond a reasonable limit. Physical body yoga is not gymnastic. It is not a sport.

Injury is always possible. A yogi should patiently work with his/her body, and expect results over a long period. One disadvantage is that a particular body derived from parents in one life, may do a pose easily, while another body from other parents in some other life, may facilitate some other pose. One should practice with reasonable expectations.

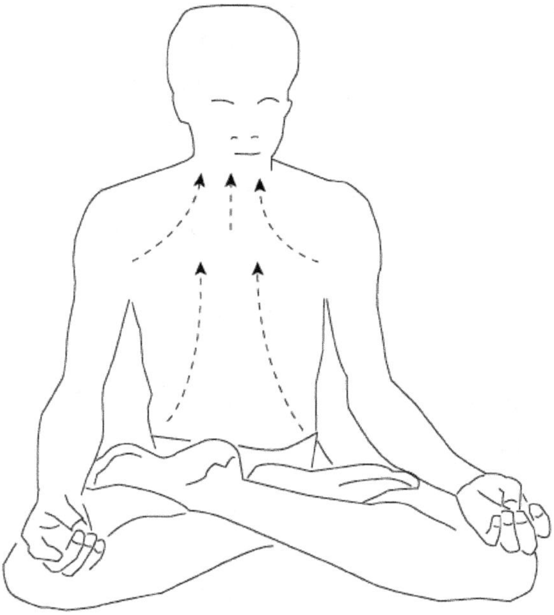

In the lotus posture above, the arrows indicate the flow of energy into the neck. To focus on this transit, the yogi should be free from pains and aches, which are due to stressed muscles and tendons. If the lower limbs and pelvis, even the vertebrae, are tense, the attention of the yogi will be drawn to those inconveniences. That will result in less focus on the flow of energy upward through the torso.

There are other constraints such as external sounds and visuals. These may rob the yogi of focus. Why? Because as the psyche is designed by Nature, it impulsively pursues objects of the senses. These are targets which the senses hunt. The eyes will hunt and apprehend visual objects. The ears will be alert for sounds which it can focus on, collect, and process. This requires energy which is extracted from one's ability to focus.

If possible, one should meditate in a dark room, or one may use a blindfold. To be protected from the hearing tendency, one should be somewhere which has no intruding noises. Even mind-created pleasant music may be a distraction, which reduces internal focus. Any mental or emotional effort which is made to ward off, or resist external targets of the senses, is a reduction in meditation focus. Hence, a stress-free environment is preferred for meditation.

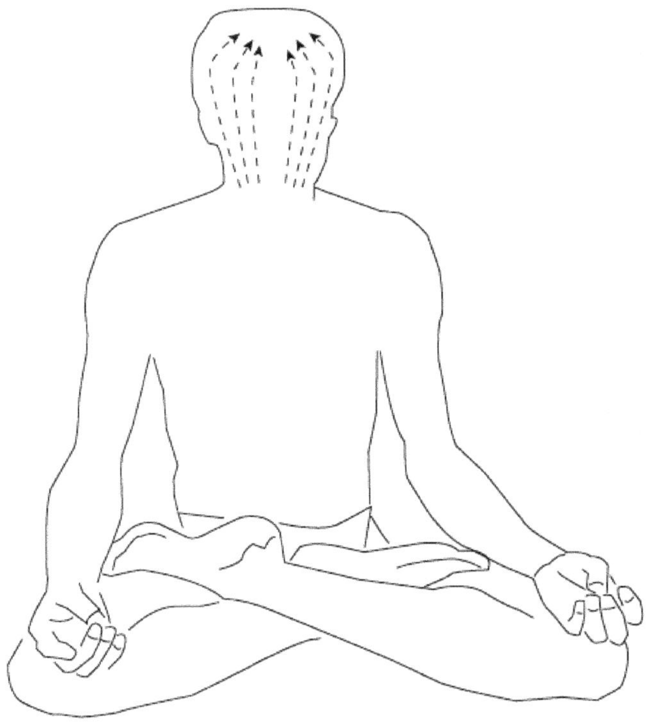

In the diagram above, the yogi sits in lotus posture. It could be some other pose. He could sit or lie on a bed or cushion. Since the physical body is affected by its position in relation to gravity, to focus on the crown of the head is easier done if the head is upright. One does not have to be in the lotus posture. One may sit on a chair or couch, where there are no aches and pains, which rob the mind of focus.

Focus Connection

The *Lotus Posture Classic* has one adoption, which is to interlock the legs and position the hands with no strain on the lower limbs. If there is strain, the yogi should use another pose. There are many such alternate postures, which are easy positions. In those, the legs may or may not be crossed. One may rest on the other.

The technicality is how the spine is slanted in reference to the floor. For those who intent to do more than fifteen (15) minutes of meditation, it is expedient to use cushions under and behind the body. The cushions which support the back of the body should be pitched a slight angle, so that the spine is tilted backward. This will allow the body to lean back from the center of gravity. This will prevent the body from falling forward.

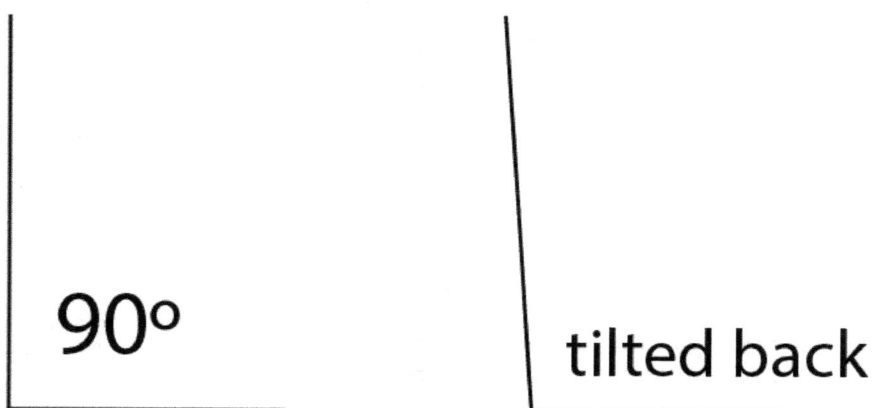

It happens that if one sits to meditate, and he/she does that for a time, say for over twenty minutes, it is likely that one will lose track of the physical body. In which case, the head may tilt to the left or right, forward or backward. If the spine is directly perpendicular to the floor, the body may fall forward. If, however the spine is tilted slightly back, the body will remain upright, even though the neck may lean to the right, left, forward or backward.

That may occur in slow motion where it is not evident to the yogi until he comes out of the meditation, and finds his body in a shifted condition. The body as it is controlled by the lifeForce may begin a downward movement. Until the yogi regains his body-related objectivity, he may be unaware of the deviation.

These meditations are some of the events through which a yogi begins to understand that his subjective self is perpetual. It does not provide objective perception on every occasion. Much happens physically and psychically, which the core cannot account for, which it did not witness, and which it has no clarification about.

Lotus Lift

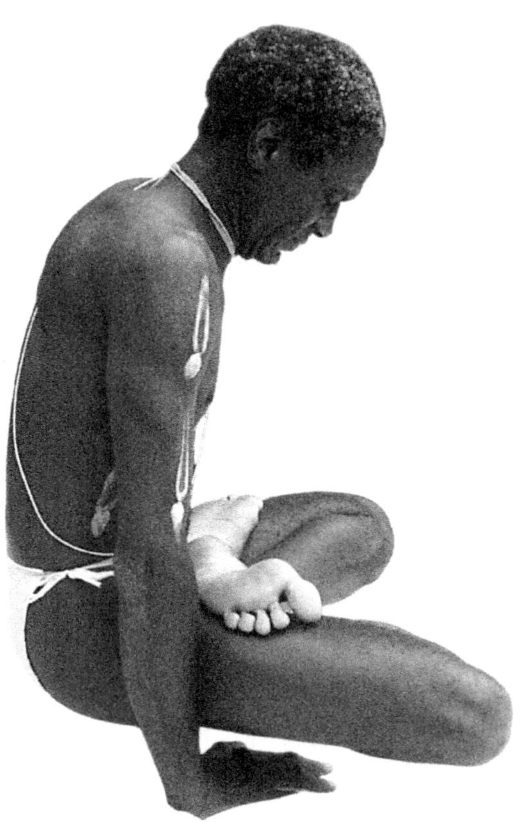

The *Lotus Lift* has many variations. It is based on having to assume the interlocked upturned feet, with no pain, nor stress in the lower limbs. It can be done otherwise, as for example if one has tight limbs and fat thighs. If, however that is the situation, the discomfort in the lower limbs and pelvic region will reduce the focus in the lifting hands, forearms, and arms. When doing this posture, the hands are the only parts of the body which contact the floor.

When from the lotus posture, the body is lifted using only the hands for support, it is likely that there will shivering in the forearms and arms. This may be tolerated for short periods, for seconds or minutes. As soon as the tolerance is reached, the yogi should slowly relax the supporting limbs. The body sits on the floor. At that time, the eyes should be closed. Meditation on the condition of the psyche should be experienced. Energy shifts, consolidations, and fragmentation, should be mapped and observed.

A check should be made to be sure that the tongue is turned upward and pushed back to the soft palate. One should meditate to find dispersed energy. It may disperse upward through the top chest region. The lower abdomen may have energy dispersing to the navel.

During the lift, energy from in the arm bone (humerus), and from the forearm bones will radiate outward. This energy should be pulled through the shoulders into the neck. When a yogi raises the buttocks, he/she should make the effort to lift the entire body, which includes the knees. If, however, that effort fails, the yogi should be certain that only the knees and hands touch the floor.

Focus Connection

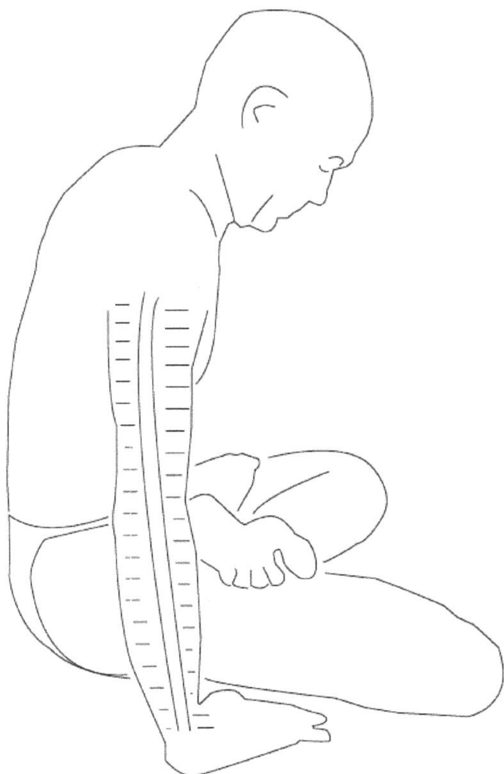

When doing the *Lotus Lift,* the supporting hands may point forward, sideward or backward. Each orientation has special effects. Usually the knees touch the floor, but the rest of the body except for the hands is elevated. The illustration above shows the body in a tight lotus. If that cannot be assumed, the yogi may use an easy pose with one leg and foot resting on the other.

During the lift, the arms, forearms and wrists may shiver. When this happens, the yogi should focus through the arms, forearms and wrists. While doing this he may notice that the elbows relaxed. He should again push up by straightening the elbows. Then again there will be shivering. He may find that unless he applies attention, the muscles which support the body, simply cannot maintain a locked elbow.

The shivering inside the elbows passes through the forearms. Like an arrow, it darts through the wrists, into the floor. A yogi may wonder how long he can give focusing energy to keep the elbows locked. He notices how the attention focus goes through the elbows, forearms and wrists.

After a time, when the arms can no longer support the body, there will be an alert that the elbows are bent. This is to allow the buttocks to rest on the floor. The arms, forearms and hands will express a happy energy. The yogi will see this. He may marvel at it. It showed him a limit at which even his will power could not maintain the pose.

When the buttocks reside on the floor, the yogi will feel an ease energy, which seems to be neither hot nor cold. It will radiate inside the forearms and wrists. Staying in this ease posture for a short time, the yogi should again raise the body as before, with the buttocks off the floor, and the knees touching the floor. Again, there will come a time, when the yogi must allow the elbows to collapse, so that the buttocks rest on the floor.

At this time, the yogi may notice that energy vibrates in the center of the trunk. That will be a shattering force, like pieces of shattered granite shifting quickly. This will be like multi-colored transparent glass. At this stage of the practice, when he finds that the elbows will not bear the weight, the yogi should again lower the buttocks. Then, he should assume an easy pose.

In that pose he should flip the astral body so that it interlocks in reverse into the physical system. The head of the subtle body will be on the floor. The feet of it will be in the air. The yogi should know that the subtle body is not as constrained as the physical one.

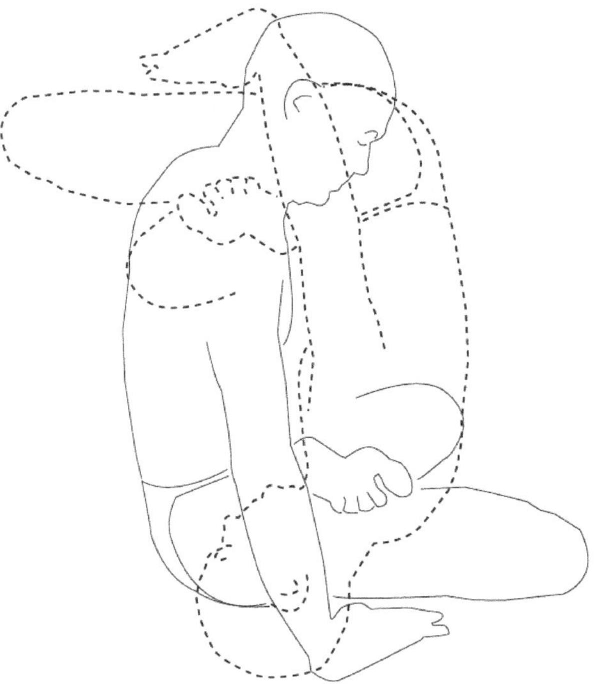

Lotus Lift – *Kukkutasana* Rooster Pose

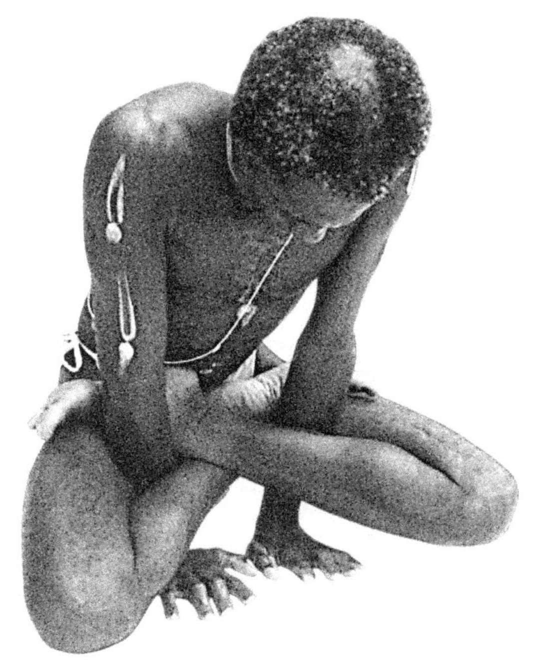

This *Lotus Lift – Kukkutasana Rooster* pose, is a variation of the rooster position, which utilizes the expertise in lotus posture. If one cannot pass the forearms through the locked lotus, this posture cannot be done. If it is only the encumbrance of friction, wetting the forearms may allow one to do this. When it is done, a yogi may find that the body slips down the forearms to the floor. However, if one is balanced, the body may slip just enough to cause the knees to touch the floor. The rest of the base will remain floating.

To do this, a yogi should first set the lotus posture with tight locking so that the soles of the feet are upturned. Then there should be a check for balance, and to set the lower spine, so that it does not sag or curve. After that, one hand should be pushed through, then the other. After this, a check should be made, to be sure that the weight of the body, is balanced.

Inner focus within the body should be achieved. If necessary, if one cannot maintain a balance, and the body slips, or the hands need to be repositioned, the yogi should withdraw the hands, unlock the lotus, and begin the posture again.

This position relies on the energy in the hands, forearms, and arms. That is the focus.

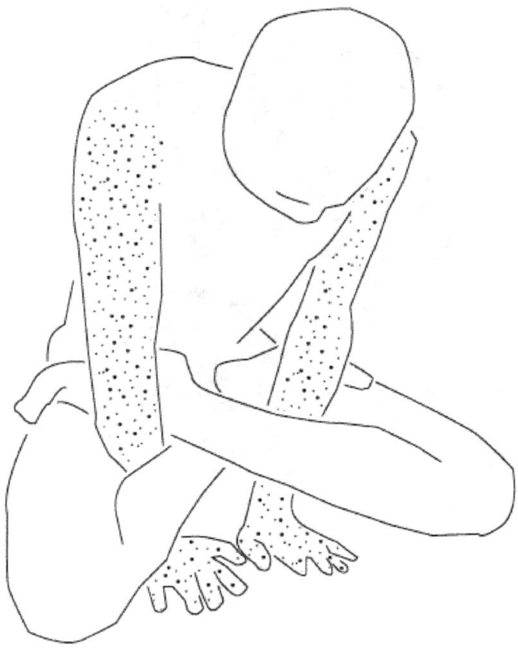

Focus Connection

The *Lotus Lift – Kukkutasana Rooster* Pose is a graduated form of the tight lotus. Yogins who cannot do the lotus, are not required to do the *lotus lift rooster* pose. First it is required that a tight lotus is achieved. The body should sit upright on the floor. The cross-leg posture is positioned. As illustrated, each hand is pushed through the vertex on either side.

The body is elevated with only the knees touching the floor. Some yogis do this with the knees lifted from the floor. It depends on the proportions of the limbs of the body. In this pose some yogis lean forward to achieve balance. Other yogis can remain upright.

If perchance a yogi cannot remain in this posture for any length of time, he should investigate this inability. He should determine if it is due to the way the body is referenced to gravity.

- What adjustment should he make?

Some yogis may unwrap the lotus posture. Sit up the body. Then do the tight lotus again. Then again push the hands through and elevate the body. If again he cannot steady the body with the knees floating or with the knees touching the floor, he should conclude that at present, he cannot assume this pose.

For anyone who can do this for a time, as soon as one relaxes from it, by lowering the buttocks to the ground, he should immediately check the inner energy. He should map the feelings. He should note the energy formations. There may be an inner screeching sound, a resonance. He should know its location.

He should extract the hands and position them on each thigh. He should then enter inner focus to check and map the energy movements. There may be an encouragement, to submerged in the upper chest area. He should follow that prompting. Then he may descend to the lower torso, which may be a blank zone. There may be some shivering.

After a time, he should resume the *Lotus Lift – Kukkutasana Rooster* pose. Then he should relax from it. He should sit in *lotus* posture. He should meditate. This may encourage the yogi to pull *chit akash* spiritual energy into his psyche. Around the coreSelf, there is a cloud of opaque mundane energy which segregates the core from the spiritual levels of existence. He should have an opening to his psyche, so that the *chit akash* energy may penetrate the dense opaque mundane shroud.

Lotus Recline Backward

This *Lotus Recline Backward* posture, requires expertise with the lotus pose. First, a yogi sits. He puts the body into a tight lotus position, with the soles of the feet facing the sky. He then uses the hands to lift the body. After this he lays backward. One may allow the thigh, legs, and feet to come up when the buttocks and head are in contact with the floor. If that is done, if the lower limbs rise, the yogi should gentle lower the thighs to the floor.

The fingers grab the feet. The yogi may hold the feet from the top with the hands facing downward. Or the hands may grab the feet from below. Once this is held, the focus should be inward. The back will be arched, but the pressure which is applied to the thighs, will cause the focus to lodge in the inner and top of the thighs. This is due to the sensations in those locations. The yogi should be absorbed. He should study the attitude of the mind when the body is in this pose.

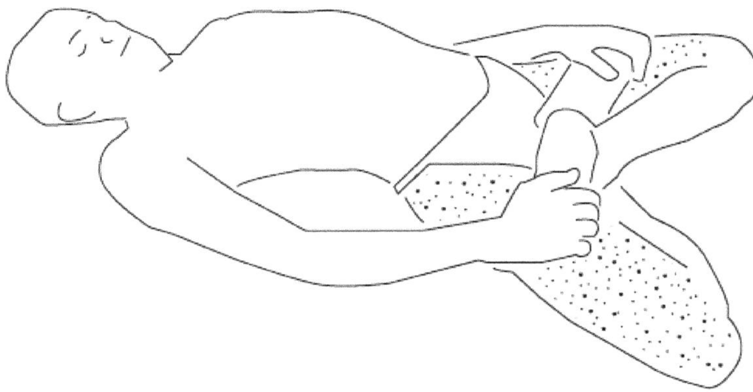

The yogi should focus on the electric sensations. This will move into a *samadhi* continuous effortless absorption into the thigh of the body. A yogi should stay in this pose for as long as he can. He should study the *samadhi* absorption.

To come out from this pose, the yogi should sit upright. Then he should release the lotus posture. He should assume an easy pose. He should meditate on the energy shifts in the psyche. It may be noticed that there are no fluctuations in the thighs as before. Rather, there may be electric micro-currents in the neck and head. A yogi should meditate. He learns how to hold a *samadhi* absorption.

Focus Connection

The *Lotus Recline Backward* posture, is a difficult event for a yogi, even for those who can easily assume the *tight lotus* pose. A yogi should be attentive when doing this. It could result in injury where a muscle, tendon, or nerve, is torn or stretched. Some yogis assume a *tight lotus*, then lay back so that the spine is on the floor but the buttocks and lower limbs are not. Then slowly the buttocks, thighs and knees are lowered to the floor. As this is done, care is taken to avoid jerks.

Once this posture is assumed, the back of the head, shoulders, buttocks, thighs, and knees, make contact with the floor. The mid-spine arches upwards. It does not touch the floor.

When a yogi assumes this pose, he may find that there is a crisis of energy. He may see that energy scatters in all directions. The self enters a spontaneous inner focus. That is a *dhyana* absorption state. A yogi should study this event.

In this pose, there may be confusion of energy. It may seem that the energy assumes a chaotic array, as if it would never become organized and stable. A yogi may become unsteady when he observes this.

After a short time, there may be energy firing through the thighs. These will feel like electric micro-darts firing through the thighs. The yogi will feel this but his tolerance may be exhausted. He will be inspired to unravel the posture.

When he does, the format of energy will be reconfigured, so that there is order in the spsyche. Sitting up, energy will normalize instantly. Then, there may be energies behind the rib cage. Bubbles, tiny ones, may form. These will dissipate as they rise upward.

He may feel as if the head is heated. It radiates heat.

Lotus – Side Face

This *Lotus – Side Face* posture, is done in the lotus position but only for those whose limbs permit doing the lotus with no stress nor muscle strain. For others, this should be done in an easy pose, even sitting on soft material. There should be no focus which is based on tension.

Use the lotus if your body can easily assume it, otherwise sit somewhere with no strain. While focusing into the body, check it to be sure that the attention powers are not pulled to a tensed area. Use the right or left hand to apply a slight pressure to the side of the face. Keep the hand there for a time. Relax the hand by placing it with palm down on the thigh area near the knee. Meditate. After a time, raise and apply the other hand. This is an observation posture. Even though it was developed for using the lotus pose, it can be done from any comfortable situation.

When a hand is against the side of the face, close the eyes and focus internally. There should be a screeching sound emanating or saturating the space at the ear where the hand presses slightly. Focus on that resonance. A yogi should experience very little interference from thoughts. There should be saturation of naad resonance, where the yogi is linked into it, or can do so with little effort in directing the focusing ability.

Focus Connection

The *Lotus – Side Face* position, is an inner sound-tracking posture. It can be done in an easy pose. However as far as possible, the spine should be erect in reference to the lower torso. A yogi should listen for inner sound(s). As soon as the hand is placed to the respective side of the face, the yogi should, with eyelids closed or blindfolded, listen in the head for inner sound. If it is noticed, he should track it.

- Where is its origin point?
- How forceful is it?
- Can it be ignored?

Once, he knows where it is located, he should connect to its node. Finding that, he should focus through the center of it. If naad resonance is operative but no origin nor location for it is found, the yogi should go to the back of the head. Then he should circle the perimeter of the head, to discover the scope of naad.

If for instance, a yogi searches for naad beginning at the right ear. He should move to the right back of the head. Then, he should rotate himself or his sound-detecting psychic instrument to the back of the head. Then he should move to the left side of the head near the left ear. Then he should rotate and listen at the front of the head. Then again, he should turn clockwise and search to the right side of the head.

Eventually a yogi should develop the determination to find inner sound. That is not a hopeless task. It can be found if one is focused to hear inner sounds. Some students fail to find naad. Others find it but regard it a nuisance. It is beneficial. It orients the yogi to a blank mind. It teaches the yogi how to focus on nothingness, on a blank mind.

Hands to Side of Face

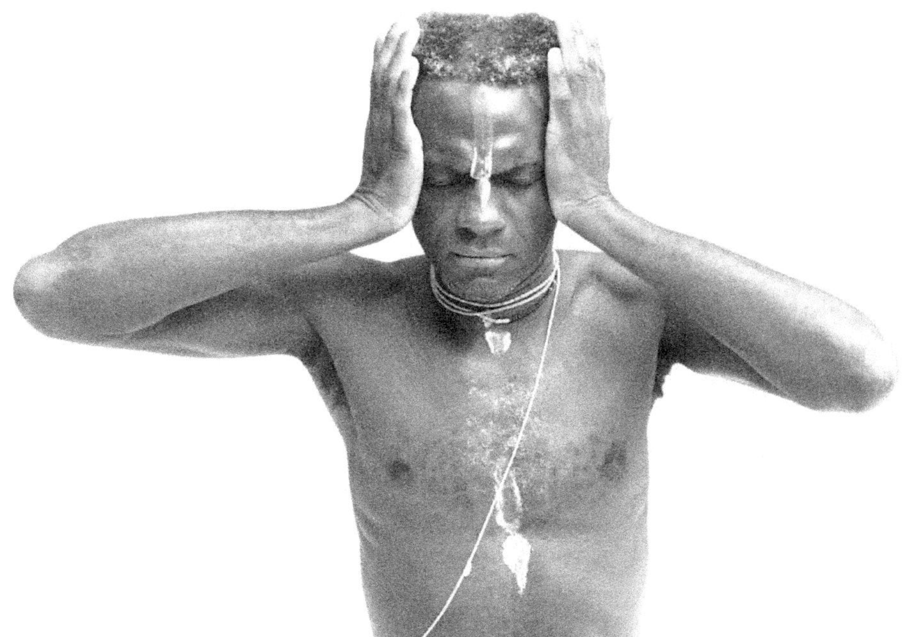

The *Hands to Side of Face* posture may be held while sitting or standing. It is best done after doing *bhastrika pranayama* breath infusion, to surcharge the subtle and physical bodies, with subtle energy, and physical fresh air. A proficient yogi who can do this while sitting in the lotus posture, and after filling the subtle body with fresh energy, will feel energy moving randomly in the subtle head.

With eyelids closed, or being blindfolded, he may feel that there is no membrane like a skull. He may feel that the skull is open, with energy surging continuously through the sky-like top of the head.

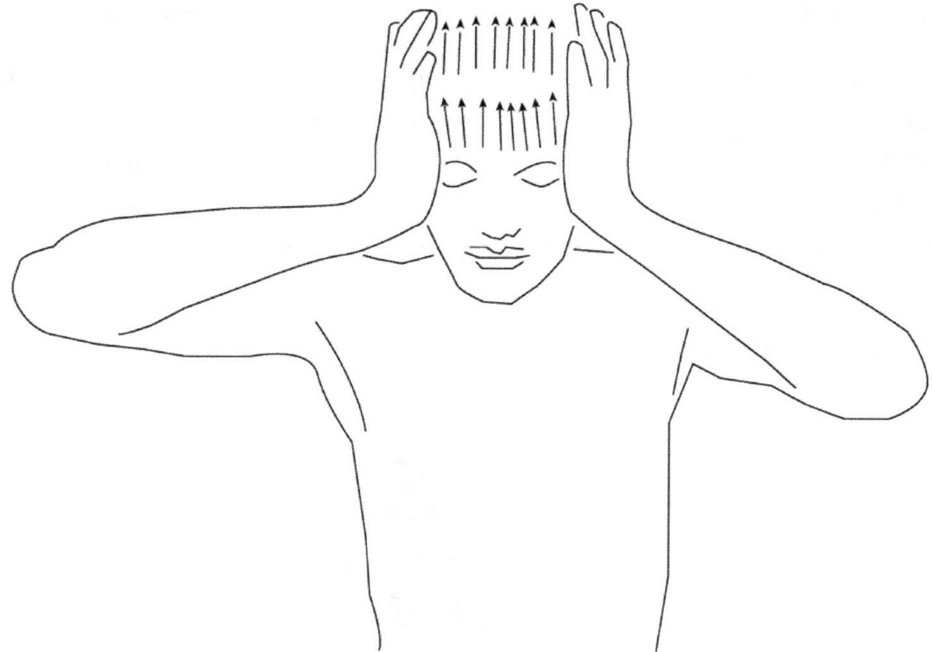

Focus Connection

The *Hands to Side of Face* posture, can be done from any siting position. A yogi may do it in the tight lotus just as well. The body should be comfortable for this meditation. It is important to be at a location which is free from external sounds, as for instance, no radio broadcasts, nor machine hums.

If external sounds are present, it is likely that the internally sounds will not be observed. This is due to the pulling force of external sounds, which pull the hearing sense to be externally alert and internally unresponsive.

There are many persons who practice meditation. Some do not hear internal sounds. Some explain that they never heard naad resonance. Others hear it as a nuisance sound which they dislike.

With no nuisance external noise within hearing distance, a yogi should map where internal resonance occurs. Look at these diagrams. These show the coreSelf as a small circle in the middle. The large circle represents the psyche perimeter. The dotted area is where naad sound saturates.

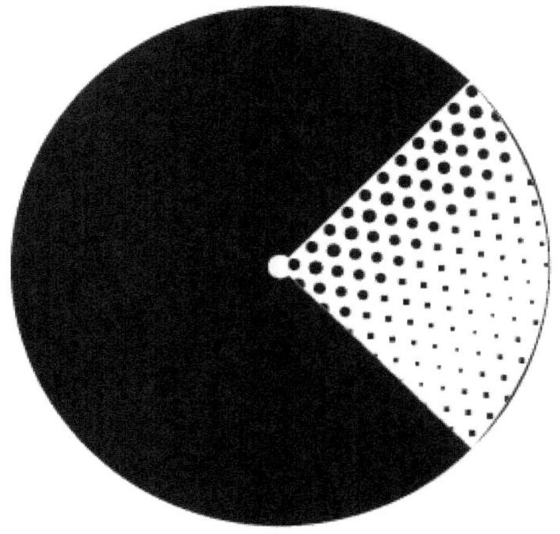

naad right

Naad right is heard as if it is involved with the right inner ear. It blares. It may be the predominant location. A yogi may notice that it has a node or source point. It can be that it has no such source and seems to be centerless. For some yogis it is the reference during meditation. It teaches the yogi how to hold the focus on inner reality.

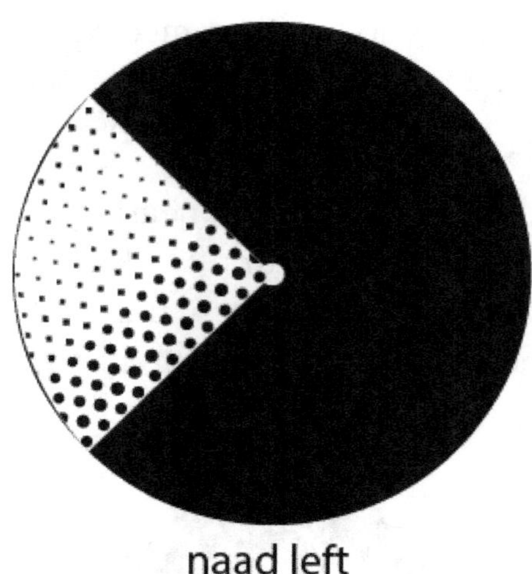

naad left

Naad left is similar to naad right. Some yogis report, that for the most part, naad is heard to the left, as if it comes from the left inner ear. For those who have the left side as the majority location of naad, the right appearance of naad is special. It happens that sometimes, during meditation, there is a sudden switch where a yogi hears naad to the opposite side. It may seem that naad ceased resonating to the left or elsewhere. It may jump to the right side as illustrated. Sometimes, the naad situation to the left is spotty, where it is not steady, where it is in and out, appearing there, then disappearing, then appearing, then disappearing. Sometimes, naad is on the left, then it switches and is in some other location. Or it may add to itself so that it is all-**surrounding**. This shows below.

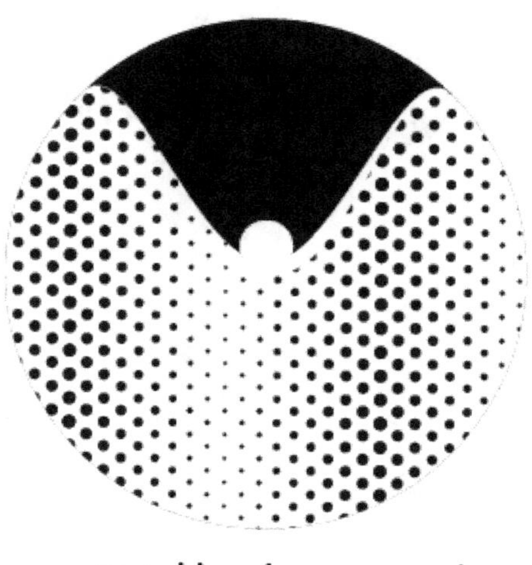

naad back surround

Sometimes, a yogi experiences naad to the **left back** or **right back** of the head.

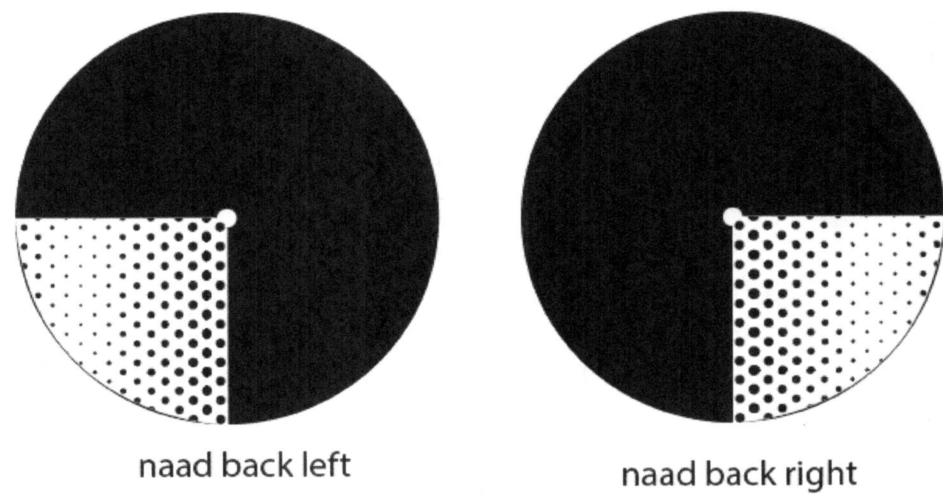

When naad is to the left or right back of the head, it may or may not be pronounced. If it blares, the yogi could listen from the center of the head. He may turn about in its zone to absorbed in it. If he turns about and enters its zone, the thought-producing part of the mind will cease operations. The yogi may notice that this cessation of thinking and ideation is a special state of mind. It gives an understanding of *dhyana* and *samadhi* states as explained by Patanjali in the *Yoga Sutras*.

Naad may be heard profusely or sparsely in the back of the head.

Its resonance in the back, where it is steady, blaring, and pronounced, is a special meditative state. A yogi takes the opportunity to be situated in the back of the head. That is a blank area. While the fontal part of the subtle head has psychic tools for ideation, imagination, and illustration of memory, the back of the head is a quiet zone. It is a shelter area where the coreSelf can escape from mental and emotional bombardment.

Sometimes when listening to naad, at the back of the head, the yogi finds that naad disappears. It ceases. Everything becomes noiseless. A careful study of this state, causes the yogi to realize that naad is ever-sounding. Its disappearance cannot happen. The yogi's experience of the vanishing naad, has to do with his consciousness switching to a state, in which naad is present, but cannot be heard. Then the yogi may be centralized in blankness.

After doing the *Hands to Side of Face* posture, the yogi should relax with the hands on the knees. He may hear the naad surround. Otherwise, there will be a free focus on the inside of the body. It will have naad as its monitor. The yogi should trace this.

Hand and Arm to Face

This *Hand and Arm to Face* posture, may be done in any sitting, or standing posture, where balance can be easily maintained. The situation should be that after sitting, the yogi, with either a blindfold or with eyelids closed, puts one palm on the side of the face, but with the fingers not covering the ear. The thumb should be below the ear.

The other hand will be pushed up so the fingers point backward, and the arm presses firmly against the corresponding face, against the temple, but not covering the ear. The yogi should inspect the energies in the psyche. This is a situation check of the mental space.

This practice should be done in an easy pose, where there are no ailments, and attention-requiring areas of the body, which cause the mind to switch to energy-demanding tension.

For the limbs which are extended upward, the arm should not touch the ear. Otherwise, there will be disturbing inner noise, from the friction between the arm and the body.

When meditating, any object which produces extraneous noises, should be disabled. Nothing should attract the attention of the yogi. An attraction which is not part of the meditation, will cause a reduction in focus.

When doing the pose, if the yogi feels to lower either arm, he should do so slowly, so as not to lose focus and internal observation. He may resume the pose soon after. Then he should reconnect to the state of consciousness, which is natural for that posture.

A yogi may in this pose, become aware of naad sound, radiating like a light which squirts energy. This energy may travel up through the top of the head.

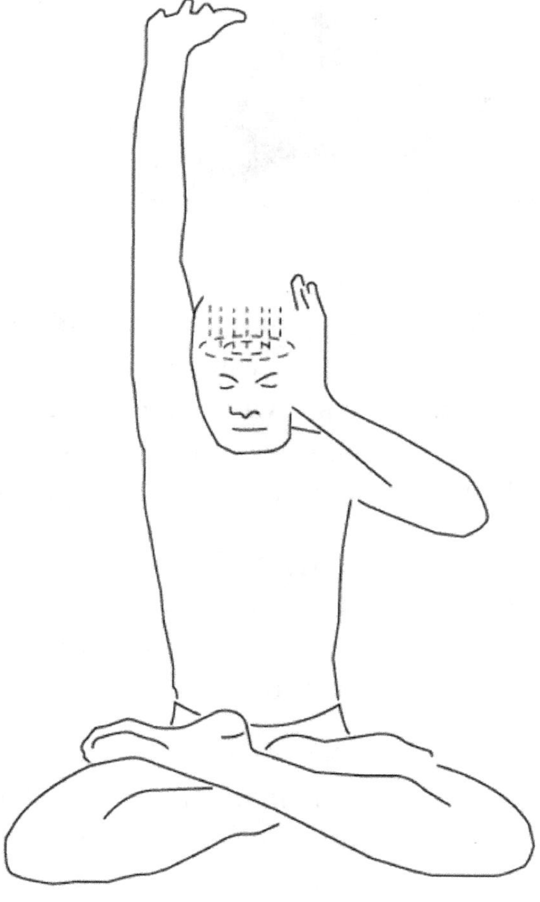

Focus Connection

The *Hand and Arm to Face* posture, can be from any sitting position, or from the tight lotus as illustrated. In this position there may be disturbance, where the palm of one hand, and the arm of the other, touches the ears. This may cause some inner sound. If that happens, the yogi should adjust to cease the friction between the involved hand, arm and ears. When the interference ceases, a yogi should listen for inner resonance.

That would be perception by the inner observing ability. At some point, the yogi may discover a mix of thought energy and naad resonance. This will have a visual appearance, like spikes of glass which reflect light, and bricks of transparent granite, being here and there at random.

Keeping the focus on this, the yogi will notice that the thoughts fade. They are no longer illustrated in the mind space. Only naad inner frequency remains. After a time, the yogi should slowly relieve the upper limbs. The hands should rest on the thighs. The muscles in the arms feel relieved, like when cinders cool after their heat dissipates, as energy radiates from them.

Back-of-Head Hold

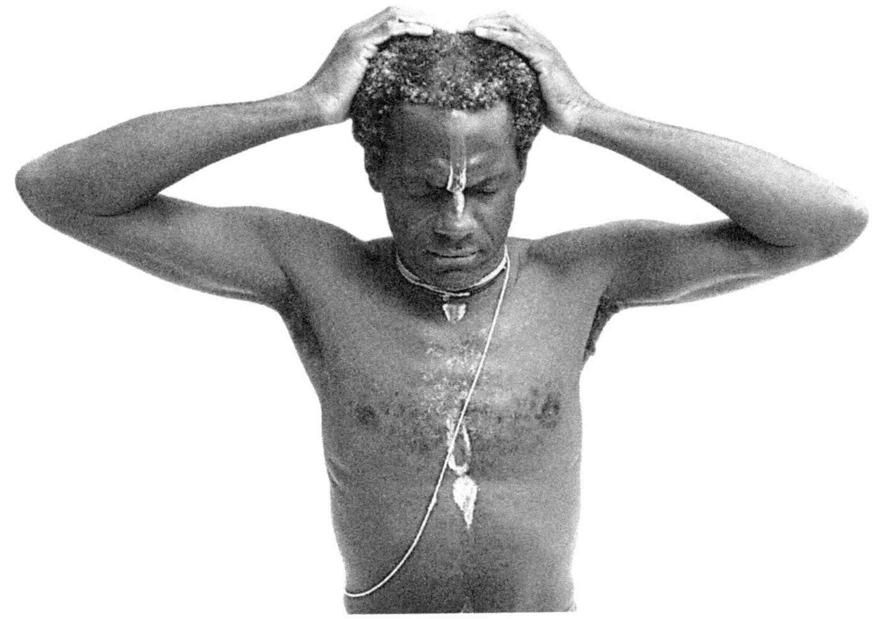

This *Back-of-Head Hold* is easy. It may be done from a sitting or standing position. One may get the best result if this is done after breath infusion, when the subtle body, lower limbs, trunk, neck, and head, have fresh physical and subtle energy.

With inner focus, with the vision interest being restricted within the body, with the hearing sense not venturing out of the psyche, the yogi should place each hand on the back of the head. The thumbs meet at the lower center back. The yogi focuses within the head and neck, to recognize how the psychic energy is arranged and focused. The situation may be chaotic.

A yogi may find that the confusion becomes settled, where the energy in the front half of the head, traverses to the rear half. The energy in the rear half will go backward but not leave the area. This is similar to an escalator which does not change location but which rotates in place. Its actions are contained.

When this posture is done, and the focus on the back of the head, is steadied, and when the yogi feels that the arms should be lowered, he may do so, allowing the hands to rest on the thighs. However, he should continue the meditation, and be aware of shifts of energy. This could lead to a state in which the yogi has a mere figment of objectivity, something that is so slight that it borders on full subjectivity. This is for a study of missing objectivity.

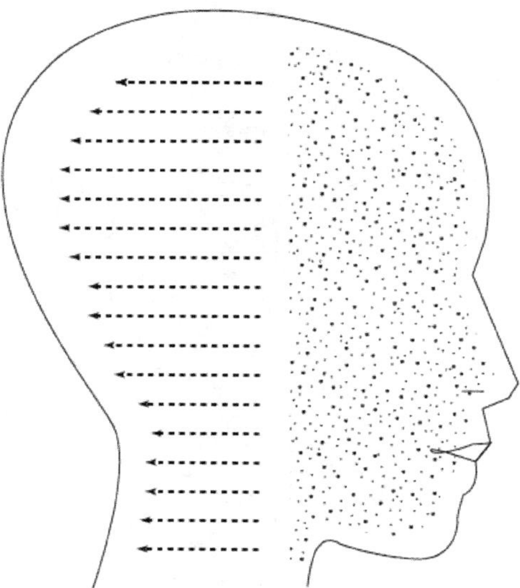

Focus Connection

The *Back-of-Head Hold* can be assumed from any sitting position. A yogi if he can, should do it from a tight lotus. He should check to be sure that adjustments are made, to make the posture become free of distracting tensions. It may be necessary to unwrap, and then rewrap the interlocking legs. Sitting erect may be readjusted as well. He should be sure that his spine is in order. He should not have a hunchback. If after making the effort to situate the body, if he still cannot align it, he should sit on a chair, or sit somewhere somehow, so that the spine is supported.

Once the hands are in position, grasping the back of the head, the yogi should restrict his attention to the inside of the psyche. His attention should be retracted from the external scenes. His interest in what is external to the physical body, should be withdrawn.

After bringing the mind to order, where it abandons its interest in the external events, the yogi should listen and be aware of what is within the head. The attention will go to the back of the head. The yogi may here naad resonance inner sound at the back right or back left of the head. It may blare loudly. It may be scanty and rarefied. He should check its location.

A yogi should check to be sure that the posture was not adjusted. If it was, he should realign it and notice which part of the body shifted. He may find that the arms or that one arm, is tense. He should relax it to ease its stress.

After a time, it will be necessary to relax from the posture. To do this, the hands should be moved to the thighs. Even so, naad should be heard. It should blare. In the mind at this time, because of the naad sound blaring, there may be clairvoyant events. These are inner perception of events, which happen hundreds of miles away.

For instance, a yogi may see a well-dressed proprietor of a hotel which is ten thousand (10,000) miles away. The vision of it will be, as if everything there was made of transparent materials. Some yogis who have that experience, may not understand the perception, and may dismiss it as being a hallucination.

Another feature of such a meditation, may be the presence of thought packages, which appear near to the coreSelf in the mind. These will not be opened by the intellect. Hence, they cannot be interpreted for the core. These psychic packages will appear and then disappear, with the yogi having no idea of their display content. A yogi should continue the meditation. After a time, he should relax. Then again, he should assume the posture. And again, he should relax.

Press Eyes

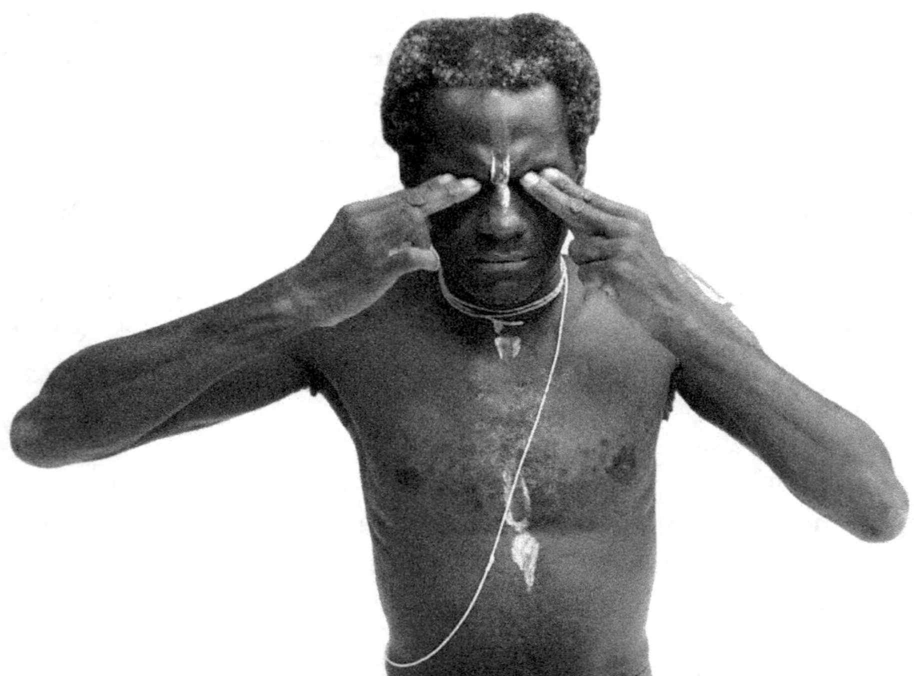

This *Press Eyes* posture concerns pressing the corneas. It may be done with two fingers and the thumb, with the thumb pressing the air canal. Every finger may press the face. Or only two fingers and the thumb may do so. If the thumb compresses the air canal, that may cause the yogi to hear resonance of a high pitched frequency.

Pressing the eyes should be with slight pressure. No pain or discomfort should be felt. The idea is to arouse the third eye chakra which is between the eyebrows. This posture may yield the best result if, it is done immediately after, or during *bhastrika pranayama* breath infusion.

When the eyes are pressed, colors may be seen in the head. It is likely that torus forms will be seen. Alternately a yogi may see discs, spots, dots, or starlike, cometlike, formations of light in various patterns, some haphazard, and some in geometrical formation.

When the pressing is withdrawn, a yogi may still see formations either for a short period or for a time.

Focus Connection

The *Press Eyes* posture causes a yogin to see inner lights. These may be random light, compressed light, moving light, or momentary stationary light. This light is produced in the physical brain and in the subtle body head-space as well. It takes much practice to know what level the light is produced in. There is a hunger for inner light. Nature has the feature of needing to perceive light. Ordinarily, this need is fulfilled by the physical perception of light. Light is a craving. In some species there is no visual perception. In those forms, the perception need is compounded, or shifted, to another sense, especially to the touching impulse.

Forms which have no developed eye, nor ear, nor nose, have all sensing functions operating to assist the touching impulse. Such forms eventually outgrow other senses. This takes time, millions of years of time. Then a rudimentary sensual organ erupts.

A yogi has to develop the divine eye. He also needs clairvoyant perception. And there are other super-sensual perceptions which he should be equipped with, before he can be liberated from his attraction to the lower levels, where survival is a brutal game.

When pressing the eyes with two, or more fingers, a yogi should press on the eyelids. The press should be gentle. It should not hurt or injure the eyeball or its socket. Pressing gently, the yogi should look ahead. There is a tendency to look down. The yogi should lift the vision focus so that it goes straight ahead or is lifted above the horizontal. One may feel a resistance to this lifting action. Due to peering down from the horizontal most of the time, there is a psychic muscle which feels strained, when the vision focus is lifted.

When pressing, if one notices that there are scattered lights ahead, random pieces of color, one should peer forward into the center of the display. One should do so and wait for a change. It may happen that a tiny star appears, either for moments, or seconds, or for a minute. The yogi should gentle stare at it. Sometimes that star will be the first display in a series of other displays. Like for instance, after the star appears, the scattered lights may disappear, or some may move away from the tiny star, as if they are afraid of it.

It may be that this star is a portal to another dimension. It may be a luminary in another dimension. If it is a portal, it will spread and open. The yogi should consider going into its environment, abandoning this physical sky where we are currently resident.

Sometimes, the star moves forward or backward. It does so slowly. If it moves away from the yogi going forward, it may get smaller and smaller. Then he will see that it begins as a tiny star again, and repeats the forward or backward movement.

In some sessions, when pressing the eyeballs, the yogi may see a round mass of color. It may be bright, even brighter than sunlight. It may be dull where in contrast to the blackness of night, it can hardly be differentiated. The yogi should keep a gentle focus in its center. It may move downward, sideways, or upward. The yogi should observe it.

Flat Hands on Face

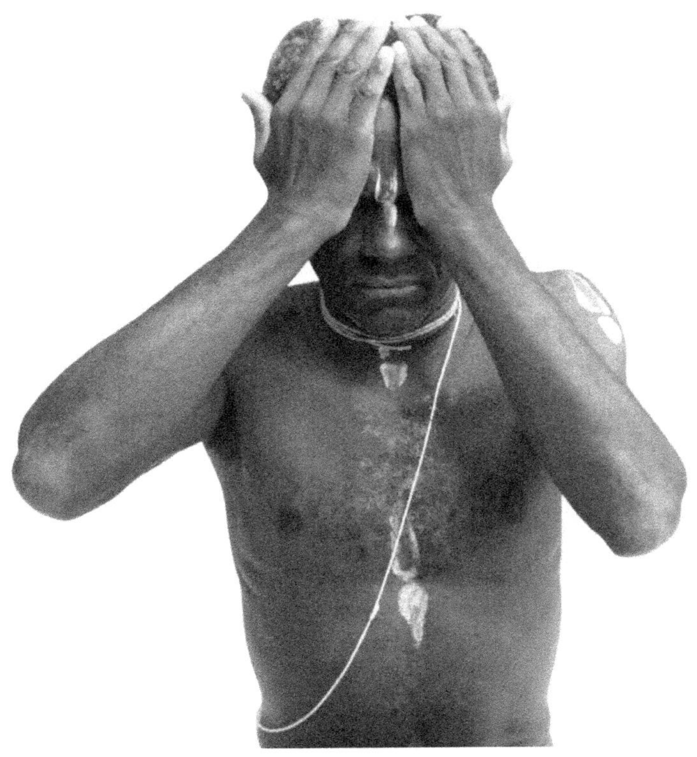

This *Flat Hands on Face* posture is easy, if the meditation occurs while the yogi sits in an easy pose. He may sit on a cushion or chair. He may stand. In this, there should be no pain, strain, nor stress. If there is, that will be a distraction, as the mind will locate the tension, and give focus to it.

Even though a yogi should be an expert at stress resistance, the involuntary system of the kundalini lifeForce, will insist that attention be allotted to any inconvenience. Hence it is sensible when meditating to avoid discomfort.

When placing the palms on each side of the face, the bottom ridge of each palm, the area which is closest to the wrist, may press slightly on each corresponding eye. One variation of this is to have the hollow part of the palm, its center, be over the eyes, such that there is air between the palms and the eyes. In this alternate method, the palms touch the face, but not the eyes.

Every so often, it will be necessary to lift the elbows. These will sag. When the yogi realizes that they did, he should slowly, with no rash movements, lift and keep them suspended. A yogi may hear naad sound, or even a throbbing sound from the heart. Naad sound resonance should be heard. That should blare like a bright light shining beyond itself.

One special benefit from this posture, is the manifestation of the touch sense. Due to the position of the hands, there may be a pervading energy, which is due to the pursuit of surfaces. This is a subtle sense. A yogi should locate it. He may discover that even though it pervades, still it does not allow itself to be discovered at a single place. It seems to be here or there or nowhere.

Focus Connection

The *Flat Hands on Face* is a simple posture, which can be done from any sitting position. It can be done from a standing pose, except that there may be other energy features in the thighs and legs, which will interact with it. It is important not to mix postures unless one has the intention, and can sort the energies which are compressed or released. Sorting the energies and configurations, can be done in one position after the other, otherwise there may be confusion.

When doing the *Flat Hands on Face* posture, the base of the palm may or may not press the eyes. If the eyes are pressed, that should be done lightly, with very little pressure. A yogi should listen for inner sound in the chamber of the head, which is behind the hands. First listen to the right side by the right ear, but on the inside. Then listen by the left ear. If you hear naad, switch attention to the other side. Observe if naad switches, or if it remains on any side, when the attention is moved to the other side.

This will inform the yogi as to if naad is flexible.

- Does it anticipate and appear where the attention will be applied?
- Does it ignore the attention, where it remains where it is expressed?

The yogi should check to know if the bases of the palms presses the eyes.

- What is the situation of the hands, wrists, forearms and arms?
- Should these be readjusted?
- Did the hands move from the face?

After checking, the yogi should resituate the hands, wrists, forearms and arms. He should check for naad.

- Is it rushing here and there, like cattle in a stampede.
- Is naad a confused, disordered array of inner sound?
- If it blares, does it have a node? Is it intense in a particular location?
- Does it hang in the space of the head?

After a time, the arms will demand attention. The yogi must provide relief for the muscles. The yogi should relax them. He should place the hands on the thigh. If he stands, he should let the arms hang freely.

Palms Pressed to Rib Cage

If someone has stiff wrists or much fat tissue on the sides of the torso, and stiffness in the forearms and arms, it is likely that this *Palms Pressed to Rib Cage* posture, will be difficult. This can be done from any sitting or standing position. It is best done from a sitting posture, an easy one, whereby there would be no stress nor imbalance.

Once the hands are placed on the corresponding sides of the torso, the yogi should internalize to check for energy distribution. Holding the mind steady, with no effort given for thinking and ideation, the yogi should map the electric sensations which occur.

- What is their direction of travel, and their spreading away from their sources?

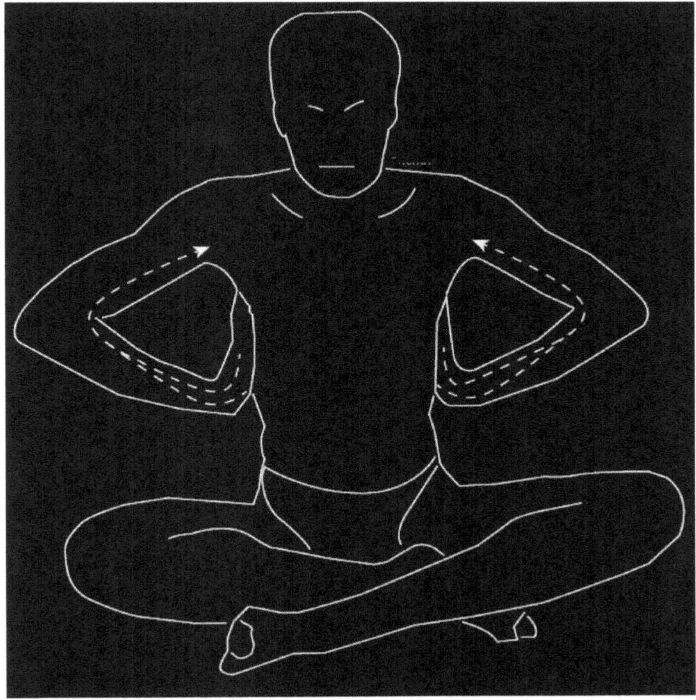

Energy may dart from the hands through the wrists and into the forearms. If held long enough, energy will stir in the trunk, then into the neck and head.

This is a practice which will help the yogi to define *samadhi*, which is the effortless continuous absorption, where a yogi investigates awareness. In this posture, the psyche itself will enter an absorption practice, a *samadhi*. The yogi should become emerged in that state for understanding what it is, as well as for knowing how one may remain in it, with no thoughts, nor ideas, being generated, either spontaneously or deliberately.

Focus Connection

A flexible yogi should do the *Palms Pressed to Rib Cage* position in an easy cross-legged pose or in the lotus posture. As soon as the hands are placed on the rib cage, the yogi should internalize the interest beam. That is a psychic instrument which emanates from the core. It should be pointed downward to track the energy shifts in the trunk.

The physical and subtle bodies are interlocked and interspaced. Activities with one of these bodies affect the performance of the other. A yogi should understand that for the most part, a physical application had a subtle act, which either follows, or even presupposes the physical one.

There may be at least two energy sweeps or darts, which are noticed in the trunk. One is slanted from the spine behind the chest to the front of the body below the navel. The other is lower, from the spine behind the navel to the genitals in the front. Even though these may be observed, the yogi will not focus on them.

There may be swinging actions, as if the elbows swing from side to side, moving just half of an inch. Naad may be perceived near the coreSelf but it may have no definition. The yogi will find that he senses it, even though he does not have the urge to listen to it.

The tendency present will be the focus which will descend into the torso. When again the yogi's interest floats up, he will become aware of naad resonance. With the attention remaining in the vicinity of naad inner sound, the elbows may sway to the left and right, moving about an inch or less.

When the yogi is attentive to the sway, his listening grip on naad will relax somewhat. He should study how his attention in combination with a single sense, shifts here or there, or even remains where it is, and projects to arrest another target.

Press Fingers

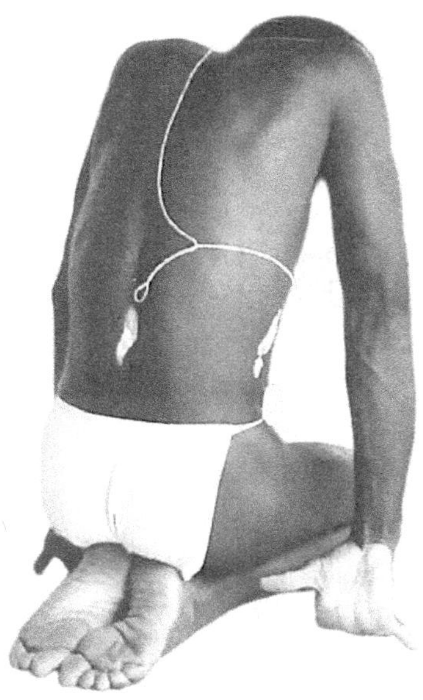

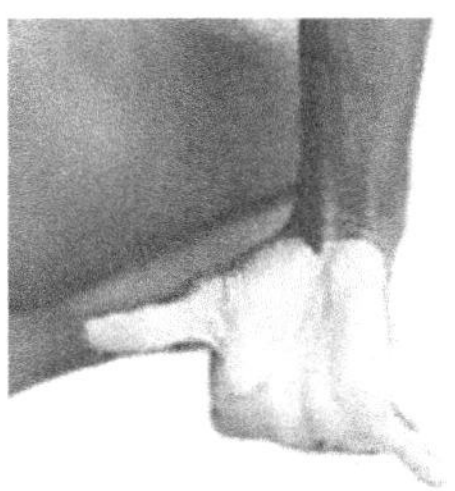

If the knee and ankles are supple, this *Press Fingers* pose is easy. It involves sitting on the heels and back of legs. Once this pose is assumed, the yogi presses the fingers to the floor. The thumb is held in the air with no pressure applied to it. The body is tilted forward, just a little. That increases the pressing force. It puts a strain on tendons and joints in hand.

The yogi closes the eyelids if he did not use a blindfold. There is inner focus to discover the format of the energy. This is done by mapping the inner feelings. At first the finger joints will exude electric currents, and will fire electric sparks and flashes. After a time, the yogi will have to release the fingers. Then he should interlock and swivel them. These actions will cause the tension which accumulated, to disperse.

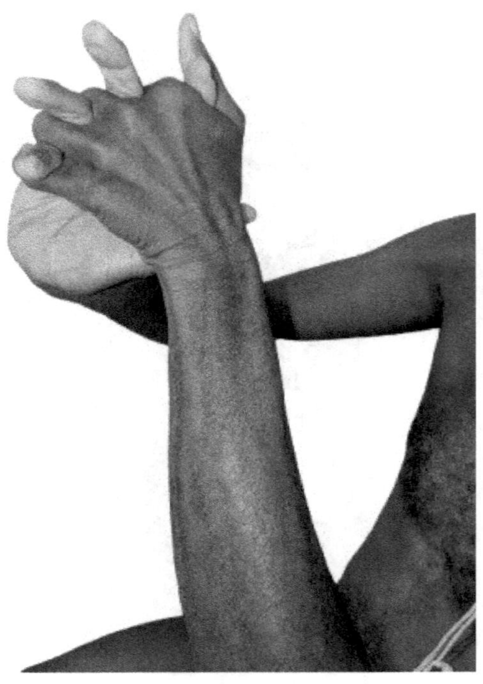

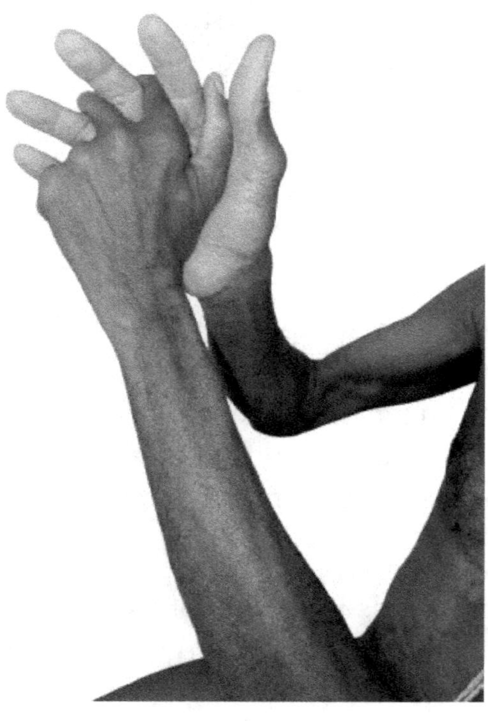

When the condition of the hands feels normal, the yogi should apply pressure to the fingers by pressing to the floor. The thumb should not be used. When the yogi feels that he should relieve the tension, he should again interlock and swivel the fingers. Then he should let the hands rest on the thighs.

He should focus to see the configuration of energy when no pressure is applied. A yogi may feel a connection, like a cable of energy running through the shoulders into the neck.

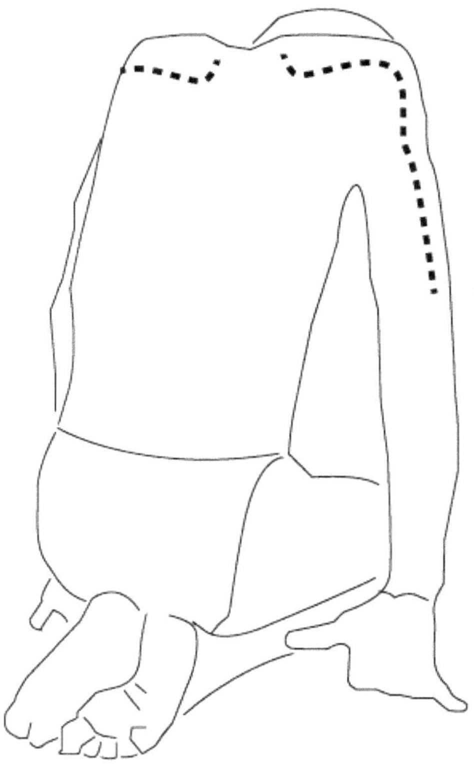

Focus Connection

The *Press Fingers* posture is done by exerting pressure on the four fingers of each hand. The thumb floats. It does not contact the floor. The yogi sits on the heels. If the body design does not allow that, a cushion may be used to elevate the buttocks. The trunk should lean forward slightly. The chin should be locked against the throat but without tilting the head.

As soon as the pressure is exerted on the fingers, the yogi should internalize, to discover the configuration of energies. There will be some tightness where the fingers meet the palms of the hands. From the fingers, lines of energy will shoot toward the palms. From the palms, energy will rush towards the fingers.

This will cause electric sensations in the form of twinkles, and rapid burst like mini-star explosions. A yogi can do so much of this. Then, he will feel compelled to relax the hands. At some point, cramp feelings will be emitted. The yogi will release the pressure.

He should interlock the fingers before his face. He should swivel the fingers back and forth as they are interlocked. He should do this until the cramp feelings and tightness dissipates.

Then, he should rest the hands on the thighs. He should listen and be alert within the body. There may be shimmering light moving through the wrist, forearms, and arms, into the shoulders. Observing and becoming fixated in this energy, he may eventually feel sparkling twinkles in the cheeks.

Lotus Stretched Back on Hands

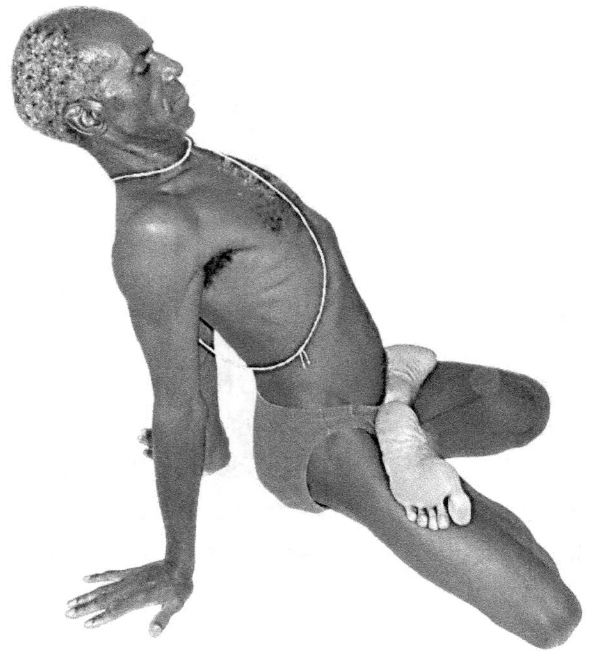

This *Lotus Stretched Back on Hands* posture, has a lift of the rib cage, with alignment of the neck. The hands are floored to facilitate the placement of the shoulders. This may be done in lotus, or in an easier pose where the legs are not interlocked. Once a yogi assumes this, he should check internally to be sure that the rib cage is lifted, and the neck is aligned. It should not be pushed forward but should be in alignment with the spine. If, however, the chin lock is not being applied, if it seems that the reverse neck lock should be used, the yogi should lift the chin as far as possible, and tilt the head back to the maximum.

Once that is achieved, and if a blindfold is not used, the yogi should close the eyelids, and focus down through the neck and trunk.

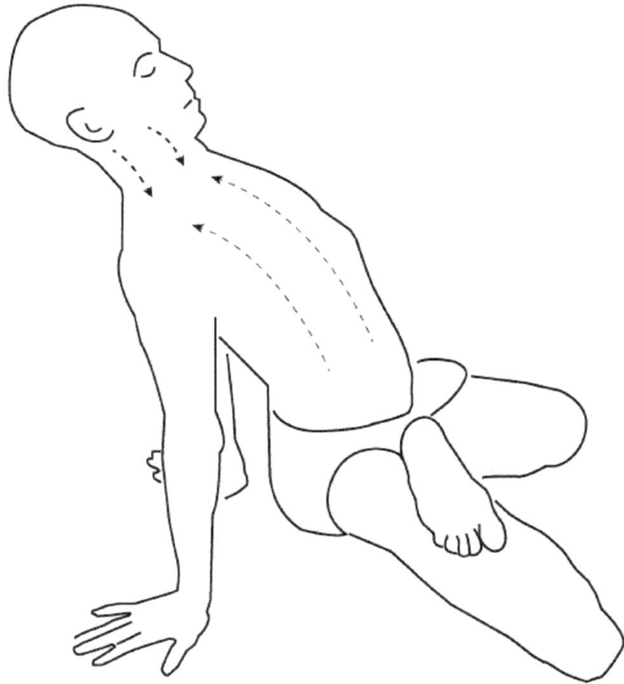

There may be release of energy from the feet and legs. This energy will run into the thighs. It will shift into the lower torso and dissipate there.

After some time, the pains in the feet and legs will cease. This may be replaced with cramp feelings. The yogi may hear naad resonance. Regardless of if the yogi hears naad or not, it will blare. It will be a steady frequency, as if the sound is dusted everywhere in the subtle head, with intensity on one side or the other, but being continuously emitted.

Focus Connection

The *Lotus Stretched Back on Hands* posture is relatively easy. It may be done in any easy pose. It can be done in a tight lotus. The yogi should be sure to apply the chin lock by bringing the chin towards the throat. The head should not be tilted in either direction.

Due to the lack of stringent tensions, there will be a natural search for events in the inner situation. When there are strain and stress, the attention is forcibly drawn to those circumstances. When there is a lack of crisis, the attention wanders in the psyche. It looks for excitements. This is in violation to the instructions of Patanjali, where he admonishes that for yoga, the *chittavritti* excitements should be curtailed. He instructed that they be terminated by the core.

Essential *chitta* is consciousness or is the energy particles which comprise consciousness. *Vritti* means the agitations within the mental and emotional environment. Due to the flashes, the coreSelf feels compelled to check, endorse and permit events to appear, develop and mutate. This makes it unlikely for someone to employ stillness.

Even in the stillness of the mind, the self is uncomfortable. It is urged to find excitement. The development of higher perception is related to the amount of stillness a yogi can endure in the mind. The more mental activity there is, the more the self is deprived of higher perception. The coreSelf needs much stillness, where it can wait for the development of higher perception.

A self is condemned to physical perception, and mundane psychic events, because it has little or no access to silence. In the *Lotus Stretched Back on Hands* posture, there is an opportunity to check inner sounds. For many yogis, naad resonance will be present. For others, naad will not be heard but the hum of psyche, or its vibration which is its consciousness, will be felt. Either of these could serve as the basis of awareness.

A yogi may notice that if he hears naad, he continues to hear it because he shifted his awareness to it. As soon as he does not point his awareness in naad's direction, that inner sound may disappear. He must apply himself but with only a little focus, to be with naad, either to be submerged in naad, or listen to it.

Once he hears naad, and once he shifts into it, or is keenly hearing it, it may come from both sides of the back part of the subtle head. It may be streaming, just as a river which glides through a valley, on its way to the sea.

Naad may be experienced coming from the lower back of the head, and streaming up to the top, traveling as it follows the curve of the back top part of the head. Naad may be loud and dominant, where the yogi feels that he must attend it.

After a short time, the yogi may realize that he travelled through a transparent tube, to go to the psychic place, where he hears physical sound. He was conveyed there. How? He may not know. But he can ponder, how even though he did not request the transit, he was transported.

- What is the reverse of this?
- How can the yogi know, and use a transit from a physical hearing place, to a transcendence hearing access?

The yogi should stay still and listen. He should realize that the stillness is due to naad's stable resonance. It is consistent. This practice is a way for the coreSelf to estimate its ability to isolate itself from physical influence, as well as from unwanted mental and emotional events.

- Does the coreSelf require a still reality to anchor itself?

That should be studied. From that, conclusions about the self may be derived.

Fingers Crimped

This *Fingers Crimped* requires an easy pose, sitting on the buttocks with the feet pulled to the body. The wrists hang over the knees. The hands are pulled back at 90^0 to the wrists. If there is tension in the thighs, where the mind is drawn to the stress or discomfort, this posture cannot be efficiently completed.

There should be tension at the wrists and in the hands. Elsewhere there should be no stress which draws the mind to other parts of the body.

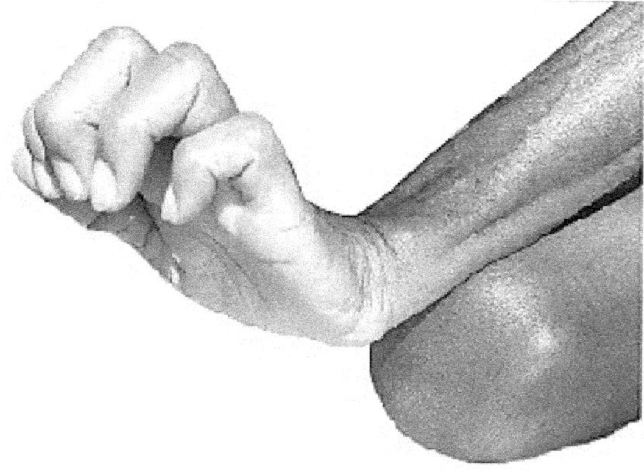

Focus Connection

The *Fingers Crimped* position can be done in any easy sitting pose, in which the knees rest on the floor. One variation has the legs crossed with knees floating due to the inability to bring the knees to the floor in that position. In that posture, the wrist may not touch the knees. The forearm may do that.

This is not a posture with much stress, except for the fingers and wrist. However, there may be a tendency for the elbows to relax. That causes them to bend. The yogi should check and recheck to certify that the elbows do not relax. If they do, or if one does, it should be straightened.

When this posture is assumed, there may be thoughts in the mind. These will appear and disappear involuntarily. The yogi may not know that a thought is running. If he discovers that it is, he will see the idea. Even sexual thoughts in reference to someone may arise. These may be current ideas which were transmitted, from an acquaintance's mind into that of the yogi. With a flash he will see a certain sexual energy, which was emitted by someone, and which entered his psyche.

The yogi may react to the thought. If he fails to do this, he will find that he must give the thought value, so that it can further reveal itself. If he participates, it will develop further. His interest in it, will give it the power to remain in the mind and be further illustrated.

If instead, once he noticed the thought, he acted as if he was not its target, that it was mistaken, even though in fact it was not, the thought will be reduced. It will diminish. This is similar to when someone rings a doorbell. He rings it. He waits. The tenant does not respond. The visitor rings again. Still, there is no response. The visitor becomes uncomfortable. The visitor goes away.

When doing this pose, when it feels that the arms and forearms should relax, the yogi should move the hands so that they rest on the knees. The fingers should be relaxed. The fingers may cup the knees.

Upper Limbs Outstretched – Fingers Crimped

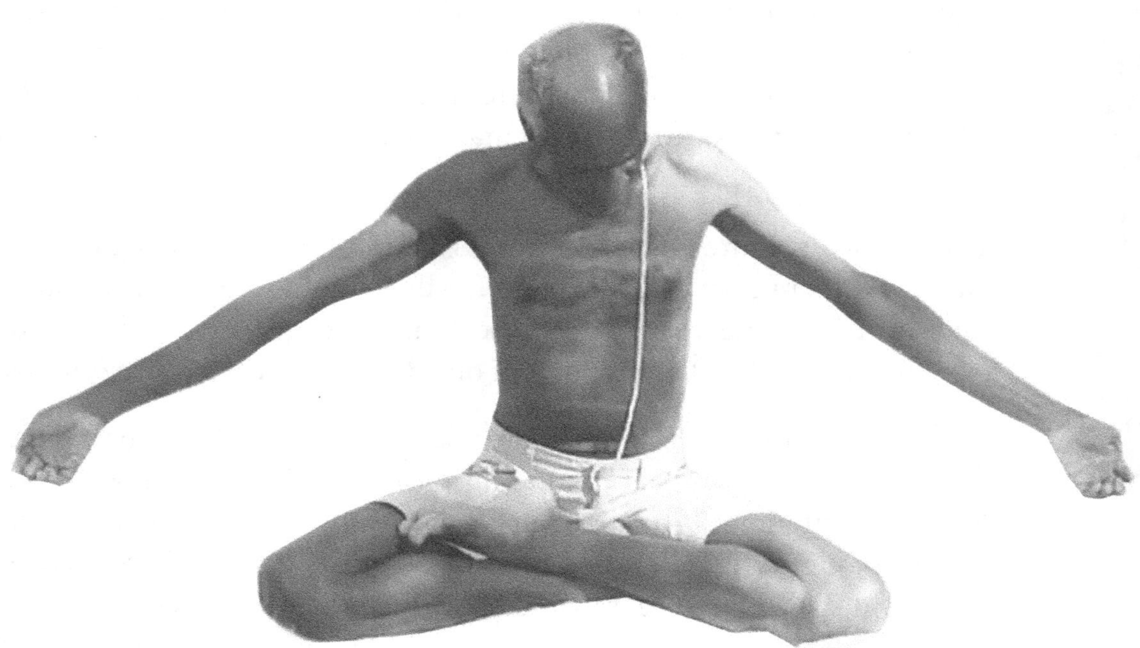

In this *Upper Limbs Outstretched – Fingers Crimped* posture, the yogi should focus within the psyche to detect energy movements and surges. At some point, he should hear naad resonance. When it is realized that the hands are no longer tensioned, the yogi should reset it.

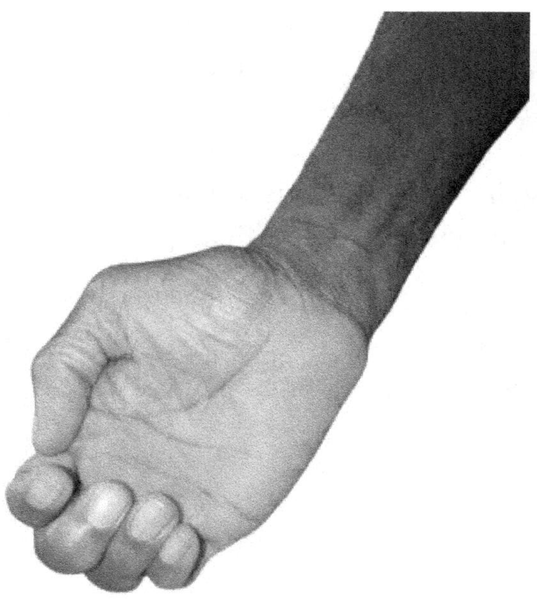

The yogi should be alert to notice when naad fades. He may investigate which force causes naad to be lost. After a time, the hands should relax, so that they change position and rest on the knee area of the thighs. Then the yogi should retreat fully into naad resonance.

Periodically, a check should be made to find if the spine collapsed, where it curves and the head drops, because the neck no longer holds the head erect. Then the yogi should slowly, not abruptly, reset the head. He should resume the meditation with naad absorption.

Focus Connection

The *Upper Limbs Outstretched – Fingers Crimped* posture, is a relatively easy pose. It may however be strenuous for the arms muscles. To hold the head in this pose, requires attention which is a type of *dharana* deliberate focus. That is the sixth of the eight processes for yoga. By studying how the arm muscles express distress, a yogi can better understand the *dharana* focusing process.

That pose should be done in the easy pose but it may be done in a tight lotus or in any cross legged posture, where the knees rest on the floor or where the knees float.

When doing this pose, the head may or may not be tilted forward. The chin lock should be applied. There should be a check within the psyche. This maps what occurs. The yogi mentally notes the outlay. He checks for areas which are blank, where there is no energy manifestation or movement.

When first assuming this pose, checking to be sure that it is done correctly, a yogi will turn to inner focus. Instead of finding an array of chaotic energy, he may discover that naad resonance streams, streamed, and will continue streaming, even if he is not attentive to it. A linkage to naad would mean access to a free focus. The yogi has neither to install, imagine, nor grip the focusing objective. It is there for the taking. It is continuous. It does not flee from the yogi.

Alongside the inner sound, there may be a thought, running in the space as well. As soon as the yogi becomes aware of it, its slow development ceases. He finds that naad is more pronounced. The thought, regardless of what it was, regarding if it is urgent or trivial, disappeares. The information is that if there are thoughts, and if there is naad resonance being acknowledged, the thoughts will disappear, if the yogi links his focus to naad. He will not have to utilize a disciplinary energy to banish the thoughts.

During this practice, the yogi will, from time to time, have the feeling to check the position of the neck.

- Is it tilted forward?
- Is it erect?

He should let the neck tilt forward just a fraction. He should lock the chin to the throat. This will provide a locked head section. Naad will seem as if it permeates only the head. It will relay that it cannot extend into the neck. The neck lock will serve as a closed valve, with no exchange of energy from the head to the torso.

At some point, the yogi will feel to relax the arms, forearms and hands. He should do so by putting the hands on the knees. There may be a burning tension in the muscles and tendons of the arms. In this posture, the yogi should notice how the arms prepare for relaxation. A yogi should go through the shoulders into the arms. There he should observe the radiation of a steady but slight pain sensation which emanates.

Then again there will be thoughts. These will open partially, so that the yogi is aware of their contents. He should swing his attention upwards to hear naad. This will cause him to observe that the energy in the arms moves to the shoulders and dissipates. Naad will be in the head area. It will appeal to the yogi to resume the free focus.

Stand – Hands Bracing Shoulders

For that *Stand – Hands Bracing Shoulders* posture, feet should be firmly placed for balance, to easily support the body. The hands are crossed behind the head but the fingers are spread and grasp the shoulder blades. The elbows are pressed backward. That creates a tension which attracts energy from the armpits. This is held, while the yogi focuses to monitor and note, where energy is released.

Immediately after doing it, one should gradually without jerks, lower the upper limbs. The hands should be brought to a position hanging to the sides with the palms facing forward. Then one should slowly lower the body, and sit in any easy pose.

Focusing inside the body, one should identify energy releases. There may be distinct releases from the armpits into the body. After a time, that will cease. The yogi should be aware of inner sound.

Focus Connection

The *Stand – Hands Bracing Shoulders* posture is an easy one, which may be strenuous or awkward for some yogis. If one has bulky shoulders, if the arms are enlarged, it may be difficult to do this. It entails grabbing the scapula shoulder blades.

When this posture is first assumed, the yogi should close the eyelids or have in use, a blindfold. He should check from within the body, to determine the position of the hands and elbows.

- Are the hands grasping the shoulder blades?
- Are the elbows pressed backwards?

There should be tension in the armpits and shoulder joints. That should be held but it should not be strenuous. The neck should be adjusted to facilitate the pose.

Once those connections are in place, the yogi should hold them in position. He should pull the abdomen. He should pull the perineum. He should be sure that the anus is uplifted. The self should mentally descend into the trunk of the body on the inside.

The yogi should release the perineum muscle, and then should immediately retract it. He should do this again and again, as if operating a pump. There is such a pump which operates in the perineum area. That pump is engaged involuntarily during sexual activity. It causes sexual fluid to squirt from the male organ, and from the clitoris in females.

By operating the perineum muscle, pulling it up and then relaxing it, the yogi isolates this biological function. It is different to the urinary muscle which concerns the bladder and its tubing. The other muscle in that area is the anus. That too is separate from the urinary ejection apparatus, and from the sexual fluid squirting system. From the inside of the body, the yogi should research to understand these systems, in regards to how energy is utilized and distributed, through the psyche.

When the yogi feels that he should relax from this posture, he should relocate his hands from the collar bones to the waist. With the hands on the hips, he should press the waist forward and relax the upper limbs.

Prayer Pose Reverse

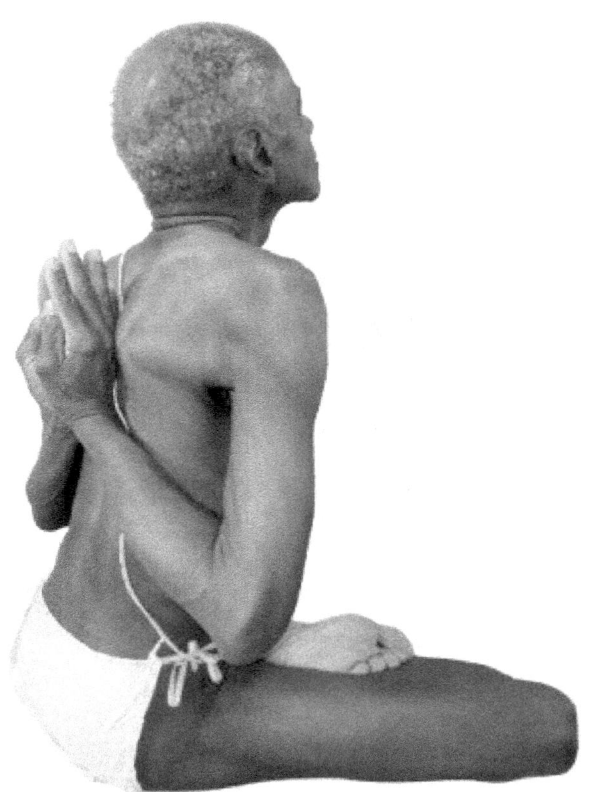

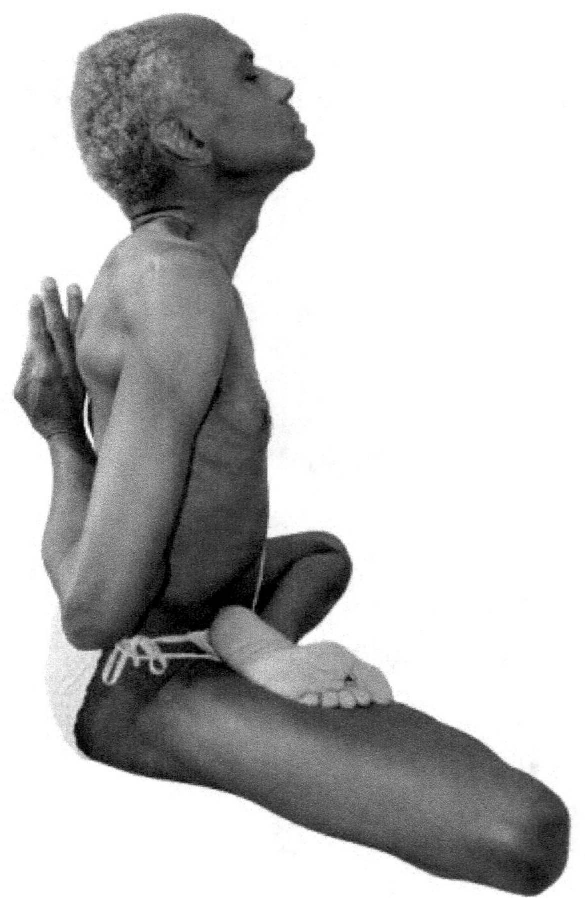

This *Prayer Pose Reverse* pose may be done from any easy sitting or standing position. There should be no tension except in the arms, forearms and hands. The spine should be kept upright. In particular, the lower abdomen should be positioned so that the upper spine does not curve forward. The head may or may not be tilted backward. If it is not, the chin should be pulled to the throat. The neck should be erect.

Tension will be in the upper limbs; the arms, forearms, and hands. The yogi when focusing internally, should notice if one upper limb radiates more energy than the other. It may seem that the backward neck lock is natural. Conversely on some occasions, it will seem as if the head should be erect and the chin should be pulled to the throat.

With the eyelids closed, or with a blindfold in place, there may be an air sound in the psyche. There may be a slight rocking, left to right, right to left. This will be in harmony with inner sound.

Focus Connection

The *Prayer Pose Reverse* position is difficult, if the arms and forearms are enlarged. Some yogis have enlarged muscular backs, which make this posture difficult to assume. It can be done in any sitting position, in an easy pose or in a tight lotus.

Once the hands are positioned, the yogi should peer through the neck. He should check the chin. There is a subtle tube running from the chin to the throat. It should be inspected.

- Is it hollow?
- What is its diameter?

The yogi should peer through the windpipe.

- Can he see through the trunk to the base of pubic area?
- Is there cloudy opaque energy when peering down?

During this pose, there may be a small tolerable tension in the arms. This will radiate a force which can be the object of focus. After a time, the yogi should relax the arms, forearms, and hands. The hands should rest either at the sides or on the thighs. The yogi should observe how the disturbed energy in the arms slowly disappear. This is like when a mist dissipates when sun rays strike it.

Press Side Chest/Breasts

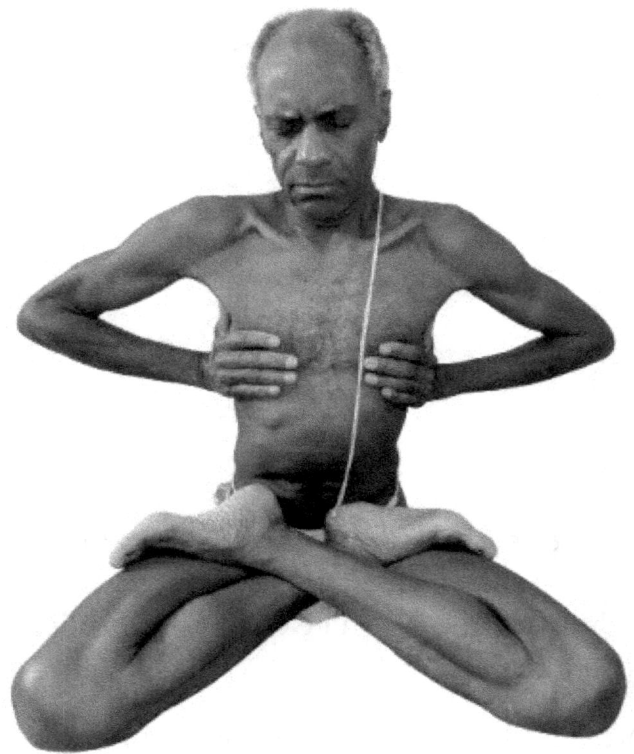

This *Press Side Chest/Breasts* posture, may be done sitting on a chair, or in any easy pose on a floor, or in any lotus posture variation. The fingers of each hand cover the chest/breasts, If the hands slide and cannot remain positioned, one may remove the shirt. Eyelids should be closed or a blindfold should be used.

The focus should be in the upper trunk, behind the rib cage. When doing this, each elbow may begin swinging to one side, then to the other. This happens because of a twisting tendency which rotates slightly to the right, then to the left, repeatedly.

After a time focusing within the chest, the yogi may realize a circular energy which emits upward torque, some on the right, and some on the left. These energies will go upward. Before reaching the collar bones, they will disappear in the upper chest

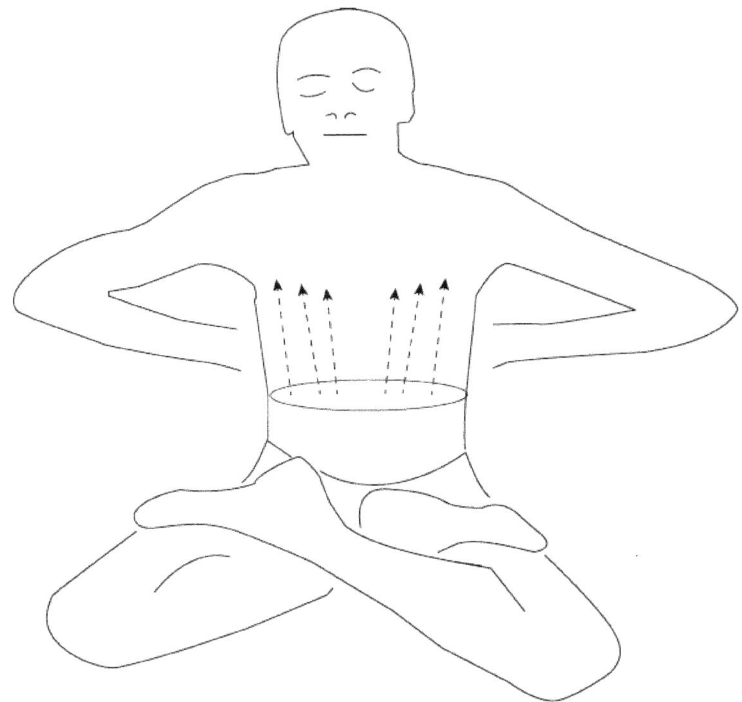

After a time, focusing on these energies, the yogi will notice that they disappear. Then, a quiescent energy will be distributed evenly in the chest areas.

Focus Connection

The *Press Side Chest/Breasts* pose, may be done from any sitting position. If the elbow joints are stiff or fleshy, that may make this posture difficult to assume.

Soon after doing this, and focusing within the psyche, the yogi may hear inner sound. That may be a blend of frequencies. When the yogi makes a movement to go down into the chest, he may discover that the inner sound is in a bowl which has a bottom where the neck intersects with the shoulders.

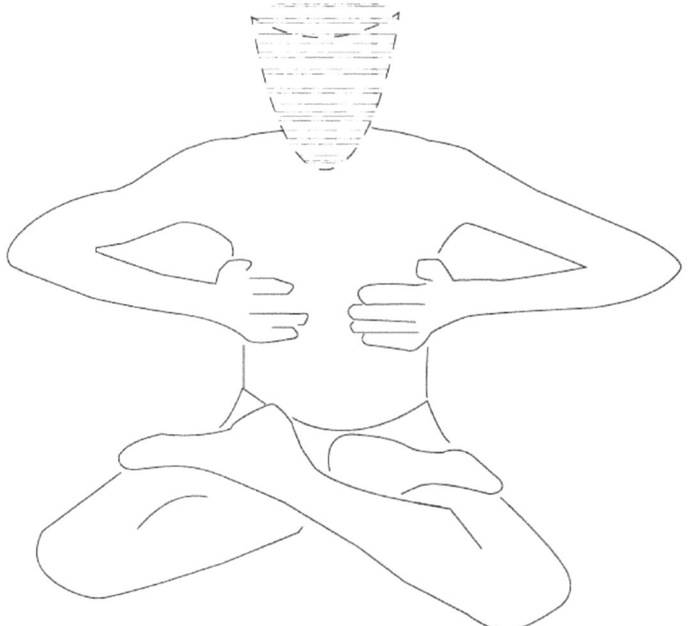

The yogi should become absorbed in that resonance. He should note its boundaries. After a time, when the hands become uncomfortable, he should release them. He should put the hands on the thighs near the knees. He may feel an immediate relief. He should again focus on inner sound. Being aware of naad resonance, he may realize that a thought develops. This thought was subliminal initially. It became evident, just as when the light of dawn increases until there is full sunlight. As the thought develops, at a certain stage he becomes aware of it. Then just his recognition, stopped it from developing. It disappeared.

Thoughts, many of them, have a power to sustain themselves, and to force the yogi to observe their development, and to interact with them. In this condition, the thoughts which arise have no display power. As soon as they are recognized as thought appearances, they flash out. A yogi notices this.

Hands to Hips

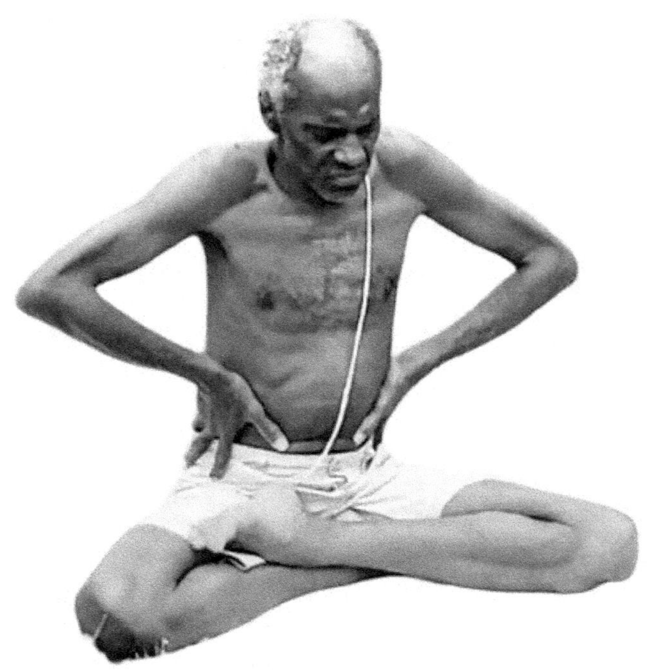

This *Hands to Hips* posture, is accomplished from an easy sitting position, either on the floor or on a chair. The body should be comfortable, so that no extra tensions interrupt the focus. Once the sitting posture is conducted, the yogi should, with the fingers pointed downward, apply the base of the hands on the hips. Each hand rests on each corresponding hip.

There may be naad ringing in the subtle head. If this is heard, the yogi should absorb and become engaged in it. Naad should be noticed.

- Does it vibrate from ear to ear?
- Does it pervade the subtle head?

From the contact between each hand and its corresponding hip, there may be a round energy zone from the center of which, there may be a streak of energy which rises upward through the trunk of the subtle body.

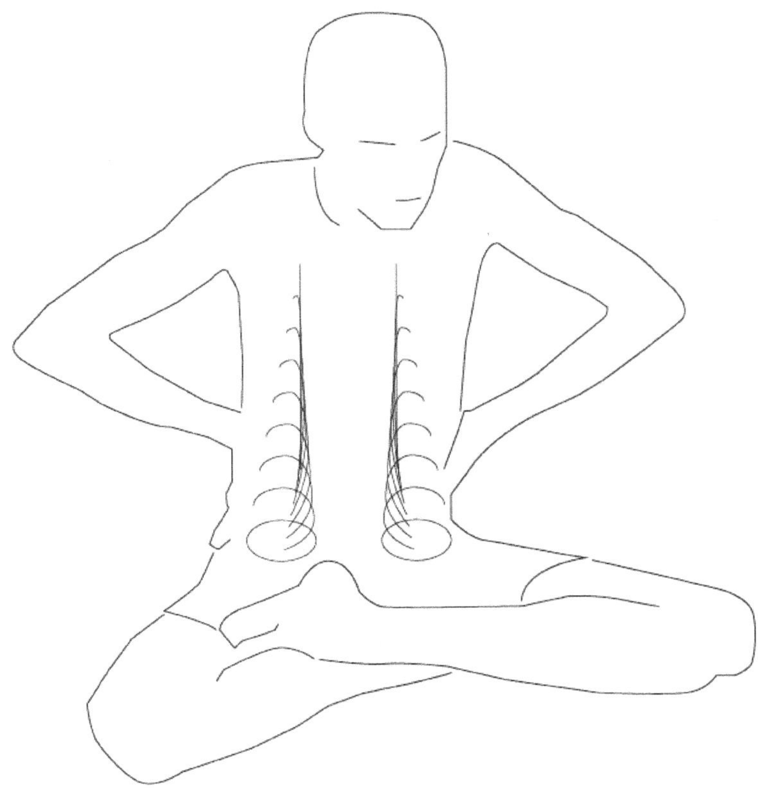

Focus Connection

The *Hands to Hips* posture is easy. It can be done from a sitting position which is easy for the yogi. Its focus for application is to be sure that the hands cradle the lower torso, and push down on each corresponding hip.

The spine should be erect for this position. As soon as the pose is formed, the yogi should check the mind space, and the torso region, for subtle movements. A yogi may realize that the inner sound blares loudly. Still, he may be aware of thoughts which arrive and develop. It may be noticed that even though the naad resonance is pronounced, even though it is persistent and loud, still any thought which arrives in the mind, absorbs the full attention of the coreSelf. The self does not have the resistance to ignore the ideas which develop.

He will notice that thoughts are like heavy metal scaffolding, and the naad sound is like the flimsy wind, which cannot affect the framing. This posture is not conducive for meditation. It is however, a posture in which the yogi can learn about thought generation and illustration, when it is contrasted to inner sound, or to any other focus which is preferred.

Grasp Back-Top Head

This *Grasp Back-Top Head* action is done with an easy posture, either sitting on a floor or other surface. The skull should be grasp with the fingers. There will be tension in the arms but it will be tolerable. Once the posture is assumed, and the eyelids are closed, or a blindfold is used, the yogi should focus internally in the head of the subtle body.

He should listen to inner sound in the back of the head.

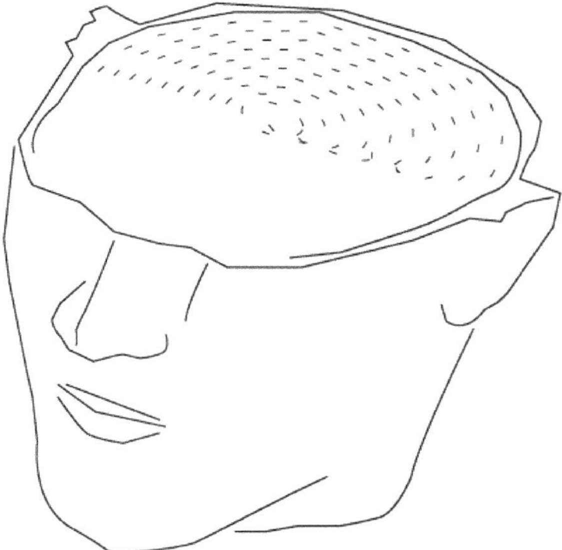

Even though naad may be heard on one side or the other, in this posture, one may hear naad blaring in the back area. In addition, the yogi should check to be sure that the neck is erect. This may cause the head and neck to feel as if floating above the trunk of the body.

When the arms are tired, the yogi should rest them on the knees. When they are relieved of tension, the yogi should slowly restore them to grasp the back of the head. When this happens, naad resonance may be heard predominantly on one side and much less on the other.

This posture can be used to indoctrinate the mind for hearing naad sound resonance in the back of the head.

Focus Connection

The *Grasp Back-Top Head* position is easy. It should be assumed from a no-tension sitting pose. The head may be tilted slightly forward. Or it may be erect. As soon as the yogi internalizes or attempts to do so, he may notice inner sound, coming from the top-right back-part of the head. This would be immediate. It should be streaming like a river coursing to the sea.

A thought may arise but it will have no power to divert the yogi. When it surfaces to display itself, the focus of the yogi will ignore it. Instead of watching the thought's development, the yogi will notice the naad resonance. He will want to investigate the situation of naad, as to its location, spread and quality.

At first, in this pose, there will be no tension. Later, the yogi should notice that a slow pain emanates from the arms. This is a muscle strain.

Noticing this, the yogi should note its precise position in each arm. He should check to see where naad is located. The quality of its energy should be observed.

Again, the pain in the arms will be noted. Then it will be that the arms relieve themselves by relaxing. The hands, forearms and arms will move as the hands rest on the thighs. The yogi will continue the internal attentiveness. He will note that the arms no longer express a slow painful muscle feeling. Instead, the entire psyche may have an interest in the inner sound. Then again, the yogi should raise the upper limbs to assume the *Grasp Back-Top Head* pose.

Jaws Braced

This *Jaws Braced* posture is done from an easy pose. It can be assumed while sitting on a chair or floor, with or without cushion. The base of a palm is used to brace the corresponding jaw. Th fingers point upward. In the mouth, the tongue is coiled up and is pushed back to the soft palate. The attention is occupied in the frontal lobe of head.

At first, the attention is in the jaw bones which are supported by the hands. When that is established and attention to anything else ceases, the attention is shifted to the frontal brain. The yogi meditates on being absorbed in the frontal lobe.

Some naad sound may be heard. It may be slight or intense. While hearing, the yogi maintains focus on the frontal part of the brain.

At some time, it will be realized that the arms tire. Then, the yogi should slowly release the jaws. He should put the hands on the knees and continue the absorption.

It may happen that there is a shift in focus, where the head has light-energy which is evenly distributed. The yogi should be absorbed in that. He should remain in that for some time. This is a training for the mind to be in *samadhi*. This is an example of a *kriya*.

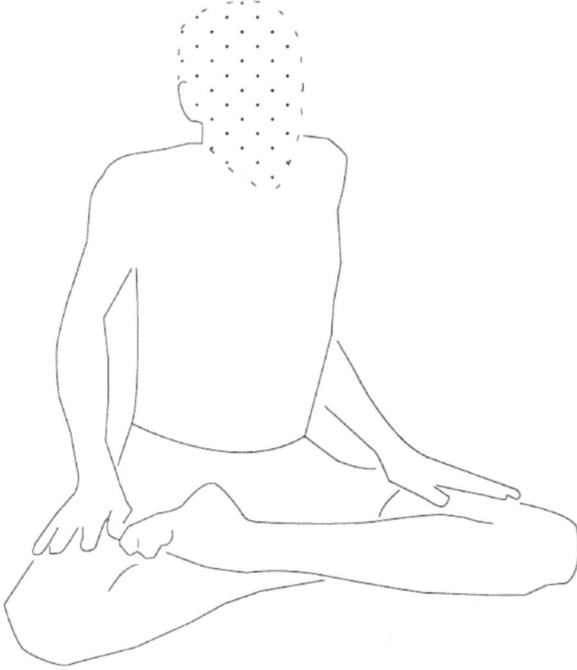

Focus Connection

The *Jaws Braced* position is an easy posture. Provided the spine is erect, it can be assumed from any sitting position. When a yogi is positioned for this, he may notice two features when he focuses internally. Those are the energy in frontal area of the head, and inner sound either to the right or left, near to the corresponding ear.

In that position, while hearing naad resonance, the yogi may see shadows of thought ideas. These will come and go, acting like shadows in the night, which showed and disappeared before they could be identified. A yogi should investigate to understand how his focus switches to a thought formation while he focused on inner resonance.

Tight Lotus Posture *(Padmasana)*

This *Tight Lotus Posture (Padmasana),* may be difficult for some yogis. If this is a tense situation, it should not be done. Or it may be done for a limited time only. There are many preliminary postures which aid a yogin in stretching the thigh and leg muscles. There is also the problem of fat in the thighs. This posture is not mandatory. If, however, one feels compelled to be proficient in it, one should consider if the body one received from the parents, is genetically capable of it.

A yogi should consider that even if he can do a posture perfectly, he may do it with incorrect focus. Hence, physical format may not correspond to subtle body. Considering this, a yogi should leave aside the idea of doing final forms of every posture.

A yogi may do a posture in a lopsided manner. Yet, internally, he may master what should done. There were lopsided yogis, like for instance Yogi *Ashtavakra,* whose body was bent (*vakra*) in eight (*asthta*) places. And yet, he was a master of yoga.

When doing meditation practice, it may happen that during the absorption, the objective awareness regarding the body is lost. If that happens the body may fall to the ground, or it may remain upright, but the head may droop when the neck muscles relax. This may happen with the yogi's awareness of it, or with his having no idea that it occurred.

The yogi's individuality on this side of existence may be suspended. When he is again aware of it, he may have full or partial recall of what happened. That may include a slight awareness of blank states, where there was no idea of existence, none whatsoever.

Each yogi should be trained to remain as still as possible in the mind space, when there is a return to objectivity on this side of existence. Any erratic or excited condition at that time, could result in a loss of memory of the transcendental events. It should be understood, that the coreSelf is different to its memory recording psychic mechanism. There is also the factor that there are several memory storage areas in the psyche. A shift away from, or a breach between the core and a memory, may result in a lack of recall. As one cannot get a clear image from a pond which has waves, so if the mind is agitated, it may not render coherent memories of the psychic events.

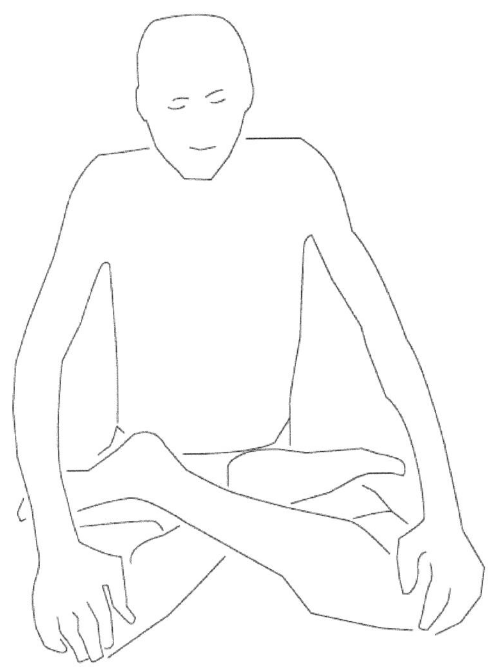

This is a difficult posture for anyone whose limbs hardly tolerate the full lotus. It is strenuous in the feet, legs, thighs and lower torso. Due to this, there may be a different result if someone does this, unless the physical body can easily slip into this.

In one body a certain pose is strenuous, while in the same body some other pose may be easy to assume. This is due to the varying designs of bodies according to the parentage. In dreams, where the subtle body flexes in any direction, someone may experience ease with a form. But that same person may be unable to assume the same pose(s) with his physical form. That gives the realization that the physical system may be designed to be at variance.

Once the full lotus is assumed, the hands should be spread over the knees. The neck should be upright with the head positioned in a balanced way. The eyelids should be closed if a blindfold was not used. The yogi should restrict focus within the head. Naad should be evident, such that it assists the yogi to keep in the center, and to be shielded from interference.

With naad resonance ringing in every direction, round-about, the yogi should experience the coreSelf as the central event in the subtle head.

Eventually this is interrupted, as somehow a thought or image appears. Then the self will find itself in an engagement with the event, but as someone who escapes the interruption, and is again absorbed in naad. That will happen. The yogi will feel the necessity to understand how the psychological instruments cause the engagement with naad, and then without giving a notice, switched the focus to thoughts and ideas. This is a study of the winding and unwinding, focusing and unfocusing, of the adjuncts in the psyche.

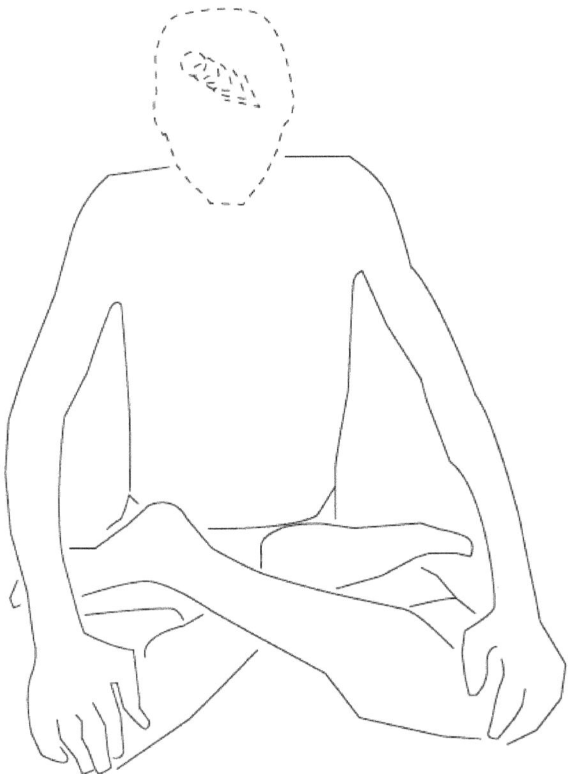

Focus Connection

The *Tight Lotus Posture (Padmasana)* is a classic pose used by many persons, even by those who do not practice the Patanjali method. It is a difficult and distracting pose for those who are not slim, and who do not have limber joints. For some it is best to substitute an easy pose where the legs are not interlocked, but where one leg is rested on the other, and where the buttocks are elevated three or four inches on a cushion.

Pain and tension can be a focus when doing internal focus *(antah dhristih)*. However, in most cases the tension and pain may be a distraction where the mind cannot use the discomfort to aid in the effort to introspect about the feelings, and the shifting energies.

Once the *Tight Lotus Posture* is assumed, the yogi should check to be sure that the body sits plumb on the buttocks. The abdomen should be properly positioned. The spine should be erect. The hands should cup the knees. If, however, the hands do not reach the knees, the hands can rest on the thighs, with palms facing up or down. Interlocking the fingers should be done, if the yogi experiences more tendency to internalize, when the fingers of one hand touch those of the other. The energy that runs from one hand to the other, though the fingers, may distract. In which case, the hands should be kept apart.

Once the posture is set, the yogi should give internal focus. He may immediately hear naad in the center back part of the head. Then he may find that the subtle body flips upward where the head of the physical one is in converse to the subtle one.

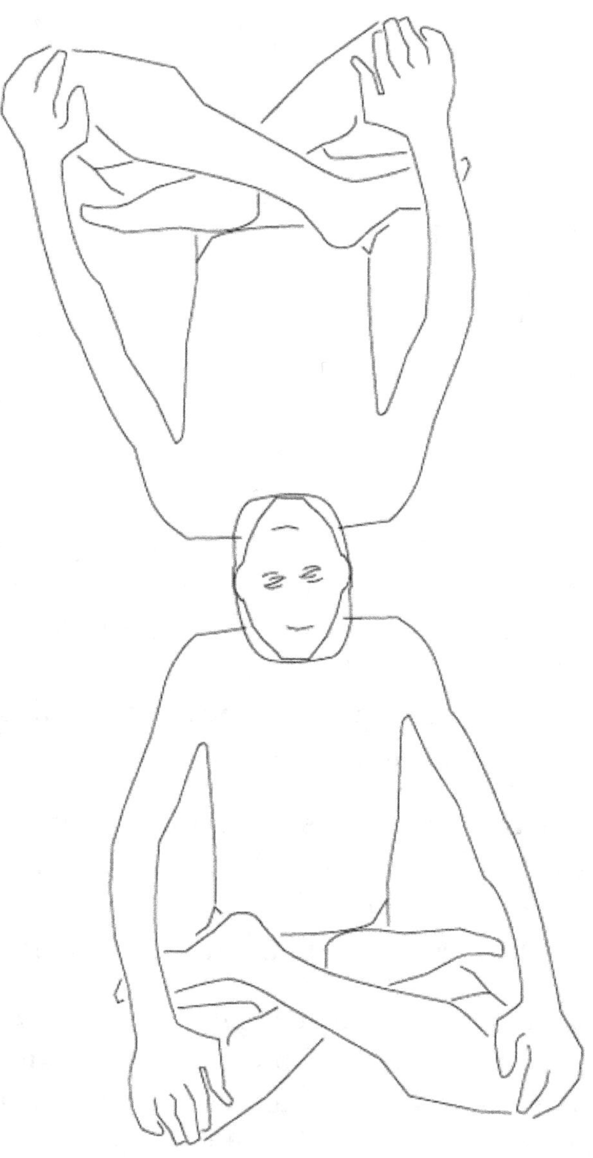

When doing the *Tight Lotus Posture,* the yogi should, periodically, check the neck and spine. There may be a tendency for the head to lean with the neck tilting to the right, left, front or back, having the head hang from the body. This may happen so that the yogi has no idea of when or why that occurred. Such movements of the physical body may be conducted by the lifeForce, which may move a part of the body without consulting the coreSelf.

The spine may not remain erect. It may curve in a convex or concave manner. The yogi should gently resituate it. If during the practice, the yogi notices that any part of the body moved, he should take note of it. He should backtrack to determine how that shift occurred, with his being unaware of it.

The yogi should study how long he can sit.

- Can it be for twenty, thirty or forty minutes?
- Should the body have spinal support when sitting for long periods?
- Can he silently track movements and shifts, to observe how the lifeForce and the earth's gravity, put parts of the body into other positions?

All-Fours on Fists and Knees

This *All-Fours on Fists and Knees,* is not strenuous, but it may be difficult to assume. Female bodies with large breast may have some discomfort and fatigue when assuming this pose. It may strain the rib cage and trunk, as the weight of the torso, which is usually conveyed through the thighs, legs and feet, will transfer through the shoulders, arms, forearms, fists and fingers. The thumbs carry no weight but the four fingers of each hand will be strained.

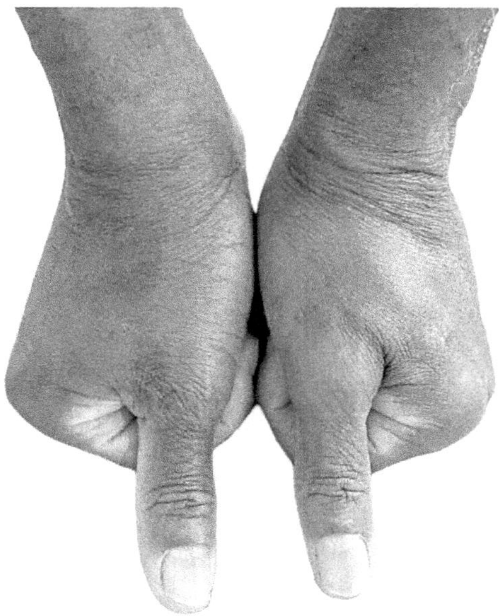

As soon as this posture is assumed, the yogi should check for energy distributions and shifts. Weight distribution should be observed. The position of the head in reference to the neck should be noted. The head should be tilted upward as much as can be tolerated. The eyelids should be closed.

There should be refocus into the shoulders, arms, forearms, wrists, and fingers. A yogi may discover energy running from the throat into the central chest. After some time, this pose cannot be tolerated. Then the yogi should slowly move backward to sit on or between the heels. While moving in this way, the body should not be jerked. Inner focus should note any energy movements and tension reliefs.

From the relief position, on or between the heels, the yogi should slowly resume the all-fours posture. This time, he should be more attentive to energy changes. There may be shivering of the shoulders. He should observe that. When it becomes unbearable, he should again sit on or between the heels.

It should be gaged as to the value of this posture, in terms of its ability to cause an absorption, with no thinking in the psyche. This will help the yogi to master higher meditation focus which is spontaneous, and which holds the focus of the coreSelf. A yogi may also study how the mind impulsively shifts, from a transcendence focus to a thought-creation mode, where the coreSelf loses objectivity, with little or no control over how it is influenced.

Focus Connection

The *All-Fours on Fists and Knees* position is easy, even for bodies which are overweight. However, it may not be tolerated for a long time. A yogi should check the neck so that it is tilted back as far as it will go, but without strain to the vertebrae. This posture reminds one of the baboon species. For them this position is normal. From this position they adjust the hind limbs and sit up.

When a yogi assumes this posture, he may at first, realize that his attention energy falls into his face. It falls into the eyes and forehead, even into the cheeks. The focus may remain in that part of the body where he may realize a shining light. That illumination may be source-less with no indication about its origination.

A yogi may hear a screeching sound from the right and left back side of the head. This will happen while perceiving the light which fell into the face. After a time, he may realize that the elbows collapsed, just a little. He should resituate them.

There will be a time, when the elbows can no longer tolerate the weight of the body. Then the yogi should sit on or between the heels. Slowly, he should put the hands on the thighs. He should sit. If this is uncomfortable, he should do the practice again but with a cushion between the heels. That will elevate the buttocks, resulting in less strain when he sits up.

The yogi should assume the *All-Fours on Fists and Knees* position again, but when necessary, he should sit up. This time, he may discover that the seeing impulse wants to position itself, so that if there is danger, it can give the psyche the optimum alert. This shows the yogi how he would behave if he used a baboon body. He would set the head, so that he could perceive risks, which would occur, if predators were in the vicinity.

Lotus Pull-up Toes

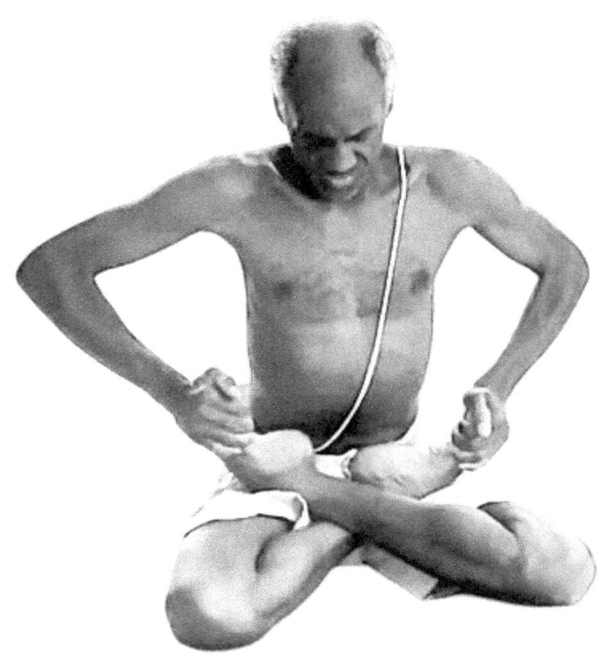

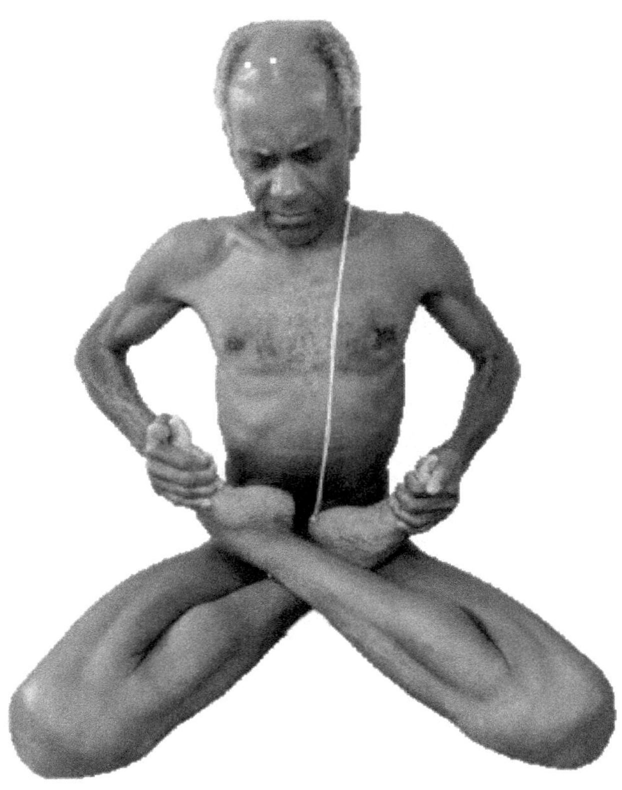

For this *Lotus Pull-up Toes*, the lotus posture is a prerequisite. However, some of this posture can be done sitting in any easy position, and using the hands to twerk and pressurize the muscles, ligaments, tendons, and nerves, in the feet. When using the hands to tense the feet, a yogi should be internally aware of the pressures which are applied. There should be no over-straining. Rather, day by day, one should apply the pressure.

At first this will be strenuous and somewhat painful. Over time, the stress will decrease. The idea is to cause the release of stagnant energy at the extremities of the feet. This is beneficial for the subtle body.

At first one should sit in a tight lotus. Using the hands on each side, one should lift the body to place it in an upright situation in reference to the floor. The back should not be curved. If necessary, one may use a cushion. This would raise the buttocks to make the posture steady.

Sitting upright, one should hold the toes with each corresponding hand. One should pull the toes upwards. This pressures the feet. At this time the focus should be within the body. No attention should be spared for external objects.

With the hands, one should keep the toes tightly drawn up. One may feel tingling sensations in the feet. In the spine, where the neck meets the shoulders, there may be an electrical current which is in the center of the vertebrae.

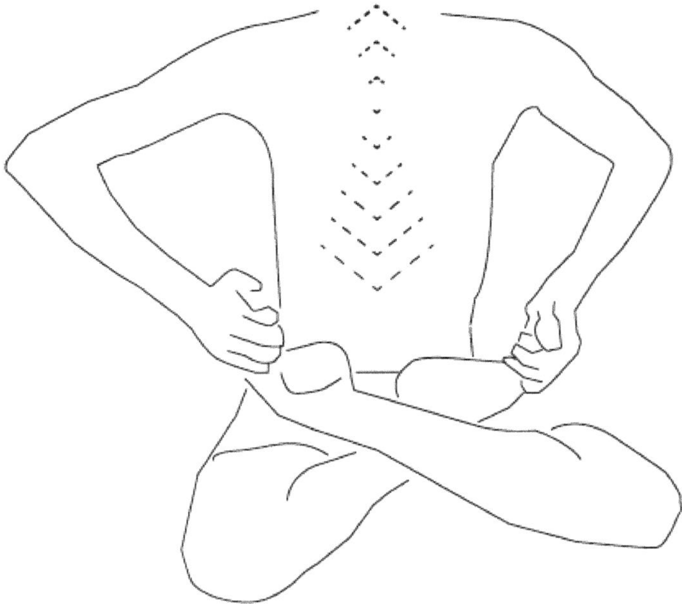

This central electric feeling is an objective of *dhyana* or spontaneous transcendent focus. The coreSelf should be absorbed in this spinal feeling. This is a method for understanding *dhyana,* the 7th step of yoga.

Focus Connection

The *Lotus Pull-up Toes* posture requires the use of a tight lotus. Once the lotus is in position, the yogi should grab the toes firmly and push them towards each other. This causes some feelings in the bone structures of the foot. It compresses the soles. When this foot lock is applied, the yogi should internalize to inspect and note the energy shifts.

He may notice that the mind is unfocused but it is not scattered. A feeling of being spaced-out will be absent. The mind's energy will be shining, blaring, just like a spotlight. It shines in all directions and shows no blaring face or projection.

During this pose, a yogi should regularly check to be sure that the toes remain locked by the gripping action of the hands. If it is discovered that the grip loosened, the yogi should slowly re-grip. He should continue the internal observations.

With the internal observation being keenly made, the yogi should sense energy descending through the center of the chest.

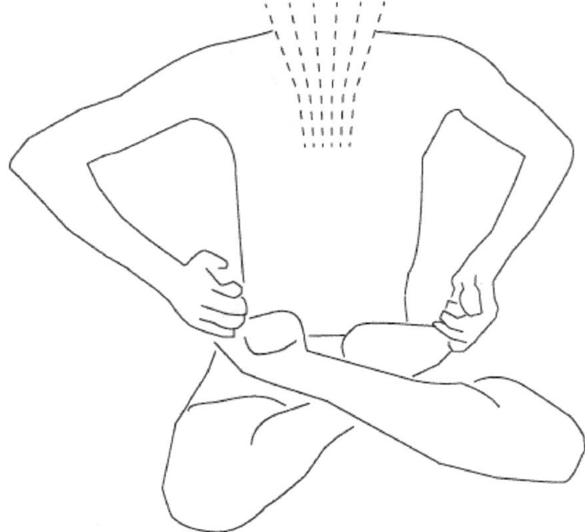

This energy will gradually move down through the torso. It will simmer though the organs and travel to the base chakra which is at the tailbone of the spine. Once the yogi senses that it reached the base, he should wait there silently. After a time, there will be a psychic light which will flash slowly. It will glow.

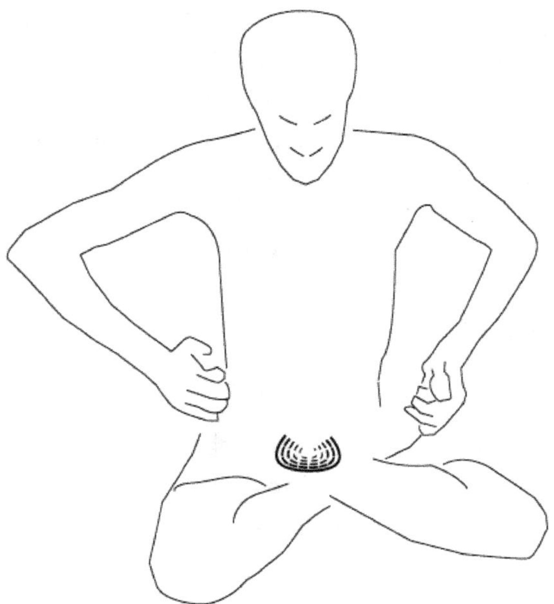

Standing- Arms 30 degrees Offset

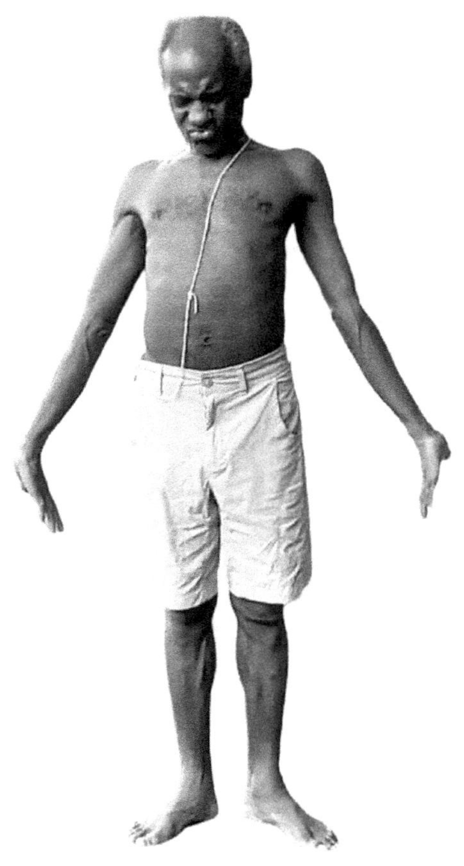

Standing with feet set for balance, with arms out at 30 degrees, with armpits turned out and hand splayed open, that is how this *Standing - Arms 30 degrees Offset* posture is done. The bottom lip is pursed tight. There should be a chair positioned behind the yogi. That will be used when it is no longer sensible to maintain the posture.

The yogi should lift the chest and keep the chin pressed to the throat. If there is no blindfold, the eyelids should be pressed. Apply inner focus to detect and track energy accumulation and dispersion. A yogi may perceive a tube of hollow white energy occurring from the throat through the trunk of the body.

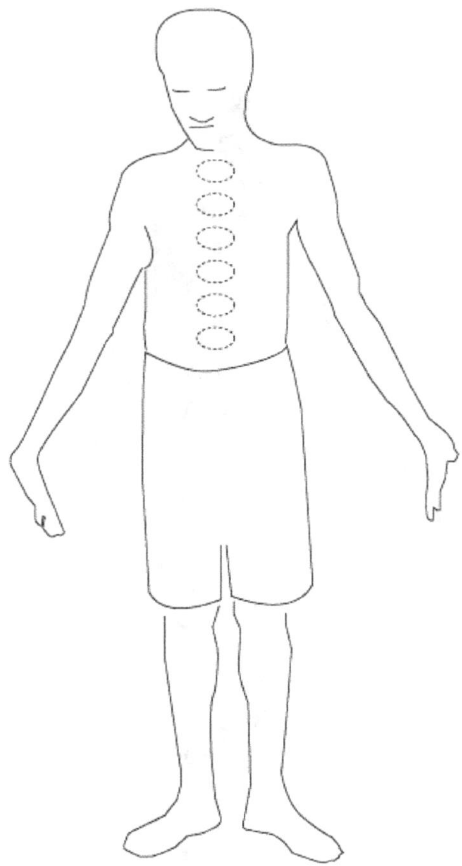

There may be a shimmering unsteadiness. If this increases, the yogi should lower the body slowly to let it sit on the chair which was placed behind.

Focus Connection

The *Standing - Arms 30 degrees Offset* position, concerns the stability of the physical body as referenced to the gravity of the earth. As soon as this position is set, there will be uncertainty, as to if the body can remain motionless. It cannot, but a yogi may shift awareness to the internal focus. Then, he may check to determine what should be done to stabilize the form.

In this posture there may arise a bulb of energy in the front center of the chest region. This bulb of energy may become hollow. There may be a whistling energy emanating from it.

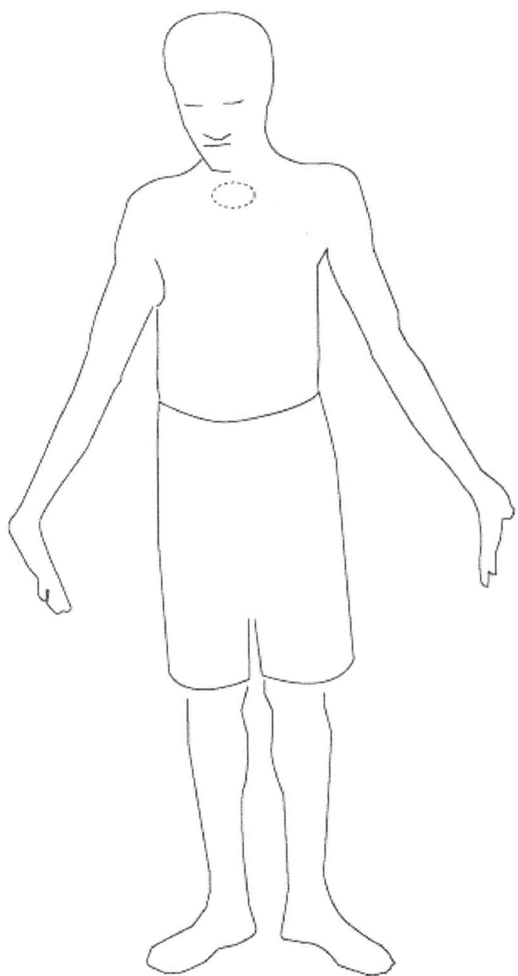

Press Hips – Raise Shoulders

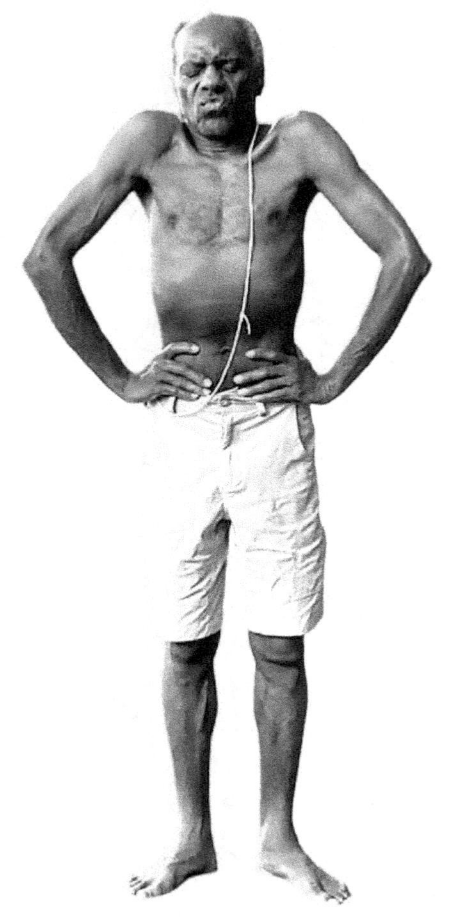

This *Press Hips – Raise Shoulders* is an easy posture. It could be done from a sitting position, but that may have varying effects. A yogi should stand firm with balance. One who has large thighs which touch, will have to position the feet to accommodate that.

The hands should press the hips. The thumbs should be to the back. The four fingers of each hand should face each other at the waist. While pressing the hips, the abdomen should be pulled back and up. The lips should be pursed. The neck should be erect between the raised shoulders. The chin should be locked against the throat. The shoulders should be pressed forward. The elbows should be pressed forward.

There should be a chair in position behind the yogi. When he does this posture, and the body is locked in it, there will come a time, when there is need to relax. The yogi should slowly bring the body into a sitting position on the chair. This should be done without disrupting the inner focus which was achieved.

Whatever inner focus was achieved while standing, should continue and should develop further while sitting. Due to confusion of energies of the psyche while doing this, focusing may be difficult.

A yogi may discover that most of the energy organization occurs in the abdomen, from the navel upward. Very little awareness of what happens below the navel, is perceived. It is like drops of water, falling on a surface at the navel area, where the water strikes the surface and splatters upward.

Focus Connection

The *Press Hips – Raise Shoulders* is an easy position to assume. However, it is made in defiance to the gravity of the earth. That causes instability and unsteadiness. Once the yogi stands and applies pressure to the hips, he must check the chin-to-throat lock. He should pull the abdomen. From inside the body, he should pull the perineum. The anus should be pulled diagonally to the center of the body. The shoulders should be locked into their respective sockets.

When the yogi checked the inside of the body, he should monitor the energy layouts and shifts. If there is confusion, he should be aware of it.

- Why is meditation not interesting in this pose?

Standing Tilted – Hands out 45 degrees

This *Standing Tilted – Hands out 45 degrees,* is a standing posture. The torso is tilted forward. The upper limbs are held at 45 degrees. The hands are arched to the wrists. The fingers are spread tautly. The feet are placed for stable balance. If during the assumption of this pose, the balance is unstable, the feet should be repositioned to establish steadiness.

If a blindfold is not used, the eyelids should be closed. The yogi should investigate the feelings in the body. He should find energy movements, accumulations and expression. If any region holds his interest naturally, he should become absorbed in it.

The energy in the bones of the arms may drain continuously. There may be doubts forming which relate a feeling, that the sense of balance should be adjusted. It may seem that the posture should cease. Nervous energy which arises, should be noted. If it seems urgent, non-jerky quiet movements should be made to reposition the feet.

A yogi may notice energy stirring in the knees. He may have to sit. If he does so, there should be no sudden jerks. Keeping the attention in the psyche, still observing the energy movements and consciousness saturation, he should be attentive. When the energy subsides, he should stand again and resume the posture. Then again, he should observe. Then again when the body becomes nervous, he should sit and observe.

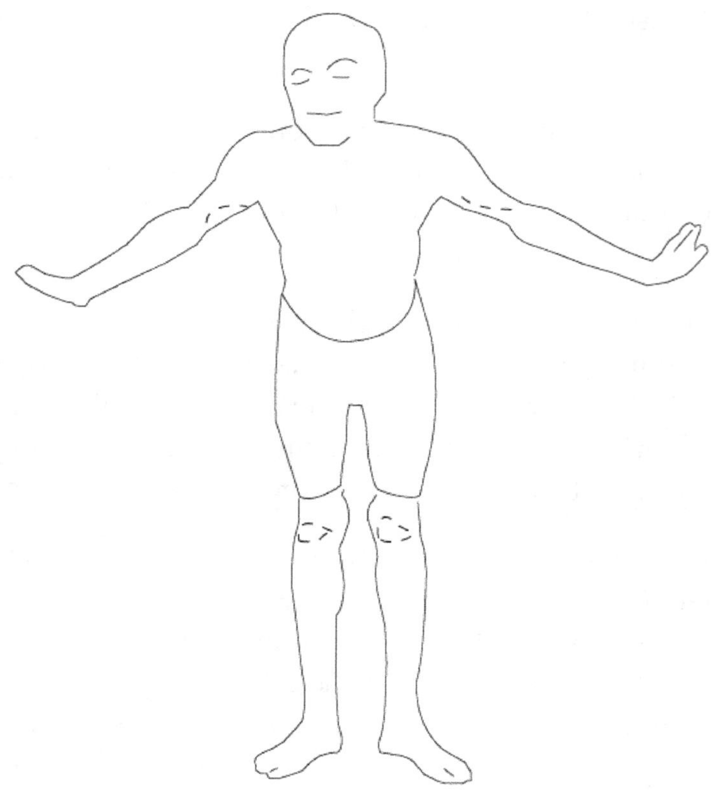

Focus Connection

This *Standing Tilted – Hands out 45 degrees* posture, may cause frontal lobe focus. It may open doors of visual perception which usually, are unavailable in the psyche of a human being. The potential for psychic visual perception exists in the subtle body. However, it may not be realized during the phase of existence when someone identifies as a physical creature.

As Nature would have it, and as revelations are bestowed, there is little chance that a yogi may experience transcendence vision. With closed eyelids or being blindfolded or even being in a room in which no light penetrates, the coreSelf may be discovered as the observing factor which can always look but may not perceive, nor identify objects in the foreground, or background, overhead or beneath.

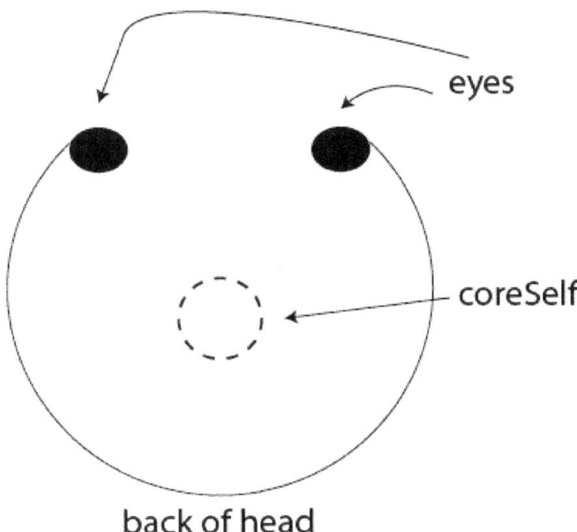

The fifth stage of yoga is *pratyahar* which is a psychic action to cease the coreSelf from venturing outward. The idea is to curtail the tendency to acquire sense objects. Instead of venturing outward to procure gratifications, the yogi practices to venture inward. Initially this is not done. After repeated efforts, it is achieved.

A yogi will, after much practice, find that the outward bound interest is curtailed. The psychic situation which is the head of the subtle body, becomes satisfied with itself. The urge to pursue, arrest, digest, and expel objects cease.

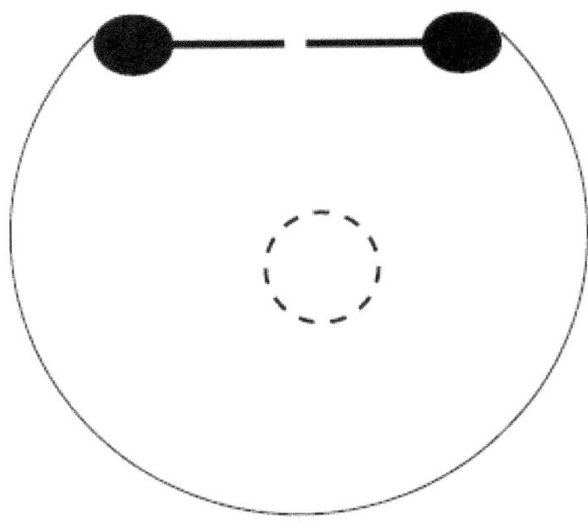

When a yogi matures in sensual energy withdrawal, he finds that the self no longer has such an intense interest in social affairs. Instead, when he sits to meditate, he experiences a rapid deceleration. He feels that the interest energy which resides in the core, no longer has an intense and greedy external interest

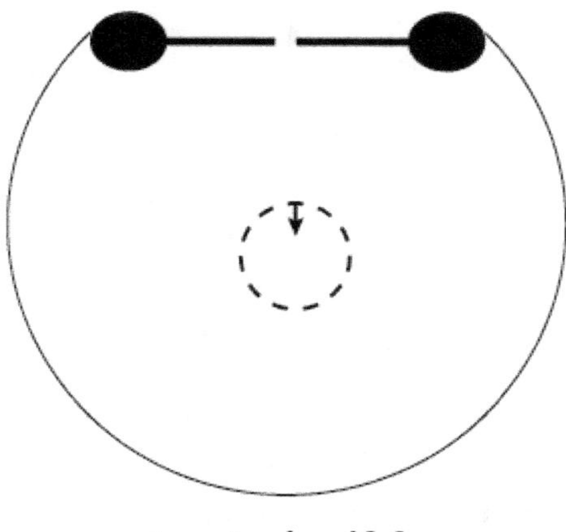

retracted self-focus

During meditation, it may be necessary to focus forward. Then the doors of perception may swing, being at least forty-five degrees. There may be no target. Instead, the energy of the yogi may pour through that door.

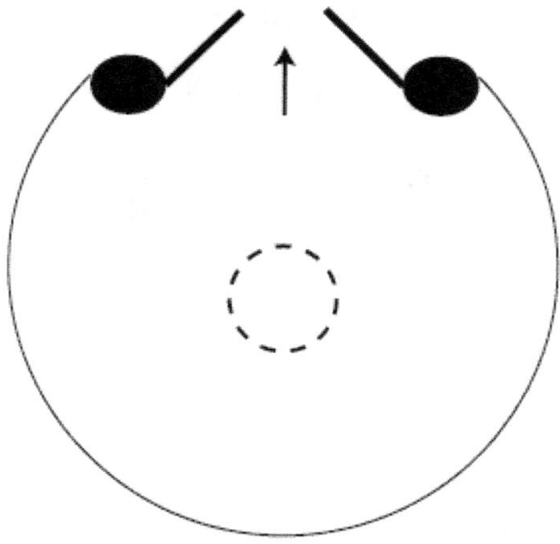

focusing visual interest

There is another important focus which may spontaneously arise. This concerns the following diagram. There we see that the doors of perception are pulled to create a vortex

pulling visual interest

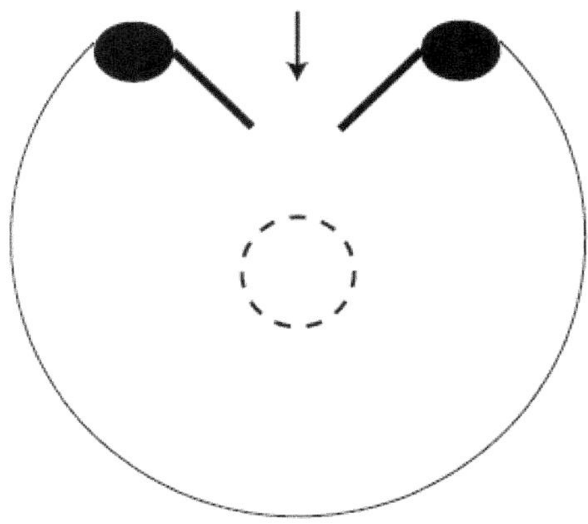

Stand- Forearms Horizontal

This *Stand - Forearms Horizontal* posture, involves standing, but it can be done while sitting. Then, the balancing need will not be required. For standing the feet should be firmly planted. The forearms should be placed parallel to the floor. The arms should be drawn back. A loose fist should be made. It should face the sky.

The forward neck lock should be applied. The backward neck lock may be used instead. For the forward neck lock, the chin should be pulled towards the throat. The head should not be tilted forward. In the backward neck lock, the head should be tilted back as far as possible. There should be inner focus.

When this posture is assumed, the yogi should check for energy movements. He should check for stress points or zones. The chest should be drawn up. The eyelids should be closed. Or the blindfold should be applied. It blocks light from entering the eyes. One may hear the heart beat at the center of the top of the chest.

Hearing that sound or feeling that pulse, the yogi should be absorbed. Lub/dub may be heard. Or it may be an electrical dazzled movement of a dart of energy, which is filled with uncertainty. It may cease, at any moment. The yogi should contemplate it. The sound or pulse may cease. It does not have to continue on and on. When the mother was pregnant with the yogi's embryo, there was another such lub/dub musical band playing. That was the mainstay, the mother's vibrating heart. That was the principal.

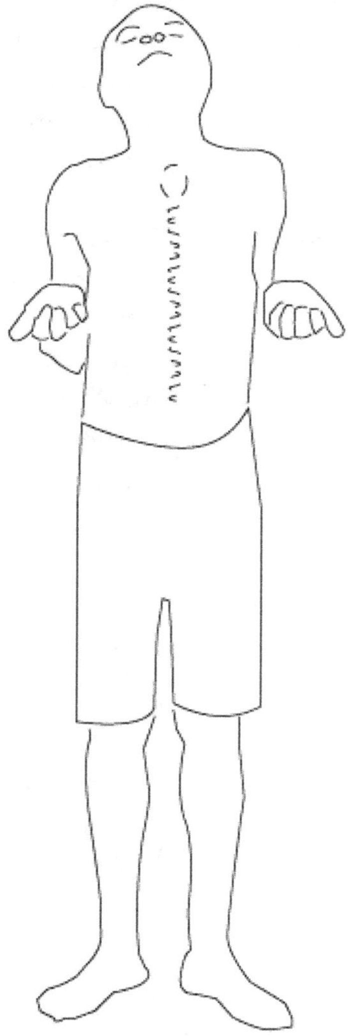

Focus Connection

The *Stand - Forearms Horizontal* posture, is a standing position, which relies on steadiness in balance, in reference to gravity. It settles the attention between the eyebrows. The main *kriya* mystic action, for arresting and using the divine vision, concerns focusing the willpower, the attention laser energy, through the center of the eyebrows. This is so essential, that it is mentioned in the *Bhagavad Gita*.

स्पर्शान्कृत्वा बहिर्बाह्यांश्	sparśānkṛtvā bahirbāhyāṁś
चक्षुश्चैवान्तरे भ्रुवोः ।	cakṣuścaivāntare bhruvoḥ
प्राणापानौ समौ कृत्वा	prāṇāpānau samau kṛtvā
नासाभ्यन्तरचारिणौ ॥५.२७॥	nāsābhyantaracāriṇau (5.27)

sparśān — sensual contact; kṛtvā — having done; bahir = bahiḥ — external; bāhyāṁś = bāhyān — excluded; cakṣuścaivāntare = cakṣuḥ — visual focus + ca — and + (eva) — indeed + antare — in between; bhruvoḥ — of the two eyebrows; prāṇāpānau — both inhalation and exhalation; samau — in balance; kṛtvā — having made; nāsābhyantaracāriṇau = nāsa — nose + abhyantara — within + cāriṇau — moving

Excluding the external sensual contacts, and fixing the visual focus between the eyebrows, putting the inhalation and exhalation in balance, moving through the nose. (Bhagavad-Gītā 5.27**)**

Even though the attention beam constantly sweeps the world for targets, it is resistant to the effort for locating portals to transcendental places. The location of positions or postures, which facilitate the search for transcendence, is required. Otherwise, a yogi will never transit from this realm of trauma.

Cross Forearms behind Shoulders

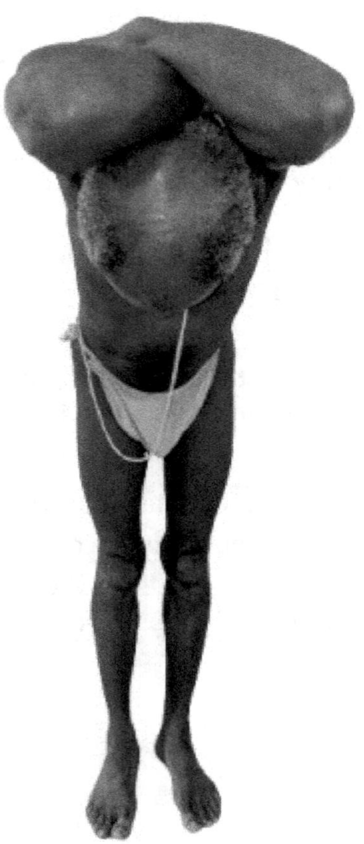

This *Cross Forearms behind Shoulders* posture, may be difficult for anyone who has enlarged shoulders, and a stiff neck. After standing firm, the yogi should cross the forearms behind the head. Each hand should grip the opposite shoulder blade, scapula. If the hands cannot accomplish that, they should rest on the shoulder blades with intentions to grip them.

Gripping the shoulder blades, the yogi should lean over less than 90 degrees. He should apply inner focus. He should hold the position, and observe the energy, either in a confused or orderly array.

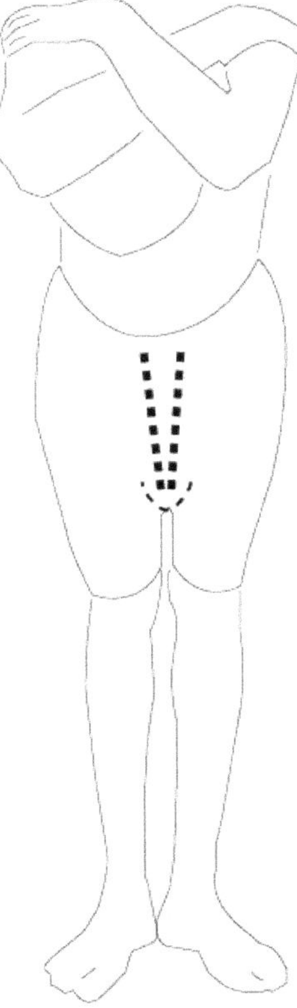

After holding this inner focus, and the grip of the shoulder blades, for a time, the yogi should slowly move the body into an upright position. Standing upright, he should focus to observe which part of the energy was adjusted. He should press the waist forward, and check to be sure that the chin is pressed to the throat.

After a time, when he feels that the system of psychic energies is normalized, he should again lean over less than 90 degrees. He should repeat this for a time. Then, sit gently to meditate. During the meditation, at first, he should note the condition of energy in the psyche. He should note if it is the same, or if it is different to what he experienced prior.

Focus Connection

The *Cross Forearms behind Shoulders* position can be strenuous. It depends in the design of the arms and forearms, shoulders and scapulas, as well as the way the vertebrae are set in the neck. A yogi should study the design of his body, and figure which postures are impractical, which can be done ideally, and which can, over time, be improved.

When doing this posture, once the hold is in place, one should check the inner energies. One may notice that there is a confusion of feelings which dash here and there. Energy may rush from here to there randomly.

The yogi should look down through the torso. This will be like shining a torchlight into a subterranean cave. When looking down like this, the yogi may be astonished to know that there is no organized energy outlay. The feelings may be slashing chaotically.

However, where the throat is located, there may be a small egg-shaped place, a blank hollow. If he can, the yogi should use that hollow for focus. He may, if he can, relocate from the head to that hollow.

Periodically, he may be distracted by a pain energy which emanates from the muscles in the arms. This energy will push out from the muscles. It may diffuse in space. It may be like a disappearing mist.

This posture is one in which, a yogi can study how to lodge a focus to a location only.

It is necessary when complying with Patanjali's instruction to cease the mento-emotional energy. A yogi should know how to make a blank space a target. In many meditations, there is no point of light nor any other attractive target. This is nothing besides blank space. A yogi must train the mind to make use of a hollow.

Full Lotus with Hands Floating

For this *Full Lotus with Hands Floating* posture, a full lotus, a tight one, is required. However, provided the elbows are not obstructed, this may be done sitting on a chair. Once the lotus is assumed, once the feet are pulled up tightly, the yogi should be sure that the spine is erect. The chest should be lifted. This draws up the vertebrae. The forearms should be extended. The palms should float above the thighs near the knees. The hands should not touch the thighs.

The yogi should check to be sure that the backward neck lock is applied. The chin should be lifted as far as possible. The yogi should examine the energy in the psyche. He should note movements and energy dispersions. When the hands cannot be held any longer, the yogi should slowly lower them so that with the palms up, they rest on the corresponding thigh.

The yogi should meditate, noticing how the energies become situated for ease of existence. When the psyche is stabilized, the yogi should again, raise the hands to float them above the thigh. He should note any energy shifts and tensions, which resume as it was before. There may be in the arms, near the elbows, an irradiation of energy, which is organized.

Repeatedly time and again, the yogi may assume the pose, relax the arms, and assume the pose again, while observing the energy organization and scattering.

Focus Connection

The *Full Lotus with Hands Floating* position, concerns balance. The hands become sensitive. They compare one side of the body, to the other. They alert the self about buoyancy. The right and left sides of the torso make an effort to contrast each other.

A yogi may realize that the body flutters silently. This is like when a bird vibrates its wet wings to remove moisture. The balancing force in the spine may be felt during this pose. It feels as if there is an edge where the spine is positioned. The intuition will alert the self if the weight is not distributed evenly.

In the upper back, below the neck, the yogi may realize a blank area. On either side of this there may be clashing energies which come to a standstill once they enter that blank space. The yogi may train the mind, to make that blank area a focus. In some meditations, there may be no pin-points, no lights, nothing. The yogi should meditate on the hollow.

An area can be the aim of focus. It may be a zone. It may be inner sound. It may be vibration. It may be the absence of everything.

After a time, it will be necessary to rest the arms. They may be placed on the thighs. The yogi should do so gentle, without jolting. To discover any changes in energy flow, or positioning, he should meditate with an observational mood.

After a time, a yogi will realize that the spine collapsed. He should reset the chest. He should firm the waist. He should check the neck. Whatever is disordered should be repositioned. He should rectify the spine so that it does not show a hunch back. If need be, the chest should be lifted.

Checking, the yogi should roll the tongue up, and push it back to the throat. He should check for mental interference. Whatever is disordered should be rectified.

Third Eye Stimulation

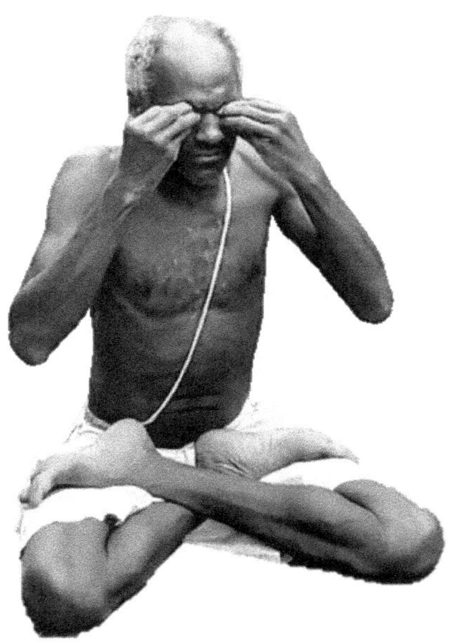

This *Third Eye Stimulation* posture may be done from any sitting position. Doing this in lotus, is the traditional way, but it is effective in easier positions. There is no guarantee that when this is done in lotus, it will cause vision-perception. For that matter in any other posture, sitting or standing, this pressing of the eyes in a gentle or firm way, may cause the yogi to see through the third eye.

It is more likely however that he will see the third eye energy in a circular or irregular shape. There is a method for this which includes hearing inner sounds in the mind space. For that, one uses the thumb to press the outer air canal. When this is done, the yogi may hear a loud screeching sound, the naad resonance. This may be a blend of frequencies. With it, due to the pressure applied with the four fingers to the closed eyelids, energy which is disordered may begin formatting itself, so that there is light in the forehead.

This could be dark or bright light. It may be like a disc or torus. It may be haphazard where no defined or recognizable shape is perceived. It may be stationary or moving in, or out, and then disappearing in the distance. It may move towards the observing self and disappear. A yogi should calmly observe it. If he becomes excited or exhibits a tendency to pursue, or to make it stationary and obedient, it may recede in the distance or simply disappear. This third eye chakra is mysterious. It is a challenge to the yogi because he lacks a method for making it steady.

Focus Connection

The *Third Eye Stimulation* is necessary in the practice of chakra perception and kundalini lifeForce activation. These are part of *kriya* yoga and *hatha* yoga practices.

The chakras or energy generating junctions which are in the subtle body, run parallel and correspond with the interconnected nerves or neurons that facilitates communication and coordination. A yogi should see these operations directly.

When the physical eyelids are pressed gently, lights may appear on the inside of the head. When doing this if the yogi does rapid breathing, he may see collective lights in the forehead. This gives some experience of the chakra formations which occur between the eyebrows. That place is addressed as the third eye or *ajna* chakra.

The third eye or brow chakra is legendary. That is due to the declarations of advanced yogi who gave descriptions of the light formations and portal openings. The list of the chakras varies but there are seven which are described by most yogis. These are.

- crown chakra top of head
- brow chakra between eyebrows
- throat chakra
- heart chakra
- navel chakra
- sex organ chakra
- anus chakra

The *Third Eye Stimulation* should be done when a blind fold is used. That causes the mind to have a steadier focus with the least distractions. One should use a sitting position but it can be done from a standing or reclining situation. The yogi should press slightly. There should be no injury.

One may see a bright light. It may be scattered and indistinct. It may be bright as to be like a high voltage spotlight. The yogi should focus to its center.

There may be a partial collapse of the spine. The yogi should check this. If the spine collapses, he should lift the waist. He should lift the chest. He should be sure that no part of the spine is curved.

After being sure that the spine is properly positioned, and holding the fingers against the eyelids, the yogi should listen for internal sounds. He should note the intensity and location. He should establish focus on the lights in the forehead. If the lights ceased, he should stare into the center of the forehead.

Press Upper Chest

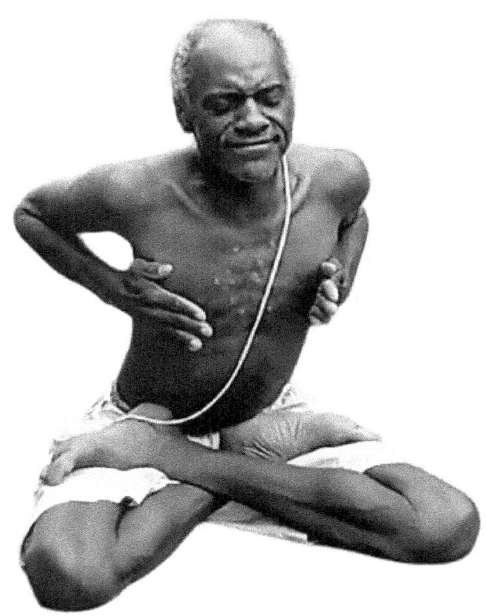

This *Press Upper Chest* posture can be done from a sitting position. It is illustrated from the lotus position in one of its variations. The yogi should be seated firmly. He should press the base of the palms to the corresponding side of the chest. The fingers point straight outward, running parallel to the floor. The thumbs may reach up into the armpits, or they may point forward.

Some pressure from the base of the palms should be applied to squeeze the chest inward. The chest should be pulled up. The spine should not curve backward. If there is no blindfold used, to keep the vision-probing sense confined in the head of the subtle body, then the eyelids should be tightly compressed on the eye.

A yogi should hear naad sound, streaming. He should absorb it, either to be in it, or to be listening attentively, while determining its core position.

Focus Connection

The *Press Upper Chest* posture may be done from any sitting position. It is required that it be from a sitting pose in which the legs and thighs are not tensioned. Once it is assumed, the yogi should internalize the focus. Then he should check the energy layout. This may provide the yogi with an organized or disordered situation.

The hands may slip. This may happen because the hands made contact with slippery skin or fabric. If the hands slip, they may rest near the waist. Noticing this, the yogi should reinstate the hands by the sides of the upper chest.

After the reset, the yogi should again note the layout of the energies. There may be a low confused state inside the head, neck and torso. This may continue for a short period. Then the energy in the head may drain into the chest.

Again, the yogi may notice that the hands which are in contact with the sides of the chest, slip. This may be repeated. The yogi, observing this, may consider lifting the hands to resume the position. While this thinking happens, the hands may slip further, near the waist. The yogi may decide to let the hands remain there for a time. This will allow the arms and forearms to relax.

The yogi can then meditate with the hands at the waist. Checking this energy, the yogi may notice that it crowds at the eyes. It will be as if the eyes have warm feelings.

Meditating in that easy posture with the hands at the waist, the yogi may drift into thinking without knowing what happened. He may become aware of a thought and simultaneously, he may realize that he drifted into a thought process. Then, he began hearing naad resonance. It was present on a mental level but since the yogi was inattentive to that plane of consciousness, it could not be heard.

The yogi was unaware of it. The state of mind shifted. Through that movement, he heard it in the distance. It came closer. It saturated his awareness.

Again, the yogi realized that he was on a level, where thoughts stream one after the other. Then he heard inner sound in the distance. He again slipped closer and closer to it. He was saturated by it.

This allows the yogi to study this process of focus slippage.

- How does it happen?
- How can the yogi operate the focus in the interest of higher meditation, where the attention remains focused as desired?

Hands Inverted with Temples Pressed

This *Hands Inverted with Temples Pressed* posture, uses the lotus as its base. It can be accomplished sitting on a chair or sitting in an easier pose. Once the sitting is made, the yogi raises the arms to position the thumbs at the temple. This is done with upturned palms. The elbows are flared back.

A slight pressure is applied to the temples with the thumbs. The fingers press against the back of the skull. In a variation, this posture is used with everything the same, except that the thumbs press the eyes slightly. When doing this pose, and hearing naad resonance or being aware of the energy in the frontal part of the head, a yogi may suddenly see a half-inch, or smaller, round orb of light, which appears suddenly in the right or left eye socket.

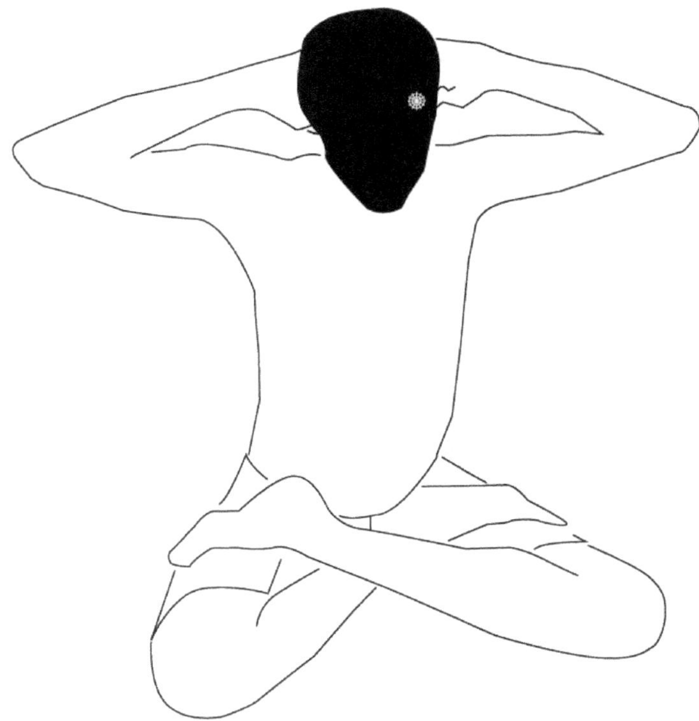

When there is pain in the arms, where it seems that there is a pipe-shaped energy which exudes pain, the yogi should slowly lower the arms, forearms and hands. The hands rest on the thighs. Naad sound may be heard blaring in the head, on this side or that side, in the front or back, up or down.

If the yogi discovers that the spine curved forward or partially collapsed, he should slowly resume the upright spine. He may continue being absorbed in naad resonance. Or, he may resume the pose with the thumbs pressing on the temples or eyes.

Focus Connection

The *Hands Inverted with Temples Pressed* posture, should be done from an easy posture. There should be no strain felt, except perhaps in the arms and forearms. If such tensions are active, the yogi should relax by lowering the forearms and hands.

In this posture, the thumbs are at the temples but the thumbs are not applying pressure. They make contact softly. The yogi should stare forward. This is done behind closed eyelids. Beyond the staring energy, there will be either blank space, space with littered non-formatted light, or with speckled multicolored light.

The yogi should stare forward with a slight force. Now and again, he may feel that he should relax the upper limbs. It will seem that the arms, forearms and hands would drop to the floor. A time will come when the yogi can no longer hold the limbs in position on the temples.

Then the yogi should relax by moving the hands to the thighs. He should observe any changes or movements. There may be a stream of energy moving from the torso through the neck. This may become blank when it enters the head. Remaining with the limbs in that relaxed condition, the yogi should observe the motion of thoughts and ideas which arise. These will manifest with their displaying power.

Now and then, inner sound will be heard. When this happens, the thoughts and ideas will cease momentarily. The yogi will find that the displaying instrument, releases itself to view thoughts and ideas. It does not stay with the naad sound, unless the coreSelf renders a force to listen to naad resonance.

This transfer of the mind to inner sound, and then to thoughts or ideas, and then again to inner sound, and again to thoughts and ideas, is a required study. The yogi must gain control of the psychological operation which causes this switching in the mind.

Press Chest/Breasts

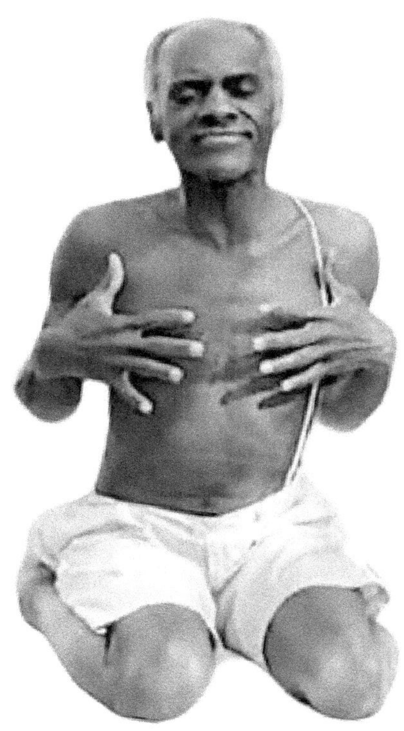

This *Press Chest/Breasts* posture has variations. It is demonstrated while sitting between the heels. It could be done with the buttocks sitting on a cushion. That would ease the knees. Tensions in the body, in places where it forces one to focus into areas, besides the ones intended, would disrupt the meditation.

This posture is for focusing on the changes in energy, which are due to applying slight pressure to the sides of the rib cage, and to the chest/breast area. For this, the fingers hug the breasts/chest area, applying a slight pressure. A yogi should check to be sure that everything is in order in other parts of the body. For instance, the chin should be pulled back to the throat. The lower abdomen should be pulled under the rib cage. The neck should upright. A second check should be made to be sure that the chin lock is applied, and the highest part of the chest to lifted.

After this posture is assumed for a time, and there is sufficient focus, the hands may be relaxed, by resting with the palms facing up on the thighs.

One should feel a slow movement of energy in every part of the trunk, neck and head. A yogi should be absorbed in this energy.

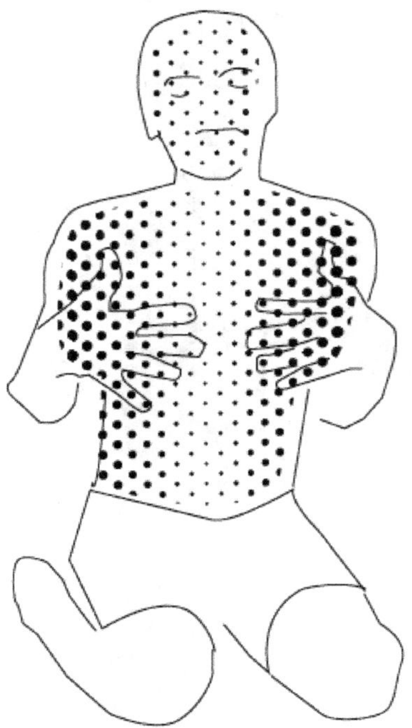

Focus Connection

The *Press Chest/Breasts* position can be assumed on a chair. On the floor, it may be on or between the heels. There should be no tension in the thighs, legs and feet. Some pressure is applied to the breasts or chest, with each hand on each corresponding side. The chin-to-throat lock should be applied. The chest/breast should be pressed forward.

Soon after assuming this posture, the yogi may hear inner sound. It may be on the right, or left, back of the head. If the yogi hears this and listens attentively, the resonance may spread to the top back. It may pervade the entire head.

During this posture, thinking may occur. It may be subliminal, where the yogi becomes aware of it, after the thinking progressed as a display for some moments. If he can, he may observe that the thought packages come from the chest. They float through the neck. They burst in the head where they are displayed legibly.

Periodically, the yogi may notice that somehow his attention became linked to inner sound. It lost track of the thinking displays. This happened spontaneously with the yogi being a passive bystander in the mind.

Once when doing this posture, there was a thinking package which came through the neck, and ledged in the left jaw. This was revealed. As soon as I noticed it, and began to read it, naad resonance was resumed. The thought vanished. This type of meditation assists a yogi in sorting thoughts, in knowing how they are stored in the psyche, and in knowing the value of inner sound.

On Heels – Crimp Fingers

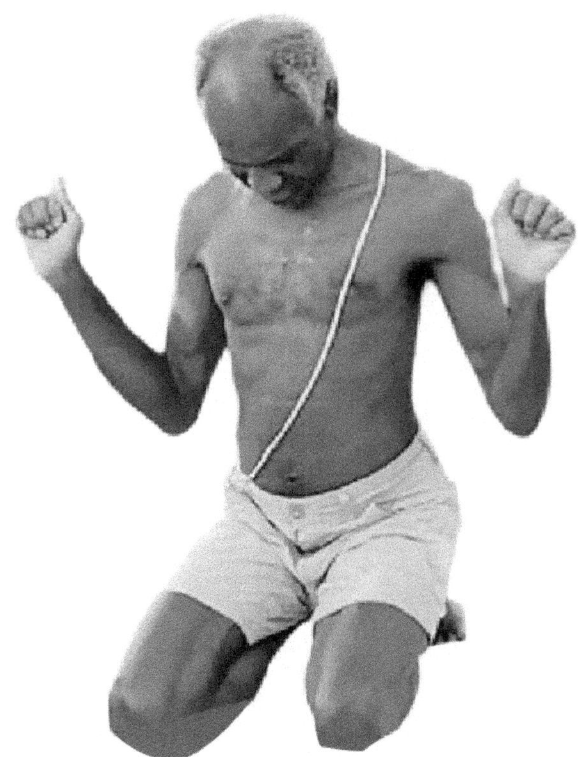

This *On Heels – Crimp Fingers* posture has several variations. It may be done sitting on heels. It could be done sitting between the heels. If a yogi can sit on the heels comfortably, he should. Then he can swing the forearms and hands back. The elbows should be as far back as possible.

The spine should be erect with the head tilted forward, or with a variation, with the head tilted back. If the head is forward, the chin should be pulled to the throat. A yogi can do this with one or the other variation, whereby the chin is dropped to the chest. This will cause a tension in the back of the neck.

The fingers should be folded. The thumbs should remain out. He should press the shoulders back. He may hear whistling in the throat and neck. He should focus through that sound. He may find a hollow area in the sound. That is a blankness place. It allows the yogi to escape from thought displays.

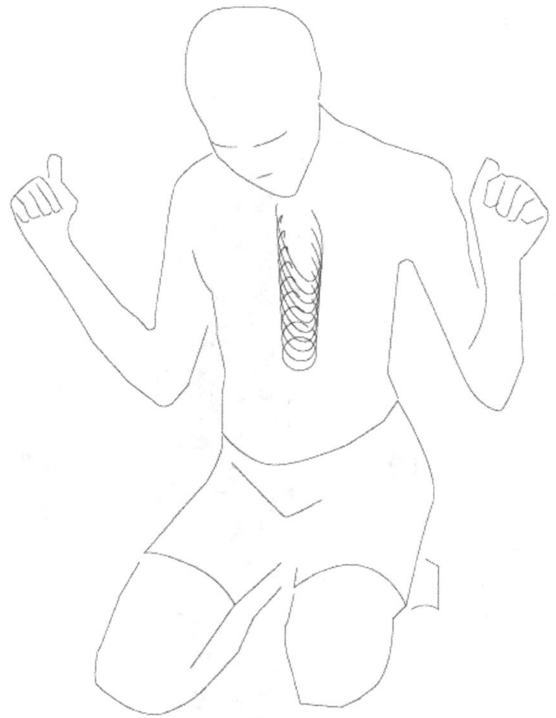

Focus Connection

The *On Heels – Crimp Fingers* position is an easy posture. It can be done from any sitting postion, or from standing even. Each yogi may decide which base posture to use, as if it should be sitting or standing. Tests can be made to observe which posture better facilitates focus, and increased removal of unfavorable energies.

This posture reveals the condition of the chest area, especially the upper chest. It gives clarity about the energy in the lower chest.

With the chin pulled to the throat, with the focusing power exerted in the chest, a yogi may feel an energy scattering in the top part of the chest.

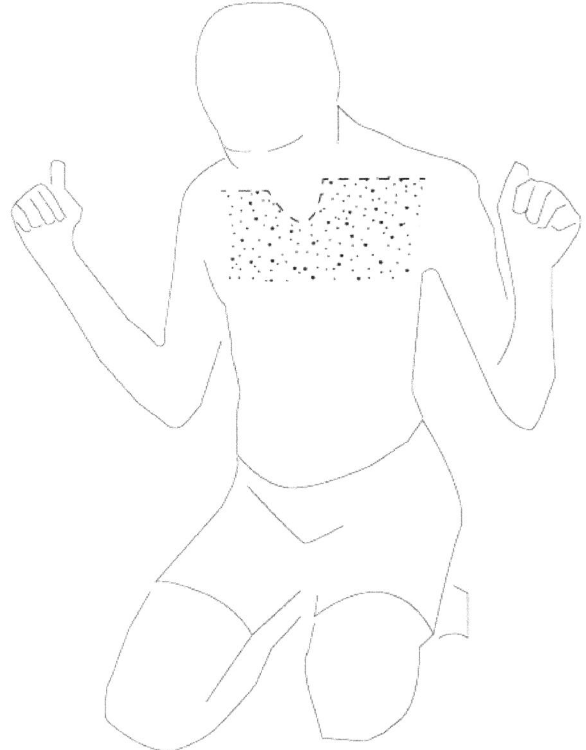

After meditating on this for a time, the situation will disappear. It may be replaced with an organized energy which configures at the bottom. It spreads from the center to each side.

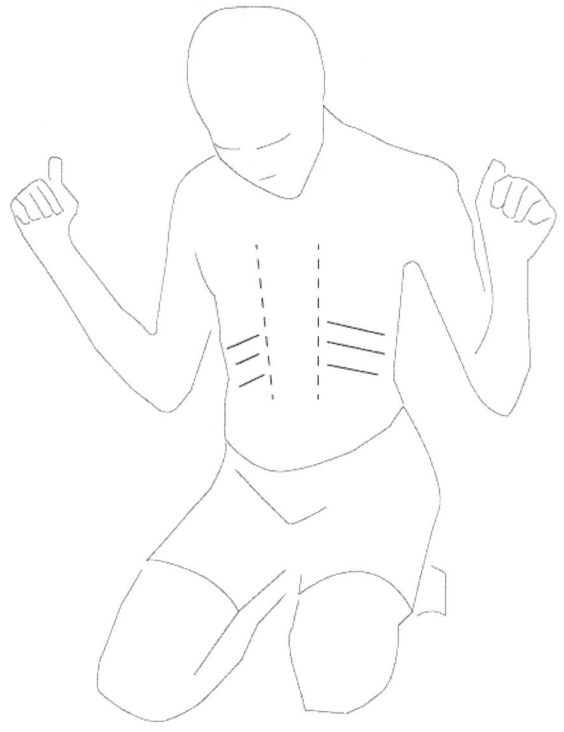

Twist Stop on the Lotus

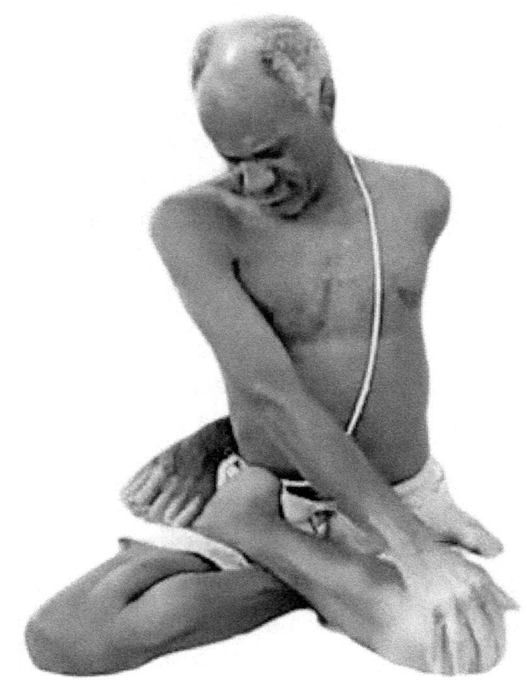

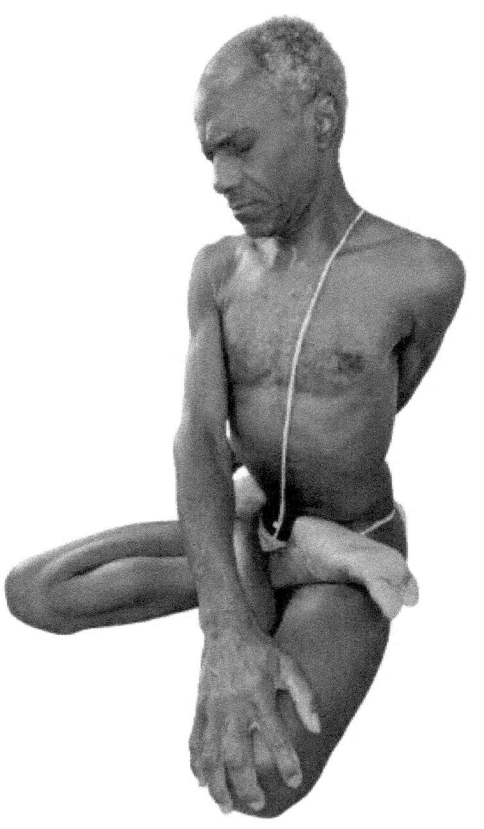

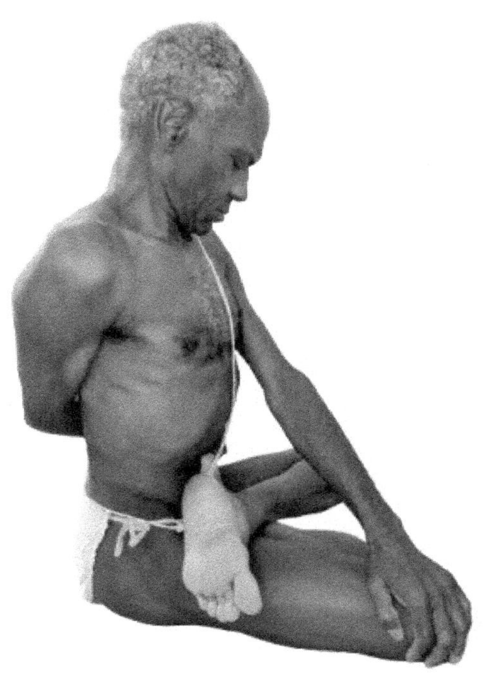

The *twist-stop-on-the-lotus* posture is not a spinal twist position. For this, the vertebrae are not torqued in one direction or another. The twist stop is concerned with feet and ankles being held tight, but using the spine as an upright non-twisting brace.

First the yogi should assume the lotus posture. He should do so with ease, with no stress for the muscles and tendons, in the thighs and legs. There may be some stress in the ankles and feet. That tightness is drawn up. The trunk is properly positioned. It is perpendicular to the floor. Some yogis may use a cushion under the buttocks.

To do this, *twist-stop-on-the-lotus* pose, the lotus is assumed. The body is lifted. It is placed upright in reference to the floor. One hand should grab the opposing knee. The other hand should be applied at the back of the body to grab the toes which it can reach. The hand, which grabs an opposing knee should firmly hold that knee. The other hand should, from the back, grab the toes.

Care should be taken, not to twist or torque the vertebrae. Instead, the abdomen should brace the hold. It should keep the spine erect, with no rotating pressure on any part of the spine.

The yogi should check the body from the inside. Once he clears that, and the posture is held with no stress on the spine, he should venture within the psyche, to investigate the energy situation. There may be a loud naad sound on the right, or left side, or in some other location.

If a thought arises, the yogi should note it. He should consider how it was generated, displayed and observed. As soon as he does that, he should return to the task of hearing naad.

After a time, the yogi should relax both hands, placing them on a thigh on each side. With a quiet focus, he should meditate.

Focus Connection

This *Twist Stop* is a brake action in the direction against the twist. No torque is made to turn the vertebrae. Instead, the body is turned away from the twist so that it reaches a stop limit. This practice is not designed to apply a twirling action to the spinal muscles and nerves. One side is done. Then the other side is completed. There is focus through the torso into the base area of the pelvic region.

The yogi should turn the body, so that from the front it turns towards the fingers of the hand, which comes from the back, to grip the toes of the corresponding foot, which is reached from the back of the body, by the waist. There should be no injury to the vertebrae, tendons or nerves in the spine. One side is done. The other side is completed with the corresponding grips

Press Eyelids

Pressing the eyelids can be done from the full lotus posture, a relaxed adjusted lotus, or any sitting position. Whatever happens when doing this in full lotus, may occur in any other sitting position. A yogi, whose lower limbs cannot assume the full lotus, should be confident that he may experience higher states, may see configurations of the third eye, and may get third eye perception, when pressing each eyelid with one, two, or three fingers. The thumb may be used to compress the ear canal. That may cause the yogi to hear inner sound.

When the eyes are pressed, even slightly, the mind increases its interest in the optic nerves. Even in the subtle body, there is spontaneous focus, which may result in seeing astral lights or spotlights, as one views the frontal focus in the mind. These may be micro-lights or bright collective lights. Staring into the void which the mind becomes, one may see a tiny star or an opening into another atmosphere. During this practice, there may be pitch-black darkness for the whole session, or for a time.

When the hands, forearms and arms tire, the yogi should slowly relax the hands on the corresponding thighs. He should inFocus. He may again press the eyes for a time. Then relax the hands for a time. He may do this repeatedly.

If the ear canal is pressed while the eyes are pressed, or even if the ear canal is pressed and the eyes are not touched, the yogi may hear a rumbling sound. As soon as he releases the press, his attention may target a high frequency resonance. He should become absorbed in this, but he should keep some focusing energy on the lights in the mind.

Focus Connection

The *Press Eyelids* action is a recommendation for those who want to see inner lights. It can be done while doing breath infusion as *kapalabhati* and *bhastrika pranayama* breath-surcharging of the physical and subtle bodies. Its natural focus is the brow chakra, the area between the eyebrows.

When the physical system is young, many colored or contrasting lights may appear between the eyebrows. The third eye (*ajna* chakra) may open, where there is opening in the opaque energy which surrounds the viewer (coreSelf). When that opening occurs, the yogi may see into another atmosphere. As the body develops and its young adult stage terminates, it is likely that the third eye rarely opens. Still, a yogi should practice the mystic actions, which facilitate this use of the third eye.

In doing this process which involves pressing gently but firmly on the eyelids, it is best to use a blindfold. This practice can be done from any sitting or standing position. There should be no tension or distraction, as that may reduce the attention which is applied.

At first when one presses the fingers, there may be no light. However, there may be inner sound. One's attention may switch to hearing the inner sound. Naad, if it imposes itself, will have a steady radiance of sound, which could be on one side or the other, by an ear or by some other place in the skull.

Naad may branch out from one zone, area, or place, to some other. A yogi, due to pressing the eyes, will notice that his attention shifted to naad resonance and lost track of the objective, which was to see lights in the frontal part of the head. Realizing this, the yogi may shift some focus to the frontal area. He may check to know if the fingers still press the eyes.

If there are no prominent lights, the yogi may see a dark space ahead. He should focus on a part of that, perhaps a central part. There may be specks of grey or washed out colors here and there, at random in the dark space. He should gentle apply focus to it.

Fingers Spread by Temples

The *Fingers Spread by Temples* posture may be done in full lotus, or in any sitting position. It should be a posture in which there are no tensions below the waist. If such tensions are felt, a different relatively easy posture should be assumed.

There are *asana* postures for physical health. There are also *asana* postures for the development of subtle meditation practice. These are two different attitudes. Postures for the sake of the healthy and athletic performance is a practice with fitness as the objective. That is not yoga practice. For yoga, whatever is done should result in graduation to higher yoga, which is *pratyahar* sensual energy enrichment, and *samyama* inner absorption stabilization.

If one thinks that yoga is for beautification of the body and for athletic performance, one does not practice according to the syllabus of Patanjali. Such yoga which does not match the *Yoga Sutras,* will not yield the benefits explained in the *sutras*.

After assuming the lotus, or some other posture, and after checking to be sure there is no tension in the lower body, the yogi should spread the fingers near to the temples. The spread should be taut, such that there is tension in the hands. No other part of the body should be stressed.

When the fingers are stretched, one should hear naad sound. If one does not hear it, one should be aware of the energy which radiates from the stretched tensioned fingers and palms. Hearing naad, or being aware of the energy which emanates from the stretched hand, the yogi should focus on naad or on the emanated energy. With full internal focus, one should lift the chest. This should be done slowly without jerks or sudden movements.

The spine should be perpendicular to the lower torso. Looking straight ahead in the head of the subtle body, a yogi may see scattered lights in the frontal lobe.

If one does not see random light, one may see formations of light in organized or chaotic patterns. If there is no such light, the yogi should check to be sure that he uses a blindfold or that he is in a dark place. He should be in a room which has no light or an outdoor area on a dark moon night.

After a time, the hands will express fatigue. Then, the yogi should lower the hands, causing them to rest of the thighs. He should be sure that the stress disappears. However, he should make any such movements quietly and with no jerks. In that way the meditative focus should continue during slight movements.

Focus Connection

The *Fingers Spread by Temples* posture, may be done from any sitting or standing position. There should be full attention applied. If not, the interference should be removed. The tension one has in a posture may be removed by changing to an easier pose.

In any position, the yogi should be sure that there is no urine in the bladder. There should be no waste in the rectum. This will allow for near-total attention to the objective. If for instance, there is urine in the body, that will deprive the self of full attention. This is due to the fact that retained urine or feces requires attention.

Failure in yoga practice has much to do with the application of fragmented focus. Indeed, it is a skill to regularly apply the full attention to the objective.

The *Fingers Spread by Temples* posture, is a mild energy focus. It is so mild that the yogi may experience a slow stir of chaotic energy which lacks clarity, but which is not violent and forceful. Thoughts may develop while the yogi notices how this energy is scattered through the psyche. However, these thoughts may not develop fully. They may develop somewhat but without clarity. Before the yogi gets a hint about them, they may collapse. Then there will be other thoughts which arise incoherently. Those too will collapse without displaying contents.

Sometimes while doing this meditation, a tube may appear in the throat and chest.

Inverted All-Fours

This *Inverted All-Fours* posture is an inverted action. It causes blood to become disoriented in terms of its usual travel to and from the heart. A yogi should lay on the back. He should situate the four limbs of the body so that they are perpendicular (at 90^0) to the floor. This means that the arms, forearms, hands, thighs, and legs, point to the sky. The feet will be parallel to the floor but the fluids in the feet will, like the rest of the limbs, be under a stress to go downward, into the trunk.

After some time of doing this posture, there may be stress in the body. Then the yogi can bring the knees to the chest, and bring the arms down to the floor. This should be done without sudden movements. The meditation in the psyche should be continuous. No movements should be made to disrupt the internal interest.

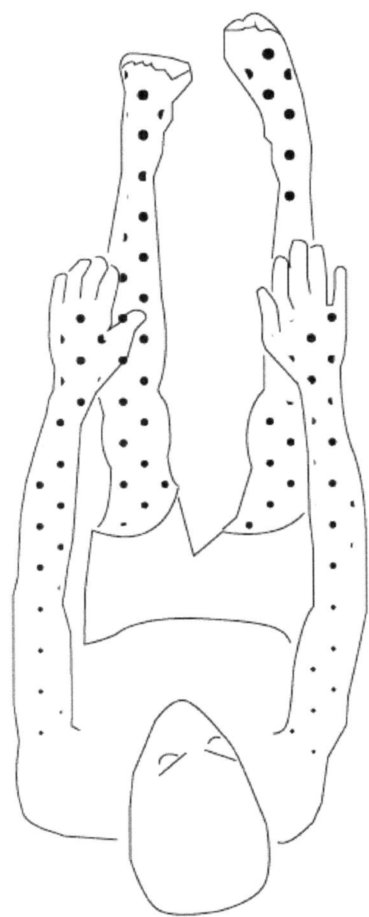

Focus Connection

The *Inverted All-Fours* position is magnificent for knowing the balancing force of gravity. After assuming this, the yogi should check the whereabouts of energy. The extended limbs will be of concern. It will be necessary to check to know if the sides of the feet touch.

- Are the fingers spread, tilting away from each other.

After a time, it will be necessary to lower the limbs. The knees may come to the chest. The fingers may cup and be lowered to touch the forehead. No extra force will be applied in lowering any limb. Gravity itself will managed this.

The yogi should study the balancing force. There may come a time, when this earth habitat is no longer available. Then it may be that everyone present on earth, may be in a state of suspension.

- Will that be experienced like this, where one exists but with no coordination or reference?

Toes Pulled in Lotus

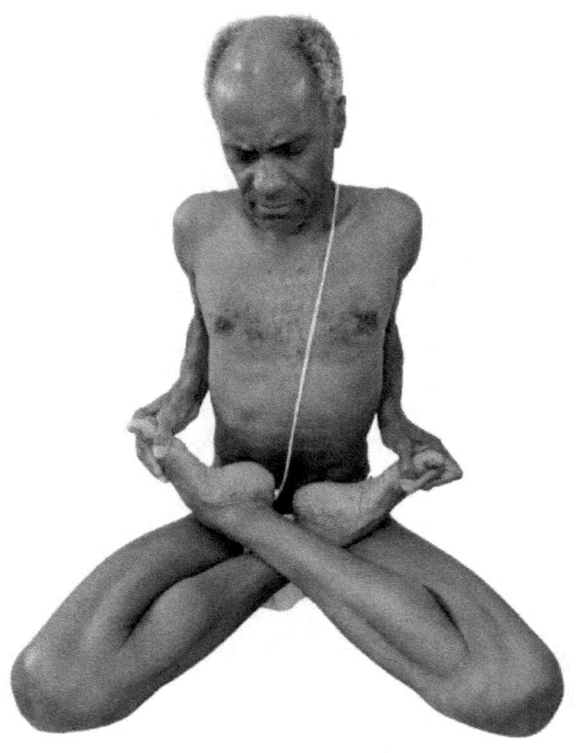

This *Toes Pulled in Lotus* posture may be done by yogis, whose bodies have no tension nor strain when in a tight lotus. Sit in lotus. Tighten the lotus by raising the body on the hands and repositioning the buttocks so that the spine is erect and does not curve. Once the tight lotus is assumed, the yogi should grab the toes. The thumbs should be above on the upturned soles. They should be used to grab the big toes. Firmly pull the feet. Close the eyelids tightly if a blindfold was not already fitted.

In this posture, there may be a chaos of energy in the psyche. However, there may be naad resonance. It may be a continuous blaring sound. Or it may be a screaming high frequency.

A yogi should consider that the hearing sense is prominent. The seeing sense may also be productive, whereby lights of a particular color or shape are perceived. The touching sense may be inactive. The smelling sense may be blank. The tasting sense may be absent.

The seeing sense may perceive sparkling clean twinkles of light, or mixed indistinct crystals of lights, which are here and there.

After a time, it will seem that the feet should be released. The yogi should release the grip on the toes. He should check for distractions, and should remain in naad resonance, with a keen observation for the bubbling of any other objects by any other sense.

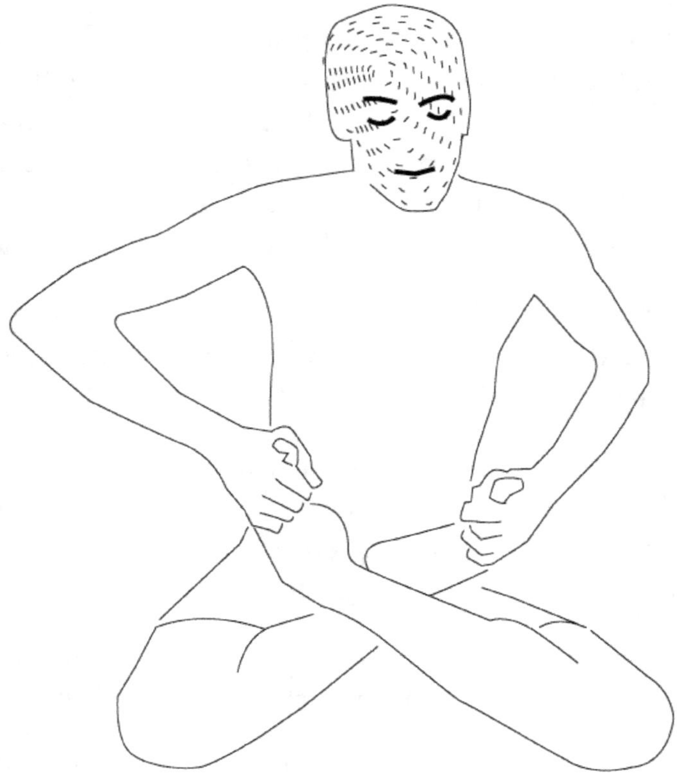

Focus Connection

The *Toes Pulled in Lotus* posture is acceptable, but only for those yogis whose lower limbs are supple. They can sit with ease in this posture, where it is required that one sit with no strain nor stress, while pulling the toes upwards in the cross-legged lotus. A yogi who cannot do this posture, should not be discouraged about the stiff, or weighty situation of the body. According to the genetic design of the body, a yogi will be facilitated or obstructed when doing postures.

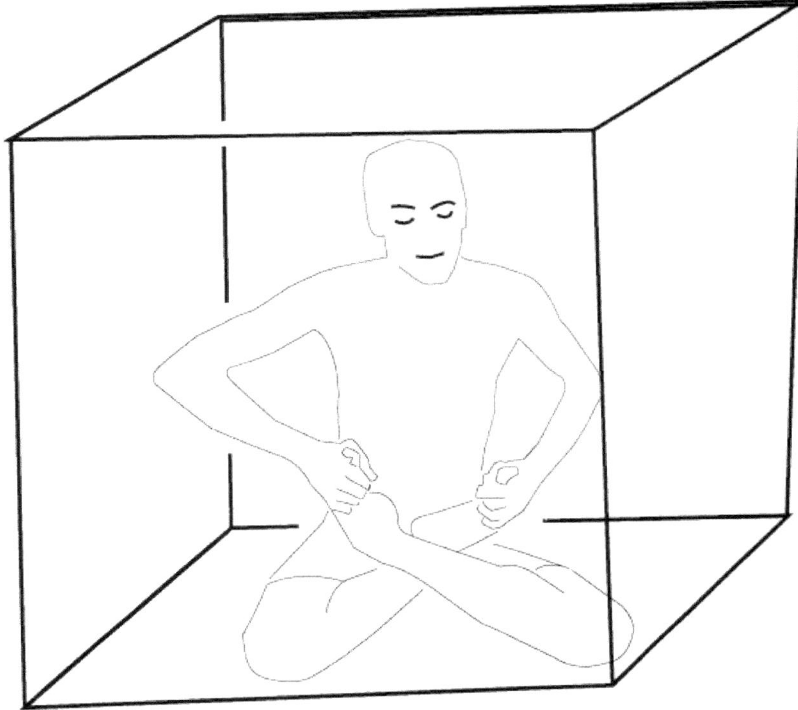

When this posture is first assumed, and the toes are pulled with the feet, a yogi may feel as if he is encased in a transparent cube. He may also hear naad resonance inner frequency blaring through the psyche. He should map this.

- What does the thinking mechanism do?
- Are there memories being displayed?
- Is there a spontaneous focus on astral light?

In the chest, the yogi may feel or see a pipe-shaped energy which sends out rays from the lower back through the torso. Elsewhere in the psyche, the yogi may feel a confusion of energies. Some are here. Some are there. They scatter with no organized design.

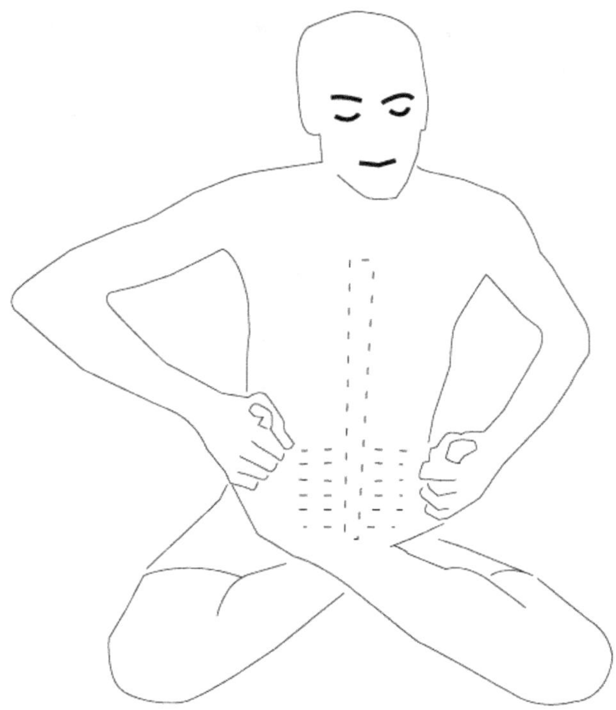

Lotus Full with Forearms Under Shins

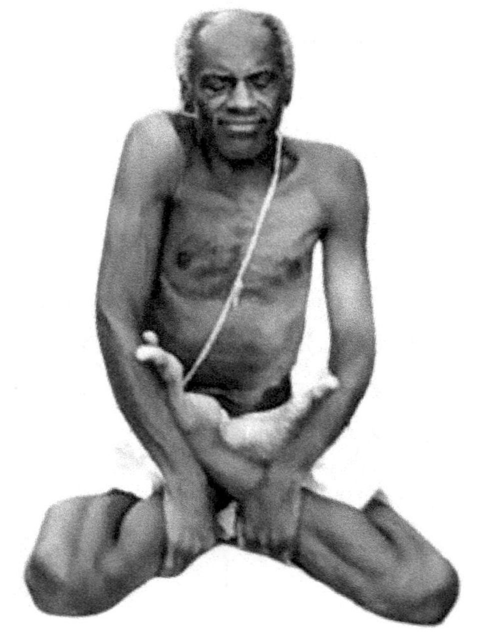

This *Lotus Full with Forearms Under Shins* posture, should not be done unless the full lotus is easily assumed. If there are stress and tension when doing the lotus, this posture is not suitable. At first, the yogi should sit in a tight lotus. That is with the feet pulled over the opposing thighs. The yogi should check to be sure that the body sits squarely on the buttocks, with the spine being erect, perpendicular to the floor. There should be no curving of the spine.

Once positioned, the toes should be grabbed. The toes should be pulled up tightly. This will cause the feet to come closer to the body. At that time the forearms should be slid under the upturned feet. The fingers should grip the shins, while the feet remain on the forearms. This is a locked position for the bottom of the body.

The eyelids should be closed. An investigation should be made to check the positions of energy in the psyche. One may hear naad inner resonance blaring, but it may not demand one's attention. Instead, one should make a special effort to remain attentive to it. It may tune in so that it is recognized. Then it may tune out, where one has no idea that it is an event in the psyche.

The yogi should observe where his recognition ability surfaces, as to what attracts it, as to why it does not remain in touch with naad. The legs will have long running sensations but these may not be demanding. If, however, the limbs involved are tensioned, the sensations will be noted as being under stress. A relief will be suggested in the psyche. To deal with this, the yogi should slowly extract the forearms and hand. He should keep the eyelids closed and continue to inFocus.

Staying in that lotus posture with the forearms and fingers in a stress-less position, the yogi should meditate. Checking in every part, he will discover that the ankles release a mist-like energy. This will be a continuous spread of a dot-like force. This will decrease incrementally until it ceases. Then, there will again be the absorption with naad resonance. It may be from one side or the other, up or down. It will be everywhere.

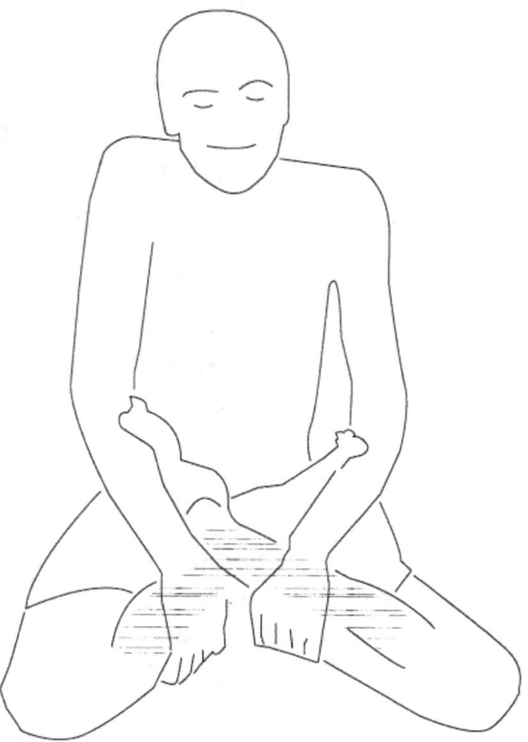

Focus Connection

The *Lotus Full with Forearms Under Shins* position, is done with no strenuous muscular feelings. This means that if one cannot easily do a tight lotus, one should not do this posture. It is no fault if the body one adopted from the parents, is unable to do some positions of yoga. It does not stop progression if one cannot do a certain pose. Skip any strenuous position, or do it partially. That is sufficient.

When this *Lotus Full with Forearms Under* Shins pose is assumed, there may be an alert that inner sound is present. The resonance is constant but sometimes the yogi is inattentive to it. In this pose a yogi may find that he hears a profound and steady stream of naad resonance. It may be loud. It may be in the chest area.

When listening to inner sound, which is not produced by the yogi, but which is evident to him, there will be lapses where the sound is heard and listened to, and then there is a blank space, where the sound is not heard, and where the listening self is itself not evident to itself.

Then again, the self will discover itself in some part of the psyche. It will be emerging to hear the naad resonance, which sounded but was not heard.

A sequence of noted events, and then no objective self in contrast, is required for study to understand the operations of awareness.

After a time, it will be necessary to relax the hands and the feet. The yogi should remain in the tight lotus, but the fingers should be relaxed on the soles of the feet. Then, the yogin should continue the meditation. Naad inner sound will be present. The yogi should attentively hear. Again, it will be experienced, that the objective range of awareness is absent. Then it will again be evident. When this happens, the yogi should have an attitude of learning about these shifts, from objectivity to subjectivity, and the reestablishment of objectivity. The yogi should question himself/herself regarding how these shifts occur.

Palms Up – Reverse Neck Lock

This *Palms Up – Reverse Neck Lock* posture, may be done in the full lotus, drawn tightly. If, however, one cannot do that, one may sit on a surface with or without a cushion. In this practice, no stress and strain should be felt in the base of the body, in the buttocks, thighs, legs and feet.

The hands should be placed on the thighs with the palms upright. The hands should be relaxed. Wherever the yogi sits, in whatever posture, his thighs, legs and feet should be relaxed. He should check to be sure that the body has no tension, nor stress energy, which demands attention.

Once the relaxation is observed, the yogi should tilt the head back. This should be done slowly with no jerking motion. There should be a check, to be sure that the focus remains within the psyche. Where the neck begins to tilt backwards, that should begin with one region going upward into the head, and another zone which goes downward into the body. Between the two there should be a blackout area which is shaped like a disc, going horizontally across the neck.

The yogi should go upward into the brain. He may feel compelled to be aware of each side of the chest. There may be a swinging energy which moves from the right to left, and left to right, continuously in the chest. That may flutter with the heart beat or the breath rhythm.

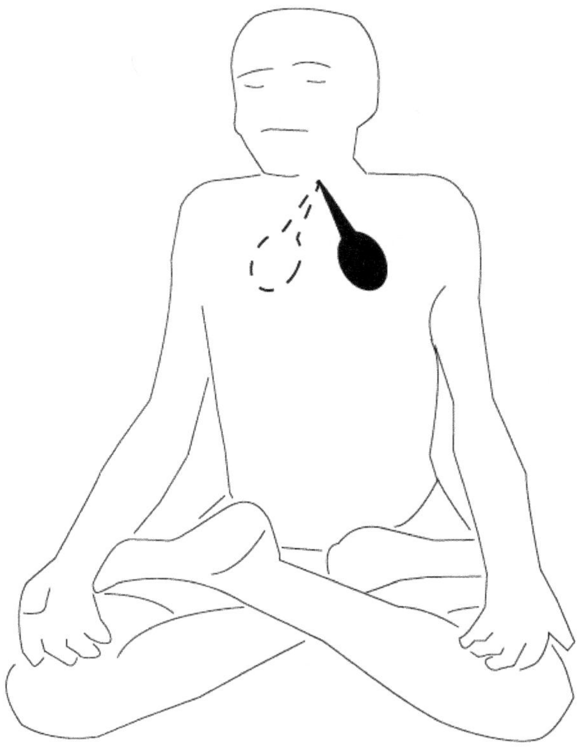

Focus Connection

This *Palms Up – Reverse Neck Lock* position, may be done from any sitting arrangement. Even while sitting on a chair or surface, it can be done. However, the palms should face the sky. The hands should be comfortable. There should be no tension nor strain to attract the attention of the mind.

In this posture, the head should be tilted back. That is the reverse neck lock. As soon as it is assumed, a yogi may hear internal sound, either to the right, left or center. It could be at the top or bottom, to the front or back. The yogi should check to observe where the energy is prominent.

There may be drifting of focus, where the yogi hears naad resonance, but then he loses that focus. Then again that focus is gained. Then it is lost again. During its disappearance, he may find that he observes thought information.

He should check to be sure that the reverse neck lock holds. If it was released, he should carefully without jerking, reinstate it. When he does so, he may focus through the face. This will happen if the head is tilted back to the maximum.

A yogi should note how there is naad resonance, then there may be a thought display, where he is aware of some part of a thought development. Then again, he may switch to full naad focus, but again, there may be a thought display that comes into focus, with the yogi not controlling this alternating focus.

Under Over Sex Energy Release

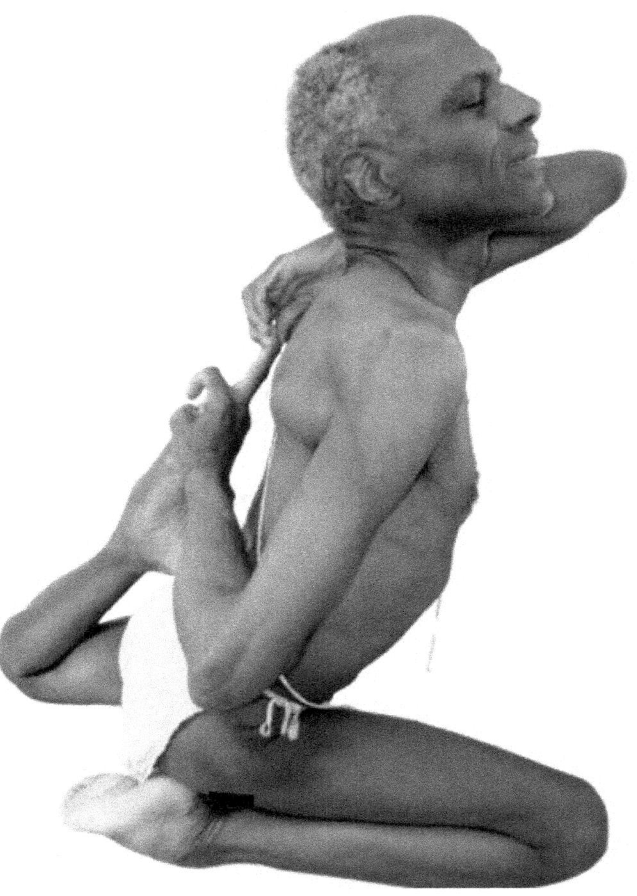

This *Under Over Sex Energy Release* posture, concerns the value of celibacy. Mental celibacy is one issue. Physical celibacy is another. And there is yet another which is emotional celibacy. Each approach requires specific adjustments from one special aspect to another. This posture begins with physical celibacy. It can assist the effort to restrain from sexual involvement. When it progresses, it can assist in emotional celibacy. When that is completed, it will accelerate mental celibacy.

This has to do with changing the sexual development of the physical body. The mere commitment, or pledge to be sexually uninvolved, is insufficient for celibacy. For that matter that commitment is repeatedly trashed by energies in the environment, which trigger the developed or developing sexual circuits in the psyche. The outlay for sexual participation is so pervasive, that mere determination to restrain from sexual expression, is breached repeatedly, sometimes in obvious actions, and mostly in covert behavior.

This posture is best done with the least clothing. The reason for this, is that the maximum stretches may not be reached if one has fabric where one part of the body contacts another. Another factor is grip. For some postures grip is required. Thus, one may require a mat. One may have to wet the hands.

To do this posture, a yogi may stretch one folded knee forward as far as it will go. The thigh should not ride on the folded leg. Most of the thigh should be on the floor. With one knee forward, one should stretch the other limb (thigh, leg, and foot) backward. Then one should fold back that foot and leg.

One should relocate that back limb so that it is as far back as possible. That limb should be grabbed with the opposing hand which grabs the foot from under.

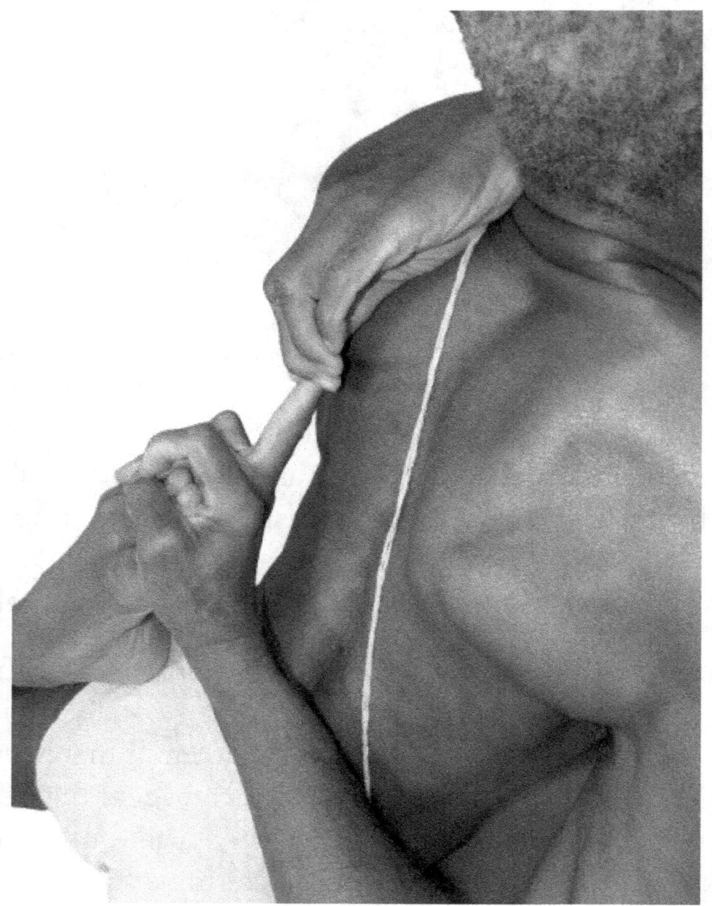

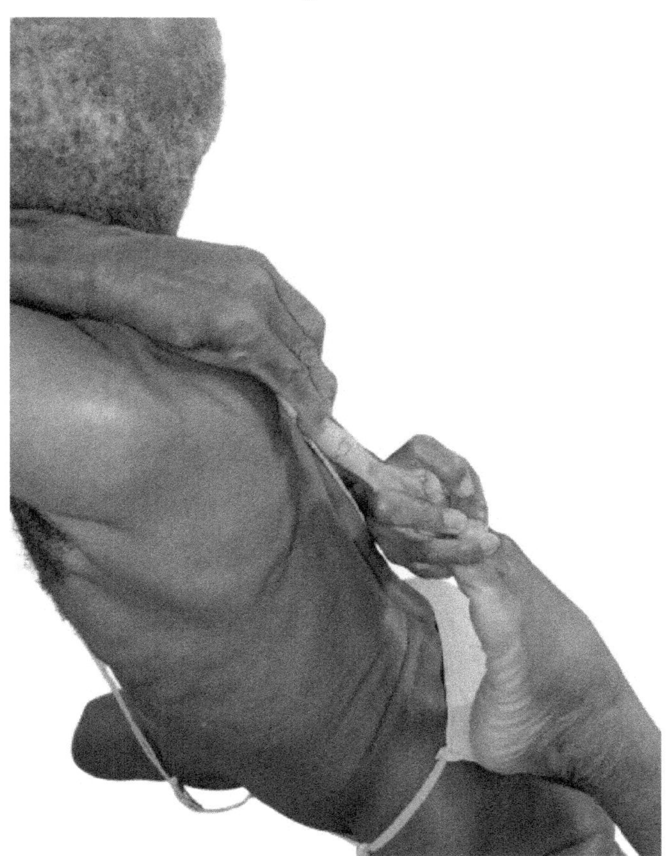

While checking this posture, one should be sure to check if the knee of the grabbed foot is as far back as possible. If the knee is not, it should be relocated. That action will cause the pelvic area to flatten towards the floor. It will spread the pelvic array of bones.

Using the other hand, one should put it over the shoulder from above. With that hand one should grab either the finger(s) of the other hand or the foot which the other hand holds. If one finds that one cannot reach that other foot or hand, one should again push the rear knee to flatten the pelvic situation.

Again, from over the shoulder, one should try to grab either the foot or hand. If again one can do neither, one should complete the posture without holding the foot or hand. Each day one should repeat this procedure.

This stretch causes reproductive energy to exude from the body, to shine from it, to radiate, and not accumulate. That is an action towards a celibate condition.

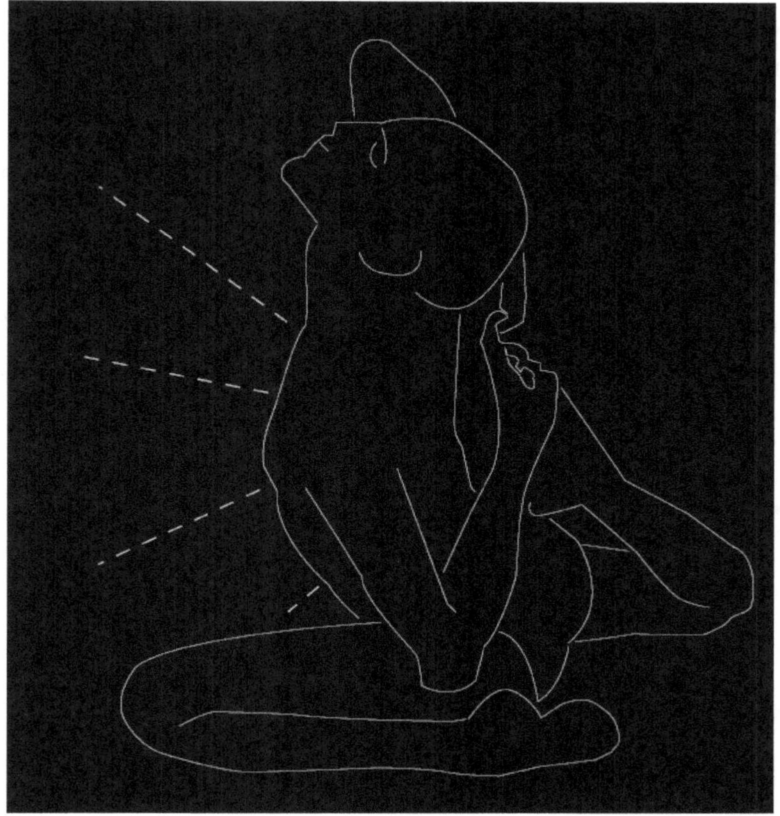

Focus Connection

The *Under Over Sex Energy Release* position is a difficult one. No one should be in a strain to assume this posture. It should be assumed slowly and carefully. If there is difficulty when practicing, it should not be done except in a partial way.

In this posture, there will be a pulling action, in the area where the front thigh connects with the lower pelvis. That is the focus area. At that place the interest energy will be focal. That is a *dhyana* meditation absorption, which when done, will use most of the attention energy. A yogi may hear inner sound. If he does, his interest energy will be split, with part going to hear inner sound, and part focusing in the pulling force, between the thigh which goes to the back, and the corresponding front pelvis area.

During this posture, a yogi may notice that any unexpended attention energy, will drift in search of objects to apprehend. Hence it is important to study the interest energy, as to its partitioning and focusing darts, which hunt and pursue objects, but which from time to time, becomes stationary or non-functional.

This book is one method of approaching the *samyama* process in the *Yoga Sutras*. A yogi can use the *asana* physical positions as a bridge to achieve inner focus. This book teaches this.

Yogeshwarananda said that many spiritual seekers have a low view of *asana* postures. These ascetics felt that *asanas* have no value. That itself was their negative view of a valuable part of *ashtanga* yoga. These fellows, he said, would get some appreciation by reading this literature. That corrective energy would cause advancement.

Index

L

M

N

O

P

Q

R

S

U

V

W

X, Y, Z

About the Author

Michael Beloved (Yogi *Madhvāchārya)* took his current body in 1951 in Guyana. In 1965, while living in Trinidad, he instinctively began doing yoga postures and tried to make sense of the supernatural side of life.

Later in 1970, in the Philippines, he approached a Martial Arts Master named Arthur Beverford. He explained to the teacher that he was seeking a yoga instructor. Mr. Beverford identified himself as an advanced disciple of *Śrī* Rishi Singh Gherwal, an Ashtanga Yoga master.

Beverford taught the traditional Ashtanga Yoga with stress on postures, attentive breathing, and brow chakra centering meditation. In 1972, Michael entered the Denver, Colorado Ashram of *kundalini* yoga Master *Śrī* Harbhajan Singh. There he took instruction in *bhastrika pranayama* and its application to yoga postures. He was supervised mostly by Yogi Bhajan's disciple named Prem Kaur.

In 1979 Michael formally entered the disciplic succession of the Brahmā - Madhava-Gaudiya Sampradaya through *Swāmī* Kirtanananda, who was a prominent sannyasi disciple of the Great Vaishnava Authority *Śrī Swāmī* Bhaktivedanta Prabhupada, the exponent of devotion to Sri Krishna.

However, yoga has a mystic side to it, thus Michael took training and teaching empowerment from several spiritual masters of different aspects of spiritual development. This is consistent with *Śrī* Krishna's advice to Arjuna in the *Bhagavad Gītā*:

Most of the instructions Michael received were given in the astral world. On that side of existence, his most prominent teachers were *Śrī Swāmī* Shivananda of Rishikesh, Yogiraj *Swāmī* Vishnudevananda, *Śrī Bābāji Mahasaya* - the master of the masters of *Kriyā* Yoga, *Śrīla* Yogeshwarananda of Gangotri - the master of the masters of *Rāj* Yoga (spiritual clarity), and Siddha *Swāmī* Nityananda the Brahmā Yoga authority.

The course for kundalini yoga using *pranayama* breath infusion was detailed by Michael in the book *Kundalini Hatha Yoga Pradipika*. This current book was composed from meditation and breath infusion notes which were originally shared in staple bound booklets as Yoga Journals.

Michael's preliminary books relating to this topic are Meditation Pictorial, Meditation Expertise, and Meditation ~ Sense Faculty (co-author). Every technique (kriya) mentioned was tested by him during pranayama breath infusion and samyama deep meditation practice.

This is a result of over forty years of meditation practice with astute subtle observations intending to share the methods and experiences. The information is published freely with no intention of forming an institution or hogtying anyone as a disciple.

Publications

English Series

Bhagavad Gita English
Anu Gita English
Markandeya Samasya English
Yoga Sutras English
Hatha Yoga Pradipika English
Uddhava Gita English

These are in 21st Century English, very precise and exacting. Many Sanskrit words which were considered untranslatable into a Western language, are rendered in precise, expressive, and modern English.

Three of these books are instructions from Krishna. **In *Bhagavad Gita* English** and **Anu Gita English**, the instructions were for Arjuna. In the **Uddhava Gita English,** it was for Uddhava. Bhagavad Gita and Anu Gita are extracted from the *Mahabharata*. Uddhava Gita was extracted from the 11th Canto of the Srimad Bhagavatam (Bhagavata Purana). One of these books, the **Markandeya Samasya English** is about Krishna, as described by Yogi Markandeya, who survived a cosmic collapse and reached a divine child in whose transcendental body, the collapsed world existed.

Two of this series are the syllabus about yoga practice. The *Yoga Sutras* of Patañjali is elaboration about ashtanga yoga. Hatha Yoga Pradipika English, is the detailed information about *asana* postures, *pranayama* breath- infusion, energy compression, naad sound resonance and advanced meditation. The Sanskrit author is Swatmarama Mahayogin.

My suggestion is that you read ***Bhagavad Gita*** **English**, the **Anu Gita English, the Markandeya Samasya English,** the ***Yoga Sutras*** **English**, the **Hatha Yoga Pradipika** and lastly the **Uddhava Gita English**, which is complicated and detailed.

For each of these books we have at least one commentary, which is published separately. Thus, one's particular interest can be researched further in the commentaries.

The smallest of these commentaries and perhaps the simplest is the one for the Anu Gita. We published its commentary as the Anu Gita Explained. The *Bhagavad Gita* explanations were published in three distinct targeted commentaries. The first is *Bhagavad Gita* Explained, which sheds lights on how people in the time of Krishna and Arjuna regarded the information and applied it. *Bhagavad Gita* is an exposition of the application of yoga practice to cultural activities, which is known in the Sanskrit language as karma yoga.

Interestingly, *Bhagavad Gita* was spoken on a battlefield just before one of the greatest battles in the ancient world. A warrior, Arjuna, lost his wits and had no idea that he could apply his training in yoga to political dealings. Krishna, his charioteer, lectured on the spur of the moment to give Arjuna the skill of using yoga proficiency in cultural dealings including how to deal with corrupt officials on a battlefield.

The second Bhagavad Gita commentary is the Kriya Yoga *Bhagavad Gita*. This clears the air about Krishna's information on the science of kriya yoga, showing that its techniques are clearly described for anyone who takes the time to read *Bhagavad Gita*. Kriya yoga concerns the battlefield which is the psyche of the living being. The internal war and the mental and emotional forces which are hostile to self-realization are dealt with in the kriya yoga practice.

The third commentary is the Brahma Yoga *Bhagavad Gita*. This shows what Krishna had to say outright and what he hinted about which concerns the brahma yoga practice, a mystic process for those who mastered kriya yoga.

There is one commentary for the **Markandeya Samasya English**. The title of that publication is Krishna Cosmic Body.

There are two commentaries to the *Yoga Sutras*. One is the *Yoga Sutras* of Patañjali and the other is the Meditation Expertise. These give detailed explanations of ashtanga Yoga.

The commentary of Hatha Yoga Pradipika is titled Kundalini Hatha Yoga Pradipika.

For the Uddhava Gita, we published the Uddhava Gita Explained. This is a large book and requires concentration and study for integration of the information. Of the books which deal with transcendental topics, my opinion is that the discourse between Krishna and Uddhava has the complete information about the realities in existence. This book is the one which removes massive existential ignorance.

Meditation Series

Meditation Pictorial
Meditation Expertise
CoreSelf Discovery
Meditation Sense Faculty

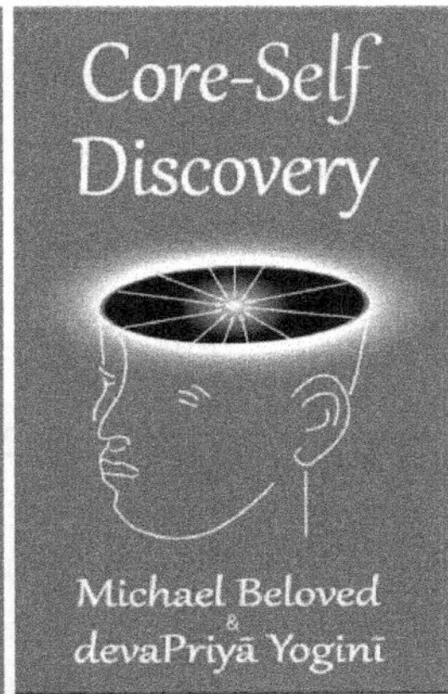

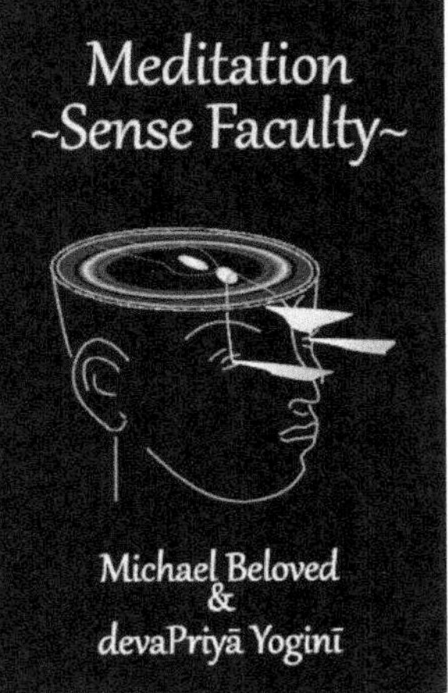

The specialty of these books is the mind diagrams which profusely illustrate what is written. This shows exactly what one has to do mentally to develop and then sustain a meditation practice.

In the **Meditation Pictorial**, one is shown how to develop psychic insight, a feature without which, meditation is imagination and visualization, without mystic experience in fact.

In the **Meditation Expertise**, one is shown how to corral one's practice to bring it in line with the classic syllabus of yoga which Patañjali lays out as the ashtanga yoga eight-staged process.

In **CoreSelf Discovery**, (co-authored with *devaPriya Yogini*) one is taken though the course of *pratyahar* sensual energy withdrawal which is the 5th stage of yoga in the Patañjali ashtanga eight-process complete system of yoga practice. These events lead to the discovery of a coreSelf which is surrounded by psychic organs in the head of the subtle body.

Meditation ~ Sense Faculty (co-authored with *devaPriya Yogini*) is a detailed tutorial with profuse diagrams showing what actions to take in the subtle body to investigate the senses faculties. The meditator must first establish the location and function of the observing self. That self must be screened from the thoughts and ideas which usually hypnotize it.

These books are profusely illustrated with mind diagrams showing the components of psychic consciousness and the inner design of the subtle body.

Explained Series

Bhagavad Gita Explained
Uddhava Gita Explained
Anu Gita Explained

The specialty of these books is that they are free of missionary intentions, cult tactics and philosophical distortion. Instead of using these books to add credence to a philosophy, meditation process, belief, or plea for followers, I spread the information out so that a reader can look through this literature and freely take or leave anything as desired.

When Krishna stressed himself as God, I stated that. When Krishna laid no claims for supremacy, I showed that. The reader is left to form an independent opinion about the validity of the information and the credibility of Krishna.

There is a difference in the discourse with Arjuna in the *Bhagavad Gita* and the one with Uddhava in the Uddhava Gita. In fact, these two books may appear to contradict each other. In the *Bhagavad Gita*, Krishna pressured Arjuna to complete social duties. In the Uddhava Gita, Krishna insisted that Uddhava should abandon the same.

The Anu Gita is not as popular as the *Bhagavad Gita* but it is the conclusion of that text. Anu means what is to follow, what proceeds. In this discourse, an anxious

Arjuna request that Krishna should repeat the *Bhagavad Gita* and again show His supernatural and divine forms.

However, Krishna refused to do so and chastised Arjuna for being a disappointment in forgetting what was revealed. Krishna then cited a celestial yogi, a perfected being, who explained the process of transmigration in vivid detail.

Commentaries

Yoga Sutras of Patañjali
Meditation Expertise
Krishna Cosmic Body
Anu Gita Explained
Bhagavad Gita Explained
Kriya Yoga Bhagavad Gita
Brahma Yoga Bhagavad Gita
Uddhava Gita Explained
Kundalini Hatha Yoga Pradipika

***Yoga Sutras* of Patañjali is** the globally acclaimed text book of yoga. This has detailed expositions of yoga techniques. Many kriya techniques are vividly described in the commentary.

Meditation Expertise is an analysis and application of the *Yoga Sutras*. This book is loaded with illustrations and has detailed explanations of secretive advanced meditation techniques which are called kriyas in the Sanskrit language.

Krishna Cosmic Body is a narrative commentary on the Markandeya Samasya portion of the Aranyaka Parva of the *Mahabharata*. This is the detailed description of the dissolution of the world, as experienced by the great yogin Markandeya who transcended the cosmic deity, Brahma, and reached Brahma's source who is the divine infant, Krishna.

Anu Gita Explained is a detailed explanation of how we endure many material bodies in the course of transmigrating through various life-forms. This is a discourse between Krishna and Arjuna. Arjuna requested of Krishna a display of the Universal Form and a repeat narration of the *Bhagavad Gita* but Krishna declined and explained what a siddha perfected being told the Yadu family about the sequence of existences one endures and the systematic flow of those lives at the convenience of material nature.

***Bhagavad Gita* Explained** shows what was said in the Gita without religious overtones and sectarian biases.

Kriya Yoga *Bhagavad Gita* shows the instructions for those who are doing kriya yoga.

Brahma Yoga *Bhagavad Gita* shows the instructions for those who are doing brahma yoga.

Uddhava Gita Explained shows the instructions to Uddhava which are more advanced than the ones given to Arjuna.

Bhagavad Gita is an instruction for applying the expertise of yoga in the cultural field. This is why the process taught to Arjuna is called karma yoga which means karma + yoga or cultural activities done with yogic insight.

Uddhava Gita is an instruction for apply the expertise of yoga to attaining spiritual status. This is why it explains jnana yoga and *bhakti* yoga in detail. Jnana yoga is using mystic skill for knowing the spiritual part of existence. *Bhakti* yoga is for developing affectionate relationships with divine beings.

Karma yoga is for negotiating the social concerns in the material world. It is inferior to *bhakti* yoga which concerns negotiating the social concerns in the spiritual world.

This world has a social environment. The spiritual world has one too.

Currently, Uddhava Gita is the most advanced and informative spiritual book on the planet. There is nothing anywhere which is superior to it or which goes into so much detail as it. It verified that historically Krishna is the most advanced human being to ever have left literary instructions on this planet. Even Patañjali *Yoga Sutras* which I translated and gave an application for in my book, **Meditation Expertise**, does not go as far as the Uddhava Gita.

Some of the information of these two books is identical but while the *Yoga Sutras* are concerned with the personal spiritual emancipation *(kaivalyam)* of the individual spirits, the Uddhava Gita explains that and also explains the situations in the spiritual universes.

Bhagavad Gita is from the *Mahabharata* which is the history of the Pandavas. Arjuna, the student of the Gita, is one of the Pandavas brothers. He was in a social hassle and did not know how to apply yoga expertise to solve it. On the battlefield, Krishna gave him a crash-course on yogic social interactions.

Uddhava Gita is from the *Srimad Bhagavatam (Bhagavata Purana),* which is a history of the incarnations of Krishna. Uddhava was a relative of Krishna. He was concerned about the situation of the deaths of many of his relatives but Krishna diverted Uddhava's attention to the practice of yoga for the purpose of successfully migrating to the spiritual environment.

Kundalini Hatha Yoga Pradipika is the commentary for the Hatha Yoga Pradipika of Swatmarama Mahayogin. This is the detailed process about *asana* posture, *pranayama* breath-infusion, complex compressions of energy, naad sound resonance intonement and advanced meditation practice.

This is the singular book with all the techniques of how to reform and redesign the subtle body, so that it does not have the tendency for physical life forms, and for it to attain the status of a siddha.

These books are based on the author's experiences in meditation, yoga practice and participation in spiritual groups:

Specialty

Spiritual Master
sex you!
Sleep Paralysis
Astral Projection
Masturbation Psychic Details
death You!
Experience You!

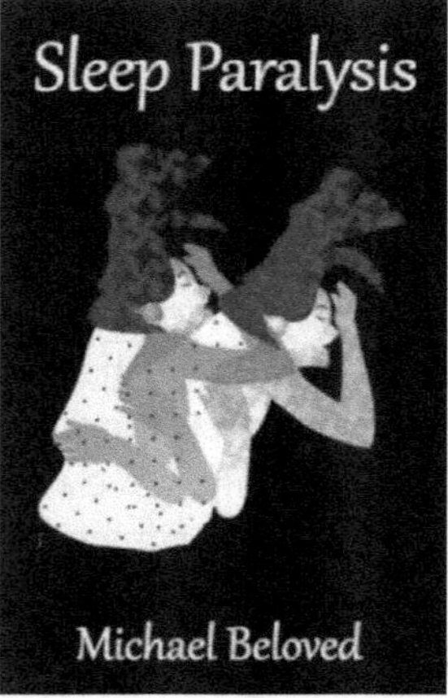

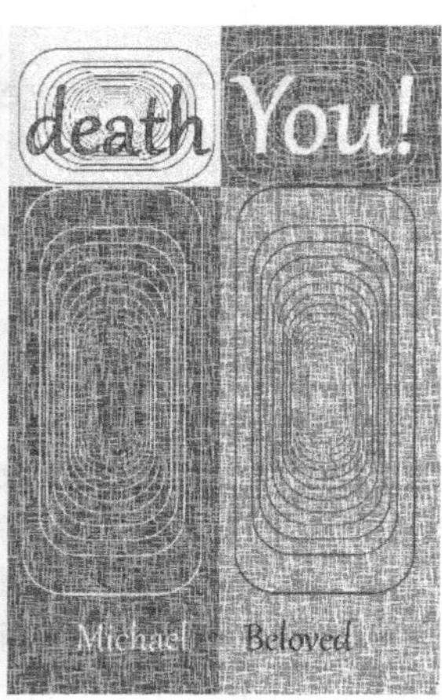

In **Spiritual Master**, Michael draws from experience with gurus or with their senior students. His contact with astral gurus is rated. He walks you through the avenue of gurus, showing what you should do, and what you should not do, so as to gain proficiency in whatever area of spirituality the guru has proficiency.

sex you! is a masterpiece about the adventures of an individual spirit's passage through the parents' psyches. The conversion of a departed soul into a sexual urge is described. The transit from the afterlife to residency in the emotions of the parents is detailed. This is about sex and you. Learn about how much of you comprises the romantic energy of one's would-be parents!

Sleep Paralysis clears misconceptions so that one can see what sleep paralysis is and what frightening astral experience occurs while the paralysis is being experienced. This disempowerment has great value in giving you confidence that you can, and do, exist even if one is unable to operate the physical body. The implication is that one can exist apart from, and will survive the loss of the material form.

Astral Projection details experiences Michael had even in childhood, where he assumed incorrectly that everyone was astrally conversant. He discusses the lifeForce psychic mechanism which operates the sleep-wake cycle of the physical form, and which budgets energy into the separated astral form which determines if the individual will have dream recall or no objective awareness during the projections. Astral travel happens on every occasion when the physical body sleeps. What is missing in awareness is the observer status while the astral body is separated.

Masturbation Psychic Details is a surprise presentation which relates what happens on the psychic plane during a masturbation event. This does not tackle moral issues or even addictions but shows the involvement of memory and the sure but hidden subconscious mind which operates many features of the psyche irrespective of the desire or approval of the self-conscious personality.

death You! is about death transit which is the shift to the psychic world with no recourse of a physical presence. Generally, human beings service a religion by consigning a dead body to a religious ceremony which promotes the idea of life hereafter in the heaven of a deity. However, the same survivors who sponsor the ceremony usually mourn the physical condition of the person's immobile body.

Experience You! is an allegoric tale from the Srimad Bhagavatam. It was narrated by Narad to King Barhi (Prachinabarhi). Its frames the life of every creature in the physical world, but it is specific for the human species. The tale opens with a wanderer named Puranjan, He was a city tenant but he had no residence. While touring the earth, he got to a place on the southern side of the Himalayan Mountains. There, luckily, he met a beautiful woman who was on the outskirts of her city. They were cordial. They agreed to live together as sweethearts for one hundred years.

inVision Series

Yoga inVision 1
Yoga inVision 2
Yoga inVision 3
Yoga inVision 4
Yoga inVision 5
Yoga inVision 6
Yoga inVision 7
Yoga inVision 8
Yoga inVision 9

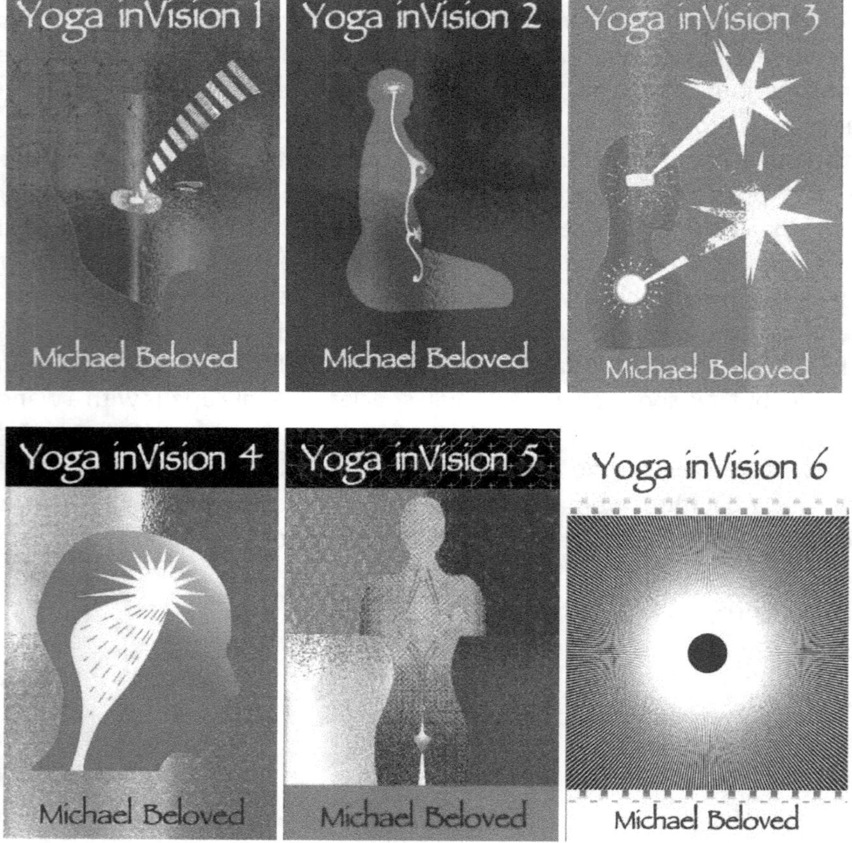
Yoga inVision 1
Michael Beloved
Yoga inVision 2
Michael Beloved
Yoga inVision 3
Michael Beloved
Yoga inVision 4
Michael Beloved
Yoga inVision 5
Michael Beloved
Yoga inVision 6
Michael Beloved

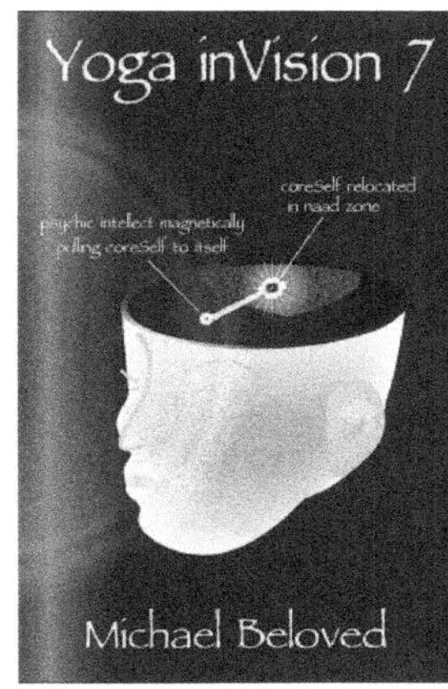
Yoga inVision 7
coreSelf relocated in naad zone
psychic intellect magnetically pulling coreSelf to itself
Michael Beloved

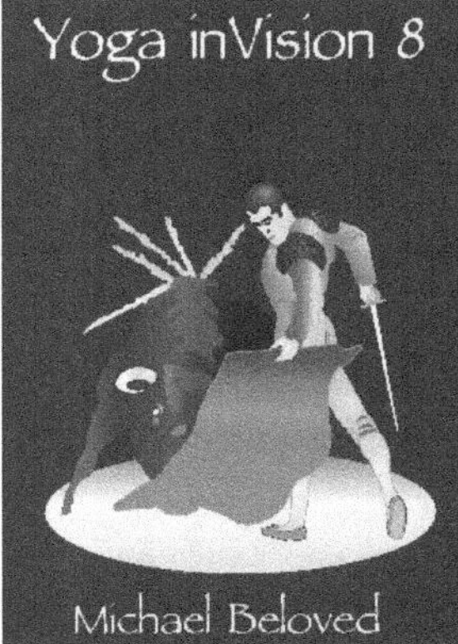
Yoga inVision 8
Michael Beloved

Yoga inVision 9
Michael Beloved

Yoga inVision 10
Michael Beloved

Yoga inVision 11
Michael Beloved

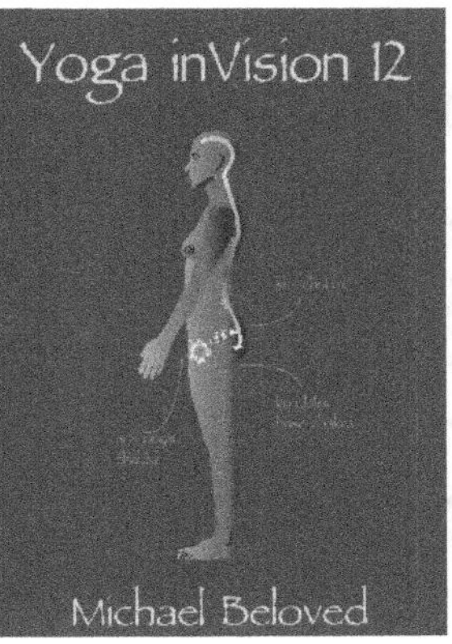
Yoga inVision 12
Michael Beloved

Yoga inVision 13
Michael Beloved

Yoga inVision 14
Michael Beloved

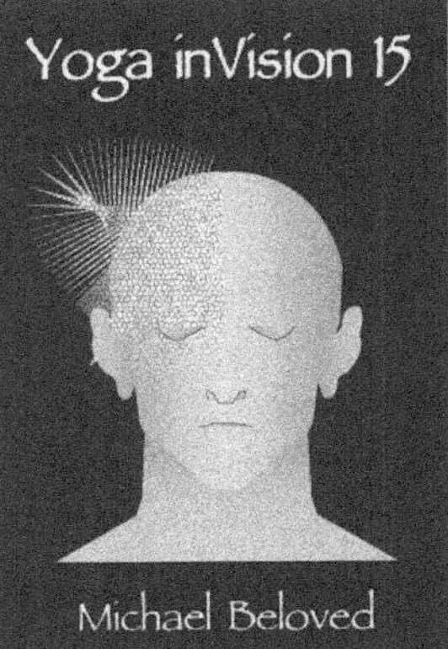
Yoga inVision 15
Michael Beloved

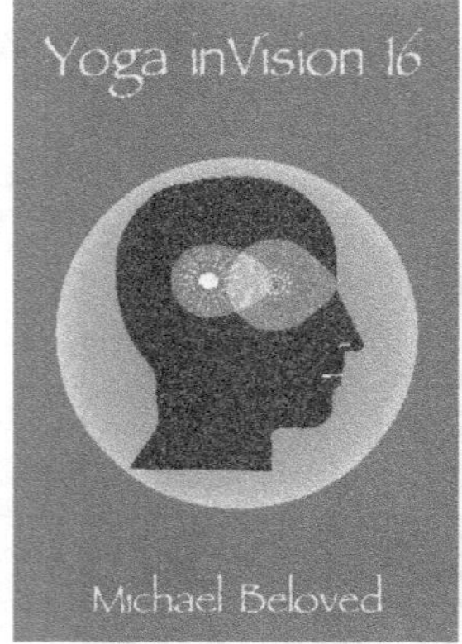

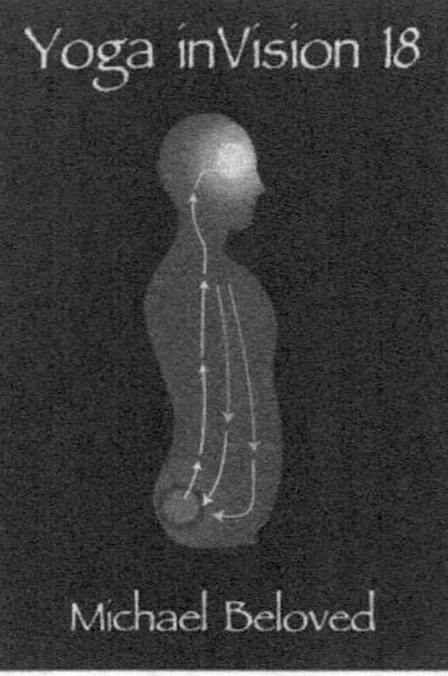

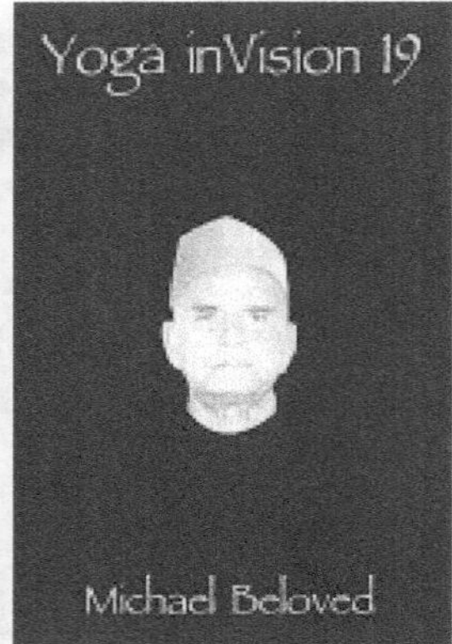

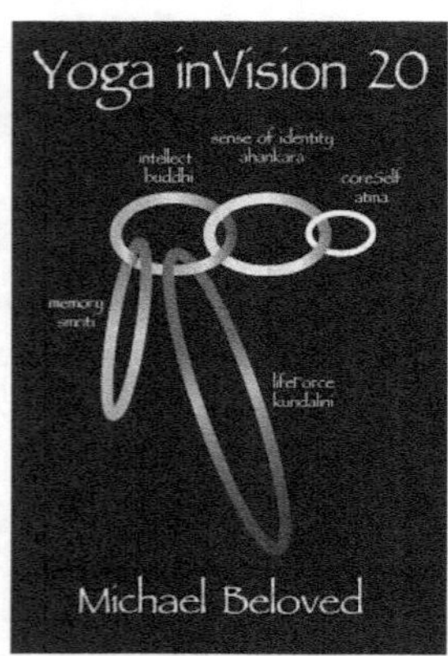

Yoga inVision 1, the first in this series, describes the breath infusion and meditation practices during the years of 1998 and 1999. There are unique, once in a lifetime as well as recurring insights which are elaborated. inFocus during breath infusion and the meditation which follows is an adventure for any yogi. This gives what happened to this particular ascetic.

Yoga inVision 2 reports on the author's experiences from 1999 to 2001. Each day the experience is unique, illustrating the vibrancy of practice. Many rare once-in-a-lifetime perceptions are described.

Yoga inVision 3 reports on the author's experiences from 2001 to 2003.

Yoga inVision 4 reports on the author's experiences from 2006 to 2009.

Yoga inVision 5 reports on the author's experiences from 2006 to 2008.

Yoga inVision 6 reports on the author's experiences in 2010.

Yoga inVision 7 reports on the author's experiences in 2011.

Yoga inVision 8 reports on the author's experiences in 2011.

Yoga inVision 9 reports on the author's experiences in 2012.

Yoga inVision 10 reports on the author's experiences in 2012.

Yoga inVision 11 reports on the author's experiences in 2012.

Yoga inVision 12 reports on the author's experiences in 2012-2013.

Yoga inVision 13 reports on the author's experiences in 2013-2014.

Yoga inVision 14 reports on the author's experiences in 2013-2014.

Yoga inVision 15 reports on the author's experiences in 2014.

Yoga inVision 16 reports on the author's experiences in 2014-2015.

Yoga inVision 17 reports on the author's experiences in 2016-2017.
Yoga inVision 18 reports on the author's experiences in 2017-2019.
Yoga inVision 19 reports on the author's experiences in 2019-2021.
Yoga inVision 20 reports on the author's experiences in 2021-2024.
Yoga inVision 21 reports on the author's experiences in 2024-2025.

Online Resources

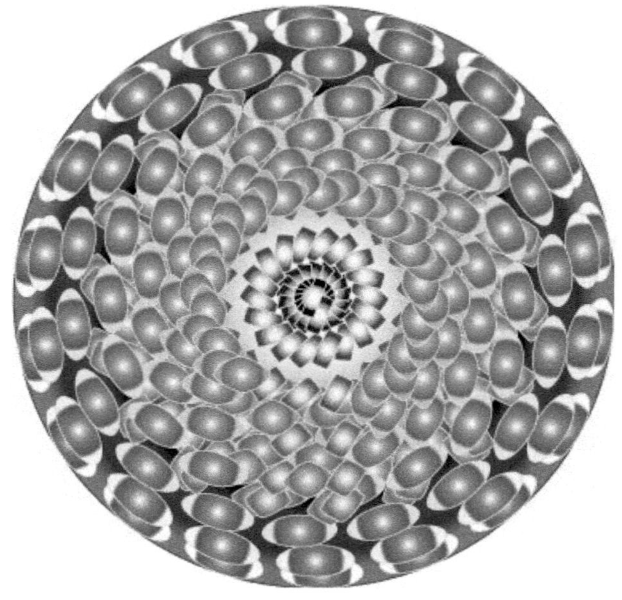

Email: michaelbelovedbooks@gmail.com
axisnexus@gmail.com

Website: michaelbeloved.com

Forum: inselfyoga.com

Posters: zazzle.com/inself

www.ingramcontent.com/pod-product-compliance
Lightning Source LLC
LaVergne TN
LVHW080329110826
845155LV00024B/135

* 9 7 8 1 9 4 2 8 8 7 6 1 4 *